The Linguistic Turn in Hermeneutic Philosophy

The Linguistic Turn in Hermeneutic Philosophy

Cristina Lafont

translated by José Medina

The MIT Press
Cambridge, Massachusetts
London, England

This book was set in Baskerville by Achorn Graphic Services Inc. and was printed and bound in the United States of America.

Lafont, Cristina, 1963–
    [Razón como lenguaje. English]
    The linguistic turn in hermeneutic philosophy / Cristina Lafont : translated by José Medina.
        p.   cm. — (Studies in contemporary German social thought)
    Includes bibliographical references and index.
    ISBN 0-262-12217-0 (hardcover : alk. paper)
    1. Language and languages—Philosophy—History—19th century. 2. Hermeneutics—History—19th century. 3. Philosophy, German—19th century. 4. Language and languages—Philosophy—History—20th century. 5. Hermeneutics—History—20th century. 6. Philosophy, German—20th century. I. Title. II. Series.
B3187.L3413   1999
121′.68—dc21   99-23900
                                                                                    CIP

To my parents

Contents

Preface to the English Edition

An early version of this study on the linguistic turn in hermeneutic philosophy appeared in Spanish in 1993. Since that time, I have become aware of many issues that arise as a natural consequence of the original study. But the attempt to address these issues necessarily led beyond the framework of the initial project; accordingly, the remarks that follow are an attempt to show how a somewhat broader framework emerges from the original one.

My original project was an analysis of the characteristic traits and problems of the linguistic turn in the German tradition of the philosophy of language.[1] This turn can be regarded as having

---

1. With the characterization of this tradition as "German" I mean to distinguish it from the other main tradition of the philosophy of language in this century, which I will call "Anglo-American." Admittedly, such labeling of traditions is always problematic, given the possible discrepancy between the nationality of an author and the effective history (*Wirkungsgeschichte*) of her work. The name "Anglo-American" may seem especially misleading for a tradition so deeply influenced by authors such as Frege, Carnap, and Wittgenstein. However, when we consider the effective history of the work of these thinkers, the label seems appropriate. At any rate, it appears less problematic than the attempt to subsume all of the diverse authors of a given tradition under the rubric of a single philosophical viewpoint. The difficulty of finding apt philosophical labels is especially clear in our own time, when the term "Anglo-American" has to include not only the analytic but also the postanalytic phase of this tradition. Equally so, the label "German" must cover not only the hermeneutic tradition (and its predecessors), but that of critical hermeneutics as well.

originated in the so-called Hamann-Herder-Humboldt tradition,[2] which received further development and radicalization by Heidegger, and which through Gadamer has extended its influence to contemporary authors such as Apel and Habermas.

This German tradition exhibits specific features that distinguish it clearly from the Anglo-American philosophy of language. Perhaps its most important feature is the explicit attempt, found in all the authors of this tradition, to break with the assimilation of all functions of language to the cognitive function (language as a vehicle of knowledge) at the expense of its communicative function (language as a means of understanding). In other words, it is a central aim of this tradition to end what Humboldt terms the "primacy of logic over grammar," a primacy that the authors in question trace to the very beginnings of Greek philosophy. The basic orientation of this tradition toward social and cultural phenomena rather than natural ones (toward the social rather than the natural sciences) explains this common motif among its authors. In keeping with this focus, the German tradition has always concentrated on the analysis of natural languages, and it has regarded these as *constitutive* of the relationship of human beings with the world at large. That is to say, this tradition's philosophical interest in the analysis of language does not stem only from the crucial role played by language in our relationship with the objective world (by allowing us to have propositional knowledge of it). Rather, language is also held to be pivotal to our relation with the social world (which is essentially dependent on intersubjective communication), and even to our experience of our own subjective worlds (which are expressible only through linguistic articulation). In this way, language is considered in its multidimensional *world-disclosing* function.

However, the differences that appear obvious at first between the German and Anglo-American traditions cease to be so upon

2. As a solution to the difficulty mentioned in the previous footnote, Charles Taylor (1985) referred to this tradition of the philosophy of language as the "Hamann-Herder-Humboldt tradition," a denomination that has now become standard.

closer analysis. Looking a bit more deeply, we find a clear convergence in their basic trends, and in the difficulties that begin to
typify *both* traditions as a result of their own internal development:
linguistic relativism, incommensurability, meaning holism, etc.
Though such a convergence is far more obvious if the German
tradition is compared with the Anglo-American philosophy of language since the 1950s (its postanalytic phase), this obviously could
not have occurred had there not been a common basis for the
linguistic turn in both traditions.

Although this book is directly concerned only with the analysis
of the German tradition, it is crucial that we identify the common
links between it and the approach of Anglo-American philosophy.
This is important, first, owing to the systematic aim of my analysis,
which is perhaps best expressed as an attempt to answer the following question: Are the difficulties mentioned in the last para-
graph a consequence of the linguistic turn *as such*? That is, are
they insurmountable problems that this turn alone has served to
bring to light? Or do they result only from a peculiar way of exe-
cuting the turn, so that they might be avoided by revising some
previously unquestioned presuppositions? I am inclined to suspect the latter, again for reasons indebted to an Anglo-American
trend that began in the 1970s—namely, the so-called theories of
direct reference.[3] This novel approach has convinced me that it
is possible to avoid the consequences of an extreme linguistic relativism without renouncing the linguistic turn as such.

In short, the common basis of the two linguistic turns in the
modern philosophy of language can be found in the way in which
each was carried out by its main figure: Humboldt in the German
tradition, and Frege in the Anglo-American. Both authors initiated their linguistic turns (it could scarcely have been otherwise)
by introducing the distinction between *meaning* and *reference*. That

---

3. My preference for this denomination over the term " 'causal' theories of reference" is not merely stylistic. As I will try to show in chapter 5, a defense of
the crucial insights of these new theories of reference does not require or even
imply the adoption of a causal explanation of reference, or that of a metaphysical-
realist viewpoint in general.

is, they realized that the peculiarity of language, in contrast with any other system of signs, is that language makes it possible to *refer to the same thing in different ways*.[4] But beyond this, both authors established this distinction *in an identical manner*, although this move is far from obvious: they generalized the meaning-reference distinction, viewing it as applicable to *all* linguistic signs (even proper names). In this way, they arrived at the general thesis that *meaning determines reference*.

But to accept this thesis as unrestrictedly valid leads to pernicious philosophical consequences. These become visible only when the claim that meaning determines reference, more or less harmless from a strictly semantic point of view, becomes burdened with epistemological tasks. Yet the linguistic turn as such seems to *require* such a burdening, given that language is no longer simply regarded as one object of study among others, but as the general paradigm for the solution of philosophical problems. In this context, the thesis that meaning determines reference is taken to imply that different linguistic expressions, with their different meanings, determine our (epistemic) *access* to their referents. That is, linguistic expressions are held to determine, if not what there *is*, at least what there *can be* for a linguistic community—or what such a community *can say* (i.e., *believe*) that there is. In this sense, the key function of language is held to lie in its *world-disclosing* capacity. For it is precisely this capacity that renders intelligible the attempt to reformulate all philosophical problems under the aegis of the philosophy of language. This also explains why the linguistic turn and the thesis that meaning determines reference seem to be one and the same. Or at least, it explains

4. Precisely because language, in contrast with other systems of signs, enables us not only to designate objects but also to classify them (i.e., to subsume different objects under the same term and the same objects under different terms), it performs a function of *world-disclosure*. That is, language allows us to have a general interpretation (and general propositional knowledge) of the world. To the extent that this function is what first makes language philosophically compelling, no linguistic turn can occur without the support of an account of this essential function of language.

why this was *considered* self-evident in both traditions for many years, and was only placed in question since the 1970s, in the Anglo-American context.

The pernicious consequences of the thesis that meaning determines reference become especially apparent once this thesis is combined with the fact of the plurality and contingency of natural languages and the worldviews peculiar to them (to use Humboldt's phrase). For this combination necessarily poses serious problems for the possibility of objective knowledge of the world and of intersubjective communication across different languages. If "what there can be" in the world diverges completely for speakers of different languages, if they cannot talk about the same reality, how can they ever communicate? Worse yet, how can these speakers achieve any knowledge about reality?

However, the problems related to the thesis that meaning determines reference have not determined the development of both traditions in the same way. The essential difference is that Humboldt, and the German philosophy of language as a whole, were always interested in the analysis of natural languages, developed through contingent historical processes. By contrast, Frege worked in accordance with the Leibnizian ideal of a perfect language, a *characteristica universalis*. His views remained closely tied to this revisionary project of constructing an artificial language. For this reason, the problems implied in defending the thesis that meaning determines reference for natural languages do not yet appear with Frege in an explicit form.[5] The parallel course of both traditions, especially as concerns the problems of linguistic relativism, became clear only at a later point: namely, when the Anglo-American tradition, in its postanalytic phase, *abandoned* the ideal of a perfect artificial language. In this way, it became sensitive to

5. Indeed, in his famous footnote about proper names in "Über Sinn und Bedeutung," Frege anticipates the problems related to the thesis that meaning determines reference when it is applied to natural languages. But he sees these problems solely as further arguments for his revisionary project, i.e., for the need to avoid the ambiguities of natural languages through the construction of a perfect formal language for the sciences.

the insurmountable character of natural languages, and thereby to the problematic implications of meaning holism.

This underlying similarity between the two traditions encouraged me to pursue a specific line of research: I set out to examine whether the questioning of the thesis that meaning determines reference, a challenge initiated by the defenders of the theories of direct reference, could also prove fruitful elsewhere. In particular, I wondered whether such questioning could be useful for identifying and problematizing the source of the reification of language (the linguistic idealism) typical of the German tradition.

Certainly, the various attempts to develop a theory of direct reference have yet to provide a full account of reference in general. But their questioning of the thesis that meaning determines reference—the common denominator of all such efforts—already goes a long way toward undermining the relativist and incommensurabilist consequences resulting from the linguistic turn in both traditions. This questioning is carried out through an analysis of the peculiarity of designation as opposed to predication (i.e., world-disclosure). As I will try to show toward the end of the book, this analysis undercuts the alleged determinative and limiting character of natural languages, and it also helps us recognize the systematic way in which the use of language is inherently related to our capacity for cognitive learning. In turn, this insight allows us to identify the fallacy involved in epistemologizing the semantic distinction between meaning and reference. Such a procedure confuses the obvious fact that our descriptions of referents (via the meanings of the words we use) *express our de facto beliefs about them* with the purported fact that our descriptions thereby *determine that to which they refer*. Whereas the former supposition is owing to the trivial truth that "the limits of my knowledge are the limits of my world" (i.e., of how I believe the world to be), the latter gives rise to the myth that "the limits of my language are the limits of my world" (i.e., of the world that I can talk about). Insofar as the latter claim extends beyond the former, insofar as it is taken in the *normative* sense that we can only refer to that which corresponds to our beliefs, it is mistaken. The expressions of a particular language with their varied meanings may determine our (epistemic) *access* to the referents. As pointed out before, they may even determine *what* a linguistic community can say that there is. But they cannot also determine what this community considers its beliefs to be *about:* they cannot determine what the linguistic community *can refer to.*

Precisely by virtue of its referential function, language enables us to *transcend the limits* of our beliefs by enabling us to refer to things *independently of how we conceive of them.* That is to say, it allows or even *forces* us to treat referents as logically independent of our particular ways of conceiving them. When we learn the referential use of linguistic expressions, we learn that the real referents of these expressions cannot be reduced to whatever happens to satisfy our descriptions. That *this cannot be what we refer to, no matter how reasonable our knowledge may be,* forces us to recognize that the descriptions of the referents that make up our alleged knowledge about them can be mistaken. Only in this way can speakers *refer to the same things,* even if they *disagree* about *how these things ought to be described.* Or rather, only in this way *can* they disagree and thereby learn from each other.

Language not only plays a crucial role in our interpretative access to the world, but has an equally pivotal role in our understanding of the world as logically independent of any particular way of conceiving it. By learning the referential use of language, we learn precisely about this independence. Thus the practice of referring involves the formal presupposition of a *single objective world,* a world *about which* our interpretations may *differ.* Without such a presupposition, as I will try to show, the entire practice of rational discussion and collective learning would utterly collapse.

However, the question that immediately arises is how to give an account of the referential function of language that is consistent with an account of its predicative function. Put differently, the challenge is to give an account of the *realist* intuitions highlighted by the linguistic function of designation (on which the epistemic intuitions regarding the objectivity of knowledge, fallibilism, etc., seem to depend), without denying the world-disclosing function of language. How can we do this without appealing to a metaphysical realism that would deny our unavoidably interpretative relationship with the world?

But it is precisely here that it would be difficult to rely on the Anglo-American tradition. For if it is possible to find in some versions of the theory of "direct" reference an attempt to *answer* this challenge (most notably in Putnam's "internal realism," on which the present book relies heavily), there are also versions of this theory which seem instead to *evade* it. Theories of "direct" reference of the latter kind tend to rely on causalist, naturalist, or metaphysical-realist strategies. In my view, all such strategies are doomed to *nullify* the linguistic turn, and to forsake much of what has been learned in the meantime about our inevitably interpretative relationship with the world.

To avoid this problem, we can draw on the resources of the German tradition of the philosophy of language. Thanks to the strong idealist tendencies of this tradition, causalist strategies of explanation—indeed, naturalisms of any kind—are quite alien to it. If anything, the problem that arises here is just the opposite. As I will try to show, the challenge is to preserve a *realist* perspective that can account for the normative presuppositions that guide our cognitive and communicative activities, while integrating it within a general *pragmatist* strategy that would also account for the interpretative or creative character of those activities.

My analysis of the view of language serving as the basis for Habermas's theory of communicative rationality is meant to answer this systematic challenge. Accordingly, this analysis is unlike the others in this book, insofar as it is not merely a reconstruction. This is owing to the singular position of Habermas's view within the German tradition.

On the one hand, the elaborate character and systematic ambitions of Habermas's view make his analysis of language incomparably more complex than the others analyzed here. This is undoubtedly owing to the broad scope of his theory of communicative rationality. On the other hand, Habermas's approach is also the only one in the German tradition that marks an *explicit* attempt to defend a universalist or rationalist perspective against any kind of relativism. For this reason, his theory is the natural place in this tradition to analyze the systematic problem at the heart of my project.[6]

Moreover, the crucial importance of Habermas's view for this project lies in the peculiar combination of theoretical strategies that he has employed from the outset. The analysis offered here of Habermas's theory of communicative rationality rests on the conviction that there is a tension in this theory between two distinct strategies. The first is of a decidedly antirealist, constructivist character. The second incorporates realist elements within a general pragmatist strategy; drawing on Putnam, I will call it *internal realism*. As developed so far, Habermas's theory does contain elements of both strategies. It is my conviction that only the latter strategy can provide adequate support for a universalist approach. For this reason, my original analysis of Habermas's philosophy of language focused on a primarily critical task: I concentrated on discrediting the viability of certain antirealist strategies that he had suggested as possible ways of completing his theory of communicative rationality.

Since the publication of the Spanish version of this book, I have repeatedly met with the following question: To what extent can the realist strategy briefly sketched in that first edition be effectively integrated and consistently developed within the framework

6. Another natural place to look, of course, would have been K.-O. Apel's view of language, from which Habermas's view of communicative rationality received decisive impulses. But owing to the complexity and systematic breadth of both standpoints, an examination of Apel's approach would have required a separate analysis in its own right. This had to remain a task for the future. On the other hand, owing to the similarities of some of the theoretical strategies favored by both authors (e.g., an antirealist conception of truth), some of the criticisms of Habermas's approach developed here are applicable to Apel's position as well. However, there is an important difference with respect to the recognition (fundamental for my criticisms) of the normative presuppositions underlying the designative use of language, for Apel has explicitly analyzed the theories of "direct" reference in a way similar to my own. Unfortunately, I became aware of this source of indirect support for my analysis only after this book was originally completed.

of Habermas's own theory? That is, to what extent can this strategy account for everything that Habermas's theory had aimed to explain?

In an effort to answer this question, I have added a new, third part to the English edition, in which I attempt to take a constructive step. In contrast with the changes introduced in other chapters, this has required advancing to some extent beyond the scope of the original project. On the one hand, this step has an obvious systematic aim, in view of which the differences between the two traditions of philosophy of language become irrelevant. On the other hand, the attempt to show the viability of developing Habermas's full theory of communicative rationality through an internal-realist strategy stands under the requirement of completeness. This entails passing outside the domain of the philosophy of language in order to disentangle, however sketchily, the problematic links between theoretical and practical reason. But in a different sense, this addition to my project represents only another step in the never-ending search for an answer to my initial question: what is the connection between reason and language?

I would like to thank Graham Harman for his indispensable help with the preparation of this new edition.

I

The Linguistic Turn in the German Tradition of the Philosophy of Language

Introduction

The linguistic turn in the German tradition of the philosophy of language, also known as the Hamann-Herder-Humboldt tradition, is characterized by two main features resulting from the identification of language with reason that is integral to this tradition. Such an identification goes beyond mere etymological reference to a common origin in the Greek *logos*. More than this, it entails two shifts that are both unprecedented in the tradition to which these authors react and unassimilable by it:

1. The view of language presupposed by the philosophy of consciousness is subjected to a critique. On this view, the role of language is relegated to that of a tool mediating the subject-object relation; consequently, language becomes a medium for the mere expression of prelinguistic thoughts. The critique of this standpoint arises by regarding language as constitutive of thought, and by recognizing accordingly the double status of language as both empirical and transcendental. In virtue of this status, language lays claim to the constitutive role traditionally attributed to consciousness, to a transcendental subject.

2. Furthermore, this transformation amounts to a *detranscendentalization* of reason. Reason comes to be unavoidably situated in the midst of a plurality of natural languages, which cannot guarantee the unity of reason in the same way as could the extrawordly standpoint of a transcendental subject.

These two central features have become commonplace in twentieth-century philosophy, with different philosophical traditions carrying out a similar linguistic turn along rather different paths. Given their apparent significance, it is important to examine whether these features have to be regarded as constitutive of the linguistic turn as such, or whether they should instead be called into question as consequences resulting only from an implausible reification of language.

To shed light on this issue, I will begin by examining Hamann's critique of Kant, which can be viewed as the starting point of the linguistic turn in the German tradition, the point at which this tradition makes a definitive break with the philosophy of consciousness (chapter 1). Next, I will proceed to discuss Humboldt's view of language, which is not only far more elaborate than Hamann's brief and fragmentary remarks, but also far more influential in the context of contemporary German philosophy[1] (chapter 2). Examining the views of these authors will provide the needed background for assessing the way in which Humboldt's conception of language is radicalized by hermeneutic philosophy (chapter 3). It will also help us to understand how Habermas develops his own view from out of this hermeneutic tradition, even while trying to recover those aspects of Humboldt's standpoint that it neglects (chapter 4).

1. Precisely because this tradition inaugurates a new philosophical paradigm, it was not well received by the dominant philosophy of its time and was confined to the shadows by the preeminence of German idealism. However, its influence on German (as well as non-German) philosophers in this century has become significant.

1

Hamann's Critique of Kant: The Role of Language as Constitutive of Our Relation with the World

The significance of Hamann's critique of Kant is certainly not due to its initial repercussions in the author's own lifetime, which were rather minimal. The weight of this critique is actually due to its anticipation of ideas that took hold only two centuries later. Hamann's critique of Kant, never read by the latter author,[1] is contained in two brief papers. The first is a review written on the occasion of the publication of the *Critique of Pure Reason,* which Hamann read while it was still in press. The second (dating from 1784) is a more elaborate if equally fragmentary paper entitled "Metakritik über den Purismus der Vernunft."[2]

We can see the *leitmotiv* of Hamann's metacritique in his claim that "reason is language, *logos,*" or that "without the word, neither reason nor world." As mentioned earlier, this theme recurs systematically in the tradition that extends down to Heidegger and Gadamer.[3] Given its great importance, it is necessary to reflect

1. For a discussion of Hamann's relationship with Kant, see F. C. Beiser (1987), pp. 16–43.

2. In the collection of Hamann's works, *Vom Magus im Norden und der Verwegenheit des Geistes.* (See the bibliography for the complete references to all works cited throughout the present book.)

3. Herder also begins his critique of Kant by pointing out that "the Greeks refer to both reason and language with a single word, *logos*" (XXI, p. 19). Although Herder's elaborate critique of Kant is interesting in its own right, I will not

on the precise meaning of the identification of language and reason by the authors in question. For it is noteworthy that no such identification can be found in Greek philosophy, Gadamer's interpretative efforts notwithstanding.

In the view of language sketched in the first book of Aristotle's *De Interpretatione,* we already find language in its mediating role between two fixed poles, namely, the "things out there" and the affections of the soul. This inaugurates a tradition, extending down to Kant, that explains the workings of language by way of a model centered in the *designation* of objects with the help of words (or names). As Aristotle explains:

Now spoken sounds are symbols of affections in the soul, and written marks symbols of spoken sounds. And just as written marks are not the same for all men, neither are spoken sounds. But what these are in the first place signs of—affections of the soul—are the same for all; and what these affections are likenesses of—actual things—are also the same.[4]

The full workings of language are thereby reduced to its designating function, such that language becomes an intraworldly tool for "representing" objects that exist independently of it. This makes it impossible to view language in its various constituting functions, in its quasi-transcendental role for our understanding of the world. And precisely this *constitutive* view of language is what lies behind its identification with reason in the Hamann-Herder-Humboldt tradition. On this point, Schnädelbach remarks as follows in his *Philosophie* (1986):

Although Aristotle means by *logos* both reason and language, he is oblivious of any perspectivism concerning languages. For him, the diversity of natural languages is no objection against the unity and permanent

---

discuss it here, for it would divert us from the general themes of the present book. For the same reason, I will discuss Hamann's critique of Kant only insofar as it anticipates central ideas of the new conception of language elaborated by this tradition, without providing an exhaustive exposition of it. For an interesting reconstruction of Hamann's critique, see J. Simon (1979), pp. 135–165.

4. *De Interpretatione* I, 16a3–8.

identity of reason, because he interprets language as a set of conventional—i.e., in principle arbitrary—signs of those affections (*pathemata*) to be found in every consciousness—which are in turn (non-conventional) signs of external objects. Given the sameness of the external world and the structure of human sensibility which is common to all men, that to which signs refer also has to be the same for all men. . . . This purely instrumental view of language, linked to the idea of an invariable human reason, constituted the unquestioned foundation of philosophy of language from Aristotle to Kant. . . . In their critical confrontation with this view of language, Hamann and Herder saw that language is not a mere instrument for fixing and communicating the experience of the world, for that which we experience is determined, "constituted," by the character of our own language. The cost of recognizing this is that reason . . . cannot be thought as "alingual" either; it has to be already, in itself, linguistic reason. Hamann and Herder criticize Kant for holding fast to a "pure" reason, independent of language. . . . Since then, "reason and language" has been the systematic central problem of all philosophy of reason in general.[5]

1.1 Language as the Hidden Common Root of Understanding and Sensibility Sought by Kant

In light of the theme sketched above, we can now consider the central features of Hamann's metacritique of Kant. The core of this critique touches on the three "purisms" pursued by Kant, which in Hamann's opinion are not feasible:

The *first* purification of philosophy consists in the attempt—partly misconstrued and partly failed—to make reason independent of all tradition and belief. The *second* reaches even further in its transcendental aspiration and ends up with nothing less than the complete independence of reason from experience and everyday induction. . . . The *third*, highest and, as it were, *empirical* purism concerns *language*, that unique first and ultimate organ and criterion of reason, with no other credential whatsoever than *tradition* and *use*.[6]

According to Hamann, this triple "purity" of reason has a single origin: the illusory attempt to separate reason from the actual

5. p. 109.

6. MK, pp. 206–207.

and historical conditions of its existence.[7] He criticizes this general tendency of the Enlightenment with a systematic objection, namely, the impossibility of "purifying" reason of language in any way, since language is the "unique first and ultimate organ and criterion of reason."

To defend this point of view, Hamann chooses the indirect path of a metacritique. That is to say, he develops his critique by examining the conditions of possibility of the very analysis carried out in the *Critique of Pure Reason*. To this extent, he understands his criticism as a metareflection on that which Kant tacitly presupposed. This metareflection is carried out by Hamann by means of a question that Kant did not answer, insofar as he "forgot" to pose it: "how is the capacity to *think* possible"?[8] Only through the prompting of such a question could Kant have discovered that "the capacity to think rests on language."[9] If Hamann succeeds in justifying the implicit assumption that language is "constitutive" of thinking, the general aim of his critique will have been achieved. If thinking is inextricably bound up with an already existing language that makes it possible, the very idea of a presuppositionless starting-point, which underlies the depiction of reason as "pure," is a mere illusion. As Gründer points out, "insofar as there can be no thinking without a language, there cannot be a suprahistoric or ahistoric reason."[10]

Hamann's justification of this claim, as we shall see a bit later, lies in his view of language as that common root of understanding and sensibility for which Kant had searched in vain. Hamann's explana-

---

7. The general line of Hamann's critique of Kant fits perfectly with the later critique of Hegel in his attempt to "dissolve the Kantian dualisms." This is recognized by Hegel himself, for whom Hamann's critique hits "at the core of the problem of reason" (*Hamanns Schriften*, in *Berliner Schriften 1818–1831*, p. 270, cited by Simon 1979, p. 158). However, the emphasis on the connection between language and reason that is characteristic of Hamann's critique is not followed up by Hegel. This is the aspect of Hamann's critique which is, in retrospect, revolutionary.

8. MK, p. 208.

9. Ibid.

10. Gründer (1982), p. 53.

tion of this view not only makes up the core of his metacritique, but also represents the key to any subsequent linguistic turn:

Words, then, have an *aesthetic* and *logical* capacity. As visible and audible objects, they belong, along with their elements, to the realm of *sensibility* and *intuition*. But according to the spirit of their *purpose* and *meaning,* they belong to the realm of the understanding and of concepts. Therefore words are as much pure and empirical intuitions as they are pure and empirical concepts: *empirical* because they cause visual and auditory sensations; *pure* inasmuch as their meaning is not determined by anything belonging to these sensations.[11]

The special character of language lies precisely in its hybrid character as both empirical and conceptual, that is, in its "aesthetic and logical capacity." Insofar as language unifies these two dimensions, it is the condition of possibility of that which can only be generated *after* the acquisition of a language—namely, the conceptual domain of meanings detachable from their sign-substratum. The abstraction of such a domain can only be explained by recourse to our linguistic capacity, in terms of our ability to use signs to represent nonlinguistic entities. This is why Hamann talks about "the receptivity of language" rather than about "sensibility," as Kant does.

Such a priority of language over the transcendental aesthetic expresses the peculiar "turn" that Hamann gives to the Kantian transcendental project. The synthesis that Kant sought in the "schematism of reason" (and that led him to the insoluble puzzle of explaining this synthesis as a causal interface between the understanding and the things in themselves) is *always already linguistically realized.* Reflection always comes too late, as it were, when it tries to "deduce" such a synthesis by means of what Hamann ironically termed a "violent, illegitimate, idiosyncratic separation of that which has been put together by nature" (p. 202).

Hamann is well aware of the scope of his critique, which questions the very idea of an a priori deduction of the principles that reason "dreams" it can give to itself as if by spontaneous generation. As he points out:

11. Pp. 210–211.

no deduction is necessary to establish the genetic priority of *language* . . . over the *seven* sacred functions of logical principles and deductions. Not only does the entire capacity to think rest on language . . . but language is also *the center of the misunderstandings of reason about itself.* (italics mine) [12]

1.2   The Untenability of the Kantian Distinction between A Priori and A Posteriori

Questioning the very idea of an "a priori deduction" is one of the central consequences of Hamann's critique of Kant. Viewed in retrospect, it is surely its most revolutionary feature, remaining unparalleled until twentieth-century philosophy.

The background to this critical move can be reproduced as follows. Hamann's metacritique radicalizes the transcendental viewpoint by asking for the conditions of possibility of an allegedly "pure reason." This radicalization culminates in the discovery of something (namely, language) that is both transcendental and empirical. But this discovery necessarily renders dysfunctional the application of the basic categorical distinctions of transcendental philosophy—for these distinctions were meaningful precisely only under the exclusion of such a possibility (that of a transcendental-empirical hybrid).

A fateful tension already appears if one tries to apply the a priori–a posteriori distinction to language. Accordingly, this distinction is strangely transformed, as Hamann expresses in his claim that the meaning and use of words is "*a priori* arbitrary and contingent, but *a posteriori* necessary and indispensable." [13] Language is

12. P. 208.

13. P. 211. The critique of Kant's a priori/a posteriori distinction implicit in this formulation of Hamann situates his metacritique in the same line as Quine's critique of the analytic/synthetic distinction in "Two Dogmas of Empiricism," Wittgenstein's reflections on the peculiar status of "propositions that hold fast" in *On Certainty,* or the transformation of the Kantian apriorism into an "*a priori* perfect" carried out by hermeneutic philosophy. For the different consequences that can be drawn from these critiques, see footnote 12 in chapter 3.

"*a priori* arbitrary and contingent" in its concrete realizations, for as a historical and factual reality, it cannot be "deduced" in any way. As opposed to any a priori claim, language is contingent or fortuitous, as the very plurality of languages attests. But "a posteriori," in accordance with its constitutive character, any given language is "necessary and indispensable" for those who speak it. It is insurmountable (*nichthintergehbar*).[14]

The recognition of these features enables Hamann to question Kant's attempt to distinguish genetically between concepts of pure reason and empirical concepts. In Hamann's view, such an attempt at a "critical self-determination" of reason can occur only as a revision or perhaps an enrichment of a particular language. In this case, it is the language in which Kant carries out his project, a language which is nothing but the product of a particular philosophical tradition. As Simon puts it in his excellent reconstruction of the metacritique:

The free and spontaneous use of language involves a receptive relation to the paths already traveled by a particular language. It is impossible to try to speak without thereby speaking a language previously structured in this sense. . . . No matter how much a philosophy can enrich language, it cannot produce, by itself, the initial fundamental concepts in their determinate relations with each other. For it lacks the "common root" of such concepts and, therefore, it finds itself in a receptive situation and—insofar as, following the Cartesian tradition, only that which is self-generated can be considered "clear"—in a situation of confusion about itself.[15]

To overlook reason's receptivity with respect to a historically given language inevitably leads to misunderstandings. As Hamann

14. The debate about the *Nichthintergehbarkeit* of language is already several decades old. The positions in this debate are divided into two poles. On the one hand, there are those who defend the *Nichthintergehbarkeit* thesis developed by hermeneutic philosophy: see Apel (1963) and (1976). On the other hand, there are those who reject it, either from the standpoint of developmental psychology (see Piaget 1970) or from a constructivist standpoint (see K. Lorenz and J. Mittelstraß 1967). An illuminating account of this controversy can be found in Holenstein (1980).

15. Simon (1979), p. 150.

emphasizes, language, as the channel for transmitting a particular fore-understanding of the world, has "no other credential whatsoever than tradition and use." Insofar as this is overlooked, language remains at "the center of the misunderstandings of reason about itself."

If Kant's system tacitly presupposes a given, historically transmitted language, it is of course vain to think of this system as the product of "pure" reason. The problem that arises from this new view of language is how to make systematic philosophy compatible with the linguistically and historically determined character of human thought. Hamann argues that a radicalization of the Kantian "critique," as an attempt to dissolve "the misunderstandings of reason with itself," has to begin with a reflection on language "just as it is." Such reflection always involves an extension if not an enrichment of the particular language in which it occurs (as Hamman remarks with respect to the terms coined by Kant). But this extension takes place in and through language itself, and therefore remains conditioned by it.

In these brief remarks on the internal problems of transcendental philosophy, Hamann anticipates most of the problems and consequences now regarded as direct results of the linguistic turn as such. In this sense, our review of Hamann's metacritique of Kant can also serve as an introduction to Humboldt's view—for as we shall see, Humboldt's approach to language remains very close to the themes originated by Hamann, even if Humboldt displays a far greater theoretical sophistication.

The Constitutive Dimension of Language According to Humboldt

The importance usually attributed to Humboldt's conception of language stems not only from its de facto influence on German philosophy (its notorious *Wirkungsgeschichte*), but even more importantly, from the wealth of perspectives that converge in his treatment of language.[1] It is difficult to find in subsequent reflections on language any conceptual distinctions that do not already have their equivalent in Humboldt's works. This rich abundance is due mainly to his rejection of any reductionism that might try to achieve systematicity at the cost of losing complexity. But perhaps as a result of this attitude, Humboldt's numerous sketches of the nature of language—usually in the form of introductions to his empirical works in comparative linguistics—do not seem to amount to a philosophical theory of language. In the present chapter, I will try to explain the advantages and disadvantages of Humboldt's particular approach.

2.1 Language as Constitutive of the World vs. Language as Tool

Given what has been said so far, we can already see the systematic role played in the German tradition by the critique of the view of

1. A good introduction to Humboldt's view of language in its philosophical dimension can be found in T. Borsche's *Wilhelm v. Humboldt.* For a more complete account of the different perspectives that inform Humboldt's view of language as well as of its leading specific features, see J. Trabant, *Traditionen Humboldts.*

language as "tool." Only through the articulation of this critique does the internal connection between language and our understanding of the world become accessible. It is precisely this connection that elevates language from its previous status of one object of study among others to the rank of a key element in tackling philosophical problems.

Humboldt enumerates the central features of this critique in his "Ueber den Nationalcharakter der Sprachen," when he writes

the diversity of languages is more than a mere diversity of signs . . . words and their syntax simultaneously shape and determine our concepts and . . . given their systematicity and their influence on knowledge and sensibility, different languages are in fact different world-views. (p. 64; IV 420)[2]

In this brief summary, we can see the three fundamental steps that separate Humboldt's position from the received view:

1. The rejection of the view of language as a mere system of signs, as a "tool" for the transmission of prelinguistic thoughts or the designation of objects that exist independently of language. His assessment of this traditional view is made explicit in his most famous work, entitled "Ueber die Verschiedenheit des menschlichen Sprachbaues und ihren Einfluss auf die geistige Entwicklung des Menschengeschlechts" (1830–1835), better known as the introduction to the *Kawiwerk:*

The [received] view is that different languages refer to the same set of independently given objects and concepts but with different words, and that they concatenate these words according to different rules which are of no importance other than for understanding the particular language in question. This view is too natural for man to be liberated from it easily, without reflecting deeply upon language. . . . The diversity of languages is to man no more than a diversity of sounds, which he

2. The quotes from Humboldt are translated from the collection of Humboldt's works edited by A. Flitner and K. Giel (vol. 3): *Schriften zur Sprachphilosophie.* I also provide the references to Humboldt's works edited by the Königlich Prussian Akademie der Wissenschaften, Berlin 1903–36, 17 volumes. When the works cited are not included in the former collection, references are to the latter edition. When page numbers are cited without accompanying volume numbers, reference is to the English edition.

uses, when aiming at objects, as mere tools to reach them. And this is precisely the view that is corrupting the study of language, the view that prevents the development of a real understanding of language and robs of its fertility the little understanding of it already available. Presumably this was the view that prevailed amongst the ancients, although it is not explicitly stated anywhere. If this were not the case, there would have flourished, out of the depths of their philosophy, different ideas about the nature of language, and they would not have concentrated only on the logical and grammatical structure of speech. (p. 153; VI 119)

2. The systematic argument justifying this standpoint is the one described in the second thesis, namely, that "words and their syntax simultaneously shape and determine our concepts," or more generally, the thesis of "the identity of thought and language" (V 433).[3] Humboldt states this crucial thesis even more sharply by adding: "Whatever man is able to think he is also able to say" (V 433).[4] It is the identity of language and thought that establishes the philosophical dimension of the study of language. As Humboldt points out repeatedly: "the true importance of the study of language lies in its participation in the formation of representations" (p. 153; VI 119). The implicit reference to Kant in this formulation is obvious. Humboldt's critical stance toward his forerunner becomes more conspicuous later on:

For man is not born as a pure spirit that only couches ready-made thoughts in sounds. On the contrary, man is born as a sounding, earthly being, whose sounds together with the system underlying their seemingly arbitrary disorder make it all develop: the Great, the Pure and the Spiritual. (p. 154; VI 120)

In this way, Humboldt situates his view in the camp of Hamann's metacritique of Kant. Against any claim to the purity of

---

3. This thesis can be regarded as the very expression of the linguistic turn. As such, it appears systematically—though in different formulations—in all the authors who later participated in the constitution of this new linguistic paradigm. For example, Peirce remarked that "each thought is an unpronounced word," and Wittgenstein that "a thought is a proposition with sense."

4. In the Anglo-American tradition we can find an almost identical insight in J. Searle's principle of expressibility, namely, "whatever can be meant can be said" (Searle 1969).

reason (any belief that it arises out of nothing in an act of self-generation), tradition, experience, and language are recognized as the only foundations of our rationality.

3. Humboldt infers from this critique of the traditional view of language that "different languages are in fact different worldviews." With this conclusion, Humboldt goes further than Hamann in his attempt to thematize language from the new standpoint. He articulates the different perspectives that participate in such a thematization with respect to an essential property of language: its world-disclosing function.

Once we have examined the internal logic that relates the new thematization of language to a criticism of the traditional view, we can enter in more detail into this criticism, which is far more elaborate in Humboldt than in the limited remarks of Hamann.

A constant feature of all of Humboldt's methodological reflections on the study of language is his rejection of any thematization that would reduce language to one system of signs among others. Thus Humboldt expresses his opposition to those who "want to annihilate the specific effect of language which arises from its peculiar substance, and view language only as a sign" (pp. 22–23; IV 30–31).

With this antisemiotic remark, Humboldt does not try to deny that words function as signs, at least not in the obvious sense that, as physical tokens, they refer to something different from themselves (namely, to "concepts,"[5] as Humboldt repeatedly says). However, the relation between sign and designatum in the case of language is very different from the relation found in other systems of signs. Whereas the things designated in these other

5. Humboldt repeatedly emphasizes that "[b]y words we understand the signs of particular concepts" (p. 70). This view of the designative function of words as "indirect," mediated by concepts (or meanings), where words are conceived as predicates rather than names, is characteristic not only of this tradition of philosophy of language, but also of the tradition initiated by Frege. Retrospectively, we can regard this view as the origin of the reification of language inherent in both traditions. It is for this reason that, as we shall see, this view has been questioned in the last few decades by the theories of "direct" reference developed by authors such as Kripke, Putnam, Donnellan, Kaplan, and others.

systems usually have an existence independent of the material elements that name them, words and concepts constitute a unity. As Humboldt remarks:

the word as designation of the concept [is related to] the sign and the symbol. But this is the place to establish these three concepts precisely, and to show that the word does indeed share properties with both of the others, but also, in accordance with its innermost nature, is different from both. Insofar as it summons forth the concept through its sound, it certainly fulfills the purpose of a sign; but it passes entirely outside the class of signs insofar as while that which is designated has an existence independent of its sign, the concept first receives its completion through the word, neither of them separable from the other. To misunderstand this, and to regard words as mere signs, is the fundamental error that destroys all science of language and all proper appreciation of language. (V 428)

As we can gather from Humboldt's remarks, the thesis of the identity of language and thought is based on the indissoluble synthesis that constitutes words and concepts, and on the immanent linguistic character of concepts that follows from this. This thesis and the critique of the view of language as a tool (i.e., as a system of signs, as a means for the designation of independently existing objects) are two sides of the same coin. They are but two ways of questioning the same traditional assumption that language has a purely *passive* character. This view arises from the objectification of language (which considers it only as an intrawordly system of signs), and renders inaccessible the functions inherent *in* language.

Against such objectification, which Humboldt regards as the foundation of the traditional mistaken view of language, he makes in the introduction to the *Kawiwerk* his most famous claim: "[language] is not a product (*ergon*) but an activity (*energeia*)" (p. 418, VII 46).

In this way, Humboldt carries out a paradigm shift that affects not only *linguistics,* whose development in the twentieth century reveals the consequences of this shift quite clearly, but also *philosophy,* for which languages (regarded as objectified systems of signs) never previously had a philosophical dimension at all. In addition, the paradigm shift carried out by Humboldt takes place in two separate dimensions.

In its *cognitive-semantic* dimension, this shift consists in viewing language not as a mere system of signs, not as something objectifiable (intraworldly), but as something *constitutive of the activity of thinking,* as the very condition of possibility of this activity. Language is thus elevated to *quasi-transcendental* status, claiming against subjectivity the authorship of the operations constituting the subject's worldview. With this transfer of powers, the analysis of language becomes indissolubly tied to the question concerning the conditions of possibility of the *objectivity of experience.* These conditions now have to be derived from the *world-disclosing function* of language (2.2).

In its *communicative-pragmatic* dimension, the shift consists in regarding this *constitutive* character of language as the result of a process or *activity:* namely, *the praxis of speaking.* In this way, language becomes the guarantor of the *intersubjectivity of communication,* the condition of possibility of *understanding* between speakers (2.3).

The scope of the perspectives combined in Humboldt's outlook, more comprehensive than in any theory since, entails a chasm between two distinct aspects of language. This is expressed clearly by Humboldt in his 1800 letter to Schiller, in which he defines language as "a sensible medium that is *at the same time* a work of man and an expression of the world" (p. 179). In what follows, I will try to explain the difficulties inherent in Humboldt's attempt to account for these two features of language without reducing one to the other.

2.2 Articulation as World-Disclosure: The Cognitive-Semantic Dimension of Language

As regards the cognitive-semantic dimension of language, Humboldt's view of language as an activity underscores the fact that language "creates" or "constitutes" something new, something that could never exist without this creating activity and which therefore cannot be considered independently of it. On this point, he remarks:

The generation of language is, from the beginning, a *synthetic process* in the most genuine sense of the term, *where the synthesis creates something that did not exist before in any constituent part.* (p. 473, VII 95)

In this genuine synthesis, which Humboldt terms "articulation" and regards as the "authentic essence" of language, we can see an anticipation of the critique of the paradigm of consciousness[6] carried out in the twentieth century (from Peirce to Saussure and from Frege to Wittgenstein). For each of its representatives, this critique is aimed at the untenable attempt to reduce linguistic articulation to a synthesis of prelinguistic representations that would somehow perfectly mirror the relation between objects in the external world. As shown by the efforts of that tradition in the philosophy of language inaugurated by Frege, the opposite is true. In fact, our representations exhibit a propositional structure analogous to that of sentences, and to that extent can only be explained by way of the latter, rather than the other way around.[7]

In this context, Humboldt remarks that "*articulation* is the authentic essence of language, the lever *through which language and thought are produced,* the culmination of their intimate mutual connection" (p. 192, VI 153).

From his reflections a few pages later, we can sense what he believes to be the role of linguistic articulation in the synthetic activity of knowledge as explained by Kant:

Subjective activity fashions an *object* in thought. For no class of representations can be regarded as a purely receptive contemplation of a thing already present. The activity of the senses must combine *synthetically* with the inner action of the mind, and from this combination the

6. As a philosophical critique of the paradigm of consciousness, this tradition's critical departure from Kant is more than a mere historical contingency.

7. For the impossibility of reducing the linguistic articulation (of the state of affairs "that *p*") to a (categorical) synthesis between consciousness and its objects, see Tugendhat's critique of Husserl in his *Vorlesungen zur Einführung in die sprachanalytische Philosophie,* pp. 161–175.

representation is ejected, becomes an object *vis-à-vis* the subjective power, and, perceived anew as such, returns back into the latter. *But language is indispensable for this.* . . . Thus the representation becomes transformed into *real objectivity*, without being deprived of subjectivity on that account. *Only language can do this; and without this transformation . . . the act of concept-formation, and with it all true thinking, is impossible.* So quite regardless of communication between man and man, *speech is a necessary condition for the thinking* of the individual in solitary seclusion. (p. 56)

Thus Humboldt argues against Kant that "intellectual activity and language are one and inseparable from each other; we cannot even consider one as generative and the other as generated" (pp. 191–192, VI 152–153). For

[i]*ntellectual activity*, entirely mental, entirely internal, and to some extent passing without trace, becomes, through *sound*, externalized in speech and perceptible to the senses. Thought and language are therefore one and inseparable from each other. But the former is also intrinsically bound to the necessity of entering into a *union* with the verbal sound; thought cannot otherwise achieve clarity, nor the representation become a concept. (pp. 54–55)

In this very sense, Humboldt also remarks later that "the word is the individual shaping of the concept, and if the latter wants to leave this shape, it can only find itself again in other words" (p. 92).

The discrepancy with Kant lies in the fact that Humboldt views the expression of thought in a linguistic articulation as the true production of it, a production without which no thought is possible. Only in the act of linguistic articulation is the unity of thought synthesized. This departure from Kant becomes clear in the inapplicability of most of the Kantian distinctions to the phenomenon of linguistic articulation. The double nature of language, its dual ontological character as *both* sensible and intelligible, precludes any attempt at dividing it. In this way, we are led to identify language as the hidden root of the two sources of knowledge (sensibility and understanding) postulated by Kant. For only in language, only "in the word . . . a dual unity, of sound and concept, comes together" (p. 70).

Precisely because human knowledge requires the receptive act of sensibility, it is only in linguistic articulation, in the discursivization of "pure" intellectual activity, that such activity becomes accessible to human experience. Only through sensibility can representations become "experienceable" objects for the subject who has formed them, and thus achieve *objectivity* without thereby losing their intelligible character, their internal kinship with subjectivity:

the nature of language consists in adhering to everything that exists, corporeal, individual, and accidental, but thereby transferring it to an ideal, spiritual, universal and necessary realm, and giving it a configuration that evokes its origin. . . . Language elevates everything inadvertently, as if by itself, to a more universal, higher level; and, on the other hand, the spiritual can only assert itself through language. (pp. 158–159, VI 124–125).[8]

In the systematic account of his position offered by Humboldt in "Über Denken und Sprechen," we find the following theses:

1. The essence of thinking consists in reflecting, that is, in distinguishing who is thinking from what is thought.

2. In order to reflect, the spirit must pause for an instant in its progressive activity, unify what is represented, and thus face it as an object. . . .

5. No thought—not even the purest—can take place without the help of the universal forms of our sensibility; only in them can we *apprehend and at the same time retain* thoughts.

6. The sensible constitution of the units in which certain portions of thought are grouped to be placed as objects before the subject, to be opposed as parts to other parts of a larger totality, is in the widest sense of the word: *language.*

7. *Therefore language arises immediately and simultaneously with the first act of reflection.* (VII 581–582)

---

8. Humboldt's criticism of Kant is peculiar because, unlike many others after him, he is not criticizing Kant's strategy of abstracting a transcendental domain or a transcendental ego from out of real, empirical egos. On the contrary, he claims that these empirical egos can only develop a transcendental domain, an ideal domain of generality (i.e., "universality and necessity"), given the double nature of language (or in Kant's terms, its double status as "transcendental" and "empirical"). For Humboldt, the generality of thought is simply the generality of language. In this sense, he claims against Kant that concepts or ideal objects "are first created through the words that designate them and exist only in them" (VII, p. 640).

As Humboldt's list of theses serves to emphasize, the true function of language begins much earlier than the transmission of information between subjects. Thus, contrary to every instrumentalist view of language, its function begins *much earlier* than communication in the strict sense. Language is the only medium through which representations can achieve *objectivity*. That is to say, it is the only medium through which they become concepts apprehensible by the subject and hence *sayable*, able to be intersubjectively shared by speakers. This is why, as we saw, Humboldt remarks that "speech is a necessary condition for the thinking of the individual in solitary seclusion."

The systematic consequence entailed by this change of perspective is simply the inverse of the discovery that the phenomenal world only acquires objectivity in a *particular language*. This is observed by Humboldt in terms not far removed from Kant's paradigm, but which for just this reason display clear relativistic consequences. He remarks:

> The interdependence of word and idea shows us clearly that languages are not actually a means of representing a truth already known, but rather of discovering the previously unknown. *Their diversity is not one of sounds and signs.* . . . The sum of the knowable, as the field to be tilled by the human mind, lies among all languages, independent of them, in the middle. Man cannot approach this purely objective realm other than through his cognitive and sensory powers, that is, in a subjective manner. (pp. 19–20, IV 27–28)

As we have seen, this reformulation of Kant's Copernican Revolution is required by the recognition that language is constitutive of our understanding of the world. The detranscendentalizing move implicit in such a reformulation yields unavoidable relativistic consequences. Once the need to reformulate the idea of an original prelinguistic synthesis into a real synthesis *within* language is made plausible, Kant's Revolution faces an unwelcome consequence. The ahistorical and strictly transcendental strategy (applied to the cognitive and sensory powers of subjectivity in order to obtain universally valid results) is untenable in the case of language. The reason that this is so can be gathered from Humboldt himself, just a few paragraphs earlier:

"Thinking is not only dependent on language in general, but, to a certain degree, on each individually determinate language" (p. 16, IV 22).

It is precisely this asymmetry between subjectivity or "consciousness in general" and language that forces us to renounce any idea of an original (and unique) synthesis. As Humboldt repeatedly points out:

language appears in reality only as a multiplicity. Talking about language in general involves an abstraction of the understanding. In fact language only appears as something particular, and moreover, only in the most individual configuration, that is, as dialect. (p. 295, VI 241)

To this extent, we cannot try to save the idea of an original synthesis, as if talking about "language in general" were enough to undo the detranscendentalizing move inherent in the linguistic turn itself. Such an attempt would make it impossible to analyze that which seems to make language relevant in the first place: its function of world-disclosure.[9] For this function could then only be reconstructed genetically, by appealing to a moment of generation or creation of language—as absurd an idea for Humboldt as it was for Hamann. The question of the origin of language arises only from a weakly defined quest: the search for an original synthesis of the two poles of language (the sensible and the intelligible). Humboldt responds to the hypothesis of the origin of language—much discussed in his day—with systematic arguments. To some extent, they anticipate the central intuition lying behind structuralism:

9. Concerning the impossibility of stopping the detranscendentalizing consequences inherent in the linguistic turn, Apel points out the systematic implications of this asymmetry. As he remarks in *Die Idee der Sprache:*

[W]hat is *a priori* in our world-view in a transcendental sense, what is always already presupposed in and by ordinary language, cannot simply be equated with the *Kantian a priori* of "consciousness in general" and its categories. It is not fixed once and for all for all men, but it is simply the totality of the fore-understanding of the world in which we find ourselves "always already" as members of a historical linguistic community in any actual world-view, e.g. in a scientific one. (p. 26)

to my deepest felt conviction, language has to be considered as immediately given to man; for it is impossible to explain it as being produced . . . by human reason. It does not help, for that matter, to assume thousands and thousands of years for it to be invented. . . . For man to be able to actually understand a single word, not only receive it as a purely sensuous affection, but really understand it as an articulated sound referring to a concept, he *already has to have the whole language and its inner structure within himself.* There are no particulars in language, each of its elements only announces itself as part of a whole. No matter how natural it seems to suppose a progressive development of language, *its invention could only take place all at once.* Man is only human through language; but in order to invent language, man would have to be already human. (pp. 10–11, IV 15–16)

The argument behind this last contention is clear. The motive for the genetic hypothesis is the attempt to reduce language to some other term from which it could have developed. But language, as the bearer of a worldview or prior constitution of meaning that determines our understanding, is the condition of possibility for all experience. Precisely for this reason, the attempt to find some foundation prior to language implies that its function of world-disclosure, its "constitutive" character, is denied. But without such constitutive status, the hypothesis itself loses all relevance.

The only way out of this situation is to reject the abstraction that is inherent in the idea of an "original synthesis." As Scharf rightly points out, "the idea of a conjunction of sensibility and intellectuality in language" can only be maintained if we understand such a conjunction "as a synthesis always already realized, which does not have to be genetically reconstructed but accepted as a [past] perfect constant of language" (Scharf 1983, p. 232).

This would involve the abandonment of the search for the ultimate foundations of knowledge sought by Kant. And it is precisely this renunciation that entails relativistic consequences.

On the one hand, the view of language as constitutive of our worldview forces us to uphold Kant's Copernican Revolution. That is, it forces us to regard the conditions of possibility of our *understanding* of the world as, at the same time, the conditions of possibility of *that which is understood in* the world. Hence knowledge of language and knowledge of the world are inextricably interwoven. On this point Humboldt remarks:

The picture of language as designating merely *objects,* already perceived *in themselves,* is not sustained by an examination of *what language engenders as its product.* By means of such a picture we would in fact never exhaust the deep and full content of language. Just as no concept is possible *without language,* so also *there can be no object for the mind,* since it is only through the concept, of course, that anything external acquires full being for consciousness. (p. 59) [10]

But on the other hand, what is now constitutive of experience has, as we saw, an irreducibly *plural* character. Thus we are forced to conclude with Humboldt that "there resides in every language a *peculiar world-view*" (p. 60). [11] The justification of this assertion, the most famous and most polemical of Humboldt's claims, contains all of the premises and consequences inherent in the view of language that he develops. We will encounter this view again in Heidegger, as well as in Gadamer. Humboldt explains the meaning of this thesis by saying:

Language is a world-view not only because it must be coextensive with the world itself, since each and every concept is to be captured by it, but also because the transformation brought about by language among the objects enables the mind to see their correlation, so inseparably tied to the concept of world. (ibid.)

It is not that language carries out the function of world-disclosure because it is a mirror of the totality of beings. Instead, it is because of its holistic structure, its character of symbolically articulated totality, that it first enables the world to appear as an *ordered*

10. This strict parallel with transcendental philosophy—which equates the case of "perception" with that of "understanding"—implies the thesis that meaning determines reference. I will discuss the problems concerning this thesis later (see pp. 59ff).

11. Thus the different "worldviews" inherent in different languages cannot claim any universal validity. Although they are regarded as constitutive of the experience and knowledge of speakers, just as the forms of intuition and the categories were for Kant, these worldviews are (as already indicated by Hamann) purely contingent and plural.

whole. As Humboldt had already pointed out against Kant, only the order of linguistic concepts entails an order of objects. This is the transformation that language "brings about among the objects" by turning what would otherwise be a disconnected flux of perceptions into objects properly so called. That is, it turns them into entities that are subsumable under general concepts and which to that extent are identifiable and reidentifiable. This is why it is only through the synthesis inherent in the holistic structure of language that "the junction of the world is revealed" (p. 224, VI 180).[12]

12. For Humboldt, this "synthesis" arises from the nature of language as a structured totality, which makes it the bearer of a worldview. In the articulation of this point (later developed systematically by Saussure) we can see the emergence of a holistic view of language, which definitively separates this tradition from the traditional instrumentalist view of language and which is inherited, as we shall see, by the philosophical hermeneutics of Heidegger and Gadamer. Humboldt remarks

> [S]ince the connection of the simplest concepts stimulates the whole network of categories of thought, the "positive"/the "negative," the "part"/the "whole," "unity"/"multiplicity," "cause"/"effect," "reality"/"possibility" and "necessity" . . . as soon as we express the connections of the simplest ideas with clarity and precision, a totality of language (including its whole vocabulary) is present. Each pronounced word prefigures or prepares the unpronounced. (p. 3, IV 4)

Humboldt holds that words only acquire meaning contextually, as parts of an articulated whole. As he repeatedly emphasizes, "in the majority of cases a word achieves its complete validity only through the context in which it appears" (p. 563, VII 173). As we saw, it follows from this that "for man to be able to actually understand a single word, he has to have already the whole language and its inner structure within himself," or in Wittgenstein's terms, that "to understand a sentence means to understand a language" (*Philosophical Investigations*, I sec. 199). Humboldt tries to give plausibility to this holistic view of language by means of the following image:

> Language can be compared to an immense web, in which every part stands in a more or less clearly recognizable connection with the others, and all with the whole. Whatever his point of departure, man always makes contact in speaking with a merely isolated portion of this fabric, but invariably does so, instinctively, as if everything that this one portion must necessarily agree with were simultaneously present to him at the same moment. (p. 69)

The Constitutive Dimension of Language According to Humboldt

To the precise extent that the fore-understanding inherent in language allows for the constitution of a world (in the strict sense of the term: *kosmos* versus *chaos*), language becomes:

• that which *determines* the objects *in* the world in which they appear.[13] Here, Humboldt adds:

Man lives primarily with objects, indeed, since feeling and acting in him depend on his representations, he actually does so *exclusively*, as language presents them to him. (p. 60)

• that which constitutes the absolute framework of reference for the individuals who find themselves within that world.[14] Humboldt continues:

By the same act whereby [man] spins language out of himself, *he spins himself into it,* and every language draws about the people that possesses it *a circle whence it is possible to exit only by stepping over at once into the circle of another one.* (p. 60)

Humboldt's explanation of this last claim clarifies the relativistic implications of his view:

To learn a *foreign language* should therefore be to acquire a new standpoint in the world-view hitherto possessed, and in fact to a certain extent

---

But, on the other hand, the fact that words only acquire meaning contextually becomes pregnant with implications when combined with the fact of the plurality of languages, that is, with the fact that the expressions of different languages "cut up the territory lying in their midst (if we may so name the object designated by them) in different ways, and contain fewer, more or different determinations" (IV 29). See footnote 14, this chapter.

13. This assumption captures what I have termed the thesis that meaning determines reference, typical of this tradition of the philosophy of language (though not explicitly expressed in these terms). See footnote 10, this chapter.

14. This holistic conception of language, characteristic of the view of language as responsible for world-disclosure, is based on two internally related insights that we have already encountered in Humboldt: the contextual nature of meaning, and the inseparability of knowledge of language and knowledge of the world. Given that the thesis of meaning holism is a common denominator among members of this tradition, I will refer to it (and its implications) in my discussion of the authors of this tradition throughout this book.

this is so, since every language contains the whole conceptual fabric and mode of representation of a portion of mankind. *But because we always carry over, more or less, our own language-view, this outcome is not purely and completely experienced.* (p. 60)

Clearly, the thesis that in every language there resides a *peculiar* worldview is simply the reverse side of the thesis that the worldviews or world-interpretations inherent in different languages are necessarily *divergent*. The relativism implied by this thesis is explicitly uttered by Humboldt in terms reminiscent of Heidegger after the *Kehre*. In "Über Denken und Sprechen," Humboldt remarks:

Every language places *definite boundaries* upon the spirits of those who speak it, and *insofar as it provides a determinate orientation, excludes others.* (VII 621)[15]

Precisely because language is deemed responsible for world-disclosure as the privileged repository of culture, it represents for the individual a power that determines her mode of thinking and configures her experience. This consequence seems to be the inverse of the rejection of the view of language as a mere intra-worldly instrument. After his previously cited remark about the tendency to regard language as a mere designator of independently existing objects (see pp. 14–15), Humboldt points out that, owing to this "objectivist" view, "[man] forgets that the mass of individual parts [of language] which keep accumulating, without

---

15. The parallel with the late Heidegger becomes even clearer if we take into consideration one of the consequences that Humboldt draws from this idea. If every language entails an historically (and therefore contingently) developed particular way of interpreting the world (i.e., a peculiar worldview, or in Heidegger's terminology a particular "understanding of being"), it follows that, "Whatever be the language, it bears within itself, at all the times of its existence, the expression of *all concepts that can possibly ever be developed within a nation*" (V 433). Heidegger will retain this idea that the particular worldview of a linguistic community has its own internal logic, in his reflections on Western culture as determined by a peculiar world-disclosure or understanding of being (namely, presence at hand), which acquires explicit expression in the history of metaphysics and fatefully drives this culture toward total destruction.

The Constitutive Dimension of Language According to Humboldt

his being aware of it, limits and dominates him" (p. 153, VI 119). He has a systematic argument for this:

Language belongs to me because I bring it forth. It does not belong to me because I cannot bring it forth otherwise than as I do, and since the ground of this lies at once in the speaking and having-spoken of every generation of mankind . . . it is language itself that restrains me when I speak. (p. 63)[16]

Keeping in mind that Humboldt regards language as a worldview rather than as just a system of rules, it is clear that:

When we think how the current *generation* of a people is governed by all that their *language* has *experienced,* through all the preceding centuries . . . it then becomes evident *how small, in fact, is the power of the individual compared to the might of language.* (p. 63)

In that set of principles that characterizes the view of language inaugurated by Humboldt, we can distinguish two aspects that are analytically distinct, yet interrelated. Each of them gives rise to different problems.

To put it schematically, we can (1) identify a set of *methodological* problems arising from this *holistic* view, problems related to the possibility of a theory of language; (2) at the same time, we can identify a set of *thematic* problems arising from the thesis that meaning determines reference. In this case, the problems pertain to the relativistic consequences of considering this conception of language as the paradigm for resolving philosophical problems.

1. As we have seen, the identification of language as responsible for world-disclosure entails the view that language is a *holistically* structured totality incapable of *objectification.* Lacking any equivalent for the transcendental subject, that is, for an extrawordly or extralinguistic subject, Humboldt's own project of a science or theory of language becomes paradoxical.

Humboldt is fully aware of this problem, and he always lands in the difficulty of trying to objectify that which in his own view

16. Heidegger will later express this same idea in almost literally the same terms with his provocative dictum: "language speaks." See chapter 3 (especially 3.1.2 and 3.1.3).

is the unobjectifiable par excellence. Concerning this point, we find the following remark in "Über Denken und Sprechen":

A second difficulty is that man is always kept enclosed within a circle by language and cannot achieve a point of view external and independent of language. As soon as he wants to go from a word to the concept designated by it, he has no other means at his disposal (if we exclude the objects of intuition) than the translation into another language or a definition which is in turn composed of words. (VII 623) [17]

As we have seen, Humboldt rejects the scientistic attitude of those who objectify language, turning it into a "dead product" (VII 45), a system of signs. Thus, although he holds that certain abstractions are essential for any comparative study of languages (and are to that extent unavoidable assumptions), he insists on the importance of recognizing them as such. That is, we should not give up on an understanding of the nature of language and its functioning that would go beyond what is allowed by these abstractions.[18] It is precisely this rejection of any objectivist view of

17. This argument shows what I mentioned at the beginning of this chapter (see footnote 5), namely, that Humboldt favors the model of predicates rather than that of names, when he talks about the designating function of language. Hence his typical remark that words designate concepts (rather than entities in the world). Humboldt assumes that designation is "indirect," that it takes place by means of concepts that are definable as such only *in* language (that is, by means of other concepts), and which therefore turn reference into something internal to language, susceptible only to an infinite process of translation. In this quote, however, we find that his assumption finds its limit in the case of names, that is, in the case (paradigmatic for the usual understanding of designation) that words designate not "concepts" but entities in the world—or as Humboldt puts it, "objects of intuition."

This is the central idea criticized by the defenders of the theory of "direct" reference when they try to dispose of the reification implicit in the thesis that meaning determines reference without renouncing the linguistic turn. I will return to this matter in chapter 5.

18. For the different aspects in which Humboldt tries to make the scientific study of language compatible with a non-objectivist view of language in its different dimensions (in the relation grammar-logic, grammar-lexicon, language-languages, etc.), see T. Borsche's exposition (1981). Borsche tries to show the internal impossibility of Chomsky's attempt to interpret Humboldt as a precursor of the "generative" view of language. Such an attempt, which Chomsky tries

language that motivates Humboldt's attempt to articulate a philosophical view of language like the one analyzed here, a view going beyond his empirical comparative studies of different languages.

But it is precisely from a philosophical standpoint that this methodological difficulty becomes an insoluble puzzle. This is the paradox of having to rely on the paradigm of language in order to construct a theory of language—or as Heidegger puts it later, "to bring language to language as language." The structural problem inherent in this situation is described by Habermas in his *Postmetaphysical Thinking:*

The objectivists are faced with the problem of having to take up a standpoint between language and reality in order to defend their thesis; but they can only argue for such a null-context from within the context of the language they themselves use. On the other hand, the relativistic

---

to render plausible by citing Humboldt's claim that language "has therefore to make infinite use of finite means" (p. 477, VII 99), finds its limit in the basic "objectivist" view that Chomsky must presuppose in order to carry out his program. In Borsche's argument, we see a sketch of the methodological problem that Humboldt faces. He compares Humboldt's view with two "dynamic" models for the study of language, Chomsky's (the generative view of language) and Weisgerber's (the "energetic" view of language). Regarding this comparison, Borsche remarks:

[I]t could seem as if Weisgerber and Chomsky had carried out, each in his own way, Humboldt's demand that linguistics subordinate the predominantly static way of treating its object to a dynamic one. . . . On Humboldt's view, the comparison between the system of language and the system of nature, in the two modern versions of dynamic linguistics, goes an important step further than the object allows. Both treat languages as subsumable under universal laws. (1981, p. 221)

And in Borsche's opinion, this is incompatible with the view inaugurated by Humboldt. He goes on to remark:

[T]he unity of a language . . . is not an underlying universal law, but its *individual character.* . . . When we consider the "functioning of language as a whole," that is, when we want to carry out a "dynamic" study of language in Humboldt's sense, we cannot look for universal concepts or rules for this functioning. Rather, we face the old difficulty, common in anthropology, of determining an *individual character,* for this is what constitutes the peculiarity of languages and their diversity. (1981, p. 222)

thesis, which concedes a perspectival right to every linguistically constituted view of the world, also cannot be put forth without a performative
self-contradiction. (p. 135)

This difficulty is an unavoidable inheritance of the German tradition. For this reason, it reappears later in philosophical hermeneutics: in Heidegger (as a paradox for "authentic thinking"),
in a more positive sense for Gadamer (as a rejection of the very
idea of a theory), and also in Habermas's view (in relation to his
attempt to construct a theory of meaning).[19]

2. The *thematic* problems arising from this holistic view of language are internally related to the methodological difficulty just
described. Language is conceived as a prior and insurmountable
totality that allows for no perspective external to it. Precisely for
this reason, this view has the tendency to *reify* language, to turn
it (in Habermas's terms) into a "contingent absolute," which by
coinciding with the limits of the world itself *determines* everything
that can appear *within* it. This calls into question in a radical way
the indispensable presupposition for a defense of the *objectivity of
knowledge:* namely, the assumption that there exists an objective
world with entities independent of language. What things *are* thus
becomes relative to that which, in a contingent manner, is linguistically prestructured in each historical language. We will find this
reification carried to its extreme in Heidegger's account of language after the *Kehre.*

To identify the origin of the reification of language (or more
exactly, of its world-disclosing function), we have to return to the
critique of the view of language as an instrument. For, as I pointed
out earlier, it is this critique that leads Humboldt to assume the
thesis that *meaning determines reference;* this thesis, in my opinion,
is responsible for the reification of language characteristic of the
tradition to which he belongs (although this will not be shown in
detail until chapter 5).

---

19. The American tradition of the philosophy of language does not escape this
difficulty either. In its own way, this tradition has been forced to recognize the
holistic character of language and, under the banner of "meaning holism," it
has been dealing for a long time with the difficulties of (or rather, the *impossibility*
of) a theory of meaning. In this connection, see Putnam (1986).

The dominant view of language from Aristotle to Kant, which regards language as an instrument for designating extralinguistic entities, reduces the power of language down to its designating function. This reduction is analyzed by P. T. Geach in his *Reference and Generality*. He traces it back to the confusion of two relations that are actually irreducible to one another: namely, *being a name of* and *being a predicable applying to*. Due to this confusion, the traditional view of language, according to which language is related to the world in the same way as names are to the objects they designate, faces the problem of determining what predicates actually "designate." This problem was already posed in the Middle Ages; the dispute about universals offers clear testimony to its depth.

This problematic conception of language—which we could term, with Geach, the "two-name theory"—is the target of Humboldt's critique. As we have seen, these criticisms are directed essentially against the illicit reduction of the functions of language to the mere designative function. They also rely on a conceptual apparatus more complex than that of the conception they criticized. In contemporary terms, we could say that Humboldt manages to articulate this critique by introducing, along with the traditional distinction between name and object, the distinction between concept (class) and object, and that between meaning and reference.

As a starting point for introducing these distinctions, Humboldt focuses on what we might call the weak point of the traditional view of language: predicates. For as we have seen, the specific difference between language and other sign-systems emerges precisely when we ask in more detail about the objects to which predicates are related. It is this question that enables Humboldt to assert the identity of word and concept. As mentioned before, he argues in the following way:

the word as designation of the concept [is related to] the sign and the symbol. But this is the place to establish these three concepts precisely, and to show that the word does indeed share properties with both of the others, but also, in accordance with its innermost nature, is different from both. Insofar as it summons forth the concept through its sound, it certainly fulfills the purpose of a sign; but it passes entirely outside the class of signs insofar as while that which is designated has an existence independent of its sign, the concept first receives its completion through the word, neither of them separable from the other. To misunderstand this, and to regard words as mere signs, is the fundamental error that destroys all science of language and all proper appreciation of language. (V 428)

Here we find an obvious departure from the view of language as a mediating instrument between prelinguistic thoughts or concepts and external objects. But even more important for Humboldt is his definitive break with the instrument-theory through his introduction of the distinction between *meaning and reference*.[20] He states this as follows:

The word acts in such a way that the object given in it is represented by the soul. This representation must be distinguished from the object; . . . along with the objective part *that relates to the object,* it has a subjective part that *lies in its manner of conceiving.* . . . In turn, we scarcely need to mention that this division rests upon [an] abstraction; [further,] that the word can have no place outside of thought, and neither can its object, if it is non-physical. . . . This remains so even in the case of material objects, since *it is never the objects directly,* but always only the representation of them provided by the word, *that is made present in the soul.* (V 418)

Note that by introducing the distinction between the referent of the word and its meaning (or the "manner of conceiving" through which the word designates its referent), Humboldt eliminates any possibility of a pure designative relation between name and object—precisely that relation which served as the paradigm for the traditional conception of language.

20. In the Anglo-American tradition, Frege is regarded as the author of this distinction, which is obviously crucial for any "linguistic turn" as such. Humboldt, however, not only introduced this distinction almost one hundred years earlier; even more interestingly, he introduced it in precisely the same way and drew the same consequences as Frege (as opposed to other possible forerunners for whom this is not clearly the case, such as Mill with his distinction between connotation and denotation). As we will see, Humboldt (like Frege) generalizes the distinction between meaning and reference to cover *all linguistic signs,* including proper names, and can therefore also maintain, as a general thesis, that *meaning determines reference.*

Accordingly, Humboldt extends this distinction beyond the realm of predicates (or "concepts") into the realm of names, including proper names. He continues as follows:

> The word conceives of every concept as general, as *always designating, strictly speaking, classes of reality,* even if it is a proper name; for thus it comprehends in itself all the various states, with respect to time and space, of that which it designates (that is, representing the referent as a class that contains the referent in all these states, just as different individuals are contained in a generic concept). (V 419)

This implicit reduction of names to predicates, or of the designating relation between names and objects to the attributive relation between a predicate and the object of predication, is what underlies the thesis that meaning determines reference. Or, put in different terms, the view of reference as *indirect,* as necessarily mediated by a meaning whose ideal identity (which Humboldt calls "concept") guarantees the identity of the referent, of that to which we refer in each case. In my view, this thesis marks the systematic point from which the above-mentioned relativistic consequences arise.

If this is not immediately evident, it soon becomes clear from a relatively simple consideration. Let us suppose, as Humboldt does, that even names are actually general concepts. (For instead of designating an object, they too, by strict analogy with predicates, can relate to their referent only in mediated fashion, as if to an object falling under a concept.) Or in what amounts to the same thing, let us suppose that names are related only indirectly to things by way of meanings or concepts. If this is the case, then the idealistic conclusion that Humboldt draws from this assumption becomes unavoidable: namely, that "man [lives] with the objects . . . *exclusively* in the way that they are conveyed to him by language" (VII 60). For, as mere exemplifications of the concepts inherent in language, objects are necessarily prejudiced by concepts. Thus the basic assumption of an exclusively indirect reference leads Humboldt to conclude that "In this way, in words of identical meaning that are found in a number of languages, there arise diverse representations of the same object, and this characteristic of the word contributes chiefly to the fact that every language yields a peculiar world-view" (V 420).[21]

This theory of language—by analogy with Geach's term, we could call it the "no-name theory"—thus falls into a one-sidedness diametrically opposed to that of the traditional view. It *reduces the functioning of language as a whole to its world-disclosing function*, a reduction achieved at the expense of its designative function. As a result of this reification of language, specific languages prejudice our experience through the worldviews that they provide. This occurs to such a degree that even the supposition of an objective world independent of language (one to which we relate through the corresponding use of our words), an assumption that lies at the basis of our notion of truth, can no longer be maintained in any intelligible sense. For we already saw that, as a result of the premises of Humboldt's conception of language, he cannot avoid the following conclusion: "Every language places *definite boundaries* upon the spirit of those who speak it, *and insofar as it provides a determinate orientation, excludes others*" (VII 621).

The absolutizing of the world-disclosing function of language has epistemological consequences just as harmful as those that occur when the designating function is absolutized. This will become clear later, when we discuss the way in which Heidegger radicalizes this view of language.

The internal logic that leads to these consequences is clear. Once we accept the symbolically mediated character of our relationship

---

21. Humboldt explains the grounds for this conclusion elsewhere, resorting more explicitly to the distinction between meaning and reference:

> If in the various languages we compare the expressions for non-physical objects, we will find only those synonyms which, because they are pure constructions, cannot contain anything more or different than what has been placed in them. All other expressions cut up the territory lying in their midst (if we may so name the object designated by them) in different ways, and contain fewer, more or different determinations. The expressions for material objects are probably synonymous insofar as the same object is thought of when they are used, but because they express a definite manner of conceiving the object, their meaning likewise varies. [For] the impression of the individual perspective of the object in the formation of the word determines also . . . how the word calls the object to mind. (IV 29)

with the world, and the dependence of this mediation upon natural languages (historically transmitted and irreducibly plural), we cannot avoid the problems posed by the contingent and determinative character of the worldview transmitted in and by language. This detranscendentalizing step gives rise to the new and paradoxical position that we saw in Hamann: namely, the acceptance of the quasi-transcendental status of language as "a priori arbitrary and contingent, but a posteriori necessary and indispensable."

Here, Humboldt finds himself pulled in two directions. He is unable to decide between them, and equally unable to resolve the dilemma by constructing a philosophical theory (and by thus becoming a sort of Kant of the philosophy of language). The significance of Humboldt's introductory philosophical writings on language is not that of a *theory* of language. Rather, they mark the inauguration of a completely new *standpoint* from which language may be studied.

On the one hand, Humboldt always remains faithful to a universalist position, and to that extent he rejects any crude relativism.[22]

22. The universalist perspective underlying Humboldt's view of language goes unquestioned in the interpretation of Humboldt in the continental tradition. This is no doubt owing to the emphasis that Humboldt places on his hypothesis of an "internal language form." The reception of Humboldt in the American tradition, on the other hand, depicts him as a defender of linguistic relativism. With the exception of Chomsky (who interprets Humboldt as a precursor of generative grammar), Humboldt is seen by this tradition as an advocate of the "principle of linguistic relativity." That is, his view is regarded as a continental contribution to the "Sapir-Whorf hypothesis." Undoubtedly, the relativistic position of Sapir and Whorf with respect to language is one of the possible consequences that can be drawn from the view of language as responsible for world-disclosure, and even a possibility suggested by many of Humboldt's assertions. However, as already pointed out, Humboldt does not settle definitively on any absolute position with respect to this question. Thus his assertions cannot be regarded as arguments for a relativistic position, at least not for one as radical as the Sapir-Whorf hypothesis.

Like Humboldt, Whorf poses his thesis in critical opposition to the classical realist view of language as an instrument. In *Language, Thought, and Reality* he remarks:

It was found that the background linguistic system (in other words, the grammar) of each language is not merely a reproducing instrument for voicing

But this intuition can no longer be made plausible through the
usual realist maneuver of postulating a world independent of

ideas but rather is itself the shaper of ideas, the program and guide for the
individual's mental activity, for his analysis of impressions, for his synthesis of
his mental stock in trade. Formulation of ideas is not an independent process,
strictly rational in the old sense, but is part of a particular grammar, and
differs . . . between different grammars. We dissect nature along lines laid
down by our native languages. The categories and types that we isolate from
the world of phenomena we do not find there because they stare every observer in the face; on the contrary, the world is presented in a kaleidoscopic
flux of impressions which has to be organized by our minds—and this means
largely by the linguistic systems in our minds. (pp. 212–213)

From this consideration, Whorf draws a consequence astonishingly similar to
the one formulated by Hamann (i.e., that a linguistic world-disclosure is "a priori
arbitrary, a posteriori necessary") and also reminiscent of the standpoint characteristic of hermeneutics, which I will discuss in the next chapter. Whorf continues:

We cut nature up, organize it into concepts, and ascribe significances as we
do, largely because we are parties to an *agreement* to organize it in this way—
an agreement that holds throughout our speech community and is codified
in the patterns of our language. *The agreement is, of course, an implicit and un-
stated one, but its terms are absolutely obligatory;* we cannot talk at all except by
subscribing to the organization and classification of data which the agreement decrees. (pp. 213–214; italics mine)

Following these considerations, Whorf introduces his "new principle of relativity": "[A]ll observers are not led by the same physical evidence to the same
picture of the universe, unless their linguistic backgrounds are similar, or can
in some way be calibrated" (p. 214).

The empirical basis of this thesis is Whorf's study of the Hopi Indian language—about which he tries to prove (*pace* Kant) the lack of a conception of
time and space comparable to the one underlying Indo-Germanic languages.

The problem inherent in this hypothesis has been repeatedly pointed out
by its critics: It cannot be defended without committing a "performative self-
contradiction." Kutschera sums up this argument in *Sprachphilosophie:* "If Whorf
were right on the thesis that our language fixes our interpretation of the world,
we could not possibly find languages with worldviews and interpretative schemes
radically different, as Whorf claims. For in that case we would always be locked
up in the worldview of our language and, therefore, we would not be able to
understand and reconstruct a radically different language" (p. 316). About this
theme, see R. L. Miller (1968) and R. L. Brown (1967). A good general exposition and discussion of the *status questionis* of this debate can be found in H.
Gipper (1972).

language, a world-in-itself that would guarantee the objectivity of knowledge. The only alternative is to appeal to the universal character inherent in language itself. Humboldt is convinced that, in Gadamer's terms, "language rejects any argument against its competence." For Humboldt, every language, no matter how "primitive" its degree of evolution, has a *universal character*. That is to say, in every language we can express every thought and every concept:

> However, and this is what is decisive in this context, to the concepts and language of each people, no matter how primitive, there corresponds a totality equivalent in extent to the unlimited human capacity for learning. From this totality it is possible to create, without external aid, everything encompassed by humanity. (p. 399, VII 29)

The plausibility of this thesis lies, for Humboldt, in the fact of *translation:*

> Experience with translation of the most diverse languages and in the use of the most primitive and less developed languages for the initiation in the most mysterious doctrines of a revealed religion, shows that *it is possible to express every concatenation of ideas in every language,* though with different degrees of success. (p. 12, IV 17)

Humboldt offers reasons for this thesis that separate him systematically from Gadamer in spite of the convergence of their views up to this point.[23] These reasons point in the direction of a *formal* view of language in which its supposed universality would be justified. Humboldt remarks:

> Since language is a universal, natural disposition of men and they all must carry with themselves the key to understand all languages, it

23. In the section on Gadamer (3.2), I will discuss his critique of Humboldt's formalism, of the hypothesis of an "internal language form" inherent in all languages. Here it suffices to point to Gadamer's systematic argument: *"Verbal form and traditionary content cannot be separated in the hermeneutic experience"* (TM, p. 441). Although this objection per se does not undermine any hope of a formal analysis of language, it constitutes a consistent internal critique of Humboldt. This is owing not to formalism as such, but to the incompatibility of the thesis that "there resides in every language a peculiar worldview" with the hypothesis of a universal "form" underlying every language—which cancels the specific sense of the former assumption.

obviously follows that the form of all languages must be essentially the same and that they all achieve the universal goal. (p. 651, VII 252)

Humboldt blocks any escape route for the defense of a realist point of view, a view that would ground the objectivity of knowledge in the unity of an objective world independent of language. Thus the only path left open to him is to seek the guarantee of the objectivity of knowledge in *language itself*. To this end, Humboldt relies on another dimension of language: its communicative function. As we shall see in what follows, he tries in this way to reformulate the question of the objectivity of knowledge in terms of the intersubjectivity of communication.

2.3 Intersubjectivity as a Dialogical Process: The Communicative-Pragmatic Dimension of Language

In retrospect, Humboldt's treatment of the communicative dimension of language seems every bit as groundbreaking as the discussion of its world-disclosing function, which I have already described. His approach to the communicative dimension can be characterized as a "pragmatic turn" that he carries out with respect to the traditional view, which regards language as a mere vehicle for the transmission of information between speakers. To this extent, such a turn is intrinsically related to the rejection of an objectivist view of language and to the defense of the constitutive character of language. With this innovative move, Humboldt anticipates insights that will only be developed much later by authors such as G. H. Mead, the later Wittgenstein, Habermas, Charles Taylor, and others.

The inauguration of this perspective was already implicit in Humboldt's famous remark against the objectivist view of language: his assertion that language "is not a product but an activity." Language cannot be regarded as an object *observable* by subjects; rather, it is tied to an activity of *understanding* in which speakers *participate*. Humboldt comments: "Language cannot be conceived as something *physical* either, finished as it were; the recipient has to pour it into the form he has already prepared for it, and this is what is called *understanding*" (p. 156, VI 122; italics mine). Thus Humboldt always insists that: "Language *only exists in ongoing speech;* grammar and lexicon are hardly comparable to their dead skeleton" (p. 186, VI 148; italics mine).

We have seen how Humboldt, with respect to the cognitive dimension of language (i.e., the language-world relation), held that the center of activity inherent in language is the synthesis that it carries out in *articulation.* In this way, Humboldt opposed the attempt to interpret this synthesis as original, ahistorical, and unique, à la Kant. Humboldt's next step in explaining this synthesis is to understand it as being in continuous creation in the *process of speech,* as an ongoing achievement of intersubjective understanding among speakers in dialogue. As Habermas points out in the references to Humboldt contained in his "Entgegnung": "The model of conversation, inspired in the ideal of Platonic dialogue, suggests the idea of a *dialogical synthesis,* which no longer yields, in the manner of the reflective force of the 'I think,' a monological unity in the diversity of representations" (p. 331).

The dialogical synthesis is Humboldt's essential shift of perspective, undertaken with full awareness of its consequences. With this shift of perspective, he passes beyond the view of language as an (intraworldly) *system* of signs, and regards it as a *process* of communication, or as dialogue:

In no way can the available vocabulary of a language be regarded as a finished and ready mass. This is . . . while this language lives in the mouth of people, *a production* and progressive reproduction of the generative capacity of words . . . *in the everyday use of speech.* (p. 480, VII 101; italics mine)

With this view, the fundamental turn is achieved. Consequently, the study of language must take as its focus the situation of dialogue, of the process of communication. For, as Humboldt puts it:

The *mutual dialogue* which is alive, a true exchange of ideas and sensations, is already, in itself, *the center of language,* so to speak. Its essence can only be thought to be simultaneously the sound and its echo, the appeal and the reply. Both in its origins and in its transformations, it *never belongs to one but to all.* It lies in the solitary depth of one's spirit and yet it only appears *in community.* The *suitability* of language for the genre of *dialogue* is, therefore, the best touchstone of its value. (p. 81, IV 435; italics mine)

Thus the defining feature of language that comes to the foreground is *intersubjectivity.* On the one hand, intersubjectivity is made possible by language; on the other hand, it is also its condition of possibility, since language exists only in the process of speech. Hence the different perspectives belonging to the situation of dialogue, by providing the intersubjectivity indispensable for all meaningful speech, are at the same time that which guarantees the objectivity of what is said. For such objectivity can no longer be regarded as derived from a prelinguistic categorical synthesis. In this connection, Habermas makes the following remark in *Postmetaphysical Thinking:*

Humboldt's interest is devoted above all to one phenomenon: in the process of linguistic communication, a synthetic force is at work that generates unity within plurality in a *different* manner than by way of subsuming what is manifold under a general rule. The construction of a number series had served Kant as a model for the generation of unity. This constructivist concept of synthesis is replaced by Humboldt with the concept of unforced agreement (*Einigung*) in conversation. In place of one unifying perspective, which the generative subject brings first to the material of sensation with its forms of intuition and categories and then to the stream of its own lived experiences with the "I think" of transcendental apperception, there now appears the unrelinquished *difference between the perspectives from which the participants in communication reach understanding with each other about the same thing.* These speaker and hearer perspectives no longer converge at the focal point of a subjectivity centered in itself; they instead intersect at the focal point of language—and as this focal point Humboldt designates the "reciprocal conversation" in which ideas and feelings are sincerely exchanged. (pp. 162–163; italics mine)

This Humboldtian interpretation, in which the objectivity of experience is dependent on the intersubjectivity of communication, is also rooted in the very core of Humboldt's references to the synthesis carried out by linguistic articulation. This is owing to the fact that the two shifts of perspective entailed by Humboldt's conception of language vis-à-vis Kant, those of the cognitive and communicative dimensions, are *always carried out jointly.*[24] They have been treated separately here only in keeping with the structure of my exposition. Thus, if we focus on the core of Humboldt's thoughts about linguistic articulation, in its role as that which constitutes the objectivity of thought, we can see that his argument was also concerned with the second aspect considered here. This argument is meant to demonstrate that "speech is a necessary condition for the thinking of the individual in solitary seclusion." But Humboldt continues, saying: "In appearence, however, language develops only *socially,* and *man understands himself only once he has tested the intelligibility of his words by trial upon others*" (p. 56).

Regarding the necessarily social character of language, Humboldt had already pointed out that "language cannot achieve reality through the individual but only in community, only when a bold attempt is followed by a new one" (p. 139, VI 27). The ultimate reason for this claim is articulated by Humboldt as follows:

The concept achieves its determinacy and clarity only through its reverberation in the thinking capacity of a fellow being. The concept is

24. Language possesses a constitutive character on two distinct levels. On the semantic level (of the cognitive relation language-world), it is constitutive by virtue of the synthesis embedded in linguistic articulation; on the pragmatic level (of the communicative relation between speakers), it is so by virtue of the synthesis that takes place in the process of intersubjective understanding between speakers. Humboldt identifies these dimensions, respectively, with the function of the verb (in the sentence) and with that of the personal pronouns (in conversation). Thus Humboldt holds that "the verb and the pronoun are the axes around which the whole of language revolves" (VI p. 346). Borsche sums up Humboldt's position by saying:

> the first condition for thinking, the mediation between subject and object through language, is designated in general grammar by the synthetic function of the verb; this is the word that configures concepts *par excellence,* the word in which the unity of sound and meaning is completed. The second condition for thinking, the mediation between subjects, is designated in general grammar by the differentiation of the three grammatical persons; through these, *speech is anchored in reality.* Precisely in this context Humboldt considers the determination of personal relations as "the most important" thing, as that through which grammar asserts its value against logic. (1981, p. 282; italics mine).

generated by being torn off from the mobile mass of representing and it becomes an object for the subject. But it is not sufficient that this rupture takes place only within the subject, objectivity is only accomplished when the subject, who is the source of the representation, really sees his thought outside himself, which is only possible in another, that is, in a being who equally has the capacity to represent it and think it. But between mental capacity and mental capacity the only mediator is language and, therefore, from here also springs its necessity for the completion of thought. (p. 201, VI 160)

In this thesis lies the heart of the shift by which Humboldt also distances himself from the classical view of the *communicative* dimension of language. In this dimension too, language cannot be considered as a "mere medium [i.e., instrument] for understanding" (p. 135, VI 23), but rather as the condition of possibility of mutual understanding—which is, in turn, the raison d'être of language. The function of language is not to provide a copy of the world. Moreover, the possibility of presenting the world objectively depends precisely on the prior understanding among the subjects who talk about it. As Humboldt remarks: "Conversing together is never comparable with a transfer of material. In the one who understands as well as in the speaker *the same thing must be evolved* from the inner power of each" (p. 57).

Thus the traditional view of language as mere intermediary between subject and object ignores the prior, essential function of language: namely, relating the subjects among themselves. Only to the extent that language yields intersubjectivity, in the subject-subject relation characteristic of dialogue, *does the objectivity specific to the subject-object relation become possible*. As Borsche points out: "Language not only connects a subject with objects, but also connects subjects among themselves. More precisely, the former relation can only be achieved to the extent that the latter is accomplished" (1981, p. 179).

For this reason, Humboldt remarks that "objectivity is only accomplished when the subject, who is the source of the representation, really sees his thought outside himself, which is only possible in another, that is, in a being who equally has the capacity to represent it and think it." The justification for this shift of perspective lies, for Humboldt, in an "ineradicable dualism" of language:

However, an ineradicable dualism underlies the original essence of language, and the very possibility of speaking is conditioned by the appeal and the reply. Thinking is already essentially accompanied by the tendency to social existence, and man, even for mere thinking, longs for a *you* corresponding to the *I*. (p. 138, VI 26)

Later, we find an explicit reference to the *intersubjectivity* achieved by the understanding in communication as the necessary touchstone for all objective thinking:

What language makes necessary in the simple act of thought-creation is also incessantly repeated in the mental life of man. . . . The power of thinking needs something that is like it and yet different from it. By the like it is kindled, and by the different it obtains a *touchstone* of the essentiality of its inner creations. Although the cognitive basis of truth, of the unconditionally fixed, can lie for man only within himself, the struggle of his mental effort toward it is always surrounded by the risk of deception. With a clear and immediate sense only of his mutable limitedness, he is bound to regard truth as something lying outside him; and one of the most powerful means of approaching it, of measuring his distance away from it, is social communication with others. All speaking, from the simplest kind onwards, is an attachment of what is individually felt to the common nature of mankind. (pp. 56–57; italics mine)

Thus Humboldt can assert: "*language must necessarily be a joint possession,* and is in truth the property of all mankind" (p. 62),[25] for "all speaking relies on a dialogue in which, even when it takes place among many, the one who speaks places himself against those whom he addresses as if against a unity. Man speaks, even in thoughts, only with another, or with himself as another" (pp. 137–138, VI 26).

From this intersubjectivist conception of language, Humboldt can attempt to explain how both the "subject-subject" and "subject-object" perspectives are possible in their specificity. Moreover, he can do this *on the basis of the structure of speech itself,* without resorting to a world independent of language that would

---

25. Humboldt's line of argument (which anticipates Wittgenstein's critique of the possibility of a private language) finds its systematic basis in the analysis of personal pronouns discussed in the following.

guarantee the objectivity of knowledge. This achievement is, at the same time, the strongest justification for his comprehensive view of language as opposed to the traditional view.

To this end, Humboldt undertakes an analysis of the personal pronouns,[26] based on an implicit critique of Fichte and the one-sidedness typical of the philosophy of consciousness, which remains hostage to the subject-object model. This analysis enables us to view language in its constitutive character, as that which "discloses" the *social* and *individual* world.[27] This innovative extension of the constitutive role of language beyond its cognitive dimension will be incorporated into the philosophical discussion only much later, in its twentieth-century development by authors such as those already mentioned above—Mead, Wittgenstein, Gadamer, Habermas, Taylor, etc.

In "Über den Dualis," Humboldt clarifies the basic features of his analysis of the personal pronouns as follows:

Thus the word has to gain its essence in a listener and responder. This archetypical fact about all languages is expressed by the pronoun in its distinction between the second and the third person. *I* and *he* are as such distinct, and as soon as one of them is thought of, they are necessarily mutually exclusive objects that exhaust everything, for they can be named, in other words, *I* and *non-I*. *Thou,* on the other hand, names a *he* that is facing the *I.* Whereas *I* and *he* are each based respectively on internal and external perception, we find in the *thou* the spontaneity of a choice. Truly, it is also a *non-I,* though not—like the *He*—*in the sphere of all beings, but in a different one, namely the one where mutual influence results in common action* [italics mine]. Thus the *he* not only consists in a non-*I,* but equally in a non-*thou;* and it is, therefore, not only opposed to one of them but to both. The fact that the same pronominal form can be found in all languages reveals that all peoples feel that speaking, in

26. In *Nachmetaphysisches Denken* (pp. 187–241), Habermas establishes an interesting correlation between the analysis of the personal pronouns carried out by Humboldt and the more recent but similar analysis of G. H. Mead. The important influence that the view of language of these authors has had on Habermas's position will become clear later on (see chapter 4).

27. About this central aspect of the conception of language inaugurated by Humboldt, see the excellent analysis, as well as the systematic development, offered by Taylor (1985), pp. 248–292.

its innermost essence, presupposes that the speaker distinguishes himself from the one addressed by his speech among all others in front of him. (p. 202, VI 161)

For Humboldt, the significance of this argument is that it shows the necessarily prior character of the subject-subject relation as opposed to the merely derivative character of the subject-object relation. Once the communicative process is taken as the frame of reference, Humboldt's argument is as forceful as it is simple. Neither subject nor object can be constituted in its specificity merely by counterposing one to the other.

The first person cannot be formed through opposition to the third person, for both comprise a universe; each of them, as opposed poles, constitutes the radical antithesis of the other. Therefore, "*I* and *he* are necessarily mutually exclusive objects that exhaust everything, for they can be named, in other words, *I* and *non-I*". From the counterposing of "I" and "he," as opposed "objects," no subject whatsoever can be formed. However, as Humboldt indicates later, "the essence of *I* consists in being a subject" (p. 204, VI 163). Therefore, its formation cannot spring from being counterposed to the third person, for in this way only the possible object-character of each would be manifested. This is shown in the fact that this relation takes place "in the sphere of all beings" (that is, in the objective world) and therefore, accordingly, in the fact that "*I* and *he* are based on internal and external *perception*." Hence this perspective does not exhaust the true essence of "I." Humboldt later remarks that "*I* is not the individual . . . within such and such spatial relations, but it is he who places himself in consciousness facing another one, at that very moment, as a subject" (p. 204, VI 163).

Consequently, the I can be constituted as such only against a "thou," for "*thou* is the *he* facing the *I,*" that is, "an object . . . *whose essence consists exclusively in being a subject*" (ibid.). And precisely for this reason, the thou "is also a non-I, but in a different sphere, in the sphere where mutual influence results in *common action*."

Only in the sphere of the social world does the first person achieve the specificity conferred by its opposition to a second person—that opposition by which "the speaker distinguishes himself from the one addressed by his speech among all others in front of him." Thus the first two persons have an irreducible character. This explains how language, as a medium of understanding, can be a mechanism that both *individualizes* and *socializes* at the same time, one which "also binds by individualizing, and [which] with the wrapper of the most individual expression contains the possibility of universal understanding" (pp. 160–161, VI 125).[28]

Once this subject-subject relation is produced through the counterposing of the first and second person, the character of the third person is transformed: "the *he* not only consists in a non-*I*, but equally in a non-*thou;* and it is, therefore, not only opposed to one of them but to both." Only by being elevated to the status of common object of the first two persons does the third achieve its character of object. In this way, it becomes an axis of a complementary perspective irreducible to the other: namely, the subject-object perspective. The I-thou perspective constitutes the sphere "where mutual influence results in common action"— that is, the social sphere centered in the subject-subject relation. The I/thou-he perspective constitutes "the sphere of all beings," the whole of everything the subjects can talk about.

This analysis of the communicative genesis of the two perspectives establishes that the dialogical sphere of the subject-subject relation is prior to the subject-object relation, which was traditionally regarded as paradigmatic. In fact, as Humboldt later argues, this latter relation can only be constituted by way of abstraction

---

28. In his "Entgegnung," Habermas remarks about this original view of language that

> Humboldt conceives the understanding as a mechanism that *socializes* and *individualizes* at the same time. In the structures of fragmented intersubjectivity that demands from the competent speakers the mastery of the system of personal pronouns, individualization without the inexorable compulsion to universality is as impossible as socialization without simultaneous individualization. (p. 332; italics mine)

from the former. His analysis lends systematic support to his attempt to "defend grammar against the primacy of logic."[29] Such primacy has biased the study of language since Aristotle, limiting it to the cognitive dimension of language and precluding, in his view, a true understanding of its nature. As Humboldt later adds:

When we only analyze thought logically and we do not analyze speech grammatically, the second person is not defined precisely and, thus, the first person is also presented in a different way. In this case, the reporter has to be distinguished only from the report, but not from a recipient and responder. Because our general grammar always starts from logic, it treats the pronoun, which is a part of speech, in a different way from the one characteristic of our discussion, in which we seek an analysis of language as such. . . . Given the different points of view from which they proceed, both considerations are perfectly correct; *it is only blameworthy that people usually stick to one of them one-sidedly, for the true, complete validity of the pronoun, also in speech, is only really appreciated when its deep root in the innermost nature of language is recognized.* (pp. 202–203, VI 161–162; italics mine)

Only the abstraction of the pragmatic dimension of speech can give rise to its characteristic monological dimension, in which language can be regarded as a mere intermediary between the world (object) and thought (subject). The ignoring of this first abstraction is precisely what makes this dimension acquire primacy over any other. As a consequence, the analysis of language is carried out without any attention to its communicative function, which becomes accessible only through the study of grammar.

In Humboldt's distinction between logic and grammar we can see the pragmatic turn underlying his intersubjectivist conception of language as mentioned at the beginning of this chapter. For the difference between logic and grammar

is expressed mainly in two important points pregnant with implications. The logical judgment and the grammatical sentence converge in all types and subtypes along the same line with respect to the connection and division of concepts. But logic treats these ideal relations merely in

---

29. As we shall see later (chapter 3), this aspect of Humboldt's view of language will be regarded as his central contribution to the understanding of language by both Heidegger and Gadamer.

and for themselves, in the realm of possibility, of absolute being. Language establishes them in a specific moment, and presents the subject as agent and recipient of what is predicated. Thus the dead concept of relation (the conjunction sign of mathematical equivalence, so to speak) is revived. There arises the verb: center and nucleus of all grammar. Besides, language always addresses the thought articulated in words to another, whether really existing or merely thought. Thus, the verb and the pronoun are the axes around which the whole of language revolves. (VI 346)

Through this shift of perspective, Humboldt sheds light on other constitutive aspects of language that could not be thematized in the classical tradition, owing to its focus on logic and its inability to conceive of language as anything other than a vehicle of knowledge. From this new standpoint, Humboldt specifies the different functions of language:

Language has, given the intensity of its effectiveness, a threefold goal.

It *mediates the understanding* and it demands, therefore, determinacy and clarity.

It *gives expression to feelings and provokes them,* and to that extent it requires force, tenderness and politeness.

It stimulates new thoughts and new connections between them, thanks to its creativity, through the configuration it gives to thoughts. (p. 76, IV 431; italics mine)

With this original redefinition of the functions of language, Humboldt distances himself from the preceding tradition in two respects. On the one hand, the cognitive function of language as a vehicle of knowledge, the only function recognized by the classical view, becomes relativized. More specifically, it becomes only one function among many of equal status. These other functions could be called "expressive" and "appelative" (which for Humboldt are complementary terms) and "poetic," following the terminology of K. Bühler (1934) and R. Jakobson (1960), respectively. On the other hand, the view of the cognitive function that, following the analogy, we could call "expository" is deeply transformed by the fact that it is reformulated in intersubjectivist terms. What we have seen so far makes clear that this function of language as a vehicle of knowledge (i.e., as the exposition of states of affairs in the objective world) can only be viewed, in Humboldt's paradigm, as embedded in the process of understanding among speakers—namely, in the mutual understanding of that which they speak about.

Borsche summarizes the two systematic consequences that follow from this transformation, consequences that we will therefore find again both in Gadamer's hermeneutics and in Habermas's own theory. Borsche remarks:

> the world then appears only in a mediated way as *that about which different subjects talk.* These are forced to articulate their representations of objects. For these representations no longer acquire determinacy through objects, but only through concepts, recognized by other subjects. Everyone who wants to find one's bearings in the world of objects must address other subjects. *Facing him there is really only another subject.* (1981, p. 285; italics mine)

With this consideration, we find ourselves once more where we were at the close of our earlier discussion, when I described the detranscendentalizing consequences tied to the view of language in its function of world-disclosure. This view seems to lead to the same conclusions in the account of both the cognitive and communicative dimensions of language. Namely, it seems to entail that the objectivity of knowledge can only be reconstructed from within the intersubjectivity of the understanding to be achieved by speakers.

But the question is whether it is possible, given all the different elements of Humboldt's conception of language, to give an account of the conditions of possibility of intersubjectivity. As we have seen, Humboldt is fascinated by the double nature of language as the *source* of both *generality* and *individuality*. That is to say, he is intrigued both by its general character, which alone allows for shared identical concepts (fulfilling an essential socializing function), and by its expressive potential, which Humboldt sees as the basis of the very possibility of individualization. Humboldt makes this clear by saying: "in language the *individualization* within a *general conformity* is so wonderful, that we may say with equal correctness that the whole of mankind has but one language, and that every man has one of his own" (p. 53).

By trying to maintain both insights, Humboldt has to recognize on the one hand that, owing to its intrinsic generality (the fact that we can share it), language guarantees the *possibility* of understanding among speakers. It guarantees, in Humboldt's words, that "nobody may speak differently to another from the way in which the latter, under similar circumstances, would have spoken to him" (p. 50). But on the other hand, such an understanding or intersubjectivity cannot be considered as *given once and for all*, but rather as the lucky outcome of the process of understanding itself, in which different individuals express their individuality or particular worldview.

Given his view of language as world-disclosing and as holistically structured, rather than as a mere system of rules, Humboldt has to acknowledge that "only in the individual does language get its last determination. . . . A nation as a whole has indeed the same language, but not all the individuals in it have . . . exactly the same one, and if one looks more carefully, every person actually has his own" (pp. 227–228, VI 183).

The consequences of this acknowledgment for the possibility of understanding are clear to Humboldt. From here, the conclusion is inevitable: "Nobody means by a word precisely the same as his neighbor does, and the difference, be it ever so small, vibrates, like a ripple in water, throughout the entire language. Thus all understanding is always at the same time a not-understanding, all agreement in thought and feeling at the same time a divergence" (p. 228, VI 183).

On the one hand, Humboldt thinks that the generality of language (i.e., the identical linguistic meanings as opposed to the intrinsically individual perceptions and feelings) should provide the guarantee for intersubjectivity. This is also the only way in which Humboldt can defend the possibility of understanding, given that he cannot appeal to a world-in-itself equally accessible to everyone, independently of any linguistic mediation or worldview. As we have already seen, Humboldt believes that language is constitutive of our relationship with the world in the specific sense that the different linguistic expressions with their different meanings determine the way the objects referred to by these expressions are understood and perceived. Therefore, *only the identity of meanings can guarantee the identity of the referents.*

But on the other hand, given the holistic nature of meaning (its contextual character as well as the inseparability of knowledge of meaning from knowledge of the world), Humboldt has to recognize that speakers cannot in fact share identical meanings. This is true to the same extent that they cannot share a strictly identical worldview. Humboldt explains this as follows:

> The picture of language as merely designating *objects,* already perceived in themselves, is also not sustained by examination of what language engenders as its product. . . . Just as no concept is possible without language, so also there can be no object for the mind, since it is only through the concept, of course, that anything external acquires full being for consciousness. But the whole *mode of perceiving* things *subjectively* necessarily passes over into cultivation and the use of language. For the word arises from this very perceiving; it is a copy, not of the object in itself, but of the image thereof produced in consciousness. Since all objective perception is inevitably tinged with *subjectivity,* we may consider every human individual, even apart from language, as a unique standpoint of the world-view. (p. 59)

But a problem now arises concerning the dialectic that takes place, as Humboldt observes, between an intersubjectivity *always already* produced, (which as a worldview "without man's being aware of it, limits and dominates him") and an intersubjectivity that in each case *has to be* produced, in the form of understanding among subjects. How can these two forms of intersubjectivity offer *criteria of validity* for such understanding concerning communication and knowledge alike?

Humboldt does not have a systematic answer to this question. Doubtless, with his view of language as the bearer of a worldview, he does not want to fall into a perspectivism that makes the objectivity of knowledge impossible. Humboldt does not want to give up either of the two poles between which his view swings: neither the *constitutive* character of our linguistic fore-understanding of the world, nor the possibility of knowledge, to which the intersubjectivity of communication must contribute. As we saw in the previous section, Humboldt remarked on the one hand that "the sum of the knowable, as the field to be tilled by the human mind, lies *among all languages, independent of them, in the middle.*" But on the other hand, he immediately added that "man cannot approach this purely objective realm other than through his cognitive and sensory powers, that is, *in a subjective manner.*" The systematic difficulties that this view of language entails, and which are shown in this counterposition, can be seen in the decidedly antirelativistic and highly paradoxical attempt to defend the possibility of objective knowledge in the following remark:

the original correlation between man and the world, on which the possibility of every knowledge of the truth relies, is recovered phenomenally in a progressive and step by step manner. For what is objective remains always as that to be recovered, and although man approaches it in the subjective manner of a peculiar language, his second effort is to isolate the subjective and detach from it the object as neatly as possible, even if only through the substitution of one linguistic subjectivity for another. (pp. 20–21, IV 28; italics mine)

Nonetheless, Humboldt does not specify how this effort could ever succeed.

3

The View of Language of Philosophical Hermeneutics

The view of language found in philosophical hermeneutics can be considered a *radicalization* of the consequences drawn from the linguistic turn by the Hamann-Herder-Humboldt tradition.

This radicalization results from a shift of emphasis with respect to the communicative and cognitive dimensions of language present in Humboldt's approach. The shift can be found in the work of Heidegger after the *Kehre*[1] in his explicit *critique* of Humboldt. As we will see, this criticism does not amount to a break with Humboldt's conception, but rather must be regarded as an "internal" critique, insofar as Heidegger's starting point is structurally identical to that of Humboldt.

In the first place, this shift of emphasis makes clear the relativistic consequences implicit in Humboldt's account of the *cognitive* dimension of language, an account in which historical natural languages were considered as bearers of different worldviews. At the same time, the *communicative* dimension, from which Humboldt hoped to extract a guarantee of the objectivity of knowledge without any paradoxical reference to a prelinguistic world-in-itself, *loses its normative potential.*

1. Heidegger himself uses the term *Kehre* in his "Letter on Humanism" to describe his shift of perspective (or rather, his *break*) with respect to the view maintained in *Being and Time*. I leave this term untranslated, as is usual in translations of Heidegger's works as well as in the non-German literature on Heidegger.

As a consequence of this radicalization, language is reified to such an extent that it is regarded as determining what can appear in the world, in a *contingent* but nonetheless *absolute* sense (3.1).

As we shall see, it is on the basis of Heidegger's shift of emphasis that Gadamer appropriates Humboldt's new approach to the communicative dimension of language. This Heideggerian approach allows him to escape the normative burden placed on the communicative dimension by the universalist claim that lay beneath Humboldt's formalism (3.2).

The radicalization carried out by Heidegger and pursued by Gadamer amounts to a consistent development of the conception of language as world-disclosing. To this extent, analyzing this development will enable us to clarify the implications of such a conception. This analysis will in turn allow us to address a crucial question concerning the view of language lying at the basis of Habermas's theory of communicative action (chapter 4). Despite his being strongly influenced by Humboldt, can Habermas avoid the relativistic implications that philosophical hermeneutics draws from this view? Or does the very attempt to construct a theory of rationality on the basis of a theory of communicative action become questionable?

3.1 The Radicalization of the Conception of Language as World-Disclosure in Heidegger's Linguistic Turn

The conception of language elaborated in the Hamann-Herder-Humboldt tradition is clearly important for Heidegger's philosophy well before the *Kehre*. This can be seen in the critique of the view of language as a tool, carried out in *Being and Time*. To this view, so typical of the philosophy of consciousness,[2] Heidegger

---

2. This attempt of Heidegger in *Being and Time* has to be regarded, however, as unsuccessful precisely to the extent that his view is still under the sway of the premises of the philosophy of consciousness. A more detailed account of this problem inherent in Heidegger's view of language, here discussed only briefly, can be found in my *Heidegger, Language, and World-Disclosure*. There I try to show that Heidegger's hermeneutic transformation of phenomenology entails a linguistic turn, which is therefore present in Heidegger's philosophy from as early as *Being and Time*, even if it is explicitly accomplished only after the *Kehre*.

opposes a nonobjectivist approach. Language is to be considered not only in its cognitive function, but also in the dialogic dimension of "talk" or "discourse." As he remarks in *Being and Time:* "Man shows himself as the entity which *talks*. This does not signify that the possibility of vocal utterance is peculiar to him, but rather that he is the entity which is such as to *discover the world* and Dasein itself" (p. 165; italics mine).

In defense of this claim, Heidegger makes explicit appeal to Humboldt's attempt "to free grammar from logic." This attempted liberation is seen as a central contribution to the destruction of the Aristotelian tradition that reduces *logos* to "assertion," thereby analyzing discourse only "on the model of *this logos*" (ibid.; italics mine).

Even so, Heidegger's forceful remarks underscoring the dialogic dimension of language as discourse already show traces of his later critique of Humboldt.

Heidegger conceives of discourse as an existentiale of Dasein, possessing the following constitutive moments: "what the discourse is about (what is talked about); what-is-said-in-the-talk, as such; the communication; and the making-known" (BT, p. 162). All four of these functions are analyzed more deeply in his 1925 Marburg lecture course, known in English as *History of the Concept of Time*. His explanation shows a clear parallel with the functions analyzed by Bühler, as mentioned in the previous chapter: expository, appellative, and expressive.

The only peculiarity comes in respect to the expository function, where Heidegger differentiates between revelation (*Offenbarung*) and predication (*Prädikation*). The former enables us to identify the referent, or "what the discourse is about"; the latter represents "what-is-said-in-the-talk, as such."

On the basis of this articulation of the functions of language as discourse (sketched in a few brief paragraphs of *Being and Time*), Heidegger wants to demonstrate "the connection of discourse with understanding and intelligibility" (BT, p. 163). That is, he aims to show the extent to which understanding and intelligibility depend on the *Offenbarung* of discourse, which accordingly must be regarded as the condition of possibility of the other functions ("communication" and "the making-known").

To render this position feasible, Heidegger draws on the fact that dialogue or conversation is possible only because "we are already with [the other person] in advance, alongside the entity which the discourse is about" (BT, p. 207). For "only he who already understands can listen" (ibid.).

Only from this standpoint does it make sense for Heidegger to define discourse or talk as "the way in which we articulate 'significantly' the intelligibility of being-in-the-world. Being-with belongs to being-in-the-world" (BT, p. 161). For Heidegger, the specific feature of a dialogic view of language is that it regards communication as possible only against the background of a shared *world*. The "intelligibility" of this world serves as the shared basis of dialogue for those who talk with one another.

This central motif of philosophical hermeneutics is precisely that which Gadamer develops under the heading of the "rehabilitation of prejudices," or the "authority of tradition." Here lies his essential departure from Humboldt, not by means of a different account of language, but through an internal critique, a consistent radicalization. More specifically, what is radicalized is Humboldt's approach to the dialectic between an intersubjectivity *always already* produced (as a worldview shared by the speakers) and at the same time as an intersubjectivity *always to be* produced (through dialogue).

As we have seen, Humboldt tried to understand this dialectic as a process resulting from two equally constitutive poles: (1) the *articulation of each historical language,* which transmits a certain worldview or concrete "intelligibility" to those who speak it, and (2) the *intersubjective process of communication* between speakers, capable of submitting to formal analysis. As already mentioned, what Heidegger does is simply carry out a shift of emphasis *within* this view of language. This change is expressed not only with the remark that "only he who already understands can listen," but even more provocatively after the *Kehre,* with the famous claim that "language speaks."[3]

To show the internal logic of this fateful shift in philosophical

---

3. In "Der Weg zur Sprache," *Unterwegs zur Sprache,* pp. 254–255.

hermeneutics, seemingly so minor, I will analyze the general features of the view of language sketched in Heidegger's *Unterwegs
zur Sprache.* This analysis will focus on two features typical of every
attempt to absolutize the world-disclosing function of language:
the thesis that meaning determines reference (3.1.1), and the thesis of meaning holism (3.1.2). Having sketched these two theses,
which are intrinsic to every such view, I will go on to consider to
what extent Heidegger's critique of Humboldt is internally justified. That is to say, to what extent does this critique follow directly
from the theses shared by both authors (3.1.3)?

3.1.1   Meaning Determines Reference

The thesis that meaning determines reference is an important
premise of Heidegger's philosophy, if a tacit one. It is present
both before and after the *Kehre,* and is already visible in his interpretation of the ontological difference. To examine this tacit
premise, we must take into account the central features of the
hermeneutic transformation of phenomenology carried out in *Being and Time.* The key to this transformation lies in two fundamental shifts through which Heidegger tries to break with the
tradition to which he belongs.

   In the first place, for the model of "perception" paradigmatic
in the philosophy of consciousness, Heidegger substitutes the
model of "understanding," which he regards as more fundamental. This transformation commits Heidegger to proving that the
primary structure of our relationship with the world can only be
analyzed as understanding. He has to show that the alleged "pure
perception" of beings is in fact only an abstraction derived
from our everyday experience of being-in-the-world, an experience in which everything appears to us as "always already" understood, or as pre-interpreted.[4] This is expressed in the thesis

4. The hermeneutic transformation of phenomenology carried out by Heidegger
has the character of an internal critique of the paradigm of consciousness. This is
emphasized by C.-F. Gethmann (1974) in his interesting interpretation of Heidegger's project of a fundamental ontology in *Being and Time.* However, this line of
interpretation neglects the break that this transformation necessarily involves.

that "presence-at-hand" (*Vorhandenheit*) is derivative with respect to "readiness-to-hand" (*Zuhandenheit*), that knowledge is derivative of understanding. The basic phenomenon Heidegger draws upon to justify this transformation is that of the "anticipation of meaning," namely, as stated at the outset of *Being and Time,* the fact that "we always conduct our activities in an understanding of being" (BT, p. 5). Starting from this phenomenon, Heidegger analyzes the "prestructure of understanding" that underlies it, determining it as the condition of possibility of our experience in the world.

In the second place, this transformation also presupposes that the traditional concept of "world" as "the totality of all beings" is replaced by what might be called the "hermeneutic" concept of world. This can be described as the view of the world as a symbolically structured whole, a whole whose "significance" (*Bedeutsamkeit*) makes possible the intraworldly experience of dealing with beings. This substitution entails a fundamental shift of perspective. The paradigmatic perspective of the philosophy of consciousness had been based on the model of the subject-object relation, which is intrinsic to the explication of knowledge. It was the model of an extraworldly observer who would stand *over against* the world, regarded as the totality of all beings. By contrast, the perspective underlying Heidegger's hermeneutic transformation of phenomenology is that of "Dasein," whose basic attribute is that of understanding—for it finds itself *within* a symbolically prestructured world.[5] This shift results in the *detranscendentalization* of inherited philosophical concepts, insofar as it precludes the appeal to an extraworldly standpoint, to a transcendental subject that would constitute the world. Thus the obligatory starting point of Heidegger's perspective is the *facticity* of a Dasein that is not a subject that constitutes the world. Instead, it participates in the "totality of meaning" inherent in this world, a world in which it finds itself always already "thrown" (*geworfen*).

These structural changes illuminate the two central premises of Heidegger's view mentioned earlier. First, there is the recognition

5. See my article "Die Rolle der Sprache in *Sein und Zeit.*"

that our access to the intraworldly is mediated and made possible by our understanding of the meanings inherent in our "being-in-the-world," an understanding "from out of which entities can manifest themselves" (BT, p. 55). This recognition expresses the assumption that meaning determines reference, insofar as the latter is only possible through the former. Second, there follows the recognition that the contexture of meanings inherent in our being-in-the-world, as a *holistically* organized totality, precludes any extraworldly perspective. That is to say, the constitution of meaning escapes *any attempt at objectification*. This implies a strong form of meaning holism. There follows the inescapability of the "circle of understanding," which Heidegger accounts for with his transformation of the Kantian a priori into the "perfect a priori" of the "always already." There follows as well the central thesis of Heidegger's hermeneutics, namely, that "disclosedness is *essentially factical*" (BT, p. 221; italics mine). Here, the process of de-transcendentalization becomes explicit.

Thus the shift entailed by the *Kehre* does not concern these premises, which are inherent in the conception of the "ontological difference" and thus make up the unvarying core of Heidegger's philosophy. Rather, there is a structural problem inherent in *Being and Time* that prevents Heidegger from following this line, while edging him gradually toward the *Kehre*. The root of this problem can be found in a specific incompatibility. On the one hand, we have the *hermeneutic transformation* sought by Heidegger, which involves the detranscendentalization of any supposed constitutor of the world. On the other, there is the *methodological* basis from which Heidegger tries to carry out this transformation: his attempt to construct a fundamental ontology based on an existential analytic of Dasein. This compels Heidegger to link the hermeneutic themes back to the subject-object schema. That is, he is forced to attempt to root the constitution of the world in the existential structure of Dasein.[6]

It is only in light of this difficulty, inherent in the project of

6. For this issue, see the excellent interpretation of the methodological difficulties internal to *Being and Time* offered by E. Tugendhat (1970).

Being and Time itself, that we can understand the internal necessity of the *Kehre*. The view of Dasein as thrown into an always already constituted world renders impossible, or empty, any attempt to then ground the constitution of that world in the existential structure of Dasein. Hence this constitution proves to be inexplicable on the basis of the methodology of *Being and Time*. As a result, the new concept of "world" (the central element of the transformation at which Heidegger aims) appears as an unjustifiable element of his approach.

On the same note, the understanding of being that establishes Dasein as the preeminent entity from the outset also becomes paradoxically elusive. There is no place for it in the dichotomy, established for methodological reasons, between intraworldly entities and a Dasein thrown into its facticity.

From this standpoint, the *Kehre* can be understood as a systematic attempt to situate this understanding of being, and consequently, to show the plausibility of the new concept of world as a symbolically structured totality. At the same time, the means employed by Heidegger to achieve these two goals allows us to interpret the *Kehre* as a linguistic turn. Consequently, the axis of this turn can be found in two central claims, resulting in the abandonment of that preeminence of Dasein dogmatically presupposed in *Being and Time*. I refer to Heidegger's famous remark that "language is the house of being" (p. 166),[7] and to his statement that "only where there is language is there world" (p. 38).[8]

With this last claim, Heidegger achieves a definitive break with those traditional premises that had still hindered the hermeneutic turn attempted in *Being and Time*. For the first time, he also explicitly elevates something other than Dasein to the rank of a constitutor of world. That is, something new becomes the condition of possibility that Dasein always already finds itself in a symbolically structured world, and thus of the possibility that entities can appear to it within the world.

7. In *Unterwegs zur Sprache*.

8. In "Hölderlin und das Wesen der Dichtung," *Erläuterungen zu Hölderlins Dichtung*.

It is this linguistic turn that links Heidegger to the central theme of the reaction against the philosophy of consciousness as described in the preceding chapters. This is the critique of the view of language as a tool, and the corresponding defense of the constitutive character of language by appeal to its world-disclosing function. It is in this context that we find Heidegger's aforementioned claim about the connection between language and world. This can be understood as an implicit critique of his own position in *Being and Time*. As he remarks in "Hölderlin und das Wesen der Dichtung":

Language serves for communicating. . . . But the essence of language is not exhausted by the fact of its being a means of communication. With this determination we do not meet with its authentic essence; rather, only one consequence of its essence is set forth. Language is not only a piece of equipment that man possesses alongside many others. Instead, *it is language alone that first provides the possibility of standing amidst the openness of entities. Only where there is language is there world.* (HWD, pp. 37–38; italics mine)

This internal connection between language and the world receives further development in "Der Ursprung des Kunstwerkes." Here Heidegger insists, following the Hamann-Herder-Humboldt tradition, that language is not restricted to the expression in words and sentences of that which is already "unconcealed" (*unverborgen*). Rather, it is responsible for the fact that the entity as such can appear at all. That is to say, it is responsible for the unconcealment itself (p. 59).

The explanation of this thesis can be found immediately thereafter:

When language names the entity for the first time, *such naming alone brings the entities to word and to appearance.* This naming nominates the entity to its being from out of this being. Such saying is a *projecting* of the clearing, in which it is announced *as what* the entity comes into the open. . . . The saying which projects is poetry. . . . [E]ach particular language is the happening of this saying in which a world is historically disclosed to a people. . . . The saying which projects is that which, in the preparation of what is sayable, at the same time brings the unsayable as such to the world. (UKW, pp. 59–60; italics mine)

In these remarks, in which Humboldt's influence is easily evident, we find an explicit assertion of the thesis that meaning determines reference. Language qua "whole of meanings" is now responsible for the intelligibility of the world that Heidegger had previously tried to ground in the formal structure of *discourse*, and thus in an existentiale of Dasein. This is so to the extent that language allows intraworldly entities to "appear." As he puts it, *by naming them it announces "as what" they must be understood or interpreted.*

With this thesis, Heidegger establishes the difference between meaning and reference in the same terms as Husserl and Frege before him. According to Frege, a name refers to an object "indirectly," through the "sense" the name expresses; this is understood by Frege, as by Heidegger, as "the mode of presentation of what is designated."[9] Insofar as language is responsible for the way in which entities appear to us, and hence is that which prejudices *what* we consider entities *as* in each case, it bears within itself the "essence" or constitution of the "being of entities" and thus their *truth.* Therefore the designation of entities by means of names cannot be understood in the sense "that something already familiar to us is provided with a name, but rather *only through this naming is the entity first nominated as that which it is.* It is in this way that it is known as an entity" (p. 41; italics mine).[10]

The other side of this view of language as "the house of being," or the view of meaning as the condition of possibility for our access to reference, can be seen in a provocative claim from *Unterwegs zur Sprache.* It is expressed in the phrase, drawn from Stefan George's poem "Das Wort," that "there is no thing where the word is lacking" (p. 163). With this claim, Heidegger establishes a dependence between thing and word, clearly not with regard to the existence of the former, but rather with regard to the possibility of our access to or understanding of the thing. In this connection, Heidegger explains:

9. G. Frege, "Über Sinn und Bedeutung."

10. In "Hölderlin und das Wesen der Dichtung," *Erläuterungen zu Hölderlins Dichtung.*

The thing is a thing only where the word is found for the thing. Only in this way *is* it. . . . The word alone supplies being to the thing, [for] . . . something only *is,* where the appropriate word names something as existing [*seiend*] and in this way *institutes the particular entity as such.* . . . The being of that which is resides in the word. For this reason, the following phrase holds good: language is the house of being. (UzS, pp. 164–166; italics mine)

With this radicalization, Heidegger advances from a more or less obvious insight into the interdependence of meaning and reference to postulate a *unidirectional* dependence, by which the world-disclosure inherent in each historical language becomes the final court of appeal for what entities are. That is to say, world-disclosure becomes a *happening of truth,* as Heidegger puts it in "Der Ursprung des Kunstwerkes." As shown by his view of the *Dichtung* of language as "creation" (*Stiftung*), and in general by his dichotomy between being and beings in the form of the ontological difference, this happening cannot in turn be caused or motivated by any intraworldly experience. For in fact, it is the absolute condition of possibility of such experience. In "Hölderlin und das Wesen der Dichtung," Heidegger explains as follows:

Poetry [*Dichtung*] is an instituting through the word and in the word . . . [for] being is never an entity. But since being and the essence of things can never be calculated or derived from the present-at-hand, they must be freely created, posited, and bestowed. Free bestowal of this kind is an instituting. (HWD, p. 41)

From this set of premises, typical of Heidegger's views after the *Kehre,* there arises the model of a linguistic world-disclosure that would prejudice every intraworldly experience without in turn being able to be corrected by it in any way. On the contrary, as a product of the "history of being," this linguistic world-disclosure is the ultimate point of validation of experience. It is a sheer "happening of truth," with no possible corrective.

By grounding the understanding of being in this linguistic world-disclosure, and by identifying it with originary "truth," the *detranscendentalizing* process initiated in *Being and Time* reaches its culmination. The guarantee of the objectivity of experience, which for transcendental philosophy was found in "transcendental apperception" (as the endowment of a likewise transcendental subject), is now located in the linguistic articulation inherent in each historically transmitted language. Thus this guarantee loses its *universal* character (which in transcendental philosophy could still be postulated, for it was methodologically secured), even while retaining its *determinative* character. As a result, this radicalization of the transcendental model (already expressed in Hamann's dictum of "a priori arbitrary, a posteriori necessary") entails conflating the objectivity of experience, of what things are, with that which is contingently "disclosed" to us in a given historical language.

This paradoxical result arises from the path taken by the radicalization in question, comprising a combination of two elements. On the one hand, there is a *detranscendentalization* of the constitution of meaning (an unavoidable consequence of the linguistic turn as such, as we saw in connection with the Hamann-Herder-Humboldt tradition). On the other hand, there is also a preservation of the conceptual apparatus of transcendental philosophy (that is, of the constitutor/constituted dichotomy that arises from its foundationalist strategy). As a result of this preservation, the detranscendentalizing process leaves unquestioned the *normative authority* of that which is made responsible for the "constitution of meaning." As a consequence, as pointed out already, this detranscendentalization goes so far as to encompass *truth* itself,[11] stripping it of all universal validity and identifying it with an incorrigible "happening," *imposed* upon us as a destiny.

The implicit preservation of the foundationalist strategy of the philosophy of consciousness can be seen in the epistemologization of the (semantic) distinction between meaning and reference, through the thesis that the former determines the latter. But the detranscendentalizing consequences actually result from the combination of this thesis with a further one, a thesis already

11. For a detailed analysis of the difficulties as well as the consequences of Heidegger's attempt to broaden the realm of detranscendentalization beyond the "constitution of meaning" to encompass the validity of truth, see K.-O. Apel (1989).

present in the Hamann-Herder-Humboldt tradition no less than in Heidegger: that of meaning holism. For the "determinative" character of the constitution of meaning derives both from its constitutive character for our access to the intraworldly, *and* from its insurmountability, from our inability to distance ourselves from it reflexively.[12]

3.1.2 Meaning Holism

We saw that in *Being and Time,* Dasein found itself always already enmeshed in the holistic structure of the referential contexture, which constitutes the world as a symbolically structured whole. This holistic structure is now inherited by language, as that which makes world possible. In this way, language possesses the same totalizing character already attributed to world, and it also lies behind the backs of the subjects who speak it. These subjects, as factical Daseins, lack all possibility of access to an extralinguistic perspective, just as in *Being and Time* they lacked any access to an extraworldly perspective. As Heidegger remarks in *Unterwegs zur Sprache:* "Language always runs ahead of us. We always speak only in repetition of it. Thus, we constantly lag behind that which we have to meet with in advance in order to be able to speak of it" (UzS, p. 179).

12. It is with regard to this point that we can see the specific difference between the consequences drawn by hermeneutic philosophy from this detranscendental-ization, that is, from the recognition of the meaning holism inherent in it, and those drawn by the authors of the Anglo-American tradition of the philosophy of language. From the "insurmountable" (*nichthintergehbar*) character of language, Heidegger like Hamann deduces the normative *necessity* of that which is "dis-closed" by language (which makes the linguistic world-disclosure "a posteriori necessary"). But Quine and Putnam, for example, draw precisely the opposite epistemological consequence, namely, *fallibilism.* Precisely to the extent that it is no longer possible to appeal to a transcendental standpoint endowed with a priori knowledge, that is to say, precisely to the extent that our linguistic worldview is unavoidably holistic and contingent (and therefore precludes any strict separation between a priori and a posteriori, between knowledge of lan-guage and knowledge of the world), these authors conclude that all knowledge is in principle *revisable.* See Quine (1953) and Putnam (1975d).

This gives support to the aforementioned thesis about the *determinative* character of the linguistic world-disclosure of each historical language. The impossibility of distancing oneself from this world-disclosure, of objectifying it and thereby making it transparent (or suspending its functioning by depriving it of its a priori character), is the price that this view has to pay for breaking with the illusions of transcendental philosophy. On this issue, Heidegger weighs in with the following:

Because we humans, in order to be those who we are, *remain included* [*eingelassen*] *in the essence of language and are therefore never able to free ourselves from it, in order to gain a view of it from elsewhere,* we always only catch sight of the essence of language insofar as we are looked at by language itself, unified in it. (UzS, p. 266; italics mine)

Paradoxically, however, this remark actually applies to Heidegger himself, at least insofar as his reflections on language try to account for the "essence" of language, "to bring language to language as language." The recognition that such an attempt is impossible establishes another of the consequences inherent in a view of language of this kind.

The difficulty already found in Humboldt's attempt to unify the different functions of language in a global view of its "nature," in a *theory* of language, becomes an impossibility. This impasse is openly acknowledged, and its origin clarified:

The peculiar thing about language, determined from out of the event of appropriation [*Ereignis*], can be known still less than what is special about language, if knowing means: to have seen something in the totality of its essence, gaining a view of it. *We are unable to gain a view of the essence of language, because we, who can only say* [*sagen*] *by repeating the saying* [*die Sage*], *ourselves belong to saying.* . . . The saying cannot be apprehended in any assertion. (UzS, pp. 265–266; italics mine)

But Heidegger regards this difficulty as "surmountable": if not for an "objectifying knowledge," then at least for a "poetizing thinking," which language itself would then have to make possible. He remarks: "In order to reflect on the essence of language, to impute to it what is its own, there is need of a transformation of language that we can neither enforce nor invent. . . . The transformation touches on our relation to language" (UzS, p. 267).

The paradoxical status of this remark (the difficulty of justifying it theoretically) is perhaps the reason that the development of this argument becomes increasingly vague, passing from argument to idle gesture. Heidegger continues:

Perhaps we could minimally prepare this transformation of our relationship with language. The experience could awaken that every reflective thinking is a poetizing, every poetizing also a thinking. Both belong together from out of that saying which has already made itself responsible to the unsaid, for it is thought as thankfulness. (ibid.)

As we shall see in the next section, Gadamer makes a virtue of necessity by interpreting this structural difficulty (which derives from the holistic structure of language) in a *positive* way. He explicitly renounces any attempt to *objectify* language, the necessary consequence of any theoretical ambition. This renunciation is possible insofar as the status of his assertions about language is no longer that of a theoretical attempt to describe that which is the case. (This was still Heidegger's aim, however paradoxically.) Rather, his assertions have the practical ("philosophical") function of making us aware of that "which happens to us beyond our willing and doing."[13]

3.1.3 Heidegger's Critique of Humboldt after the *Kehre*

Following this sketch of the central features of Heidegger's view of language, I will discuss the aforementioned radicalization that it entails in connection with the themes elaborated in the Hamann-Herder-Humboldt tradition. This radicalization can be clearly seen if we examine Heidegger's critique of Humboldt in his lecture "Der Weg zur Sprache" (also included in *Unterwegs zur Sprache*).

The target of this critique is the attempt to view language merely as a *human activity*, as the capacity to speak. Heidegger

---

13. In *Gesammelte Werke II, Wahreit und Methode: Ergänzungen*, p. 438.

regards Humboldt as a paradigmatic representative of this pragmatist point of view. He remarks:

One represents language from the standpoint of speaking with respect to articulated sounds, the bearers of meaning. Speaking is *a kind of human activity*. Through many transformations . . . this representation of language has remained the enduring and guiding representation through the centuries in Western or European thinking. (UzS, pp. 245–246; italics mine)

This conception of language "reaches its high point in Humboldt's reflections on language, which culminates in the great introduction to his work on the Kawi language of the island of Java" (ibid.).

The point of departure for Heidegger's critical remarks is Humboldt's most famous claim about language, already cited in the previous chapter: "this [language] is not a product (*ergon*) but an activity (*energeia*) . . . it is the eternally repeated labor of the spirit to make the articulated sound capable of expressing thought" (p. 418, VII 46).

Heidegger's objection to Humboldt's view of language as *energeia* is that this be understood, as he puts it, "in a completely un-Greek way, following Leibniz's *Monadology* in regarding it as the *activity of the subject*" (UzS, p. 249). Thus language is reduced to something else; it becomes an instrument of the "labor of the spirit," or that which mediates the subject-object schema. Heidegger explains:

Humboldt represents language as a *special* "labor of the spirit". . . . According to the teaching of modern Idealism, the labor of the spirit is positing (*Thesis*). Since spirit is conceived as subject and is therefore represented in the subject-object schema, positing must be the synthesis between the subject and its object. What is thus posited in this way gives *a view of the whole of objects*. That which the force of the subject works on, that which it posits through the work between itself and the objects, Humboldt calls "*world*." In such a "world-view," a civilization brings itself to expression. (UzS, pp. 247–248; italics mine)

In view of what we have seen so far, the diagnosis that Humboldt's view is trapped in the subject-object model does not seem to do justice to the specific character of his linguistic turn. (This becomes particularly clear in the concept of world that Heidegger so inappropriately attributes to him.) [14] Following this diagnosis, we find the objections that characterize Heidegger's general critique of the philosophy of consciousness.

Heidegger's critique is developed at three different levels. In my opinion, though, his general criticisms of the paradigm of the philosophy of consciousness as such do not in fact touch upon Humboldt's view of language. Accordingly, I will only consider that level of criticism which in my opinion has *internal* relevance to the themes inaugurated by Humboldt.

On the one hand, Heidegger (like Gadamer after him) criticizes the *formalism* of Humboldt's view, the attempt to derive the different worldviews (*Weltansichten*) inherent in different languages from the "internal form of language" (*innere Sprachform*) underlying them. From Heidegger's holistic point of view, a view shared by Humboldt, any appeal to the form/content distinction becomes highly problematic. However, the scope of this critique cannot be settled a priori, but will depend in each case on how much plausibility a theory can lend to this distinction. This topic will be examined later when we discuss the Gadamer-Habermas debate, which shares structural features with Heidegger's criticism of Humboldt.

On the other hand, in keeping with the complaint that Humboldt reduces language to an instrument of subjectivity (in my view, an unjustified complaint), Heidegger criticizes him for his understanding of language as one expressive means of the spirit *among others*. That is, it is taken to be just one constitutive element

14. On this point there is a radical difference between Heidegger's reception of Humboldt and Gadamer's. The latter will see in Humboldt's view of language as bearer of a worldview the rejection of the subject-object perspective, the rejection of the concept of "world" as a totality of entities (objectified by the subject), and the subsequent elaboration of a new concept of world adequate to the subject-subject perspective (as a symbolically structured totality *in which* speakers find themselves). However, as we shall see in the next section, this does not prevent Gadamer from appropriating the central aspects of Heidegger's critique of Humboldt.

of a worldview among other elements (one of the elements of the
"objective spirit," of culture). This critique, however, does not
take into account the evolution that occurs in Humboldt's own
view. Humboldt does indeed start from the standpoint criticized
by Heidegger, but he opts for a systematic, comparative analysis
of languages only once he has recognized the primacy of language
with respect to other cultural manifestations. That is to say, he
only begins his systematic study of languages once he has recognized the intimate connection between language and worldview.[15]

But most interesting for our purposes is Heidegger's systematic
argument against any pragmatist reduction of language to the human capacity to speak. This argument concerns the appropriate
relation between the semantic dimension of language in its function of world-disclosure and the pragmatic dimension of language
in its function as medium of understanding, of communication
(and hence as the condition of possibility of intersubjectivity).

Heidegger makes clear that the relation between these dimensions cannot be that established by a reduction of the former to
the latter. As he remarks: "Language needs human speaking, and
is nonetheless not the mere product of our linguistic activity"
(UzS, p. 256).

With this remark, Heidegger does not oppose treating language
as discourse, for this is precisely the view in which he coincides
with Humboldt. Like Humboldt, he opposes any objectivist view
of language as a system of signs. However, if we consider the view
of language as dialogue that he sketches in "Hölderlin und das
Wesen der Dichtung," we find an essential point of difference
with Humboldt, a shift of emphasis of the kind pointed out above:

[Language] *happens* authentically only in dialogue. . . . But what is a
"dialogue"? Obviously, speaking-with-one-another about something. . . .
But the unity of a dialogue consists in the fact that in each case in the
essential word *one and the same thing* is manifest [*offenbar*], that about
which we agree, that on the basis of which we are . . . in agreement. Our
Dasein is sustained by dialogue and its unity. (HWD, pp. 38–39; italics
mine)

15. See J. Trabant (1990), pp. 37–38.

This characterization of what happens in a dialogue is then summarized by Heidegger, when he asserts that "since language happens authentically as dialogue . . . *a world appears*" (HWD, p. 40). In this account, we can see Heidegger's essential opposition to any attempt to subject the dialogic dimension of language to a pragmatist reduction, that is, to reduce language to the human activity of speaking.

Heidegger's systematic reason against such an attempt, underscored by his view of conversation or dialogue as a "happening," concerns the relation between discourse and intelligibility. This was already clear in *Being and Time*, and Heidegger underlines it here even more clearly. The condition of possibility of dialogue, understood as "reciprocal talking about something" is that "one and the same thing be manifest, that about which we agree, that on the basis of which we are . . . in agreement" (HWD, p. 39).

With this conflation of that about which an agreement must be reached in dialogue and that which constitutes the basis of agreement, the figure of the circle of understanding developed in *Being and Time* is replicated. Heidegger already pointed out in his analysis of the forestructure of understanding that, to reach an agreement about something in dialogue, that something must first appear as one and the same thing about which agreement can, in principle, be reached. Therefore the condition of possibility of dialogue between speakers is that there be a common language available that guarantees, through its world-disclosing function, the unity and identity of the world—a unity on the basis of which speakers can then discuss specifically what is or is not the case. As Gadamer later puts it, any disagreement presupposes a prior "sustaining agreement."

To that extent, since only identical meanings can guarantee identical reference (the fact that speakers talk about the same thing), the semantic dimension of language in its world-disclosing function is necessarily prior to its pragmatic dimension. For in fact, the former must be seen as the condition of possibility of communication itself. Thus the pragmatic dimension (regarded as merely derivative) is *deprived of the role* attributed to it by Humboldt: namely, to *contribute to the very constitution of that world-disclo-*

sure. This is attributed instead to a demiurgic language, alien to any intraworldly activity.

This consequence is underscored by Heidegger's conflation of that about which speakers *must reach* an agreement with that on the basis of which speakers are *always already* in agreement. For when things are considered in this second way, there can only be disagreement in a conversation in a *relative* sense, against the background of a prior, unquestioned agreement that first enables speakers to talk about "the same thing."

Against the background of this view, Heidegger's argument against Humboldt becomes transparent. When he asserts that the conception of language as discourse cannot amount to the transformation of language into "the mere product of our linguistic activity," he is expressing his opposition to Humboldt's attempt to ground the constitution of the linguistic world-disclosure in the activity of talking as such. Heidegger's argument is systematic. By considering Humboldt's own account of the semantic dimension of language, in which language appears as constitutive of the linguistic worldview available to individuals, it becomes clear that this worldview cannot then be interpreted as the product of the activity of those individuals. As we have seen, they are unconsciously dominated by it. It is precisely for this reason that the function of language as a medium of understanding must be seen as *subordinated* to its world-disclosing function.

Heidegger develops this argument precisely by drawing attention to what happens when we talk in a conversation, that is, when language is used as a medium of understanding. He remarks:

It is necessary to bring the peculiarity of language closer to us. In this connection too, language shows itself in the first instance as our speaking. We now pay attention only to all that also speaks [*mitspricht*] in speaking, always already and according to the same measure, whether noticed or not. (UzS, p. 250)

It is from this standpoint that Heidegger later says:

We not only speak language, we speak *from out of it.* We are able to do this only for the reason that we have always already listened to language. What do we hear there? We hear the speaking of language. . . . Language speaks by saying, i.e., by *showing.* (UzS, pp. 254–255; italics mine)

The View of Language of Hermeneutics

In "Hölderlin und das Wesen der Dichtung," it was precisely this "showing" of language that figured as the condition of possibility for the fact that "one and the same thing be manifest," or that "a world appear." Thus Heidegger remarks:

What is essential to language is saying [*Sage*] *as showing* [*Zeige*]. Its showing is not grounded in whatever signs, but rather all signs stem from a showing, in whose domain . . . they can be signs. In view of the structure of saying, we are *permitted to ascribe showing neither exclusively nor decisively to human acting* [italics mine]. . . . Even there where showing is achieved by our saying, this showing as an indicating is preceded by a letting-itself-be-shown. (UzS, p. 254)

Beyond the reification of language[16] (and its "intentions") that becomes patent in these remarks, it becomes clear that the creation of language (or of signs) by speakers, as well as the intersubjectivity of the communication between them, is only possible on the basis of a transmitted language that is already presupposed. This language carries out the function of world-disclosure (that is, the "showing") that has always already occurred, beyond the will of individuals. Therefore it cannot be understood as the result of their activities, but as the necessary condition of possibility of these activities (for any attempt at showing takes place only within the framework of a prior "letting-be-shown").

This is what Heidegger wants to underline with his provocative claim that "language speaks," and what was already pointed out in *Being and Time* with the phrase "only he who already understands can listen." Heidegger connects with this motif here too by remarking: "Speaking is in itself a listening. It is listening to the language we speak. Therefore speaking is not simultaneously, but *beforehand*, a listening" (ibid.; italics mine).[17]

Given the esoteric and provocative way in which the motifs of Heidegger's view of language are presented, they are not always amenable to a critical discussion; nor are they always commensurable with other, more prosaic (or perhaps "profane") accounts

16. On this theme, see the interesting interpretation in Rorty (1991).

17. This aspect of Heidegger's hermeneutics is developed systematically by M. Riedel (1990).

of language. All of these motifs will be developed at length in Gadamer's philosophical hermeneutics, which in this respect can be regarded, in Habermas's words, as an "urbanization of the Heideggerian province."[18] The essential reason is that Gadamer both takes for granted the central premises of Heidegger's view of language and tries to develop their consequences. On this basis, as we shall see, Gadamer appropriates Humboldt's view of language as dialogue, but understands this in Heidegger's sense of a "happening" (i.e., as something liberated from any normative dimension).

Precisely because Gadamer relies on and presupposes what Heidegger had elaborated, it is difficult to assess in the terms of his argument the plausibility of its own background assumptions. To that extent, it has been indispensable to provide a brief discussion of the central premises behind Heidegger's radicalization of the Hamann-Herder-Humboldt tradition. For these premises constitute the background against which Gadamer appropriates the earlier tradition.

3.2 Gadamer's Reception of Humboldt and Heidegger: Linguistic World-Disclosure as the Condition of Possibility of Understanding

Gadamer explicitly acknowledges the internal connection between his account of the hermeneutic experience in *Truth and Method* and Heidegger's analysis of understanding[19] as developed in *Being and Time*.[20] In connection with Heidegger's aspiration to carry out a hermeneutic transformation of phenomenology, Gadamer chooses the term "hermeneutics" for his own investigation in *Truth and Method*.[21]

18. See J. Habermas: "Urbanisierung der Heideggerschen Provinz."

19. The term "understanding" will be used in what follows to refer to the agreement among speakers (that is, "*Verständigung*" and not "*Verstand*," as in Hamann).

20. See *Truth and Method*, pp. 242–271; see also *Hermeneutik II*, p. 440.

21. See *Hermeneutik II*, Gesammelte Werke Bd. 2, p. 446. Hereafter GW 2.

However, Gadamer also emphasizes that the underlying motif of his analysis is the attempt to "level the field toward the later Heidegger" (GW 2, p. 10), insofar as Heidegger's view after the *Kehre* "liberates the hermeneutic problem, making it come back to itself" (GW 2, p. 446). Given what we have seen about Heidegger's later views on language, this standpoint is substantiated by Gadamer's remark about his own phenomenological treatment of language, according to which "language is not exhausted by the consciousness of speakers and is, to that extent, more than mere subjective behavior" (ibid.). In what follows, I will discuss how Gadamer lays the foundations of his theory of hermeneutic experience, "taking language as a guide." In the course of this discussion, it will become clear to what extent Gadamer's view of language coincides in its central features with that of the later Heidegger.

However, a decisive difference separates these authors from the outset. In *Truth and Method,* we encounter a reception of Humboldt that differs from Heidegger's own in two important respects.

In the first place, Gadamer acknowledges that the view of language he wants to develop in *Truth and Method* is marked by a continuity with the view of the Hamann-Herder-Humboldt tradition. Despite all the differences with Humboldt that Gadamer will air explicitly, the continuity lies in approaching language through its dimension of world-disclosure. In light of this common theme, Heidegger's attempt to reduce Humboldt's view to the objectivist conception of language held by the philosophy of consciousness seems implausible.

In the second place, and more importantly, the account of language in the third part of *Truth and Method* has to provide the basis of the theory of hermeneutic experience sketched in the earlier parts. For this reason, as we will see, the *communicative dimension* of language (which was developed in Humboldt's work) acquires a significance that has no analogue in the view of language as "discourse" found in Heidegger.[22]

22. An interesting interpretation of the view of language developed by Gadamer in *Truth and Method,* which assesses its similarities and differences with respect to Heidegger's view, is offered by Kathleen Wright (1986).

But this does not mean that Gadamer's treatment of the communicative dimension of language amounts to a break with Heidegger's view, as discussed in the previous section. On the contrary, the peculiarity of Gadamer's view of language in *Truth and Method* is precisely that he receives Humboldt's dialogic concept of language as a medium of understanding *against the background of Heidegger's view*. In Gadamer's interpretation, there appears a new and complementary relation between the two points of view. Even though this approach results in a more harmonious image of the different dimensions of language than that which we found in Humboldt, it still suffers from a certain degree of one-sidedness. This arises, no doubt, from the specific case of hermeneutic experience on which *Truth and Method* focuses: that is, the interpretation of the classical texts of a tradition.[23] But as we shall see, this can be avoided without endangering the model as a whole.

To grasp the full constellation of perspectives encompassed by Gadamer, it is necessary to keep in mind both the basic structure and central motifs of *Truth and Method*.

To begin with the motifs, it is clear that the common basis of Gadamer's philosophical hermeneutics and Heidegger's hermeneutics of facticity is the attempt to counterpose the *finitude of human existence* (and hence of human reason) to the Enlightenment ideal of an absolute reason. In this respect, Gadamer repeatedly emphasizes that the background determining the hermeneutic phenomenon is "the *finitude of our historical experience*" (TM, p. 457). It is precisely in this context that Gadamer situates his appeal to language. He adds: "In order to do justice to [the finitude of our historical experience], we followed the trail of language, in which the structure of being is not simply reflected; rather, in language the order and structure of our experience itself is originally formed and constantly changed" (ibid.).

---

23. Gadamer explicitly acknowledges in the preface to the second edition of *Truth and Method* that "within the universal nexus of the moments inherent in understanding I have given primacy to the direction of the appropriation of past and tradition" (GW 2, p. 447).

In this interpretation of the linguistic turn, typical of both Heidegger and Gadamer, it can be seen that they have recourse to language insofar as it is something *supersubjective*. Language in its world-disclosing function is both the condition of possibility of experience and its limit. Thus it is inevitably found behind the backs of subjects, "for there is no point of view outside the experience of the world in language from which [language] could become an object" (TM, p. 452). Language thus becomes "something to be counterposed to the ideal of complete self-possession and self-consciousness" (GW 2, p. 9), or what is the same, it becomes the "reality that limits . . . the omnipotence of reflection" (TM, p. 342). This background is what accounts for the references to language as a "happening."

In addition to this motif, which Gadamer shares with Heidegger, there is another one specific to *Truth and Method* (and aimed against the radicalization of the Enlightenment ideal carried out by historicism).[24] The motif in question is that of the *rehabilitation of the authority of tradition*. The treatment of historical consciousness carried out by historicism involves the reification of tradition, which as a result is no longer regarded as a possible "source of truth" (TM, p. 279), but is reduced to an object of scientific investigation, deprived of any authority. With his analysis of language, Gadamer not only tries to show the power of tradition as a transmitter of a linguistic world-disclosure, "constitutive" of everything that can appear in the world (as we saw in Heidegger); rather, he also wants to restore the *binding* normative power of tradition for all those individuals who are immersed in it or who appropriate it via interpretation.

Indeed, after the de facto loss of the authority of tradition that characterizes modernity, Gadamer cannot but acknowledge that "even the most genuine and pure tradition does not persist be-

---

24. At the end of *Truth and Method*, Gadamer reconstructs both motifs in explicit connection with his account of language. He remarks: "We formulated this universal hermeneutics on the basis of the concept of language not only in order to guard against a false methodologism that infects the *concept of objectivity* in the human sciences but also to avoid the idealistic spiritualism of a Hegelian *metaphysics of infinity*" (TM, p. 476; italics mine).

cause of the inertia of what once existed. It needs to be affirmed, embraced, cultivated" (TM, p. 281). For this, Gadamer needs to go beyond the model developed by Heidegger after the *Kehre*, in which language is reified as a "contingent absolute," predetermining everything that can appear within the world. Moreover, he must find a model in which tradition does not have to be understood only as a *vis a tergo* (TM, p. 360)—whose power "does not depend on its being recognized" (TM, p. 301)—but in which tradition can also demand recognition.

This is what leads Gadamer to go beyond the subject-object model underlying historicism (which "objectifies" tradition, depriving it of authority). Instead, appealing to the same perspective that Humboldt proposed to overcome this model, he interprets tradition as a *vis a fronte,* as that which is not objectifiable par excellence, as a "Thou." This systematic role acquired by the communicative dimension in the account of language as a medium of understanding is what distinguishes Gadamer's view from Heidegger's.

Unlike his view, Gadamer's not only emphasizes as a condition of possibility of understanding that what the speakers must achieve an understanding about be "manifest as one and the same thing," owing to the world-disclosure they share. It is also emphasized that the interlocutor with whom we want to reach an agreement must be taken seriously in her claim to truth for what she says.

With this second point, Gadamer incorporates into his own view of language the dialectic found in Humboldt: that between an intersubjectivity always already produced (guaranteed by a shared world-disclosure) and an intersubjectivity always in the making. The difference lies in the fact that Gadamer does not understand this dialectic as a movement between two poles of equal status. Humboldt's account had already been criticized by Heidegger; as we shall see, Gadamer persists in this critique. The understanding between speakers cannot be interpreted as the conscious self-production of a world-disclosure that takes place in a "zero context." Rather, it can only be achieved by speakers *within* a shared constitution of meaning, always already given. Thus this constitution of meaning or worldview is the condition of possibility of understanding, and hence also that which guarantees the validity of this understanding. Then its insurmountability is not only *factual,* as suggested by Humboldt (who opposes it to the regulative ideal of a world-in-itself), but also *normative.* For the linguistic world-disclosure is at the same time a *happening of truth* (for it constitutes what things are). Therefore our explicit appropriation of it in hermeneutic experience demands the recognition of our *belonging* to it as well as of the *truth* it contains.

This double response to historicism leads Gadamer to develop the model of dialogue in its proper complexity, which had not yet occurred either in Humboldt's account or in Heidegger's. The constitutive moments of dialogue considered by Gadamer are as follows:

• the telos of understanding between *speaker* and *hearer* . . .

• *about something* on which they have to reach an agreement . . .

• against the background of a *shared world-disclosure* that is the condition of possibility of their understanding.

This model makes it possible to integrate the world-disclosing dimension of language with its function as a medium of understanding. On the basis of this model, Gadamer will try to give support in the last part of *Truth and Method* to his theory of hermeneutic experience, whose "phenomenology" has been exhibited in the earlier parts.

However, I will proceed here in inverse order, discussing first the central premises of the view of language developed by Gadamer (3.2.1 and 3.2.2). I will then show the internal logic by which Gadamer's interpretation of hermeneutic experience derives from his view of language (3.2.3).

3.2.1 Gadamer's Reception of Humboldt's View of Language as World-Disclosure

In part 3 of *Truth and Method,* Gadamer shows the systematic importance of Humboldt's account of the world-disclosing dimension of language by offering a historical reconstruction of the different conceptions of language throughout Western history. In this reconstruction, there appear again the central premises inherent in the conception of language as constitutive of our understanding of the world, which we already saw in Humboldt's approach, namely:

• The rejection of the view of language as a mere instrument, as a system of signs;

• the assertion of the identity between language and thought (between word and concept); and

• the view of language as bearer of a worldview.

Gadamer considers these premises historically, as the result of a process of evolution. Since no later than Humboldt, this evolutionary process has split in half. On the one hand, there is a scientistic tradition guided by the ideal of the *mathesis universalis* and dedicated to the construction of artificial languages as perfect systems of signs (without the ambiguities of ordinary language). In this tradition, which has roots in Greek philosophy, language is reduced to a mere instrument. On the other hand, there is the tradition to which Gadamer wants to contribute, in which language is thematized in its constitutive dimension of world-disclosure (the Hamann-Herder-Humboldt tradition).

Since the core of the critique of language as an instrument has already been repeatedly discussed, I restrict myself here to the specificity of Gadamer's historical reconstruction in contrast with that of the authors already discussed.

The first difference lies in the fact that Gadamer does not regard the instrumental view of language as a perspective "natural to man," as Humboldt did. On the contrary, Gadamer shows through a historical reconstruction the lengthy process of rationalization involved in the process by which the word becomes "sign."[25]

25. Of course, this rationalization is regarded by Gadamer as a negative evolution promoted by those who do "not accept the intimate unity of word and subject matter" (TM, p. 403). However, Gadamer's explanation of this evolution is instructive independently of his assessment of it. At the end of this book I will try to provide arguments to defend the purely rational character of this evolution, arguments showing the internal connection between the designative function of language and the possibility of cognitive learning.

The View of Language of Hermeneutics

To illustrate this point, Gadamer begins his reconstruction with "the Greeks." The aim of this starting point is not to emphasize the identification of language and reason in the Greek word *logos,* as was typical of the Hamann-Herder-Humboldt tradition. Rather, the aim is to underscore, as Heidegger previously did in *Being and Time,*[26] that "the *Greeks* . . . did not have a word for what we call language" (TM, p. 405). Thus Gadamer wants to illustrate a characteristic feature of language that is and has been constitutive of it: the "unconsciousness of language." This is its unobjectifiable nature (due to its quasi-transcendental status), its necessary disappearance in speech, precisely so that we can employ language to refer to things and not just back to language.

In this genuine characteristic of language, already thematized in the writings of Heidegger,[27] the primitive unity of word and thing becomes clear:

> In the earliest times the intimate unity of word and thing was so obvious that the true name was considered to be part of the bearer of the name, if not indeed to substitute for him. In Greek the expression for "word," *onoma,* also means "name," and especially "proper name"—i.e., the

26. Heidegger had already remarked in *Being and Time* that "the Greeks had no word for 'language'" (p. 209). The context of this assertion can serve to illustrate the position of Gadamer that I discuss in what follows:

> Among the Greeks, their everyday existing was largely diverted into talking with one another. . . . Is it an accident that . . . they defined the essence of man as ζῶον λόγον ἔχον? . . . Man shows himself as the entity which talks. This does not signify that the possibility of vocal utterance is peculiar to him, but rather that he is the entity which is such as to discover the world and Dasein itself. (pp. 208–209)

27. In *Unterwegs zur Sprache,* Heidegger remarks:

> [W]herever and however we speak a language, language itself is precisely never brought to word in this way. In languages, many things are spoken, above all those things that we discuss: a state of affairs, an incident, a question, or an object of inquiry. In everyday speaking language does *not* bring itself to language, but rather stays within itself. Only because of this fact are we able to speak a language straightaway, to concern ourselves with and about something. (p. 161)

name by which something is called. The word is understood primarily as a name. But a name is what it is because it is what someone is called and what he answers to. It belongs to its bearer. The rightness of the name is confirmed by the fact that someone answers to it. Thus it seems to belong to his being. (TM, p. 405)[28]

The "breakthrough of philosophical inquiry into the territory over which the name had undisputed rule" (ibid.) entails the differentiation of "word" and "thing," of the name and the thing named. This step taken by the "Greek Enlightenment" is the beginning of an evolution which, in Gadamer's opinion, has negative consequences.

Once this differentiation is in place, the relation between word and thing can be interpreted according to two contrasting models. Both are discussed in Plato's *Cratylus:* the conventionalist account of the word-object relation, and the opposed theory that argues for "a *natural* agreement" between word and object.

Gadamer's critique of these two views coincides with the critique of language as tool already present in the Hamann-Herder-Humboldt tradition. Gadamer remarks: "Language is not a mere tool we use. . . . Both these interpretations of language start from the existence and instrumentality of words, and regard the subject matter as something we know about previously from an independent source. Thus they start too late" (TM, p. 406).

The situation is not improved by Plato's proposal, which also rejects both of these theories. In fact, Plato's proposed solution, his "discovery of the ideas," only makes matters worse. For it introduces a further differentiation: the distinction between sign,

---

28. Both from a phylogenetic and from an ontogenetic point of view, Gadamer's thesis seems to be correct. From a phylogenetic point of view, the rationalization implicit in the progressive differentiation between language and reality, between sign and what is designated by it, takes place in the rationalization of mythical worldviews. This rationalization is repeated in ontogenesis: *after* learning language, the child must learn this differentiation, that is, she must learn not to conceive of a name as a constitutive element of that which bears it (see J. Piaget 1929). For the implications of the rationality of this kind of differentiation, see chapter 5.3.

designatum, and concept. Thus Gadamer emphasizes: "The net result, then, is that Plato's discovery of the ideas conceals the true nature of language even more than the theories of the Sophists" (TM, p. 408).

By tracing the relation between word and thing to a prior correlation, in the sphere of the *logos,* between the noetic and the things themselves, language is definitively consigned to a merely secondary role. It becomes a tool, an intermediary of that essential relation: "If the sphere of the logos represents the sphere of the noetic in the variety of its associations, then the *word,* just like the number, becomes the mere *sign* of a being that is well defined and hence pre-known" (TM, p. 412). Thus it becomes clear that on this view,

it is *not word but number* that is the real paradigm of the noetic; number, whose name is obviously pure convention and whose "exactitude" consists in the fact that every number is defined by its place in the series, so that it is a pure structure of intelligibility, an *ens rationis* . . . in the strong sense of perfect rationality. This is the real conclusion to which the *Cratylus* is drawn, and it has one very important consequence, which in fact *influences all further thinking about language.* (TM, p. 412; italics mine)

With this reduction of the word to a mere sign, language is understood exclusively in accordance with its *designative* function—the telos of which is no doubt the greatest possible univocity. Thus this account of language can be seen as the beginning of a process that culminates in the ideal of replacing natural languages with a perfectly univocal artificial language, one free of the metaphorical nature of a natural language. As soon as the word is conceived as a cumbersome intermediary between thought and thing,

thought is so independent of the being of words—which thought takes as mere signs through which what is referred to, the idea, the thing, is brought into view—that the word is reduced to a wholly secondary relation to the thing. It is a mere instrument of communication. . . . It follows that an ideal system of signs, whose sole purpose is to coordinate all signs in an unambiguous system, makes the power of words (*dunamis ton onomaton*)—the range of variation of the contingent in the historical languages as they have actually developed—appear as a mere flaw in their utility. This is the ideal of a *characteristica universalis*. (TM, p. 414)

This initial "forgetfulness of language in Western thought" is remedied to some extent, not by a *Greek*, but by a *Christian* idea of special significance in the Middle Ages: the idea of *incarnation* (TM, p. 418). With this idea, it is possible to view the relation between thought and language not merely as instrumental, but as a "revelation" (*Offenbarmachen*) in which the word is not distinguished from that which it reveals, but is something that "has its being in its revealing" (TM, p. 421). The medieval account of the relation between God's word—the origin of creation—and the human word makes it possible to think of "a real affinity between word and concept" (TM, p. 438).

However, this affinity is interpreted as an internal "correspondence" between the multiple human languages and the one divine truth. Accordingly, it is this concordance, and not language itself, that "the Christian Platonist is concerned with. Essential for him is the fact that all human speech is related to the thing, and not so much the fact that human knowledge of things is bound to language. The latter represents only a prismatic refraction in which there shines the one truth" (TM, p. 438).

After this excursus, Gadamer goes on to discuss the conception of language of the Hamann-Herder-Humboldt tradition, focusing on the third member of this trio.

Although Gadamer's discussion of Humboldt's view appears under the heading "language as experience of the world," his presentation of Humboldt as the "founder of the modern philosophy of language" already suggests a critical hindsight that later becomes explicit. The *formalism* inherent in the project of developing a science of language through the comparative study of natural, historical languages is the feature of Humboldt's view of language that Gadamer first criticizes.

Owing to the formalism underlying Humboldt's view, his correct recognition of the unity of thought and language becomes disfigured in a peculiar way. As Gadamer points out: "The path of investigation that Humboldt follows is characterized by *abstraction down to form*. . . . [H]e thereby limited the universality of the connection between language and thought to the formalism of a faculty'' (TM, p. 440). This entails the consequence that "as the formalism of a faculty, [language] can always be detached from the determinate content of what is said" (TM, p. 441). And this is what Gadamer finds objectionable in the "abstraction" underlying Humboldt's hypothesis about an "inner form" of language. The unity of thought and language is understood only in a formal sense, as an inseparability in principle. Against this formalism, Gadamer appeals to the fact that *"verbal form and traditionary content cannot be separated in the hermeneutic experience"* (TM, p. 441).

As was anticipated, if Gadamer's critique of Humboldt were to rely on this claim alone, it would be, if not entirely implausible, at least very limited. That is, it would remain correct only as long as the opposite was not demonstrated. However, Gadamer can advance his objection as an *internal* criticism of Humboldt's position, insofar as they both start from essentially the same view of language.

If we consider Gadamer's argument as an internal criticism, it becomes clear that his critique draws its force from a contradiction in Humboldt's view. As already pointed out in chapter 2, there is an incompatibility between the supposition of the universality of language (supported by the abstraction of an inner form underlying all natural languages), and the thesis (arising from his account of the world-disclosing function of language) that "there resides in every language a *peculiar* world-view." It is only against the background of this tension that Gadamer's critique becomes plausible. This is made plain by the argumentative context of the thesis cited above:

Nevertheless this concept of language constitutes an abstraction that has to be reversed for our purposes. *Verbal form and traditionary content cannot be separated in the hermeneutic experience.* If every language is a view of the world, it is so not primarily because it is a particular type of language (in the way that linguists view language) but because of what is said or handed down in this language. (TM, p. 441)

Gadamer's thesis against formalism draws its force in the context of this argument, insofar as it uncovers an *internal difficulty* in Humboldt's view. As we saw, the latter tried to save the possibility of objective knowledge by reinterpreting the constitutive character of the worldview transmitted by a language. He tried to convert its *normative* status, as that which structures the intraworldly as such, into the merely *factual* status of an unavoidable obstacle for the genuine task of reaching the "world in itself." (That is, "the sum of the knowable . . . as the field to be tilled by the human mind," which, as we saw, "lies among all languages, independent of them, in the middle.")

Gadamer's critique of this attempt is certainly consistent. If language is recognized as responsible for world-disclosure, as what makes accessible the intraworldly as such, then the knowledge of what appears in that world cannot be grounded in the impossible task of "separating the object as neatly as possible" from the "subjectivity of language."[29]

However, the consistency of this critique depends precisely on a recognition of the fundamental insight of Humboldt's view of language, a recognition utterly lacking in Heidegger. That is, it is necessary to understand Humboldt's view of language as an attempt to "[show] that *a language-view* [*Sprachansicht*] *is a worldview* [*Weltansicht*]" (TM, p. 442). As Gadamer later remarks:

Language is not just one of man's possessions in the world; rather, on it depends the fact that man has a *world* at all. The world as world exists for man as for no other creature that is in the world. But *this world is verbal in nature*. This is the real heart of Humboldt's assertion (which he intended quite differently) that languages are worldviews. By this Humboldt means that language maintains a kind of independent life *vis-à-vis* the individual member of a linguistic community; and as he grows into it, it introduces him to a particular orientation and relationship to

---

29. This problem has its origin in the reification of language as world-disclosure inherent in the thesis that meaning determines reference. Indeed, it cannot first be postulated that the access to referents is only possible by virtue of meanings (which show the way in which the referents are given, or in which we refer to them), only to revoke this later on—when knowledge is explained as the attempt to gain access to objects by avoiding the indirect, subjective route of linguistic articulation. The solution to this problem cannot be found *from within* this view of language, but only by breaking with it. This issue will be discussed in chapter 5.

the world as well. But the ground of this statement is more important, namely that language has no independent life apart from the world that comes to language within it [*zur Sprache kommt*]. Not only is the world world insofar as it comes into language, but *language, too, has its real being only in the fact that the world is presented in it.* Thus, that language is originally human means at the same time that man's being-in-the-world is primordially linguistic. (TM, p. 443)

In what follows, Gadamer systematizes that which, in his opinion, is involved in the recognition of the world-disclosing dimension of language. A fundamental implication is the *distance* with respect to the "environment" (*Umwelt*), according to which "having world" results from having language. This distance establishes a definite difference between man and animals:

unlike all other living creatures, man's relationship to the world is characterized by *freedom from the environment.* This freedom implies *the linguistic constitution of the world* [italics mine]. Both belong together. To rise above the pressure of what impinges on us from the world means to have language and to have 'world.'" (TM, p. 444)

This *distance,* arising from the symbolic mediation of the world, is due to the *propositionally structured* character of the world in accordance with its linguistic configuration. Therefore, as Gadamer remarks, "animals have a language only *per aequivocationem*" (TM, p. 445):

[L]anguage is a human possibility that is free and variable in its use. For man language is variable not only in the sense that there are foreign languages that one can learn but also variable in itself, for it contains *various possibilities* for saying the same thing. . . . Animals do not have this variability when making themselves understood to one another. This means, ontologically, that they make themselves understood, *but not about states of affairs, the epitome of which is the world.* (TM, p. 445; italics mine)

This intrinsic variability of language, which by creating "possibilities" also creates the distinction between truth and falsity, is what Gadamers terms "its unique *factualness*" (*Sachlichkeit*). This feature of language must be regarded as constitutive, since to speak is always to speak "about something." This is the only one of its features taken into account in Greek philosophy: "Greek ontology is based on the factualness of language, in that it conceives the essence of language in terms of statements" (TM, p. 446).

Against the one-sidedness of this view, Gadamer then points out another constitutive aspect of language that also underlies its world-disclosing dimension, and which was also present in Humboldt's view. This is its character as a medium of understanding: "it must be emphasized that language has its true being only in dialogue, in *coming to an understanding*" (TM, p. 446).

This assertion should not be read, however, as if it meant to indicate "the purpose of language." On the contrary, it is only in dialogue that the true importance of the world-disclosing function can be assessed. In this manner, Gadamer continues Heidegger's critique of Humboldt. The relevance of the world-disclosing function of language as a *condition of possibility for the understanding* between speakers becomes patent only when we take into account that "*coming to an understanding is not a mere action, a purposeful activity*" (TM, p. 446; italics mine). And here, in relation to the connection between the cognitive and communicative dimensions of language (between its world-disclosing function and its function as a medium of understanding), Heidegger's critique of Humboldt explicitly reappears. Gadamer remarks:

human language must be thought of as a special and unique life process since, *in linguistic communication, "world" is disclosed* [*offenbargemacht*]. Reaching an understanding in language places a subject matter before those communicating. . . . Thus the world is the common ground, trodden by none and recognized by all, *uniting all who talk to one another* [italics mine] . . . language . . . fully realizes itself only in the process of coming to an understanding. That is why it is not a mere means [*Mittel*] in that process. (TM, p. 446).

As Heidegger already argued, given the priority of language as *constitutive for that about which an understanding must be reached*, it cannot be viewed as a mere instrument for achieving understanding *about something that exists independently of this instrument*. The difference between language and such an instrument is illustrated by Gadamer's remark about artificial languages:

For this reason invented systems of artificial communication are never languages. . . . It is well known that the consensus by which an artificial language is introduced necessarily belongs to another language. In a real community of language, on the other hand, *we do not first decide to agree but are always already in agreement.* . . . The object of understanding is not the verbal means of understanding as such but rather the world that presents itself to us in common life and that embraces everything about which understanding can be reached. Agreeing about a language is not the paradigmatic case but rather a special case—agreeing about an instrument, a system of signs, that does not have its being in dialogue but serves rather to convey information. (TM, pp. 446–447; italics mine)

This contrast with artificial languages underscores that the essential function of the world-disclosure of natural languages is to guarantee the identity of the world, the world against the background of which speakers try to reach a mutual understanding. Therefore, it is inherent in the *priority* of the linguistic world-disclosure over any conversation that this "disclosure" as well as the world structured by it lies behind the backs of the subjects who converse. Speakers reify the intraworldly, that about which they speak, rather than language in general or the world in which they find themselves and therefore presuppose:

Our verbal experience of the world is *prior* [italics mine] to everything that is recognized and addressed as existing. *That language and world are related in a fundamental way does not mean, then, that world becomes the object of language.* Rather, *the object of knowledge and statements is always already enclosed within the world horizon of language* [italics mine]. That human experience of the world is verbal does not imply that a world-in-itself is being objectified. (TM, p. 450)

This view, central to the account of language that Gadamer defends, is already pointed out in a final remark with which Gadamer introduces the third part of *Truth and Method*. There, the implications of this view are unpacked:

Our first point is that the language in which something comes to speak is not a *possession at the disposal* of one or the other of the interlocutors. Every conversation presupposes a common language, or better, creates a common language. . . . Hence reaching an understanding on the subject matter of a conversation necessarily means that a common language must first be worked out in the conversation. This is not an external matter of simply adjusting our tools; nor is it even right to say that the partners adapt themselves to one another but, rather, in a successful conversation they both come under the influence of the truth of the object and are thus bound to one another in a new community. To reach an understanding in a dialogue is not merely a matter of putting oneself forward and successfully asserting one's own point of view, but being transformed into a communion in which we do not remain what we were. (TM, pp. 378–379; italics mine)

These highly compressed remarks already indicate the framework within which Gadamer will situate the different dimensions of language. As already pointed out, the essential difference between Gadamer's account and those of Humboldt and Heidegger lies in the complexity that the model of conversation acquires for him. From this model, Gadamer will proceed to give a more complex account of the communicative dimension of language.

Taking as our background the view of the world-disclosure of language as the condition of possibility of understanding, I will now discuss the central features of Gadamer's account.

3.2.2 Language as Medium of Understanding: The Model of Conversation

The view of language as the medium in which understanding takes place is defined by contrast with that of language as a mere instrument for the transmission of information. This contrast makes plain the significance of the supposition that language is constitutive of our understanding of the world. Because our access to reality is symbolically mediated, the information to be transmitted by means of language possesses, as Gadamer remarks, an irreducible variability. And to that extent, it is necessarily subject to interpretation. Thus the univocity of the linguistically transmitted "message" can only be achieved through the mutual understanding about the subject matter that takes place *in* and not *prior to* the conversation itself.[30] Therefore understanding constitutes a telos inherent in all discourse.

30. This is what Gadamer terms the "speculative" structure of language, which emerges "not as the reflection of something given but as the coming into lan-

Hence the aim of this account of discourse or conversation as oriented toward reaching an understanding about some subject matter is to overcome the objectivism characteristic of every instrumental view of language. This is the common denominator of Gadamer's and Humboldt's views. Gadamer's treatment of the communicative dimension of language, following the model of conversation, can be seen as attempting to break with the primacy of the subject-object relation (which distorts the nature of language). It does so through an account of this relation similar to Humboldt's, though incomparably more intricate regarding the intersubjectivity that typifies such relation (3.2.2.a).

However, the essential difference in comparison with Humboldt is still the same that we found in the later Heidegger's critical radicalization of Humboldt. This difference is underscored by the persistent interpretation of conversation as a "happening," which has no parallel in Humboldt (3.2.2.b). Against this backdrop, the view of language developed by Gadamer can be seen as a middle ground between Humboldt's position and Heidegger's.

We seen that these authors drew opposite conclusions from the same phenomenon, that is, from what Gadamer calls the "speculative structure of language" (or the symbolic mediation of our relationship with the world). Both Humboldt and Heidegger recognized that, given this phenomenon, our relationship with the world becomes an infinite *interpretative* task. For the world

---

guage of a totality of meaning" (TM, p. 474). A constant assumption made by Gadamer is that what "comes into language" is "a totality of meaning." This assumption is perhaps correct in the particular case of the interpretation of texts, but not in the normal case of talking about states of affairs in the world. It is this assumption that leads Gadamer to assert the universality of hermeneutics in radically idealistic terms, namely, in the sense that "*being that can be understood is language*" (ibid.). This reification of language, adopted by Gadamer from Heidegger and subjected to a further development, has its origin in the thesis characteristic of this view of language—the view that that meaning determines reference. So it is only logical that Gadamer asserts this thesis in this context. He remarks: "To come into language does not mean that a second being is acquired. Rather, *what something presents itself as belongs to its own being*" (TM, p. 475; italics mine). For "that which comes into language is not something that is pregiven before language; rather, the word gives it its own determinateness" (ibid.).

ceases to be the totality of entities given independently of language. It is rather a totality of possible states of affairs, from which speakers must decide in each instance which particular one is the case. This recognition led Humboldt to redefine the objectivity of our experience in the world, and our knowledge of it, in terms of the intersubjectivity achieved by speakers in the process of mutual understanding.

But Heidegger, in his analysis of the conditions of possibility of the process of understanding, emphasized that talk is only possible against the background of a world linguistically disclosed and shared by speakers. A shared world is what makes possible both speakers' initial disagreement and their eventual agreement (for as we have seen, "only he who already understands can listen"). The consequence of this viewpoint could be clearly seen in "Hölderlin und das Wesen der Dichtung." There, with respect to the linguistic world-disclosure, Heidegger *conflated* that about which speakers must reach an agreement with that on the basis of which they are always already in agreement. For indeed, the agreement reached by speakers cannot go beyond the limits of the world they share. To that extent, it is necessarily included in that all-encompassing, prior, and tacit agreement. As we shall see, the originality of Gadamer lies in maintaining *both* points of view, each of them one-sidedly maintained by Humboldt and Heidegger, respectively.

Gadamer shares with Humboldt the view that, since there is no fixed, pregiven world (not susceptible to interpretation) in relation to which speakers confine themselves to the mutual transmission of "information," it is *only* in the process of mutual conversation that a common perspective can emerge, on the basis of which speakers can reach an understanding: "Language is the medium in which understanding among the speakers and agreement about the thing at issue take place" (TM, p. 384). The "thing itself" about which speakers must reach an understanding is not at their disposal *before* the understanding is reached, but only *if* it takes place, and therefore *after* it takes place. Hence an essential component of conversation is "the coming-into-language of *the thing itself*" (TM, p. 378; italics mine). As we shall see, this consideration is essential for the philosophical hermeneutics developed by Gadamer in the early chapters of *Truth and Method*. This is what enables him to carry out an analysis of the conditions of possibility of the understanding between speakers. This analysis is characterized by two distinct features:

• on the one hand, unlike Heidegger's approach, it does not reduce these conditions to the single assumption of an always already shared world-disclosure (an assumption that led Heidegger to regard as irrelevant how a factual agreement is reached in each case);

• and on the other hand, going beyond Humboldt's approach, it captures the specificity of the participants' perspective in the conversation (that is, of the subject-subject relation). That is, it shows the indissoluble connection between meaning and validity, a connection that Humboldt sensed in the structure of dialogue, but could explain only in metaphorical terms.

3.2.2.a *Conversation and Understanding*

As already indicated, the background against which Gadamer's development of the model of conversation should be considered is his critique of objectivism in the human sciences. This holds in particular for the historicist attempt to apply the methodology of the natural sciences to the study of social, historical, and cultural reality. To this end, Gadamer realizes that it is not enough to appeal to the difficulties arising from the attempt to apply science's ideal of objectivity to a reality in which the investigator is unavoidably involved (and whose essentially open character precludes any definitive results). These difficulties explain the methodological concern with guaranteeing this ideal, present ever since the human sciences started to be differentiated as such. However, Gadamer's arguments are aimed at the very ideal of objectivity involved in the interpretation of these difficulties.

Gadamer must show the inadequacy of this scientific ideal for the methodological self-interpretation of these sciences so that it loses its status as a regulative idea, as something desirable but difficult to achieve (as, for example, in Humboldt's view). For this reason, it is not enough to join Heidegger in appealing to the symbolically mediated character of our relationship with the world (or in Heidegger's terms, to the primacy of understanding over knowing, or as Gadamer puts it, to the "universality" of the hermeneutic phenomenon). The recognition of this fact only complicates our understanding of how the objectivity of science is nonetheless still possible. For the efficacy of science in its increasing domination of nature cannot be doubted, and it would therefore be absurd to prescribe how science ought to function. Undoubtedly, "the objectifying procedures of natural science and the concept of being-in-itself, which is intended in all knowledge, proved to be an abstraction when viewed from the medium that language is" (TM, p. 476). The idea that the subject-object perspective arises as an abstraction from a prior subject-subject perspective could already be found in Humboldt's view. But this idea does not involve questioning the subject-object perspective as such (nor, obviously, is it Gadamer's intention to do so).

What Gadamer has to show is that the "abstraction" of the subject-object perspective is *structurally inapplicable* to the realities that transcend the natural sciences. It is not just a "difficult" perspective to apply (as suggested by the methodological reflections of historicism) but rather, in this particular case, an *unacceptable* perspective.

Thus Gadamer will try to show that our experience of these social, historical, and cultural realities can *only* take place within the framework of a relation prior to the abstraction of the subject-object perspective: namely, the *subject-subject relation*. Therefore this experience can be understood only from the standpoint of what is most specific to the subject-subject relation—that which Gadamer calls "the experience of the Thou." Hence the challenge faced by Gadamer's account of this relation, in his development of the model of conversation, will be to show why in this case the abstraction underlying the subject-object perspective is unacceptable.

As pointed out earlier, the model of conversation necessarily involves a more complex structure than the subject-object relation. For as we have seen, what must take place in a conversation is both "the understanding between participants" and "the consensus about the thing" at issue. The understanding toward which a conversation is directed is always an understanding *with someone* and *about something*. Since this "something" about which an agreement must be reached is not accessible as an entity in itself, but is linguistically prestructured, the understanding of it is unavoidably subject to interpretation (this is the moment of "application" inherent in any understanding, a moment that Gadamer repeatedly underlines). It follows from this that the agreement about the thing at issue can only take place by means of the different interpretations of the participants in the conversation. That is, it can only occur insofar as they achieve a mutual understanding.

This is why Gadamer analyzes the conditions of possibility of understanding by way of an account of the specificity of the "experience of the Thou," which in Gadamer's opinion constitutes "the essence of hermeneutic experience" (TM, p. 346).

Gadamer begins his analysis by opposing the objectivist reduction of the concept of experience to the model of perception, to the subject-object paradigm. The abstraction or idealization that science carries out, with the aim of developing such a paradigm from out of the "primary experience" of the lifeworld, was already shown by phenomenology, especially by Husserl. However, the experience upheld by Gadamer's argument is completely different from the instrumental-pragmatic experience of the lifeworld. It is the "experience of the Thou"—an experience that precedes the idealizations of science. Gadamer emphasizes that what is specific to this experience is, in Humboldt's terms, that "the Thou is not an object but is in relationship with us" (TM, p. 358). Therefore the I-Thou relation cannot consist in a perception of the external world, but rather in the understanding of others by interacting with them. As Humboldt argues, this relation does not take place in the sphere of all entities, but in that of "interaction"—namely, in the social world. Gadamer makes this point as follows: "Since here the object of experience is a *person*, this kind of experience is a *moral phenomenon*—as is the knowledge acquired through experience, the understanding of the other person" (TM, p. 358; italics mine).

Thus what is specific about this experience is that "the Thou is *acknowledged as a person*" (TM, p. 359; italics mine), and not perceived as an intraworldly object. Gadamer explains this specificity as follows:

This relation is not *immediate* but *reflective*. To every claim there is a counterclaim. This is why it is possible for each of the partners in the relationship reflectively to outdo the other. One claims to know the other's claim from his point of view and even to understand the other better than the other understands himself. In this way the Thou loses the immediacy with which it makes its claim. It is understood, but this means it is co-opted and pre-empted reflectively from the standpoint of the other person. Because it is a mutual relationship, it helps to *constitute the reality of the I-Thou relationship itself.* The inner historicity of all the relations in the lives of men consists in the fact that there is a constant struggle for mutual recognition. (TM, p. 359; italics mine)

Gadamer characterizes this mediated relation inherent in the experience of the Thou as a relation of "openness." In his explanation of this concept, Gadamer tries to underscore that it goes beyond that which the social sciences call the "double contingency" of human interaction. What is most specific about the I-Thou relation cannot be captured from the one-sided standpoint characteristic of the social sciences, which work with "a clichéd version of scientific method" (TM, p. 359) and whose only goal is the "calculus" of the behavior of others. If, discarding this monologic perspective, we take the model of conversation as our starting point, it becomes clear that in order to "let something be spoken by another" we cannot overlook the other's claim. This is what Gadamer calls the openness toward the other, which requires that she be "recognized."

Gadamer justifies this claim through an analysis of what he terms "the *logical structure of openness* that characterizes hermeneutical consciousness" (TM, p. 362). This analysis, carried out under the heading of "The Hermeneutic Priority of the Question," is meant to sketch the structure of the conversation directed toward understanding. The logic underlying this kind of conversation is what Gadamer calls the "logic of question and answer."

In light of all that has been seen so far, we can easily understand the following connection. The priority of the question corresponds to the fact that that about which speakers must reach an agreement is accessible only through understanding, and thus only through interpretation. What is characteristic of this situation is that which Gadamer calls "the openness of being either this or that" (TM, p. 362). This openness can only be closed off by speakers through questions and answers that allow them to reach a common perspective or interpretation. For as Gadamer points out, "the essence of the question is to have *sense*. Now sense involves a sense of direction. Hence the sense of the question is the only direction from which the answer can be given if it is to make sense. A question places what is questioned *in a particular perspective*" (TM, p. 362; italics mine). But for this very reason, Gadamer adds: "Posing a question implies openness but also *limitation*. It implies the explicit establishing of presuppositions, in terms of which what still remains open *shows* itself" (TM, p. 363; italics mine).

These considerations allow him to uncover the "essential relation" between question and knowledge, for only when the presuppositions to which something is subject are fixed can we find an answer: "For it is the essence of knowledge not only to judge something correctly but, at the same time and for the same reason, to exclude what is wrong. Deciding the question is the path to *knowledge*. What decides a question is the preponderance of reasons for the one and against the other possibility" (TM, p. 364; italics mine).

It is evident that conversation as such requires this structure of question and answer. Gadamer remarks:

To conduct a dialogue requires first of all that the partners do not talk at cross purposes [*aneinander vorbeireden*]. Hence it necessarily has the structure of question and answer. The first condition of the art of conversation is ensuring that the other person is with us. . . . To conduct a conversation means to allow oneself to be conducted by the subject matter to which the partners in the dialogue are oriented. (TM, p. 367)

Indeed, it is a necessary condition of any conversation that its participants converse *about the same thing*. For this, they must construct a common perspective, such that that which they talk about can be identified as "the same." Hence: "As the art of conducting a conversation, dialectic is also the art of *seeing things in the unity of an aspect* [*sunoran eis hen eidos*]—i.e., it is the art of forming concepts through working out *what is meant in common* [*gemeinsam Gemeinten*]" (TM, p. 368; italics mine). To this extent, the only thing that precedes the conversation guided by the logic of question and answer is the "anticipation of meaning" from which the participants in the conversation generate questions and answers. The conversation takes place "on the basis of expectations of meaning drawn from our own prior relation to the subject matter" (TM, p. 294). That is, it occurs on the basis of "expectations of meaning that proceed from the relation to the truth of what is being said" (ibid.). As Gadamer proceeds to argue, this is owing to the fact that:

There can be no tentative or potential attitude to questioning, for questioning is not the positing but the testing of possibilities. . . . To understand a question means to ask it. To understand an opinion is to understand it as the answer to a question. (TM, p. 375; italics mine)

In this reconstruction of the logic of question and answer, Gadamer finds the arguments that enable him to wage war on two fronts. First, he opposes the historicist "objectivism" that tries to isolate understanding from any evaluating perspective (destroying in the process the binding validity of the tradition that is thus "understood"). Second, he fights the attempt to guarantee the absolute validity of understanding, its absolute "objectivity," through the development of a methodology that secures its scientific character. I will discuss the former opposition in what follows, saving the latter until the next section.

As we shall see in the next section, the conclusion reached in Gadamer's reconstruction of the logic of question and answer makes up the core of his interpretation of hermeneutic experience. This is so insofar as it allows Gadamer to assert the inexorable connection between meaning and validity inherent in understanding (but denied by historicism). Gadamer explicitly draws this implication from the argument quoted above:

This is the reason *why understanding is always more than merely recreating someone else's opinion.* Questioning opens up possibilities of meaning, and thus what is meaningful passes into one's own thinking on the subject. (TM, p. 375; italics mine)

In conversation we cannot help taking seriously the truth claim of another if we want to understand what she is talking about. Precisely so, in the specific case of hermeneutics (the understanding of the texts of a tradition) we must take seriously the truth claim that "speaks" in the tradition if we are to understand what is said in it. For "just as each interlocutor is trying to reach agreement on some subject with his partner, so also the interpreter is trying to understand what the text is saying" (TM, p. 378). This hermeneutic consequence, which Gadamer discusses under the heading of "the fore-conception of completeness" (i.e., the principle of charity), will be examined in more detail at the end of this chapter.

With his analysis, Gadamer has shown that the logic of conversation cannot be guided by anything other than criteria internal to the search for understanding, to the achievement of an intersubjective perspective shared by speakers. For it is only in virtue of this understanding that there can be consensus about the subject matter. Only in this way can that which the conversation is *about* become accessible as the *same* thing.

But what we have described so far is an analysis of the logic of conversation *from the perspective of its participants.* This is the perspective from which Humboldt had already thematized the communicative dimension of language as a medium of understanding (as a process characterized by intersubjectivity). Gadamer's account, though, is undoubtedly more sophisticated and richer in philosophical implications. However, in view of the logic of question and answer, Gadamer does not restrict his analysis of the model of conversation to this perspective, but extends it to a further issue: namely, the *conditions of possibility of the understanding* that takes place in conversation. Thus Gadamer simultaneously elaborates the perspective from which Heidegger analyzed language as discourse, a perspective that made visible the internal connection between the communicative and world-disclosing dimensions of language (which had no connection for Humboldt).

3.2.2.b Conversation as a "Happening"

Given the logic of question and answer, the analysis of the model of conversation has made clear that *prior* to the conversation we cannot view as "given" (or as fixed beforehand) that about which speakers must reach an agreement.[31] The only thing that is given, prior to understanding, is the anticipation of meaning that guides understanding and thus makes accessible what the conversation is about. This is why Gadamer regards conversation as a "happening," owing to its dependence on an anticipation of meaning or fore-understanding that makes the conversation possible, and therefore cannot produce itself.

This view of conversation as happening was already implicit in the explanation of the logic of question and answer. In this sense, Gadamer will later remark that "the dialectic of question and answer *always precedes* the dialectic of interpretation. *It is what determines understanding as a happening*" (TM, p. 472; italics mine). The justification of this claim is to be found in Gadamer's central argument in his reconstruction of the logic of question and answer: namely, "there can be no potential attitude to questioning," for "*to understand the questionableness of something is already to be questioning*" (TM, p. 375). As already indicated, this peculiarity of questioning has a further consequence. And this is what is essential for Gadamer's critique of historicism, which aspires to find a methodological guarantee for the absolute "objectivity" of understanding. Gadamer puts it as follows:

The priority of the question in knowledge shows how fundamentally the idea of method is limited for knowledge, which has been the starting

---

31. The presupposition of an object given independently of the subject who perceives it is what characterizes the subject-object relation distinctive of science. In fact, as Gadamer already pointed out at the beginning of his argument, this presupposition is the result of an abstraction from the context of the life world, where the "constitution" of what science (oblivious of this abstraction) takes as something "in itself" has always already taken place.

point for our argument as a whole. *There is no such thing as a method of learning to ask questions, of learning to see what is questionable.* (TM, p. 365; italics mine)

This analysis of conversation, as structured by the logic of question and answer and oriented toward understanding, could suggest the possibility of interpreting understanding as a total self-enlightenment. Perhaps it could be viewed as the achievement of an absolutely valid intersubjectivity, one that would be at the free disposal of the participants in a conversation. But nothing could be more alien to Gadamer's view.

The logic of question and answer cannot be at the disposal of the conversants, insofar as they cannot determine a priori what becomes questionable in it. As we saw, this logic can proceed only from the anticipation of meaning that guides the understanding of speakers. From this context, Gadamer derives a *systematic argument* against any claim of a total self-reflection lying behind the historicist ideal of objectivity. He makes explicit appeal to the view developed by Heidegger and remarks: "*The anticipation of meaning* that governs our understanding of a text *is not an act of subjectivity*, but proceeds from *the commonality that binds us to the tradition*" (TM, p. 293; italics mine).

As we saw, Heidegger arrived at this conclusion in his critique of Humboldt. There, he argued that in order for the perspectives of the participants in the conversation to become unified, *that about which* they have to reach an agreement must already be manifest as one and the same thing. Gadamer also underscores this point by saying that "the common subject matter [*die gemeinsame Sache*] is what binds the two partners" (TM, p. 388) in a conversation. Thus he goes on to argue that "inasmuch as we understand, [we] participate in the development of a tradition" (TM, p. 293). And precisely for this reason, "the most basic of all hermeneutic preconditions remains one's own *fore-understanding*, which comes from *being concerned with the same subject matter*" (TM, p. 294; italics mine).

It is impossible for speakers to refer to the "same thing" and to have a conversation about it without this fore-understanding that feeds their interpretations. For it is this shared background knowledge that alone enables the world to appear as one and the same in the understanding of the participants in the conversation. Therefore the first condition of every conversation and every understanding is the "belonging" (*Zugehörigkeit*) to a tradition, for tradition guarantees "the *commonality of fundamental, enabling prejudices*" (TM, p. 295; italics mine):

Hermeneutics must start from the position that a person seeking to understand something has *a bond to the subject matter* that comes into language through the traditionary text and *has*, or acquires, *a connection* with the tradition from which the text speaks. (TM, p. 295; italics mine)

Thus by inquiring into the conditions of possibility of understanding in conversation, Gadamer obtains two conditions that enable us to see the limitations of any objectivist perspective with respect to hermeneutics. Gadamer argues that the task of hermeneutics

is not to develop a procedure of understanding, but to clarify the conditions in which *understanding takes place*. But these conditions do not amount to a "procedure" or method which the interpreter must of himself bring to bear on the text; rather, *they must be given*. The prejudices and fore-meanings that occupy the interpreter's consciousness *are not at his free disposal*. He cannot separate *in advance* the productive prejudices that enable understanding from the prejudices that hinder it and lead to misunderstandings. Rather, this separation must *take place* in the process of understanding itself. (TM, pp. 295–296; italics mine)

On this basis, we can understand why Gadamer introduces his account of the model of conversation in Part III of *Truth and Method* with the following remark: "*Understanding* or its failure is *like an event that happens to us*" (p. 383; italics mine).

The conditions of possibility of understanding in conversation (or its failure) are traced back to a shared background knowledge. This knowledge cannot be entirely "brought to consciousness," for given the holistic character of language, and hence of the world that is "disclosed" by it, such reflection would always have to rely on other background assumptions.[32] This is the reason that Gadamer views conversation as a "happening."

We can see that Gadamer's view coincides with Heidegger's in holding, *pace* Humboldt, that the *intersubjectivity* necessary for a conversation to take place can only be regarded as a condition already given. It is not considered to be the result of a procedure at the disposal of speakers, a procedure that would enable them to achieve an understanding from a zero context, free of prior assumptions. In "Die Universalität des hermeneutischen Problems" (1966), Gadamer underscores the implausibility of the latter view with a rhetorical question: "Isn't it the case that there is something like a '*sustaining agreement*' that underlies every misunderstanding?" (GW 2, p. 223; italics mine). In light of all that we have seen, Gadamer's answer is quite predictable. Echoing a motif that is central for Heidegger, both early and late, he remarks: "an agreement is presupposed whenever there is a distortion of it" (GW 2, p. 186). Therefore "agreement precedes disagreement" (GW 2, p. 187).

At the beginning of his account of language, in Part III of *Truth and Method,* Gadamer implicitly asserts this perspective when he refers to language as the precondition of conversation. He remarks:

Every conversation obviously presupposes that *the two speakers speak the same language.* Only when two people can make themselves understood through language by talking together can the problem of understanding and agreement even be raised. (TM, p. 385; italics mine)

The seemingly trivial character of this consideration disappears when Gadamer emphasizes later that "for there to be language a common world . . . must be presupposed" (TM, p. 406). Similarly, in "Die Universalität des hermeneutischen Problems,"

32. In *Hermeneutik II* Gadamer remarks: "The reflection of a given fore-understanding puts in front of me something that, without this reflection, would happen behind my back. Something, but not everything; for the consciousness subject to effective history is unavoidably more being than consciousness" (p. 247).

Gadamer remarks that "the '*linguistic constitution of the world*' appears as a consciousness subject to effective history, which *previously schematizes all our possibilities of knowledge*" (GW 2, p. 228; italics mine).

Gadamer's initial claim appears trivial only from the perspective of a view of language that would reject the notion that language "precedes experience" (TM, p. 350). For given language's world-disclosing function, the presupposition of a shared language is equally the presupposition of *one* symbolically structured and shared world, a world in which the participants in the conversation can talk about *the same thing* and reach an understanding.

Gadamer's view gives primacy to the experience of understanding mediated by ordinary language (by the subject-subject relation), as opposed to the abstraction of the objectifying experience of science. This primacy is later identified by Gadamer in a passage summarizing all those central features of his account of language that we have considered so far:

This structure of the hermeneutical experience, which so totally contradicts the idea of scientific methodology, itself depends on the *character of language as event* that we have described at length. It is not just that the use and development of language is a process which has no single knowing and choosing consciousness standing over against it. (Thus it is literally more correct to say that language speaks us, rather than that we speak it. . . .) A more important point is one to which we have constantly referred, namely that *what constitutes the hermeneutical event proper is not language as language,* whether as grammar or as lexicon; it consists in *the coming into language* [*Zursprachekommen*] *of what has been said in the tradition:* an event that is at once appropriation and interpretation. Thus here it really is true to say that *this event is not our action upon the thing, but the act of the thing itself.* (TM, p. 463; italics mine)

Only from this perspective can we understand Gadamer's characterization of the conversation, and of the understanding that can take place in it, as a "happening." Conversation and understanding constitute the pursuit of a process not at the disposal of the speakers, a process that they can therefore only follow. Thus, as Gadamer concludes at the end of *Truth and Method*, "in understanding *we are drawn into a happening of truth* and arrive, as it were,

too late, if we want to know what we are supposed to believe"
(TM, p. 490; italics mine).

3.2.3 Consequences for Hermeneutic Philosophy

Given the above reconstruction of the view of language developed
in the last part of *Truth and Method,* its internal coherence with the
phenomenology of hermeneutic experience, presented in earlier
parts of the book, becomes clear. Gadamer inherits the Hamann-
Herder-Humboldt view of language (as a world-disclosure shared
by speakers and forming the condition of possibility of understanding). And on the basis of ideas developed previously by Heidegger, he applies it to the interpretation of hermeneutic
experience. It is this view of language alone that enables him to
uphold the central ideas and motifs of *Truth and Method.* As we
have seen, these motifs revolve around the dispute with historicist
objectivism.

As I pointed out at the beginning of this chapter, the guiding
aim of this dispute with objectivism is to rehabilitate the authority
of tradition. Gadamer attempts to carry out this rehabilitation on
two fronts, both of which gain their plausibility from the view of
language that I have been trying to reconstruct.

1. On the one hand, as we have seen in all the authors of this
tradition, the view of language as responsible for world-disclosure
entails both the thesis that *meaning determines reference* and the thesis of *meaning holism.* Both theses depart from the external perspective characteristic of the subject-object relation by *situating*
the subject in a symbolically structured world, a world whose intelligibility is assured by the "constitution of meaning" inherent in
the language *shared by the subject with other subjects.* This constitution
of meaning, or "fore-understanding," is the condition of possibility of the *access to the intraworldly* as well as of the *understanding
between speakers.* Further, it is responsible for the "anticipation of
meaning" that feeds the speakers' interpretations, and therefore ultimately for the understanding that these interpretations
make available to the participants in a conversation. To this extent, the "participation" in the constitution of meaning (or to

put it differently, the relation to the tradition) is a condition *sine qua non* of all understanding.

This view of language not only allows Gadamer to regard the "prejudices" that guide understanding as its very condition of possibility; by means of this consideration, he can also rehabilitate the authority of tradition.

Gadamer does not only want to underline the de facto dependence of all understanding on the prejudices of the interpreter. This "circle of understanding" is well known, and it is precisely what motivates the search in the human sciences for a methodological way to avoid it. Beyond this, Gadamer claims that these prejudices (i.e., our relation to the tradition) can once again be regarded as "a source of truth"—modernity notwithstanding (TM, p. 279). As we saw at the end of the previous section, the issue is precisely to demonstrate that "insofar as we understand, *we are included in a happening of truth* and always arrive too late when we want to know what we should believe" (TM, p. 490; italics mine).

Gadamer does not explicitly develop this standpoint in *Truth and Method,* but borrows it from Heidegger, and in fact takes it for granted. As we saw, such a standpoint results directly from the reification of language as world-diclosure present in Heidegger's writings after the *Kehre*.[33] If language is responsible for world-disclosure, and thus for the constitution of the beings that can "appear" in this world, this constitution obviously predetermines what can and cannot be predicated meaningfully of those beings. Hence it predetermines the possible truth and falsity of our beliefs about them. In this sense, then, it is a "happening of truth." This is the idea underlying Heidegger's thesis of an originary sense of truth as unconcealment. In the same vein, Gadamer remarks as follows in "Die Universalität des hermeneutischen Problems":

In fact, it is the historicity of our existence that grounds the idea that prejudices, in the literal sense of the term, constitute the guidance prior to any capacity to experience. They are preconceptions [*Voreingenommenheiten*] of our world-disclosure and, for that very reason, what makes it

33. See my *Heidegger, Language, and World-Disclosure.*

possible that we can experience something, that that which we encounter be meaningful to us. (GW 2, p. 224)

As we saw in Heidegger, the "constitution of meaning" inherent in the linguistic world-disclosure determines the "essence" of beings, *what* they are. In this sense, it is the final court of appeal for our knowledge about them. It is thus the originary truth, which nothing within the world can contradict, for it is the very condition of possibility of the intraworldly. To precisely this extent, it is a "happening of truth."

Only against the background of this view of language (in particular, the "epistemologization" of the thesis that meaning determines reference) is it feasible to confer a normative status upon the prejudices that guide our understanding. For they are elevated to the rank of final court of appeal for our knowledge. They are, as Gadamer wants to show, a "source of truth" (if not the only source).

With this argument, he has established the *normative* "power" of tradition, if only as *vis a tergo*, as a force lying behind our backs. It is now a detranscendentalized equivalent of the constitution of the world, one that can no longer be attributed to the transcendental endowment of an extraworldly subject. This constitution of the world has always already taken place; it happens in the form of a cultural tradition and is therefore the corrective for any utopia of a "complete enlightenment." Hence its power "does not depend on its recognition" (TM, p. 301). Consequently, we "arrive too late when we want to know what we should believe" (TM, p. 490). Its inevitably holistic character, derived from an equally holistic language, is at the same time the "reality . . . in which the omnipotence of reflection meets its limit" (TM, p. 342).

2. On the other hand, the view of language as a condition of possibility for understanding allows Gadamer to break with the subject-object model of historicism. This model was meant to serve as the guarantee of objectivity in the understanding of tradition. Gadamer's analysis of the hermeneutical experience makes us aware that, owing to the symbolically mediated nature of our relationship with the world, all understanding *is*

interpretation. Such an interpretation, in turn, can only draw on the *fore-understanding* or background knowledge from which we want to understand the tradition. Hence it seems obvious that we can only have *access* to what the text says from the perspective of our own beliefs about the subject matter.[34] And these include our assessment of the validity of the author's opinion. Structurally speaking, the hermeneutical experience is no different from a normal conversation. We can only hope that we have interpreted correctly (or better, *admissibly*), if in the light of our interpretation, that which the author wanted to say seems plausible. As Gadamer argues, there can be no *potential* attitude toward this plausibility or "convincingness" (*einleuchtend*). Therefore it can be argued against the objectivist ideal of historicism that "understanding is always more than merely recreating someone else's opinion" (TM, p. 375). What can be understood "is always more than an unfamiliar opinion: it is always *possible truth*" (TM, p. 394; italics mine).

With this argument, Gadamer obtains another important hermeneutic consequence from his conversation-based account of language as a medium of understanding. This is what Gadamer calls "the fore-conception of completeness," more commonly known as the principle of charity. However, given the perspective of Gadamer's argument, this principle cannot be understood in the usual sense of an unavoidable methodological presupposition that is merely formal. That is, it cannot be understood in the sense that "only what really constitutes a unity of meaning is intelligible" (TM, p. 294). Beyond this usual consideration, which actually arises from the subject-object perspective itself, what Gadamer's development of the model of conversation has shown is as follows. It is not possible to understand someone else, to grasp or reconstruct the argument that structures her opinion, *without taking seriously the truth claim* that makes such argument possible.

34. This point makes especially clear the similarities between the presuppositions of understanding that derive (in very different ways) from the approaches of Gadamer and Davidson, which converge in the principle of charity. For the problems related to the unrestricted use of this principle, see the following footnote.

For we can only reconstruct an argument as being *plausible* insofar as it *seems plausible to us* in the light of "our own fore-understanding of the subject matter." Insofar as the tradition we attempt to understand aims to transmit an understanding *about something*, it speaks to us as a "Thou" in a conversation; hence it is inappropriate to reduce it to an object of inquiry. To this extent, the conditions that guide the achievement of understanding in a conversation and those that guide the interpretation of a tradition are structurally identical. In a conversation, mutual understanding becomes impossible if the participants adopt an external perspective to the conversation from which the interlocutor is "explained" rather than "understood." If we take this into account, Gadamer claims, it would appear that in the genuine case of hermeneutical experience, "it is only when the attempt to accept what is said as *true* fails that we try to 'understand' the text, psychologically or historically, as another's opinion" (TM, p. 294; italics mine).

However, what Gadamer then counterposes to the "failure" of interpretation certainly goes beyond the presuppositions inherent in the pursuit of understanding in conversation. He adds: "The prejudice of completeness, then, implies not only this formal element—that a text should completely express its meaning—but also that what it says should be *the complete truth*" (TM, p. 294).

No doubt, this consideration supports Gadamer's attempt to rehabilitate the authority of tradition. But it is not justified, as he claims, by his reconstruction of the model of conversation. Indeed, as has been objected repeatedly, the alternative that Gadamer offers cannot be applied to the normal case of a conversation oriented toward understanding. The symmetry presupposed in this situation (from which Gadamer derived his arguments for dissolving the asymmetry of the subject-object model) precludes the reduction of possible outcomes either to a failure of understanding or to an acknowledgement of the opinion of the "Thou" as "the whole truth."[35] It is in this sense that the

35. The difficulties concerning how to set limits on the logic of the principle of charity have also been discussed in the Anglo-American tradition. In "Language and Reality," Putnam argues (as does Habermas, as we shall see; see

model of conversation oriented toward understanding, a model in which Gadamer's philosophical hermeneutics is grounded, can be turned against him. This will be seen in our discussion of Habermas's critique of Gadamer.

As we have seen, Gadamer's reconstruction of this model is not meant to situate us in a *symmetrical* relation with tradition. Rather, it is intended to restore the *authority* that tradition has lost since the Enlightenment. Gadamer thinks he can carry out this task by appealing to the telos of "understanding" lying beneath the model of conversation. But he relies on other premises that are not drawn from the internal logic of this model. (These are the

---

4.2.1.b) that if the only prior and general criterion that would make understanding possible is the principle of charity (i.e., the maximization of agreement or truth), it is clear that an unrestricted use of this principle must lead us to project our own beliefs onto that which we want to understand. The options seem to be the following: Either the other has essentially the same beliefs we have, or insofar as she does not (in cases of deep disagreement), we cannot understand her at all. Once the linguistic turn is embraced (and thus once it is accepted that it is not possible to appeal to a world in itself, independent of language, to ensure understanding), it seems that the only basis available for understanding and interpretation is our own beliefs about the subject matter. Putnam, however, draws on the basic insights of a theory of direct reference to defend other normative presuppositions underlying referential acts that can limit the unrestricted use of the principle of charity. Putnam subsumes these presuppositions under the headings "the principle of the benefit of the doubt" and "the principle of reasonable ignorance," which are conceived as a counterbalance to the principle of charity. The basic idea is that, insofar as we can suppose that the person we want to understand also tries to refer to a world that is logically independent of her particular way of conceiving it, we can also reasonably suppose that she would be willing to change her descriptions of objects in case of deep disagreement with our descriptions of the same things, insofar as we can show her the steps through which we ourselves became convinced that our current descriptions are better than hers. That is, given that the correct description of objects is in dispute, the interlocutor should be willing to regard her descriptions as wrong descriptions of the same objects, and not as necessarily correct descriptions of (by definition) different objects, inaccessible to our system of beliefs (or incommensurable with it). This view becomes a plausible alternative only if we have a theory of reference that can question the assumption, generally accepted since the linguistic turn, that meaning determines reference. I will discuss this issue in detail in chapter 5.

ones we considered in our discussion of Gadamer's account of language as world-disclosure, and his resulting characterization of conversation as a "happening.") These presuppositions, of Heideggerian origin, are in fact precisely what support his contention that once the truth claim of tradition is *taken seriously,* we cannot help *acknowledging its authority.*

Given the context in which Gadamer talks about the rehabilitation of authority and tradition, it is clear that he tries to establish the authority of tradition by appealing to "the past's normative significance." This significance "has been . . . dissolved by sovereign historical reason" (TM, p. 286). In this way, Gadamer presupposes that the tradition dealt with by the interpreter is characterized by "a notable mode of being historical" (TM, p. 287) contained in the normative significance of "the classical." That is, it is a tradition marked by "the historical process of *preservation* [*Bewährung*] that, through constantly *proving itself* [*Bewährung*], allows something *true* [*ein Wahres*] to come into being" (ibid.).

This primacy of tradition does not depend on the understanding attained in conversation, at least not in the sense that it can be "decided" in it. Rather, this primacy is decided beforehand. And herein lies Gadamer's rehabilitation of the authority of tradition. This is made clear in his explanation of the normative significance of the classical: "The classical is something that resists historical criticism because its historical *dominion,* the *binding power of the validity* that is preserved and handed down, *precedes all historical reflection* and continues in it" (TM, p. 287; italics mine).

Despite Gadamer's efforts to convince us that "*authority* has to do not with obedience but rather with *knowledge*" (TM, p. 279; italics mine), the former has something that differentiates it from the latter, and which is precisely in need of rehabilitation according to Gadamer. He proceeds:

That which has been sanctioned by tradition and custom has an authority that is nameless, and our finite historical being is marked by the fact that the authority of what has been handed down to us—and *not just what is obvious on the grounds of reasons*—always has power over our attitudes and behavior. . . . This is precisely what we call tradition: *what is valid without foundation.* (TM, p. 281; italics mine)

To understand precisely what Gadamer wants to rehabilitate, and in what sense this goes beyond what is "obvious on the grounds of reasons," we must take into account two central assumptions of *Truth and Method:*

1. First, from his view of language as world-disclosure (and the thesis inherent in this view that meaning determines reference), Gadamer derives the "normative" authority of tradition. In this way, tradition serves as a stand-in for the transcendental subject, that which "constitutes" the world and the intraworldly.

Tradition is what preserves and transforms the linguistic disclosure of the world that has always already taken place behind the backs of subjects (who find themselves constantly determined by it). In light of this, it is clear that the explicit contact with tradition, the attempt to understand it (which is at the same time an attempt at self-understanding), must lead to the *acknowledgment of the normative authority of tradition over our own current understanding of the world.* Tradition itself is a "happening of truth" that has always already determined what can seem plausible or absurd, convincing or preposterous. To this extent, then, it also determines what we can recognize as true or false.

2. Second, as mentioned earlier, Gadamer shares with Heidegger the emphatic sense of truth as unconcealment (*Unverborgenheit*). He too holds that the *true* goes beyond the correctness of statements, that the true is tantamount to the *meaningful.*

This is an essential presupposition for the explicit task of *Truth and Method:* namely, the attempt to preserve a sense of truth that goes beyond the scientific kind. Taking this into account, we can see that the authority Gadamer talks about does not proceed from a superiority in reasoning, from knowledge in the strict sense. Nothing would be more inappropriate with respect to Gadamer than to try to situate his interpretation of hermeneutics in the strictly scientific realm of explaining "what is the case." Throughout *Truth and Method,* Gadamer repeats insistently that his hermeneutic philosophy does not try to compete with science, and claims no superiority over it. This becomes explicit in his "Replik zu Hermeneutik und Ideologiekritik," when he remarks that "the fundamental presupposition of the hermeneutical task has always been the appropriation of a superior *meaning*" (GW 2, p. 264; italics mine).

This consideration is already evident from the closing remarks of *Truth and Method,* which note that to the meaning transmitted by tradition belongs the kind of truth inherent in everything "meaningful," its being "convincing" (*einleuchtend*). In light of this, it becomes clear that the "truth" that Gadamer, like Heidegger, wants to save for those cultural phenomena that *go beyond scientific knowledge* (aesthetic or religious experience, the appropriation of history, etc.), does not arise from a cognitive orientation toward what is the case. That is, this truth does not necessarily maintain an internal connection with reasoned argumentation. Rather, as we saw in Gadamer's account of what is most specific to the experience of the "Thou," it belongs to the realm of the "moral" (in Gadamer's broad sense of this term).

The recognition of the other, recognizing oneself in her in virtue of a mutual belonging to the (same) tradition, was underscored by Gadamer in the explanation of the logic of conversation as something that cannot be produced in the conversation itself. It is rather something that necessarily belongs to the conditions that must be satisfied for understanding to take place. In connection with his postulate of a sustaining agreement (as the condition of possibility for every understanding between the participants in a conversation), Gadamer would later explain in "Replik zu Hermeneutik und Ideologiekritik" that "whenever *understanding* is possible, *solidarity* is presupposed" (GW 2, p. 269; italics mine).

Insofar as there is a sustaining agreement underlying the tradition to which we belong, a tradition that makes possible the (ethical) self-understanding of the individuals within it, this tradition contains a "truth" that goes beyond knowledge and reasoning. It constitutes the source of solidarity (i.e., identity) of a group that recognizes itself in this tradition.

This ethical rather than cognitive orientation, which Gadamer uses to account for the hermeneutical experience, already lay behind his argument against the possibility of understanding a "Thou" (or a tradition) from an objectivist standpoint. Gadamer established the equivalence between these two situations in the following terms:

It is like the relation between I and Thou. A person who reflects himself out of the mutuality of such a relation changes this relationship and destroys its *moral bond. A person who reflects himself out of a living relationship to tradition destroys the true meaning of this tradition in exactly the same way.* (TM, p. 360)

From this ethical perspective, we can grasp the emphatic sense of "understanding" to which Gadamer appeals in his reconstruction of the experience of the Thou as a "dialectic of recognition." The same ethical perspective is presupposed as paradigmatic of the appropriation of tradition. Only by taking this into account can we understand the remark quoted above:

To reach an *understanding* in a dialogue is not merely a matter of putting oneself forward and successfully asserting one's own point of view, but *being transformed into a communion in which we do not remain what we were.* (TM, p. 379; italics mine)

What remains open is whether this understanding "without reasons," which arises from the sentiment of *belonging* to a tradition that is mobilized by our appropriation of it, can be convincingly explained by appealing to the model of conversation oriented toward understanding. That is, by appealing to a situation in which understanding is mediated precisely by the explicit assent of the participants. For it seems impossible to rely on this situation without also embracing an unwelcome consequence, one touching on the indissoluble connection shown by Gadamer between meaning and validity (between understanding and assessing). This connection does not seem to ground the *asymmetry* necessary for the rehabilitation of authority. Instead, as we will see, it may actually underscore the *symmetry* that most likely produced the very loss of authority that Gadamer so greatly regrets.

II

The Conception of Language in Habermas's Theory of Communicative Action

Introduction

The conception of language underlying Habermas's theory of communicative action can be viewed, in retrospect, as a development and deepening of the perspective inaugurated by the German tradition of the philosophy of language. We have discussed the general features of this tradition in the preceding chapters.

The complexity that we find in Habermas's development of his forerunners' views corresponds to the greater level of theoretical elaboration that he undertakes. However, this complexity is undoubtedly also due to Habermas's reception of (and actual *use* of) the *other* important tradition of philosophy of language in this century. I refer, of course, to the Anglo-American tradition, whose analytic and conceptual apparatus is clearly more elaborate than that of the German philosophy of language.

The importance of these two traditions for what has been called Habermas's "Linguistic Turn of Critical Theory"[1] is explicitly recognized by Habermas himself. Reflecting on the evolution of his own view in the preface to the second edition of *On the Logic of the Social Sciences,* Habermas remarks:

The appropriation of *hermeneutics* and *linguistic analysis* convinced me then [in the 1960s] that critical social theory had to break free from the conceptual apparatus of the philosophy of consciousness flowing from Kant and Hegel. (LSS, p. xiii; italics mine)

However, despite the importance of Habermas's appropriation of different views from the Anglo-American philosophy of language, his conception of language is decisively influenced by the basic premises developed in the German tradition (especially in Humboldt's and Gadamer's views).[2] These are premises that, as

1. See A. Wellmer (1977).

2. In an interview with A. Honneth, E. Knödler-Bunte and A. Widmann in 1981 (see *Die Neue Unübersichtlichkeit*), Habermas remarks:

I owe the central intuition which is made explicit in my *Theory of Communicative Action* to the reception of the theory of language both in its hermeneutical and its analytic versions, or better, to a reading of Humboldt illustrated by

already mentioned in the preface, cannot be regarded as equally central for the Anglo-American tradition.

In light of what has been analyzed so far, we can see Habermas's conception of language as an intermediate standpoint between those of Humboldt and Gadamer. For Habermas's critical approach to Gadamer leads him to vindicate certain key aspects of Humboldt's view (such as its universalism and formalism) that had been decidedly rejected in the hermeneutical critique. The result is a view unparalleled in complexity and scope among the authors discussed so far.

However, Habermas's specific development of this view suffers from a particular form of one-sidedness. It is limited to considering language in its *communicative* dimension, while disregarding its *cognitive* dimension. Because of this one-sidedness, Habermas did not feel compelled until well into the 1980s to deal with the problem that has accompanied this tradition from its beginning: namely, the reification of language as world-disclosure.

This problem of the reification of language, which lies at the core of the current rationality debate (and fuels the various radical critiques of reason), has been underscored by a peculiar convergence of different philosophical movements in this century. The Anglo-American philosophy of language in its postanalytic phase (Quine, Goodman, Davidson, Putnam), post-structuralism (Derrida, Foucault), and neo-pragmatism (Rorty) have all converged on some of the central ideas traditionally associated with hermeneutics.[3]

---

analytic philosophy. I am referring to the intuition that the telos of mutual understanding is inherent in linguistic communication. This is the guiding thread that leads to the concept of communicative rationality. (p. 173)

3. The latter positions are undoubtedly influenced by the view of the later Heidegger. Hence it is understandable that there arises in them the problem of the world-disclosing function of language. This problem has a different origin in Anglo-American philosophy of language, where it arises as a result of the internal evolution of this tradition.

Generally speaking (and considering it from the standpoint of our discussion), the Anglo-American tradition starts from the conception of language as "tool" inherent in the ideal of attaining a perfect language or, as Gadamer calls it, a

Except in the case of the Anglo-American tradition, this convergence can be traced back to a central motif characteristic of all of these movements—a global critique of reason, one that radicalizes the detranscendentalization inherent in the linguistic turn to the point of advocating an absolute contextualism. The insurmountability of the worldviews inherent in natural languages turns any universalist position into a mere illusion, the illusion of achieving a "God's eye point of view" (as Putnam puts it). It would seem as if the linguistic turn as such lends support to a contextualist position.

Habermas has opposed this position since the mid-1980s (in *The Philosophical Discourse of Modernity* and *Postmetaphysical Thinking*). However, his confrontation with it highlights the

---

characteristica universalis (Russell, Carnap, or the early Wittgenstein). It is only in its later evolution that this tradition breaks with this ideal and subordinates its analysis to the explanation of the working of natural languages, undergoing a shift of perspective that was already characteristic of the German philosophy of language. That is, there is a transition from the external perspective of an observer facing a language as a "system of signs" to the internal perspective of participants in communication who share a common language (see Apel 1963). And it is only from this latter perspective that the problems concerning the world-disclosing dimension of language become accessible. In the Anglo-American tradition these problems are treated under the heading of "meaning holism," which has become an important challenge to the theoretical ambitions that had historically characterized this tradition (i.e., the construction of a theory of meaning, of reference, of truth, etc.).

This convergence seems to encourage the suspicion that the origin of the problems concerning the world-disclosing dimension of language, given their vast scope (i.e., given that they seem to affect the whole spectrum of current philosophical positions), may lie in the linguistic turn itself, however unrenounceable it may seem.

However, in my opinion, the common denominator of this convergence is not the linguistic turn as such. Rather, it is a reification of language thought to be entailed by the linguistic turn and which should be rejected by any view that, in principle, does not want to give up its theoretical ambitions. Support for this claim can be found in the view elaborated in recent decades by those authors of the Anglo-American tradition who have opposed the reification of language without renouncing the linguistic turn as a whole. Among these authors are Putnam, Kripke, Donnellan, and Kaplan, who have tried to work out a theory of direct reference. The views of these authors will be discussed in chapter 5.

consequences of the one-sidedness that, in my opinion, character-izes the development of Habermas's views. For under his concep-tion of language as developed so far, it seems impossible to give a convincing answer to the challenge posed by the reification of language inherent in the view of language as world-disclosure.

In support of this claim, I will reconstruct the central features of the conception of language that underlies Habermas's theory of communicative rationality. As already pointed out, what charac-terizes the development of this conception is that it views language exclusively in its *communicative* dimension: that is, as a *medium for understanding* (chapter 4).

In this way, the account developed by Habermas from this per-spective is directly linked to Gadamer's views in *Truth and Method.* Habermas will incorporate new aspects of language that Gadamer did not take into account (see 4.1). But by doing so, he will also encounter new difficulties concerning the formalism and univer-salism of his view, features that distinguish it from Gadamer's (see 4.2). These difficulties, in turn, will lead him to modify some of his initial assumptions (see 4.3). But in light of these modifications, already present in his *Theory of Communicative Action,* the weak-nesses of Habermas's approach to address the problems concern-ing the world-disclosing function of language become even clearer (see 4.4). By examining Habermas's proposed solutions to these problems, I will try to show that the acceptance of certain fundamental premises of the hermeneutic conception of lan-guage makes it impossible to find an adequate alternative to the contextualism inherent in the view of language as world-disclosure.

As we shall see, Habermas's account of the *communicative* di-mension of language makes room for important insights that Ga-damer either failed to take into account (such as the potential for critique of actions oriented toward understanding), or sub-jected to a one-sided treatment (due to the asymmetry he presup-posed between the participants in a conversation).[4] However, this

4. Habermas's criticisms of Gadamer can be found in ''Zu Gadamers *Wahrheit und Methode*'' and in ''The Hermeneutic Claim to Universality.'' We will discuss the latter paper shortly (4.1).

development is not sufficient for a defense of the universalist perspective inherent in Habermas's view. That is, it cannot support his claim that the analysis of action oriented toward understanding should be understood as a theory of *communictive rationality*. In my opinion, Habermas *assumes* in his analysis the central premises that underlie the hermeneutic view of language. Thus, despite his internal revisions of this view (admittedly of a fundamental character), Habermas cannot convincingly respond to a challenge directed against its very premises.

However, we can find a theoretical locus in which Habermas's view of language can be distinguished from that of hermeneutics by analyzing more closely his few remarks about the *cognitive* dimension of language. This is not surprising if we recall that it is precisely here that the problems concerning the world-disclosing function of language arise, and only here where a solution to these problems should be sought. We can thus find in Habermas a perspective that is perhaps capable of giving a satisfactory answer to the problems we have discussed. To clarify this issue, I will examine the assumptions that enable Habermas to introduce the notion of *discourse* (whose normative sense sharply distinguishes Habermas's analysis of action oriented toward understanding from Gadamer's). Habermas introduces this notion in chapter 1 of his *Theory of Communicative Action*. There, we find a genuine connection between language and the capacitiy for cognitive learning. In my opinion, it is this connection that guarantees the central intuition dividing the theory of communicative action from hermeneutics: namely, that the sustaining agreement between speakers contains counterfactual elements that allow for a potential questioning of any given factual agreement. Despite the importance of this connection in Habermas's theoretical system, he has neither developed nor recognized it up till now (owing, no doubt, to the fact that the cognitive dimension of language has been systematically "forgotten"). In my opinion, however, this is the systematic standpoint from which it is possible to show the untenability of the reification of language as world-disclosure (see chapter 5).

To lend plausibility to this thesis, so central to my interpretation, I will rely on a new approach to language developed in recent decades by several authors in the Anglo-American tradition: the so-called theories of direct reference (Putnam, Donnellan, Kripke, Kaplan, and others). In my opinion, they provide powerful means for identifying and avoiding the problems resulting from the reification of language that has accompanied the linguistic turn up to the present day.

These theories try to rehabilitate the *designative function* of language, which we have seen to be systematically neglected in the German tradition (Habermas included). They do so by revealing the internal connection of designation with the possibility of *cognitive learning* (see 5.2). From this perspective, we can see the untenability of the central thesis underlying the view of language as world-disclosure: the thesis that meaning determines reference. In this way, it becomes clear why internal difficulties arise in the attempt to defend this thesis (see 5.1). Only by questioning it do we see why it is wrong to reify language into a *demiurge,* into something that "happens" as a fate and predetermines every intraworldly process. Quite the contrary—language is precisely an essential element for our intraworldly procesess of learning (see 5.3).

4

Language as Medium of Understanding: The Communicative Use of Language

The importance of Habermas's view of language cannot be adequately assessed by merely situating it within the framework of the philosophical movements that have contributed to the linguistic turn in this century, for the systematic role of language in his theory does not proceed only from the conceptual and methodological advantages of the paradigm of language over the paradigm of consciousness (which limits itself to the subject-object relation and is fraught with methodological difficulties pertaining to introspection and intuitionism). The linguistic turn carried out by Habermas during the 1970s cannot be understood simply as a way to pursue the philosophical enterprise by other means. It has a more substantive significance: In the *communicative* use of language Habermas finds a specific kind of rationality that enables him to carry out two fundamental tasks (tasks at which, in his opinion, Critical Theory had not succeeded). One is to overcome the narrow concept of instrumental rationality dominant in the theory of science and theory of society. The second is to give a convincing answer to the central question for any theory of society: How is social order possible?

To this end, Habermas relies on the view of language elaborated by the Hamann-Herder-Humboldt tradition, which extends as far as Gadamer. On this view, language is not considered as a mere instrument, as a "medium without properties" (PMT, p. 161) for the transmission of information. Nor is it reduced to an object, as implicitly required by the abstraction of the structure of language from the praxis of speaking. On the contrary, according to this view, "the core of language is conversation" (ENT, p. 328). Thus the model of conversation as directed toward understanding is the paradigmatic use of language in Habermas's theory, just as it was for Humboldt and Gadamer.

In light of what we have seen so far, Habermas's development of this model can be characterized as a gradual shift:

• *from* an initial perspective (developed in the 1970s) in which Habermas, like Humboldt, views the interaction oriented toward understanding as a process of achieving intersubjectivity between speakers that depends, at bottom, on the formal-pragmatic presuppositions of speech (see 4.2);

• *to* a perspective developed in the 1980s that restores the dialectic (already present in Gadamer's approach) between an intersubjectivity *to be* produced through communication, and an intersubjectivity *always already* produced, thanks to the "lifeworld" shared by speakers (as a sort of "conservative counterbalance" that bridles the risks of disagreement inherent in action oriented toward understanding) (4.3).

I will try to show that this gradual shift of perspective responds to the internal needs of Habermas's theory. To this extent, it should be viewed as an unavoidable evolution, and not as an accidental one.

In the course of this evolution, however, problems will arise similar to those faced by the passage from Humboldt's to Gadamer's views. For these problems, as indicated earlier, Habermas's theory does not provide an adequate answer. In my opinion this shortcoming is due to Habermas's reliance on the same conception of language as that of the authors we have been discussing. To this extent, Habermas cannot escape the conclusions that result from the very premises of this conception, as we saw in our discussion of Gadamer. Habermas has become aware of these implications only gradually during the development of his own theory. However, the source of the problems that will be discussed is not an internal paradox in Habermas's theory, or a blind alley into which this theory falls. Instead, the source of these problems is to be found in the decisive influence of the later Heidegger on various philosophical movements in the second half of the twentieth century (not only in Germany, but in France and the United States as well). As pointed out earlier, this influence has resulted in a generalized "suspicion" concerning reason. Habermas is thus confronted with the problem of how his theory of communicative rationality can respond to the challenge raised by such suspicion. And as we shall see, this is where Habermas's theory shows a peculiar weakness. The internal logic of this weakness is the theme of the present chapter.

To analyze the steps in the evolution of Habermas's treatment of the communicative dimension of language, I will first discuss his article "The Hermeneutic Claim to Universality." This is one of the first papers by Habermas in which we can find *in germ* the project of a theory of communicative action. But more importantly, this paper allows us to examine the genesis of Habermas's theory precisely from the standpoint of his explicit confrontation with Gadamer's *Truth and Method*.

In this confrontation, Habermas already points out the difficulties underlying the hermeneutic view, and he also indicates the path that must be taken to avoid them. Examining these hints will enable us to assess, at the end of the present chapter, the following questions. Can Habermas's actual development of the theory envisioned in the aforementioned paper escape the difficulties it describes? Or rather, would this require a reelaboration of some of the initial assumptions of his theory?

4.1. The Reception of the View of Language of Philosophical Hermeneutics in "The Hermeneutic Claim to Universality"

In "The Hermeneutic Claim to Universality," Habermas opposes the theses set forth by Gadamer in "The Universality of the Hermeneutic Problem."[1] To assess his reception of the view of

1. In *Hermeneutik II*, pp. 219–231.

language of philosophical hermeneutics, it is convenient to examine briefly an earlier paper in which Habermas discusses the hermeneutic view: "On the Logic of the Social Sciences."

In this earlier paper, Habermas explicitly underscores the superiority of the view of language found in philosophical hermeneutics over two others: the "phenomenology of the lifeworld" constructed by A. Schütz (from a Husserlian standpoint) and the "positivist analysis of language" in the two phases of its evolution (as exemplified by the early and later Wittgenstein).

In light of what we have seen so far, the superiority that Habermas attributes to hermeneutics consists in the fact that it overcomes the view of language as an instrument, a view that in his opinion underlies both of the other positions. This superiority constitutes, in turn, the *implicit* common denominator of Habermas's *explicit* criticisms of these positions:

• with respect to the comprehensive sociological approach of phenomenology, Habermas's main criticism emphasizes that this approach remains trapped in the *paradigm of the philosophy of consciousness*. This is so insofar as it views language as one system of signs among others, one rooted in the apperceptive operation of a transcendental ego (LSS, p. 116–117); and

• with respect to the positivist analysis of language, the core of Habermas's critique is that this analysis (explicitly in the early Wittgenstein, but implicitly even in the later Wittgenstein)[2] is trapped within the limits of the model of formalized languages. In this sense, it does not escape the typically *empiricist* view of language as a system of signs for the transmission of information (LSS, pp. 149–150).

By way of contrast with the instrumental view of language shared by the philosophy of consciousness and empiricism, Habermas proceeds to show the superiority of the view of lan-

---

2. The interpretation of the view of language of the later Wittgenstein that we find here is different from the one Habermas currently holds (as discussed, for instance, in *Postmetaphysical Thinking*). The references that follow are meant only to illustrate Habermas's take on hermeneutics, and not his views on Wittgenstein.

guage found in philosophical hermeneutics. His characterization of this superiority is interesting in the present context, insofar as it allows us to identify the basic features of the view of language that Habermas shares with philosophical hermeneutics. He remarks:

> Wittgenstein linked the intersubjectivity of ordinary language communication to the intersubjective validity of grammatical rules: following a rule means applying it in an identical way. The ambiguity of ordinary language and the imprecision of its rules are an illusion. . . . For someone who connects linguistic analysis with the self-reflection of ordinary language, the opposite is obvious. The lack of ambiguity in calculus languages is achieved by means of their *monological structure,* that is, by means of a construction that *excludes dialogue.* Strictly deductive connections permit derivations, not communications. *Dialogue is replaced by the transfer of information.* Only languages free of dialogue are perfectly ordered. Ordinary languages are imperfect and do not ensure lack of ambiguity. For this reason the *intersubjectivity* of communication in ordinary language is continually interrupted. *It exists because consensus is, in principle, possible; and it does not exist, because reaching an understanding is, in principle, necessary.* Hermeneutic understanding begins at the points of interruption; it compensates for *the discontinuous quality of intersubjectivity.* (LSS, pp. 149–150; italics mine)

It is a very specific perspective that makes possible such a description of what is distinctive about ordinary language in contrast with any other system of signs. Namely, language is the medium in which understanding takes place, and hence that which guarantees intersubjectivity. This perspective is the common background that Habermas shares not only with Gadamer, but also, as previous chapters made clear, with the Hamann-Herder-Humboldt tradition.

Only against the background of these common presuppositions can we assess Habermas's confrontation with the view of philosophical hermeneutics in "The Hermeneutic Claim to Universality." In this confrontation, Habermas attempts to demarcate his view from Gadamer's. However, he does this not in order to break with Gadamer's basic conception of language, but rather to compensate for its structural shortcomings (see 4.1.2).

4.1.1 The Superiority of the Nonobjectivist Conception of Language in Hermeneutics

The context of Habermas's appropriation of the view of philosophical hermeneutics is formed by his methodological reflections directed toward a "foundation of sociology in terms of a theory of language." These reflections date back to the late 1960s; their most representative expression can be found in *On the Logic of the Social Sciences*. There already, Habermas singles out as the fundamental contribution of philosophical hermeneutics its "excellent critique of the objectivistic self-understanding of the *Geisteswissenschaften* [in] historicism" (LSS, pp. 153–154). In "The Hermeneutic Claim to Universality," Habermas summarizes the core of this critique as follows:

It follows from the hermeneutic situatedness of the interpreting scientist that *objectivity in understanding* cannot be secured by an abstraction from preconceived ideas, but only by reflecting upon the context of effective history *which connects perceiving subjects and their object.* (HCU, pp. 186; italics mine)

As Habermas remarks later, what makes this critique possible is that "hermeneutics has taught us that *we are always a participant as long as we move within the natural language* and that *we cannot step outside the role of a reflective partner"* (HCU, p. 191; italics mine).

This standpoint typical of hermeneutics derives, as we saw in chapter 3, from the recognition of the symbolically mediated character of our relationship with the world. This recognition led to the abandonment of the extraworldly perspective of a constituting subject over against the constituted object (which lay at the basis of the subject-object model). Instead, the subject was seen as situated *within* a symbolically structured world *shared* by other subjects. It was this shift of perspective that unmasked the naivete of the "objectivist" claim of historicism. With this claim, it attempted to guarantee the objectivity of understanding by methodological appeal to the perspective of a disengaged observer, one who would not participate in the processes that constitute that which she wants to understand. After such a shift of perspective, objectivity can only be grounded in the *very conditions under which understanding takes place,* not outside them. Only the conditions that guarantee the *intersubjectivity* of communication can guarantee the *objectivity* of understanding. Thus the analysis of the conditions of possibility of intersubjectivity becomes the core of the hermeneutic treatment of language.

In keeping with this view, Habermas's account of hermeneutic experience reproduces Gadamer's account, found in *Truth and Method,* of the communicative dimension of language as medium of understanding. This account carried out the analysis of the model of conversation oriented toward understanding from a twofold perspective. On the one hand, it analyzed the structure characteristic of this model from *the perspective of the participants* in a conversation (see 3.2.2.a). On the other hand, it investigated the conditions of possibility of such conversation, which have to be *given* for understanding to be possible at all (see 3.2.2.b). This double perspective is reproduced in Habermas's characterization of the two constitutive moments of hermeneutic experience. As pointed out above, these moments are grounded in the fact that "the intersubjectivity of everyday communication is principally as unlimited as it is discontinuous" (HCU, p. 182).

1. The first moment of hermeneutic experience that Habermas emphasizes is characterized by what he calls the peculiar *self-referentiality* inherent in natural languages (and that is missing in any other system of signs). He describes it as follows:

[The speaking subject] can draw upon the *self-referentiality* of natural languages for paraphrasing any changes metacommunicatively. It is, of course, possible to construct hierarchies of formal languages on the basis of everyday language as the "last metalanguage." . . . The formal construction of such language systems excludes the possibility that for individual sentences the rules of application be determined *ad hoc,* commented on or changed; and the type-rule prohibits metacommunication about sentences of a language on the level of this object language. *Both these things are, however, possible in everyday language.* The system of natural language is not closed, but it allows the rules of application for any utterance to be determined ad hoc, commented on or changed; and metacommunication can only employ the very language which is simultaneously spoken about as the object: *every natural language is its own metalanguage*. This is the basis for that *reflexivity* which, in the face of the type-rule, *makes it possible for the semantic content of linguistic utterances to contain, in addition to the manifest message, an indirect message as to its application*. . . . Thanks to the reflexive structure of natural languages, the native speaker is provided with a unique *metacommunicative maneuvering space*. (HCU, pp. 182–183; italics mine)

As we shall see later, from this "singularity" of ordinary language Habermas will draw the conditions of possibility of intersubjective understanding underlying communicative action through a formal-pragmatic analysis. In this analysis, Habermas will appeal to the same structural connection between meaning and validity that Gadamer underscored earlier with his analysis of understanding. However, Habermas will thereby attempt to overcome the limitations which, in his opinion, are the origin of the one-sidedness of Gadamer's account of the model of conversation oriented toward understanding. The status of Habermas's analysis as an *internal* improvement of this account is made clear in *On the Logic of the Social Sciences,* in his characterization of the inherent shortcoming of Gadamer's view. As Habermas puts it: "Gadamer fails to recognize the power of reflection that unfolds in understanding" (LSS, p. 168).

2. Immediately thereafter, Habermas characterizes the second moment of hermeneutic experience by contrasting it with the first:

The reverse side of this freedom of movement is *a close bond with linguistic tradition.* Natural languages are informal; for this reason, speaking subjects cannot confront their language as a closed system. Linguistic competence remains, as it were, *behind their backs:* they can make sure of *a meaning-complex explicitly* only to the extent to which *they also remain tied to a dogmatically traditioned and implicitly pregiven context.* Hermeneutical understanding cannot approach a subject matter free of any prejudice; it is, rather, unavoidably biased by the context within which the understanding subject has initially acquired his *interpretative schemes.* This *preunderstanding* can be thematized and it has to prove itself in relation to the subject matter in the course of every analysis undertaken within hermeneutic awareness. But even the modification of these unavoidable pre-conceptions does not break through the objectivity of language *vis-à-vis* the speaking subject: in the course of improving his knowledge he merely develops *a new pre-understanding which then guides him as he takes the next hermeneutical step.* (HCU, p. 183; italics mine)

On the basis of these two moments that characterize "hermeneutic consciousness," Habermas can determine the kind of reflection that takes place in hermeneutics. As he remarks:

Hermeneutic consciousness is thus the outcome of a process of self-reflection in which a speaking subject recognized his *specific freedom from, and dependence on, language.* This leads to the dissolution of a semblance, both of a subjectivist and an objectivist kind, which captivates naive consciousness. *Self-reflection* throws light on experiences a subject makes while exercising his communicative competence, but *it cannot explain this competence.* (HCU, p. 186; italics mine)

With his remarks on the structural shortcomings of the hermeneutic view as such, Habermas begins his explicit attack on the hermeneutic claim to universality.

As the title of Habermas's paper indicates, this attack is the explicit guiding motive of his discussion. However, I will not examine all the lines of criticism developed in Habermas's discussion. Given the retrospective standpoint from which we approach the initial sketches of the theory of communicative action, I will focus only on the internal structure of Habermas's critique of Gadamer's view, and only insofar as it enables us to envision the fundamental features of the project of the theory of communicative action that he will carry out later.

There are systematic reasons for this limitation. Only by isolating this line of criticism from the whole of his argument does it become clear to what extent Habermas's critique fails to achieve a sufficiently radical distance from the basic premises of hermeneutics. For despite the multiple fronts on which he questions the hermeneutic claim to universality (ranging from developmental psychology to the critique of ideologies, and passing through constructivism and psychoanalysis), he does not in fact break with the central features of Gadamer's underlying conception of language. But as we shall see in the course of this chapter, only such a break would have allowed Habermas to truly avoid the danger of reifying language that is inherent in hermeneutics, as Habermas already explicitly recognizes in the paper under discussion.

4.1.2 The Need for a Theory of Communicative Action

Our discussion of Habermas's critique of Gadamer's view in "The Hermeneutic Claim to Universality" will focus on Habermas's attempt to overcome the limitations of philosophical hermeneutics (thus opposing its claim to universality) without thereby breaking with its conception of language. This attempt is not surprising if we keep in mind that Habermas regards this conception as distinctly preferable to its alternatives. We can characterize Habermas's confrontation as the result of two separate but complementary lines of criticism. These are internally related to the twofold characterization of the "singularity" of natural languages already discussed.

On the one hand, according to Habermas, the analysis of the "self-referentiality" of the communicative use of language should explain "the power of reflection that unfolds in understanding," which was systematically disregarded by Gadamer. For such an explanation, Habermas considers it indispensable to abandon the perspective of self-reflection that is characteristic of philosophical hermeneutics (but which also limits its scope). He endorses, instead, the perspective of "an explicit *theoretical reconstruction*" (HCU, p. 203; italics mine) aimed at the construction of a theory of communicative competence. Such a theory would necessarily go beyond the reflective level characteristic of hermeneutics. For "[i]f the claim to present such a theory were justified, then an *explanatory* understanding would be possible which transcended the limit of the hermeneutical understanding" (HCU, p. 189–190; italics mine). And thus this theory would enable us to "refute the hermeneutic claim to universality" (HCU, p. 190).

On the other hand, a theory of communicative competence should be able to differentiate the factual consensus rooted in the unavoidable "belonging" to a cultural tradition (in virtue of being socialized in a given natural language) from the normative conditions (or counterfactual consensus) underlying communicative competence. Undoubtedly, the factual consensus sustains and guides the understanding of participants in communication, just as Gadamer claims. But given the counterfactual consensus, speakers are also able to distinguish (if only tentatively and in retrospect) between a valid understanding and a pseudo-understanding. It is the need to articulate this distinction that makes it necessary to go beyond Gadamer's philosophical hermeneutics, not only because of the lack of theoretical ambition of this view, but more importantly because of its unacceptable normative consequences.

Thus considered, it is clear that the heart of the confrontation between Habermas and Gadamer lies in this second point. For the question of whether it is possible to give a rational reconstruction of communicative competence is not to be decided a priori, but only on the basis of whether such an attempt ever succeeds. For this reason, Habermas devotes the third and last part of the paper to discussing this issue, so central for the hermeneutic claim to universality.

After sketching the development of a theory of communicative competence that would have to cover "the forms of the intersubjectivity of language and causes of its deformation" (HCU, p. 202), Habermas discusses the essential difference between his position and Gadamer's. This discussion is to be situated against the general critical background that Habermas himself characterizes as "*the questioning of the ontological self-understanding of the philosophical hermeneutic* which Gadamer propounds by following Heidegger" (HCU, p. 203). He remarks:

Gadamer turns *the context-dependency of the understanding of meaning,* which hermeneutic philosophy has brought to consciousness and which requires us always to proceed from a pre-understanding that is supported by tradition as well as to continuously form a new pre-understanding in the course of being corrected, to *the ontologically inevitable primacy of linguistic tradition.* Gadamer poses the question: "Is the phenomenon of understanding adequately defined when I state that to understand is to avoid misunderstanding? Is it not, rather, the case that something like a 'sustaining consensus' precedes all misunderstanding?" We can agree on the answer, which is to be given in the affirmative, but not on *how to understand this preceding consensus.* (HCU, p. 203; italics mine)

This passage makes it clear that Habermas's critical attitude toward Gadamer's conception of language has the character of an *internal* improvement. Again, the task is to *redefine* the internal relation between the two poles of the dialectic that is analyzed by all the authors we have discussed so far. It is the dialectic between an intersubjectivity *to be* produced through action oriented toward understanding, and an intersubjectivity *always already* produced and guaranteed by the linguistic world-disclosure shared by speakers.

Habermas carries out the redefinition of this dialectic (in the context of his project of a theory of communicative competence) through a critique of the primacy granted in Gadamer's account to one of the poles over the other. That is, it is the "factual consensus" guaranteed by belonging to a tradition that is privileged over "the power of reflection that unfolds in understanding" and which enables speakers to distinguish between a merely factual consensus and a true consensus.

Habermas shows how the hermeneutic view leads to the "absolutization of tradition," by which the reflection inherent in communication oriented toward understanding loses all its critical force. He underscores this is in the following brief characterization of Gadamer's view:

> If I understand correctly, then Gadamer is of the opinion that the hermeneutical clarification of incomprehensible or misunderstood expressions always has to lead back to *a consensus that has already been reliably established through converging traditions.* This tradition is objective in relation to us in the sense that *we cannot confront it with a principled claim to truth.* The pre-judgmental structure of understanding not only prohibits us from *questioning that factually established consensus which underlies our misunderstanding and incomprehension,* but makes such an undertaking appear *senseless. . . .* It would be senseless to abstractly suspect this agreement, which, admittedly, is contingent, of being false consciousness since we cannot transcend the dialogue which we are. *This leads Gadamer to conclude as to the ontological priority of linguistic tradition over all possible critique;* we can consequently criticize specific traditions only on the basis that we are part of the comprehensive context of the tradition of a language. (HCU, p. 204; italics mine)

Habermas opposes Gadamer's conclusion by arguing as follows: "Insight into the pre-judgmental structure of the understanding of meaning does not cover the identification of actually achieved consensus with a true one. This identification leads to the *ontologization of language* and to the *hypostatization of the context of tradition*" (HCU, p. 205; italics mine).

This dead-on analysis of the consequences of hermeneutics (which Habermas subsumes under the heading "linguistic idealism") is not accompanied, however, by a correct identification of their causes. That is, Habermas does not analyze why, for Gadamer, "insight into the pre-judgmental structure of understanding" is tantamount to the recognition of the factual sustaining agreement as the true one.[3]

As we shall see, the identification of these causes would have led to a deeper break with hermeneutics than the one that resulted from Habermas's critical standpoint. For it would have forced him to abandon some of the central premises of the hermeneutic conception of language, premises that he assumes without full awareness of their implications.

Thus Habermas's argument against the reification of tradition does not enter deeply into the grounds of the "ontologization of language" (inherited by Gadamer from Heidegger). Instead, Habermas simply underscores the reflective and critical potential of the communication oriented toward understanding, a potential entirely disregarded by Gadamer. But in so doing, Habermas fails to articulate an account *different* from Gadamer's of one of the poles of the dialectic mentioned above: namely, the intersubjectivity that is always already produced by a linguistic world-dis-

3. As we saw in chapter 3, Gadamer and Heidegger give a normative status to this "sustaining agreement" by characterizing it as a "happening of truth." This status proceeds from the constitutive character ascribed to linguistic world-disclosure, or in other words, from the thesis that meaning determines reference. As we shall see throughout this chapter, this is the presupposition that Habermas does not succeed in identifying, due to his one-sided attention to the communicative use of language at the expense of its cognitive use (or as he puts it in his "Entgegnung," due to the fact of having "neglected the 'world-disclosing' function of language," p. 336). As we shall see later (4.4), it is because of this neglect that the theory actually developed by Habermas so far appears as a weaker alternative to hermeneutics than the one he sets out to develop in the paper now under discussion.

closure and is transmitted by tradition. Habermas focuses, instead, on the other pole of the dialectic, trying to transfer to it all the normative weight of his argument. It is along these lines that he argues against Gadamer:

It would only be legitimate for us to equate the sustaining consensus which, according to Gadamer, always precedes any failure at mutual understanding with a given factual agreement, if we could be certain that each consensus arrived at in the medium of linguistic tradition has been achieved without compulsion and distortion. . . . A critically enlightened hermeneutic that differentiates between insight and delusion . . . *connects the process of understanding to the principle of rational speech,* according to which truth would only be guaranteed by *that* kind of consensus which was achieved *under the idealized conditions of unlimited communication free from domination* and could be maintained over time. . . . It is only *the formal anticipation of an idealized dialogue* . . . which guarantees *the ultimate sustaining and counterfactual agreement* that already unites us; in relation to it we can *criticize* every factual agreement, should it be a false one, as false consciousness. . . . To attempt a systematic justification we have to develop . . . a theory which would enable us to deduce *the principle of rational speech* from the logic of everyday language and regard it *as the necessary regulative for all actual speech,* however distorted it may be. (HCU, pp. 205–207; italics mine)

Here we find Habermas's explicit formulation of the difference between his view and Gadamer's concerning the sustaining agreement which is the condition of possibility of understanding. With this formulation, Habermas points in the direction already taken by Humboldt and proposes a *formal analysis* of the ideal conditions that regulate any conversation oriented toward understanding. With this analysis, he wants to contrast the factual sustaining agreement presupposed by hermeneutics with a "counterfactual agreement" underlying the principle of rational speech. This contains *in germ* the project of a theory of communicative action that, from a formal standpoint, must reconstruct the counterfactual conditions that guarantee the intersubjectivity of conversation. This project is intended to underscore "the power of reflection that unfolds in understanding." Therefore, as Habermas put it earlier in *On the Logic of the Social Sciences,* it must also contain "a system of reference" that makes possible "the self-limitation of the hermeneutic approach" (LSS, p. 170).

Habermas transfers the normative weight that hermeneutics one-sidedly placed on "belonging" to a tradition to the conditions that allow the participants in a conversation to achieve an intersubjective understanding. However, insofar as this transfer of normative status does not involve a break with the background assumptions of the hermeneutic view of language, Habermas possesses limited resources to combat Gadamer's systematic arguments against Humboldt's similar project. Habermas anticipates this difficulty in *On the Logic of the Social Sciences,* when he points out not only the need for a "system of reference" such as the one sketched in "The Hermeneutic Claim to Universality," but also the weakness of such an attempt at a "self-limitation" of the hermeneutic approach. He remarks:

Gadamer has a systematic argument on hand. The right of reflection requires the self-limitation of the hermeneutic approach. It requires a system of reference that transcends the context of tradition as such. Only then can tradition be criticized as well. But how is such a system of reference to be legitimated in turn except through the appropriation of tradition? (LSS, p. 170)

As we can see, this difficulty is already identified by Habermas in the late 1960s. Nonetheless, it will be shown later that the theory of communicative action which is meant to escape the problem seems unable to provide a satisfactory answer to it, at least in the current version of the theory.

4.2. The Analysis of Communicative Action in "What Is Universal Pragmatics?"

As underscored in the foregoing discussion of Habermas's project of a theory of communicative action, the direction in which Habermas wants to transform the hermeneutic account of the communicative dimension of language coincides with the perspective already found in Humboldt. That is, Habermas's project seeks an analysis of the conditions of intersubjectivity in communication characterized by the following features:

a. It is to be carried out through a *formal* analysis. From the formal-pragmatic presuppositions of speech, it should be possible to deduce *general conditions* for the communicative use of language (i.e., for action oriented toward understanding). These conditions as such do not depend on a factual "sustaining consensus" that arises from belonging to a particular linguistic tradition.

b. It has a *universalist* aim, for it seeks a rational reconstruction of those universal presuppositions that underlie the communicative competence of *every speaker* (see 4.2.1).

As we saw in "The Hermeneutic Claim to Universality," Habermas takes the normative role of the factual sustaining consensus identified by Gadamer as a condition of possibility of understanding, and he attempts to assign it to a counterfactual consensus that arises from the underlying presuppositions of rational speech. But this attempt is laden with difficulties that can easily be anticipated in light of what we have seen in previous chapters. Insofar as the conditions of possibility of understanding are thematized only from the perspective of participants in communication (*intentione recta*), the conditions that must be factually given for action oriented toward understanding to take place are left unspecified. Both Gadamer and Humboldt analyzed these conditions in their account of the *cognitive* dimension of language, that is, its world-disclosing function. However, Habermas leaves this dimension out of the picture, owing to a tacit "division of labor" (which, as we will see, has highly negative consequences). Habermas takes it for granted that the articulation of a theory of communicative action (essential for a theory of society) requires only the analysis of the *communicative* use of language. Thus its cognitive use can be relegated to the *savoir faire* of formal semantics.

The untenability of this tacit division of labor will become clearer throughout this chapter. More specifically, it will become clearer through our discussion of internal difficulties, which, however independent and unconnected they may appear, can be traced back to a single origin if we take into account our prior discussion of Humboldt's and Gadamer's views. As we shall see, Habermas will find himself continuously bedeviled with problems concerning both the *formal* standpoint (4.2.2.a) and the *universalist* claim of his approach (4.2.2.b). Ultimately, these problems will appear as the result of his "neglecting" (ENT, p. 366) the analysis of the cognitive use of language, of its world-disclosing function.

Only by confronting hermeneutics *at this level* (which is actually its "strong side," as we saw in the criticisms lodged against Humboldt) can it be determined whether it is possible to *transfer the normative weight* that Gadamer placed on the linguistic world-disclosure (as a "sustaining agreement" that constitutes a "happening of truth") to the *formal structures* underlying the *cognitive* use of language. That is, we have to determine whether there is an equivalent of the formal and universalist perspective defended by Habermas with respect to the communicative use of language for the thematization of its cognitive use. I will come back to this question once it has been shown why providing an answer for this question is an internal requirement of Habermas's approach (rather than just one possible extension of it).

4.2.1   The Presuppositions of Action Oriented toward Understanding: The Validity Basis of Speech

In the central theses of "What Is Universal Pragmatics?" we can already recognize the basic premises that Habermas shares with Humboldt. We can also sense the similarity between Habermas's universal pragmatics and Humboldt's formalist and universalist account of language. At the beginning of his paper, Habermas specifies the tasks of universal pragmatics and the fundamental assumptions on which it relies. These can be summarized as the following theses:

• the task of universal pragmatics is to *identify and reconstruct the universal conditions of possible understanding;*

• at the sociocultural stage of evolution, language is the *specific medium of understanding;*

• thus, the conditions of possible understanding coincide with the *universal presuppositions of communicative action;*

• communicative action (i.e., action oriented toward understanding) is *fundamental,* insofar as other forms of social action (belonging to the model of strategic action) can be considered as *derived* from it; and

• given the importance of language with respect to understanding, this analysis of communicative action is justified in privileging *explicit speech acts* (over nonverbalized actions, bodily expressions, and so forth).

After elucidating the fundamental assumptions of his project of a universal pragmatics, Habermas not only goes on to determine the universal presuppositions of possible understanding. More importantly, he also offers a determination of their *status.*

Regarding the thematization of this status, we can certainly find more detailed remarks in later writings. Even so, the initial intuition remains the same. As we saw, the intersubjectivity of natural language is discontinuous. "It exists because consensus is, in principle, possible; and it does not exist, because reaching an understanding is, in principle, necessary" (LSS, p. 150). To this extent, understanding is the telos inherent in the communicative use of language; as such, it is also a goal that may or may not be achieved. Hence the conditions of possibility of understanding are to be regarded as *normative* conditions.

Here, Habermas already explicitly raises the question of how this normativity is to be understood (so as to avoid the identification of his project with the "transcendental pragmatics" proposed by Apel). But it is only much later that we find a sufficiently precise explanation of this normative status (in "Entgegnung"). The conditions of possibility of understanding are normative in a twofold sense: (1) as *constitutive* conditions (since they have the validity of any regulation), and (2) as *evaluative* conditions (since they determine whether or not the sought goal can be "achieved").[4]

4. With this distinction, Habermas wants to attribute to these presuppositions a sense of "validity" distinct from (and more ambitious than) the mere validity underscored by Wittgenstein's concept of "following a rule." What follows from our transgressing a constitutive presupposition of a language game (or of a game in general) is that we are not playing this game, but some other game (or none at all). What follows from our transgressing a necessary presupposition for the

But precisely because these conditions may or may not be achieved, they are not, strictly speaking, "transcendental":

> They resemble transcendental conditions insofar as we cannot avoid certain general presuppositions in the communicative use of language oriented toward understanding. But, on the other hand, they are not transcendental conditions in the strict sense: a) because *we can also act otherwise,* in a noncommunicative way, and b) because the inevitability of these idealized presuppositions *does not imply their factual satisfaction.* (ENT, p. 346; italics mine)

The normativity typical of the necessary presuppositions of understanding distinguishes them not only from transcendental conditions in a Kantian sense, but also (insofar as they are *counterfactual* presuppositions) from the factual sustaining agreement that hermeneutics considered to be the condition of possibility of understanding. Precisely because understanding is not the normal case of everyday communication (as made clear by hermeneutics), it cannot be regarded as something that has always already taken place. Rather, it has to be traced back to counterfactual presuppositions that regulate those actions that are oriented toward understanding.[5] In an openly hermeneutic vein, Habermas

---

achievement of understanding, the telos inherent in communicative action, is not that this action does not take place, but rather that the attempt to achieve understanding has *failed.* So it is clear that the normativity of these presuppositions results from the emphatic normative sense of "understanding" as Habermas uses the term. I will come back to this issue later (4.4).

5. With this remark, I do not endorse the viability of Habermas's project in "The Hermeneutic Claim to Universality" of substituting the factual "sustaining agreement" of hermeneutics for a "counterfactual" one in his analysis of communicative action. If we take into account the two perspectives from which Gadamer analyzed the conditions of possibility of understanding, it becomes clear that the difference between these two kinds of sustaining agreement is to be traced back to a difference in *levels of analysis,* and therefore cannot be regarded as offering a genuine alternative (or substitution).

The present analysis of the presuppositions of communicative action proposed by Habermas is intended to thematize the possibility of understanding from the perspective of the participants who try to achieve it. In this sense, Habermas's analysis constitutes an unquestionable improvement over Gadamer's analysis of the logic of conversation (3.2.2.a), not only for its incomparable degree of elaboration, but above all for its normative consequences (as opposed to those drawn

remarks: "If full agreement . . . were a normal state of linguistic communication, it would not be necessary to analyze the process of understanding from the dynamic perspective of *bringing about* an agreement. The typical states are in the gray areas in between: on the one hand, incomprehension and misunderstanding . . .; and, on the other hand, pre-existing or achieved consensus" (WIUP, p. 3).

For Habermas, the counterfactual presuppositions that enable speakers to distinguish intuitively between understanding and misunderstanding, between agreement and incomprehension, constitute "the validity basis of speech." He systematizes these presuppositions as follows:

[A]nyone acting communicatively must, in performing any speech action, raise universal validity claims and suppose that they can be redeemed. Insofar as he wants to participate in a process of reaching understanding, he cannot avoid raising the following—and indeed precisely the following—validity claims. He claims to be:

a. *Uttering* something understandably;

b. Giving [the hearer] *something* to understand;

c. Making *himself* thereby understandable; and

d. Coming to an understanding *with another person.*

---

by Gadamer). These consequences derive from the thematization of that which Habermas found missing in Gadamer's analysis, namely, "the power of reflection that unfolds in understanding."

The counterfactual "background consensus" that Habermas appeals to and subsequently thematizes (the very core of his theory of communicative action) does not lie at the same level as the factual "sustaining agreement" to which Gadamer appeals. That is, the Habermasian consensus is not an attempt to account for the conditions of possibility that must be *given* for understanding to be possible (or rather, for communicative action as such to be possible). So it cannot be understood as an equivalent answer or proposal to that contained in Gadamer's argument. That is, it cannot be understood as a perspective that can undermine the normative consequences drawn by hermeneutics from the need for a factual sustaining agreement. Precisely for this reason, when Habermas later faces the problem of providing a foundation for the presuppositions of communicative action as such (that is, when he discusses at a more fundamental level the conditions of possibility of communicative action), the linguistic function of world-disclosure appears as an *unresolved* problem.

The speaker must choose an intelligible [*verständlich*] expression so that speaker and hearer can understand one another. The speaker must have the intention of communicating a true [*wahr*] proposition (or a propositional content, the existential presuppositions of which are satisfied) so that the hearer can share the knowledge of the speaker. The speaker must want to express his intentions truthfully [*wahrhaftig*] so that the hearer can believe the utterance of the speaker (can trust him). Finally, the speaker must choose an utterance that is right [*richtig*] so that the hearer can accept the utterance and speaker and hearer can agree with one another in the utterance with respect to a recognized normative background. Moreover, communicative action can continue undisturbed only as long as *participants suppose that the validity claims they reciprocally raise are justified.* . . . Agreement is based on recognition of the corresponding validity claims of *intelligibility, truth, truthfulness, and rightness.* (WIUP, pp. 2–3; italics mine)

If we compare Habermas's account of "the validity basis of speech" with Gadamer's account of the peculiarity of the "experience of the Thou," the continuity between them becomes clear. Habermas's analysis of the conditions of possibility of understanding in communication (i.e., his account of intersubjectivity), can indeed be understood as an analysis of what it means to "take seriously the claim of another" (and to what extent this is necessary). This is what Gadamer appealed to when he discussed the need of "recognizing the other." But this recognition now loses its moral connotation and is more clearly appreciated in its internal relation with understanding as such.

As we shall see in what follows, through his analysis of the communicative use of language, Habermas explains why the *interactive* perspective (underscored by Gadamer's "dialectic of recognition") cannot be left out of an account of the conditions of possibility of understanding (4.2.1.a). However, some of the consequences of this analysis will to some extent undermine the continuity of Habermas's account with the hermeneutic view (4.2.1.b).

4.2.1.a The Double Structure of Speech
As we saw in Gadamer's analysis of the model of conversation, the conception of language as a medium of understanding, rather than as an instrument for the transmission of information, led

him to consider the conditions of possibility of understanding from a *twofold perspective*. He underscores this when he remarks that in a conversation two different things take place:

(a) the understanding between interlocutors, and

(b) the agreement about the subject matter.

The indissoluble interdependence between these (between the interactive and cognitive dimensions of conversation) explains why Gadamer considered the recognition of the claim of another as an indispensable element in understanding what the other says. However, insofar as this analysis appeals to the need to "recognize the other as a person," the validity claims inherent in communication are interpreted as a specifically moral phenomenon. In this way, the sought-for connection with the phenomenon of understanding in general loses plausibility.

Habermas avoids this problem by tracing the twofold dimension of the communicative use of language (as both cognitive and interactive) back to the singularity of natural languages already emphasized in "The Hermeneutic Claim to Universality." That is, he traces it back to the self-referentiality or reflexivity specific to ordinary language.

Habermas relies implicitly on this reflexivity for his characterization of the validity basis of speech, that is, for his differentiation of levels in which speakers communicate with one another *simultaneously* whenever they speak. This reflexivity is made explicit in the second part of "What Is Universal Pragmatics?" through an analysis of what Habermas terms the *double structure of speech*. This analysis makes up the core of his account of the theory of speech acts (a central element of universal pragmatics for the construction of a theory of communicative action).[6]

Habermas first discusses speech act theory by appealing to what he calls elsewhere the "discovery of the communicative use of language" by the later Wittgenstein (VSGS, pp. 79ff.). Here, in his discussion of Austin, Habermas explains this discovery as follows:

6. An excellent account of the core ideas of the universal pragmatics that Habermas conceives in this paper can be found in T. McCarthy (1978).

Language as Medium of Understanding

The principal task of speech act theory is to clarify the *performative status* [italics mine] of linguistic utterances. Austin analyzed the sense in which I can utter sentences in speech acts as the *illocutionary force* of speech actions. In uttering a promise, an assertion, or a warning, together with the corresponding sentences I execute an action—I try to *make* a promise, to *put forward* an assertion, to *issue* a warning—I do things by saying something. (WIUP, p. 34)

Thus every speech act is at least implicitly constituted by an illocutionary component (M) and a propositional component (p), represented schematically as Mp. The former fixes the "mode" in which the latter is to be understood, for both components can vary independently; the same propositional content can be asserted, asked, promised, requested, etc. This "uncoupling" of the illocutionary and the propositional components of speech acts is, for Habermas, "a condition for the differentiation of the *double structure of speech,* that is, for the separation of two communicative levels on which speaker and hearer *must simultaneously come to an understanding* if they want to communicate their intentions to one another" (WIUP, p. 42; italics mine). Habermas describes these two levels of communication as follows:

(1) the *level of intersubjectivity* on which speaker and hearer, through illocutionary acts, establish the relations that permit them to come to *an understanding with one another,* and (2) the *level of experiences and states of affairs,* about which speaker and hearer try to reach an understanding in the medium of the communicative function fixed by (1). (WIUP, p. 42; italics mine)

As pointed out above, this analysis of the double structure of speech offers direct support to Gadamer's thesis that a conversation comprises both the understanding between interlocutors and their agreement about the subject matter. Habermas goes on to connect this analysis with the "reflexivity" inherent in ordinary language. He remarks:

A basic feature of language is connected with this double structure of speech, namely its inherent *reflexivity*. The standardized possibilities for directly and indirectly mentioning speech only make explicit the *self-referentiality* that is already contained in *every speech act*. In filling out the double structure of speech participants in dialogue *communicate on two levels simultaneously*. They combine communication of a content with communication about the role in which the communicated content is used. (WIUP, p. 42; italics mine)

These two levels of communication explain why we must take seriously the claim of another in order to understand what she means. For as soon as a propositional content is uttered by a speaker with communicative intention in a speech act, as soon as it is embedded in an illocutionary act, it becomes linked to validity claims. And the "success" of the speech act as such depends on the *recognition* of these claims by the hearer (WIUP, p. 63).

To explain this peculiarity of the communicative use of language (i.e., its possessing not only a cognitive dimension tied to a propositional content, but also an interactive dimension), Habermas appeals to the difference between the mere production of a grammatically correct sentence and its use in a situation of possible understanding. This difference

can be made clear with regard to the *relations to reality* in which every sentence is first embedded *through the act of utterance*. In being uttered, a sentence is placed in relation to (1) the *external reality* of what is supposed to be an existing state of affairs, (2) the *internal reality* of what a speaker would like to express before a public as his intentions, and, finally, (3) the *normative reality* of what is intersubjectively recognized as a legitimate interpersonal relationship. It is thereby *placed under validity claims* that it need not and cannot fulfill as a nonsituated sentence, as a purely grammatical formation. (WIUP, pp. 27–28; italics mine)

It is precisely the situated character of the communicative use of language that explains why the achievement of understanding between speaker and hearer requires that they be able to agree on the *presuppositions of reality* that are inherent (whether implicitly or explicitly) in their speech acts. That is, speaker and hearer must share the *knowledge* implicit in the propositional content of the speech act (and hence must accept the *truth* claim of the utterance). They must share the normative presuppositions inherent in the interpersonal relationship established by the illocutionary act (i.e., they must accept the claim of normative *rightness* inherent in it). Further, they must trust in the *truthfulness* with which the speech act is uttered.

In this context, Habermas talks about "the rational basis of illocutionary forces," which results from the fact that these validity claims can be thematized and tied to arguments. For the implicit presupposition of every "successful" speech act is that either the validity claims involved are redeemed, or, if they become problematic, they can be justified. This presupposition is tied to validity claims that are open to *cognitive examination*. The fact that the obligations inherent in speech acts "*are connected with cognitively testable validity claims*" (WIUP, p. 63) explains why the illocutionary offer of the speaker does not limit itself to producing a suggestive effect on the hearer. Instead, it can actually move the hearer to accept the offer on a rational basis.

This last point, however, refers to another aspect inherent in the reflexivity that characterizes the communicative use of language.

4.2.1.b Communicative Action and Discourse: The Reflective Force Inherent in Understanding

Thus the peculiar character of the communicative use of language (of action oriented toward understanding) as analyzed by Habermas is emphasized through two of its features:

a) communicative action involves the *recognition* of validity claims that participants in communication set forth with their illocutionary acts.... (WIUP, p. 63)

b) [T]his recognition need not follow irrationally, since the validity claims have a *cognitive* character and *can be checked*. (WIUP, p. 63; italics mine)

With this last remark, Habermas appeals to the peculiarity that distinguishes communicative action, which is directed toward understanding, from any other type of action. Habermas discusses this peculiarity at the beginning of "What Is Universal Pragmatics?" where he remarks:

Coming to an understanding is the process of bringing about an agreement on the presupposed basis of validity claims that can be mutually recognized. . . . As soon as . . . the presupposition that certain validity claims are satisfied (or could be redeemed) is suspended . . . *communicative action cannot be continued*. One is then basically confronted with the alternatives of switching to strategic action, breaking off communication altogether, or *recommencing action oriented to reaching understanding at a different level, the level of argumentative speech* (for purposes of discursively examining the problematic validity claims, which are now regarded as *hypothetical*). (WIUP, pp. 3–4; italics mine)

It is just this peculiarity of the action oriented toward understanding (the fact that it cannot be continued if the "counterfactual agreement" is suspended), that enables Habermas to postulate a "communicative rationality" inherent in this type of interaction. It is in virtue of this rationality that we can assess whether or not the goal of the interaction (i.e., the achievement of "understanding" in a normative sense) has been attained. In his Christian Gauss Lectures (1970–71), Habermas already provided a typology of possible "discourses" that would be correlated with the different validity claims that ground the normative sense of "understanding." As Habermas explains:

If understanding is not a descriptive concept, what characterizes a rational consensus as opposed to a purely contingent consensus that, we say, cannot be "firm," nor serve as the ground of anything? A *rational consensus,* we have said, *is achieved in discourses* . . . . Discourses are acts organized so as to reason about cognitive utterances. . . . In discourse we try to arrive at shared convictions through reasons. . . . We initiate a *hermeneutic discourse* when the validity of the interpretations of expressions in a given linguistic system is called into question. We initiate a *theoretical-empirical discourse* when the validity of assertions and explanations with empirical content must be checked. We initiate a *practical discourse* when what is in question is the validity of recommendations (or warnings) that involve the acceptance (or rejection) of standards. (VSGS, p. 115; italics mine)[7]

Habermas goes on to explain the singular character of those argumentative practices that he calls discourses as follows:

7. Habermas expands this typology of possible "discourses" in *Theory of Communicative Action I* (pp. 20–23) by including types of argumentation that relate to the validity claim of "truthfulness" (which does not appear here). These are "aesthetic criticism" and "therapeutic criticism," which, however, do not amount to "discourses" insofar as they do not satisfy certain general conditions (the former because it involves a discussion about cultural values that cannot claim to have universal scope, the latter because of the unavoidable asymmetry between physician and patient).

Participants in argumentation commonly *assume* something like an *ideal speech situation*. What characterizes the ideal speech situation is that every consensus that can be achieved under its conditions can be considered, *per se*, a rational consensus. My thesis is then the following: the *anticipation of an ideal speech situation is what guarantees that, through a factually achieved consensus, we can lay claim to a rational consensus*. At the same time, this anticipation is the *critical element* that enables us to call into question any factually achieved consensus and proceed to check whether it can be considered as sufficient ground for real understanding. . . . With respect to the distinction between a true consensus and a false one, we call ideal that situation in which communication is not disturbed, neither by contingent, external influences nor by constraints resulting from the very structure of communication. The ideal speech situation excludes the systematic distortion of communication. It is only then that the peculiar unforced force of the better argument exclusively prevails. This force can lead to a competent and methodic verification of assertions, or it can rationally motivate a decision concerning practical issues. Now, no constraint results from the very structure of communication if and only if there is a symmetric distribution of opportunities to choose and execute speech acts for all participants. For it is then that there is not only a universal interchangeability of dialogic roles, but also an actual state of equal opportunity for the realization of these roles. From this condition of *universal symmetry* we can deduce special rules for each of the four kinds of speech acts introduced [corresponding to the four validity claims]. (VSGS, pp. 118–120; italics mine)

It is necessary to take into account this condensed characterization of what Habermas calls discourse in order to assess the continuity and the differences between his analysis of action oriented toward understanding and that provided by Gadamer in *Truth and Method*.

1. There is a strong continuity between Gadamer's and Habermas's analyses with respect to the first structural feature distinguished above. I am referring to Habermas's basic conceptualization of action oriented toward understanding as a type of action intrinsically tied to the mutual recognition of validity claims.

This continuity will become much more explicit in the *Theory of Communicative Action*. There, relying on the analysis of the conditions of possibility of communicative action, Habermas opposes "objectivist" approaches in the social sciences. In doing so, he tries to emphasize (as did Gadamer in *Truth and Method*) the indissoluble, internal connection between meaning and validity, between "understanding" what the other says and implicitly "assessing" its plausibility.

Although the degree of specificity in Habermas's defense of this thesis is undoubtedly greater than that afforded by Gadamer's analysis, the core of the argument is the same in both. Since understanding another speaker is only possible against the background of validity claims recognized by all speakers, to understand what the speaker means entails assessing this in the light of validity claims. This assessment can either take place implicitly, insofar as the validity claims are not regarded as problematic; or it can occur explicitly, by reconstructing the reasons the speaker would have given to defend her claims as justified had they been problematized. And as Gadamer argues, this reconstruction of reasons does not leave room for a potential attitude. Habermas makes the same argument when he says: "reasons are of such a nature that they cannot be described in the attitude of a third person, that is, without reactions of affirmation or negation or abstention. . . . [For] one can understand reasons only to the extent that one understands *why* they are or are not sound, or why in a given case a decision as to whether reasons are good or bad is not (yet) possible" (TCA I, 115–116; italics mine).

2. But precisely at this point, which corresponds to the second structural feature distinguished above, we begin to find discontinuities between the accounts of Gadamer and Habermas. As anticipated in our discussion of Gadamer's argument in Chapter 3, it is precisely the internal connection between "understanding" and argumentation through reasons—or "discourse"—that has as a necessary consequence the structural *symmetry* between speaker and hearer. That is, it has the consequence that neither of them can apply the principle of hermeneutic charity (or "the foreconception of completeness") in such a way as to grant the other the "authority" that everything she says is "the whole truth." As Gadamer remarked, understanding what the other says involves taking seriously her truth claim (that is, assessing this claim in the

light of one's own beliefs about the subject matter). But it is for just this reason that the problematization of this claim can arise at any point and in any direction.

The possibility of this problematization cannot be ruled out a priori, precisely insofar as we cannot have a potential attitude toward understanding. The path to discourse cannot be closed off in any direction if mutual understanding is to be achieved.

Thus, in *Theory of Communicative Action,* Habermas can distance himself from Gadamer in the following way:

> To be sure, Gadamer gives the interpretative model of *Verstehen* a peculiar *one-sided twist.* If in the performative attitude of virtual participants in conversation we start with the idea that an author's utterance has the presumption of rationality, we not only admit the possibility that the interpretandum may be exemplary *for us,* that we may learn something from it; *we also take into account the possibility that the author could learn from us.* Gadamer remains bound to the experience of the philologist who deals with classical texts. . . . The knowledge embodied in the text is, Gadamer believes, fundamentally superior to the interpreter's. In opposition to this stands the anthropologist's experience that *the interpreter by no means always assumes the position of a subordinate in relation to a tradition.* (TCA I, p. 134–35; italics mine)

This *potential for critique,* which cannot be placed under control, is inherent in action oriented toward understanding as such. And this is precisely what makes it impossible to assimilate this type of action to the kind of "ethical self-understanding" through which a group ascertains its identity. The latter is what Gadamer appealed to when he described understanding in conversation as "being transformed into a communion in which we do not remain what we were" (TM, p. 379).[8]

8. The "ethical self-understanding" underlying the model of conversation developed by Gadamer (which is the "source" that guarantees social integration and can guide action) cannot be regarded as the paradigm of understanding for communicative action as such (i.e., for a kind of action that requires the *explicit agreement* of participants in conversation and which, therefore, is necessarily linked to reasoning). The reasons for this can be found in Habermas's reflections in *Nachmetaphysisches Denken:*

> That social order is supposed to produce and reproduce itself by way of processes of consensus formation might seem at first glance to be a trivial

But moreover, this potential for critique inherent in action oriented toward understanding, that is, the "ability to say 'no'" which marks the specific feature of this kind of action, is "the power of reflection that unfolds in understanding" (LSS, p. 168). And this is what Habermas, as early as his *On the Logic of Social Sciences,* found to be missing from Gadamer's analysis. But it is only now that Habermas can give plausibility to his critique of Gadamer's view. If we take into account the internal connection between communicative action and discourse, as well as the potential for critique inherent in the latter, it becomes clear that the possibility of criticizing tradition does not involve any objectification of tradition. On the contrary, as Habermas remarks,

The same structures that make it possible to reach an understanding also provide for the possibility of a reflective self-control of this process. It is this *potential for critique* built into communicative action itself that the social scientist, by entering into the contexts of everyday action as a virtual participant, can systematically exploit and bring into play outside these contexts and against their particularity. (TCA I, p. 121; italics mine)

As we saw, it is this singular reflexivity that allows for a "meta-communication" about the very communication that is taking

---

notion. The improbability of this idea becomes clear, however, as soon as one reminds oneself that every communicatively achieved agreement *depends on the taking up of "yes"/"no" positions with regard to criticizable validity claims.* In the case of communicative action, the double contingency that has to be absorbed by all interaction formation takes the particularly precarious shape of an ever present risk of disagreement that is built into the communicative mechanism itself, whereby every disagreement has a high cost. . . . If one considers that every *explicit agreement* to a speech act offer rests on a double negation, namely the repudiation of the (always possible) rejection of it, then the communicative processes operating by way of criticizable validity claims *do not exactly recommend themselves as reliable rails along which social integration might run.* Rational motivation, which rests on the fact that the hearer can say "no," constitutes a *maelstrom of problematization* that makes *linguistic consensus formation appear more like a disruptive mechanism.* (pp. 84–85; italics mine)

[Translator's note: the chapter of *Nachmetaphysisches Denken* from which these quotes are drawn has not yet been published in English; see footnote 14.]

place, that is to say, for the transition from communicative action to discourse. This reflexivity entails:

• a problematizing potential which is not subject to control, as well as

• the possibility of achieving understanding (through the indirect, reflexive path to discourse).

Precisely because the "*path from communicative action to discourse* . . . is always ingrained in the very structure of action oriented to reaching understanding" (TCA I, p. 130), Habermas can provide a rebuttal to one of Gadamer's central objections. Against Habermas's approach, Gadamer had argued that the "social critic" vindicated by Habermas could only be, in fact, a "social technocrat" in disguise. For to carry out her critique, she would have to break the symmetry of communication oriented toward understanding. It is with this objection in mind that Habermas later remarks:

In thematizing what the participants merely presuppose and assuming a *reflective* attitude to the interpretandum, one does not place oneself *outside* the communication context under investigation; one deepens and radicalizes it *in a way that is in principle open to all participants.* (TCA I, p. 130; italics mine)

With this reconstruction of the similarities and differences between Habermas's and Gadamer's accounts of action oriented toward understanding, we have discussed only *one* level of the confrontation between their positions. Accordingly, we have examined only one line of argument among the many that make up their debate.[9] Later, we will discuss another key aspect of the confrontation between Gadamer and Habermas (4.4). This discussion will require that we first reconstruct the internal difficulties of Habermas's view in order to analyze other aspects of his debate with Gadamer.

9. For a good review of the central aspects of the Gadamer-Habermas debate, see U. Nassen (1982); D. Misgeld (1976); and A.R. How (1980), pp. 131–143. For a broader perspective on this debate, see D. Ingram (1983), pp. 86–151 and M. Jay (1982), pp. 86–110.

4.2.2 Two Structural Shortcomings

In our previous discussion of Habermas's project of a universal pragmatics (a necessary step in the construction of a theory of communicative action), we only examined the structural features of his account of the communicative use of language in "What Is Universal Pragmatics?" This enabled us to bring to light the similarities and differences between Habermas's and Gadamer's views. But we have not yet explicitly examined the methodological issues that Habermas discusses at length in that paper, issues central for an assessment of the project of a universal pragmatics as such.

Since Habermas's project has been transformed in recent decades (not only in the *Theory of Communicative Action,* but also in his later reflections in *Nachmetaphysisches Denken,* see pp. 63–152),[10] I will not expand on the details of his initial project. Instead, given the reconstructive tenor of my discussion, I will pass directly to an analysis of the structural shortcomings of this project. For it is possible to understand the changes introduced in *Theory of Communicative Action* as an internal development resulting from the attempt to avoid these shortcomings (see 4.3).

A cursory glance at the numerous critiques aimed at Habermas's project from its origins to the present would be enough to forestall any attempt to systematize everything that has been regarded as problematic in this project.[11] For this reason, it is nec-

10. Translator's note: These pages correspond to chapter 4 of *Nachmetaphysisches Denken* ("Handlungen, Sprechakte, sprachlich vermittelte Interaktionen und Lebenswelt"), which is not contained in the English translation of this work. Thus I translate the author's quotes from this chapter from the German original (with the abbreviation "NMD"). All other quotes from *Nachmetaphysisches Denken* are taken from the English translation (with the abbreviation "PMT").

11. A representative selection of critical perspectives on Habermas's theory of communicative action can be found in A. Honneth and H. Joas (1986). Here one can also find a bibliography of the literature on *Theory of Communicative Action* compiled by R. Görtzen (1986, pp. 406–416). A broader bibliography of the literature on Habermas, also compiled by R. Görtzen but not limited to that work, can be found in Görtzen 1990, pp. 114–140.

essary to clarify what is meant here by the project's "structural shortcomings."

There are two sorts of methodological decisions at the basis of our analysis, which allow us to group the multiple constellations of problems facing this project around two specific shortcomings.

On the one hand, the reconstructive nature of the present book leads us to consider the evolution of Habermas's view from what can be termed an internal perspective. That is, this evolution will be treated as the result of the process of overcoming the difficulties arising with the development of the project itself. At the end of this process, however, one type of problem will appear to be insoluble by means of surface modifications (to use Quine's expression). That is, it will become plain that these problems are due to difficulties inherent in the very conception underlying Habermas's view as a whole.

On the other hand, the thematic perspective of this book allows us to focus exclusively on the *conception of language* underlying Habermas's view. Moreover, taking into account the earlier schematization of the authors of the German tradition, I will consider only the *improvements* or *difficulties* that the specific differences in his view entail, with respect to a nucleus of problems constantly present in this tradition (namely, those resulting from the connection between reason and language). Given this perspective, it is only natural that the shortcomings to be discussed will revolve around the two methodological decisions that this tradition has always criticized. These are formalism (4.2.2.a) and universalism (4.2.2.b).

4.2.2.a The Formal Point of View

Habermas's project of a universal pragmatics represents a continuous development of the perspective from which Humboldt projected a "comparative science of language." In "Entgegnung," Habermas explicitly underscores this continuity in his reply to Taylor's criticism (which stems from an appropriation of Humboldt very different from Habermas's own). However, this continuity can already be implicitly identified in the central premises of Habermas's project in "What Is Universal Pragmatics?" if we keep in mind our earlier discussion of Humboldt's view.

As we saw at the beginning of this chapter, Habermas opens his paper by stating the central thesis that "language is the *specific medium of understanding* at the sociocultural stage of evolution" (WIUP, p. 1; italics mine). No matter how obvious this claim may seem in the context of the present book, Habermas is perfectly aware of the compatibility problems[12] involved in his attempt to combine this view of language with the conceptual apparatus of the Anglo-American tradition of philosophy of language.

To render this view of language plausible, Habermas appeals to Humboldt on two central issues:

• regarding the demarcation of the object domain of his analysis, Habermas appeals to Humboldt's *differentiation* between language

12. These compatibility problems are of two kinds. On the one hand, there are problems arising from the primacy given to the cognitive use of language over its communicative use, not only in Anglo-American philosophy but from the beginnings of Greek philosophy (as repeatedly noted and lamented by hermeneutics). This primacy entails such broad differences not only in methods but also in content (differences concerning the very problems that are recognized and discussed), that the possibility of unifying the philosophical results of the thematizations of these two uses is not guaranteed in advance. This feeling of mutual exclusion is conveyed, for instance, by M. Dummett (1986) when he remarks: "Language is both an instrument of communication and a vehicle of thought; it is an *important* question of orientation in the philosophy of language *which role we take as primary*" (p. 470; italics mine).

On the other hand, as Dummett's remark makes clear, the account of the communicative dimension of language in the Anglo-American tradition usually involves the conception of language as an instrument for the transmission of information (which covertly preserves the primacy of the cognitive over the communicative use of language). As a result, the attempt to thematize in Humboldt's manner the communicative use of language in its "constitutive" functions (with respect to the objective, social, and subjective worlds), must first "demonstrate" its philosophical status—that is, its status as a conceptual (and not merely empirical) analysis.

These two "difficulties" constitute the background that structures Habermas's central methodological discussion in "What Is Universal Pragmatics?" (and that gives the paper its title): the defense of a "pragmatic" perspective against the traditional "absolutization" of the semantic perspective.

as "structure" (*ergon*) and language as "process" (*energeia*) or "speech";

• regarding the methodological viability of a philosophical analysis of speech, he proposes to adopt a *formal* point of view.

Habermas remarks:

> It is certainly legitimate to draw an abstractive distinction between language as structure and speaking as process. . . . [But] the separation of the two analytic levels, language and speech, should not be made in such a way that the pragmatic dimension of language is left to exclusively empirical analysis—that is, to empirical sciences such as psycholinguistics and sociolinguistics. I would defend the thesis that not only language *but speech too*—that is, the employment of sentences in utterances—*is accessible to formal analysis.* Like the elementary units of language (sentences), the elementary units of speech (utterances) can be analyzed in the methodological attitude of a reconstructive science. (WIUP, pp. 5–6; italics mine).

So a formal analysis of the structures underlying speech is the methodological route for carrying out the task of universal pragmatics, namely "to identify and reconstruct universal conditions of possible understanding" (WIUP, p. 1). Once this is established, Habermas provides a more detailed specification (1) of the level of analysis that converge in a universal pragmatics, and (2) of the levels of abstraction needed to obtain a formal perspective.

1. With respect to the different levels of analysis, the distinction between the cognitive and communicative uses of language, reflected in the double structure of speech (i.e., in the two components of every speech act, *Mp*), results in a "division of labor" between semantics and formal pragmatics:

a. "*Formal semantics* examines *the propositional content* of elementary propositions" (WIUP, p. 33). . . . Its object domain is "the acts of *reference and predication*" (ibid.; italics mine).

b. "The *theory of speech acts examines illocutionary force* from the point of view of the establishment of legitimate interpersonal relations" (ibid.; italics mine).

The object domain of speech act theory (that is, the establishment of interpersonal relations) renders this theory "central" for a theory of communicative action (WIUP, p. 34). Thus Habermas goes on to specify the second differentiation of levels mentioned above, namely, those that allow for a formal perspective at this level of analysis.

2. To provide this second kind of specification, Habermas draws on Searle's view. More specifically, he appeals to the methodological principle set forth by Searle in *Speech Acts*, the principle of expressibility. This principle makes it possible to restrict the analysis of speech acts to their standard form, to explicit and propositionally differentiated speech acts "made up of an *illocutionary* and a *propositional* component" (WIUP, p. 36).

The difficulties inherent in this principle (central for any speech act theory) become clear in the explanatory context in which Habermas discusses it. He introduces this principle when he points to a further step of abstraction needed to carry out a *formal* analysis of speech acts:

[W]e shall exclude those explicit speech actions in standard form that appear in *contexts that produce shifts of meaning*. This is the case when the pragmatic meaning of a context-dependent speech act *diverges from the meaning of the sentences used in it* (and from that of *the indicated conditions of a generalized context* that have to be met for the type of speech action in question). Searle's "principle of expressibility" takes this into account: assuming that the speaker expresses his intention precisely, explicitly, and *literally*, it is possible in principle for every speech act carried out or capable of being carried out *to be univocally specified* by a complex sentence. (WIUP, p. 39; italics mine)

From Habermas's proposal to exclude those "contexts that produce shifts of meaning" in speech acts, we can indirectly infer the supposition implicit in this principle, which accounts for both its theoretical (and methodological) importance as well as the impossibility of its application. The proposed contextual abstraction that makes the formal analysis of speech acts possible involves the supposition that there exists a "zero context" or "literal meaning,"[13] according to which we can distinguish univocally determined speech acts from ambiguous ones.

13. There is another fundamental element in Habermas's discussion which, though relevant for the identification of the background assumptions underly-

Searle discusses the difficulty of defending this point of view when he introduces a crucial modification in his speech act theory. I refer to his recognition of the "background" as an indispensable element for the analysis of speech acts in *Expression and Meaning* (1979a). Putting aside the long and complex debate about literal meaning that has taken place since at least the late 1970s,[14] we can group the difficulties inherent in the supposition of a univocal "determinacy" of meaning (i.e., an "identity" of the meanings shared by speakers) around the central arguments Searle provides in the introduction of *Expression and Meaning*. These arguments are usually discussed under the heading "meaning holism."[15]

The thesis defended by Searle in the introduction is made explicit in his exposition of the perspective from which he will discuss "literal meaning" (1979a, p. 117–136). He writes:

I shall argue that in general the notion of the literal meaning of a sentence only has application *relative to a set of contextual or background assumptions* and finally I shall examine some of the implications of this alternative view. The view I shall be attacking is sometimes expressed by saying that the literal meaning of a sentence is the meaning that it has in the "zero context" or the "null context." (1979a, p. 117; italics mine)

---

ing his project, cannot be examined here. This element is implicit in Habermas's remark that "conditions of a generalized context" are indicated in "the speech act itself." This supposition is internally related to the singular view of the "self-referentiality" of ordinary language that Habermas expresses by saying that "speech acts identify themselves." The claim of "self-transparency" implicit in this supposition will be discussed later (4.4.1).

14. An aspect of this debate that will not be considered here concerns the possible defense of the thesis of "literal meaning" as regards "pragmatic meaning." That is, the issue of whether the "serious" use of speech acts (the use in which the speaker means what she explicitly says) can be regarded as "fundamental," and the other uses regarded as parasitic on it, as Searle maintains against Derrida. See Searle (1977), Derrida (1977), Culler (1982), and also Habermas (PDM), pp. 219–247 and (NMD), pp. 242–266. This issue will appear only indirectly in my discussion of Habermas's defense (required by the foundational issues examined in the next section; 4.2.2.b) of the "fundamental" character of action oriented toward understanding (more specifically, the thesis that strategic action is "parasitic" on communicative action).

15. See Putnam (1986), pp. 405–426.

Searle devises an ingenious list of possible variations of the meaning of the assertion "The cat is on the mat" by means of a thought experiment in which the context of the utterance is significantly transformed (as, for example, by assuming the absence of gravitational force). He concludes that the meaningful use of this sentence (i.e., the univocal fixation of its truth conditions) requires the specification of the background assumptions that constitute, in each case, the "normality" conditions that the speaker assumes when she utters the sentence. These assumptions cannot be derived from the semantic structure of the sentence. The reasons Searle cites are of two kinds (corresponding to the two peculiar features of these assumptions):

a. Background assumptions cannot be completely *objectified*, for they are indefinite in number and holistically structured.

[T]here are . . . two reasons why these extra assumptions could not all be realized in the semantic structure of the sentence, first they are *indefinite in number*, and second, whenever one is given a literal statement of these assumptions, the statement *relies on other assumptions for its intelligibility*. (1979a, p. 128; italics mine)

However, Searle goes on to argue, the thesis that the semantic structure of a sentence cannot guarantee its intelligibility[16] in virtue of its grammatical correctness should not be understood as a "technical difficulty" faced by the attempt to objectify something that is indefinite in number and has a circular structure. Rather, it expresses an impossibility *in principle*. This is owing to the other peculiarity of background assumptions (which also represents the key consequence of meaning holism):

(b) It is not possible to draw a sharp boundary between those background assumptions that concern the meaning of a sentence and those that concern the empirical knowledge it conveys.

This is the conclusion that Searle arrives at in his argument in defense of his initial thesis:

16. I will discuss later the problems concerning the validity claim of "intelligibility" encountered by Habermas (4.4.2).

The thesis I have been advancing is that for a large class of sentences the speaker, *as part of his linguistic competence,* knows how to apply the literal meaning of a sentence *only against a background of other assumptions.* If I am right, this argument has the consequence that *there is no sharp distinction between a speaker's linguistic competence and his knowledge of the world.* (1979a, p. 134; italics mine)

The "meaning" of a speech act becomes determinate only in light of certain background knowledge that speakers have *in virtue of their linguistic competence.* Therefore the mere utterances of speaker and hearer in the form of standard and explicit speech acts can no longer be regarded as the most basic units of analysis of speech act theory. Rather, we must begin with a background of shared presuppositions (which involve an undifferentiated stock of knowledge of both language and the world) as the condition of possibility for the success of speech acts; for otherwise, they would lack "univocal" meaning.

The modification of Searle's speech act theory introduced in *Expression and Meaning* lies at the basis of one of the central developments of Habermas's project, from its initial sketch in "What Is Universal Pragmatics?" to its realization in *Theory of Communicative Action.* This is the introduction of the concept of the lifeworld as a necessary correlate of communicative action.

The connection between this systematic improvement introduced in *Theory of Communicative Action* and Searle's modification of his speech act theory is explicitly stated by Habermas, in his 1980 "Reply to My Critics." There, he remarks that

a difficulty of orthodox speech act analysis . . . has in the meantime caused me to expand my basic formal-pragmatic assumptions. The methodological limitation to the standard form goes a step too far in *neutralizing context.* The model of the speech act has to take into account not only such familiar elements as utterance, action situation, speaker, hearer and the yes/no position he or she takes, but *also the background of the lifeworld shared by speaker and hearer* and thus *the culturally transmitted, prereflexively certain, intuitively available, background knowledge from which participants in communication draw their interpretations.* In coming to an understanding about something by way of their speech acts, participants in communication not only take up a *frontal relation* to three worlds: in doing so, they have *at their backs* a context-forming lifeworld that *serves as a resource for processes of achieving understanding* [italics mine]. (p. 271)

We can assess in greater detail the implications of this "correction" of Habermas's initial project if we take into account, anticipating a later discussion (see 4.3.1), the characterization of the lifeworld he offers in "Remarks on the Concept of Communicative Action." According to this characterization, the lifeworld:

• "as a resource . . . plays a *constitutive role in the processes of understanding*" (RCCA, p. 591; italics mine);

• constitutes the "*linguistically* organized stock of background assumptions, which is reproduced in the form of a cultural *tradition*," "occupying a *somewhat transcendental* position" (ibid.; italics mine);

• and therefore "allows participants in the interaction to find a connection between the objective, the social, and the subjective world, a connection which is *interpreted beforehand* as far as *content* is concerned." (ibid.; italics mine)

In light of this characterization of the lifeworld, the "correction" of the formalist excesses of "What Is Universal Pragmatics?" seems to point in the direction of the evolution (examined in previous chapters) that led from Humboldt to Gadamer. For the analysis of action oriented toward understanding carried out by Habermas in the wake of this correction is characterized by the following modifications:

• Habermas no longer considers the conditions of possibility of understanding exclusively from the perspective of participants in communication (*a fronte*); he also considers the conditions of possibility that must be *given* (*a tergo*) for understanding to take place;

• therefore, like Gadamer, he regards as constitutive moments of action oriented toward understanding not only (a) the telos of understanding between *speaker and hearer*, (b) *about something* on which they have to agree. Equally constitutive is the fact that this process can only take place (c) against the background of *a linguistically structured and shared world*, transmitted by a cultural tradition that guarantees that speakers can talk about the same thing (i.e., that guarantees the "identity" of shared meanings);

• and, in this way, Habermas reintroduces the *inseparability of form and content* (already defended by Gadamer against Humboldt), at least for the "hermeneutic experience" of participants in communication (if not for philosophical analysis).

In view of the systematic significance of these "corrections," one might conclude that Habermas now regards the linguistic function of world-disclosure as a constitutive element of the analysis of action oriented toward understanding (by combining the communicative and cognitive dimensions of language as hermeneutics did, thus inheriting the difficulties resulting from the form/content distinction). But this conclusion is correct only in retrospect. Although the aforementioned corrections of his initial view certainly played a crucial role, Habermas became aware of the need for an explicit thematization of the linguistic function of world-disclosure only *after* the writing of *Theory of Communicative Action*.[17]

The difficulties involved in this issue will be addressed later, when I discuss the structural problems of Habermas's theory (IV.4), after examining the "improvements" introduced in *Theory of Communicative Action* (4.3).

4.2.2.b Foundational Problems

As pointed out at the beginning of this chapter, formalism and universalism are indeed the key points both for linking Habermas's project of a formal pragmatics (sketched in "What Is Universal Pragmatics?") to Humboldt's view, and also for distinguishing it from Gadamer's. The problematic character of this formalism has already surfaced in relation to the inseparability of form and content implicit in the introduction of the holistic concept of lifeworld. But I have not yet discussed the consequences of this holism for the viability of a formal analysis.

To examine the problems concerning the universalism that is characteristic of Habermas's project, we must keep in mind the central theses that he formulates at the beginning of "What Is

---

17. See Habermas, *The Philosophical Discourse of Modernity*, "Entgegnung," and *Nachmetaphysisches Denken*.

Universal Pragmatics?'' There, he remarked that the task of universal pragmatics is "to identify and reconstruct universal conditions of possible understanding" (p. 1), and that these conditions have to be derived from the presuppositions of action oriented toward understanding.

In his conceptual demarcation of the notion of understanding, Habermas underscores its *normative* sense. In this context, "understanding" does not have the minimalist sense of referring merely to the identical comprehension of a linguistic expression. Rather, it is defined as "the process of bringing about an agreement on the presupposed basis of *validity claims that can be mutually recognized*" (WIUP, p. 3; italics mine), a "rationally motivated agreement."

Although Habermas does not address here the foundational problems inherent in this kind of "normativity," he does identify their theoretical locus as well as their scope. He defines communicative action as that action which is oriented toward understanding in a normative sense, toward a "rationally motivated understanding". To this extent, the analysis of such action only involves, per se, the reconstruction of *a particular possible praxis.*

Habermas underscores the universal scope of this kind of action by considering its analysis as a reconstruction of "the universal conditions of possible understanding." But to guarantee the universality of this kind of action, or in other words, to assert its underlying "principle of rational speech . . . as the necessary regulative for *all actual speech*" (HCU, pp. 206–207), it is necessary to *show* that this type of action is more "fundamental" than any other type of action. However, we already find a reservation on Habermas's part concerning this point, in his enumeration of the central theses of "What Is Universal Pragmatics?" After asserting that he takes "the type of action aimed at reaching understanding to be fundamental," Habermas remarks:

I start from the assumption (*without undertaking to demonstrate it here*) that other forms of social action—for example, conflict, competition, strategic action in general—are *derivatives* of action oriented to reaching understanding. (WIUP p. 1; italics mine)

When Habermas takes up the task of demonstrating the fundamental character of communicative action (a thesis fraught with normative assumptions), his initial project undergoes methodological transformations. These will be examined later, in my discussion of the systematic "improvements" introduced in *Theory of Communicative Action* (4.3.2).

Certainly Habermas's remark might suggest that this issue does not concern the explicit themes of "What Is Universal Pragmatics?" However, a remark added in 1983 hints at a systematic locus where this problem cannot be ignored (unless it is "resolved" via definition).

Habermas wants to base his theory of communicative action on a formal-pragmatic analysis of speech acts. As we saw, the key to this analysis lies in the investigation of "*illocutionary force* from the point of view of the establishment of legitimate *interpersonal relations*" (WIUP, p. 33; italics mine). By granting primacy to this investigation, Habermas assigns a secondary role to the formal-semantic analysis of the propositional content of speech acts.

The heart of this investigation is its analysis of the "pragmatic" meaning that illocutionary force adds to the purely linguistic meaning of the sentence uttered in a speech act. It does this by fixing the "mode" of the sentence. For the peculiarity of pragmatic meaning is that it *situates* the sentence "in relation to reality" (i.e., in relation to the objective, subjective, and social worlds). Thus it establishes an internal link between the sentence and "validity claims" (truth, truthfulness, or rightness; see WIUP pp. 45–46).

From this contribution of the "pragmatic" meaning of illocutionary force to the mere "linguistic" meaning of the sentence there follows the fundamental thesis of the formal-pragmatic analysis of speech acts, namely, "we understand a speech act when we know what makes it acceptable." For we cannot know how the sentence uttered in the speech act is to be understood unless we can relate it to the specific reality at issue, and thus to universal validity claims that can be discursively redeemed.

The importance of this thesis lies in the fact that it bears the *normative* weight that results from postulating an *internal*

connection between meaning and validity (which, as we saw, both Gadamer and Habermas do). This thesis enables Habermas to link
"the validity basis of speech" (WIUP, p. 1) to "the rational foundation of illocutionary force" (WIUP, p. 59). That is to say, given
this link, Habermas can demonstrate that there is an *internal connection* between communicative action and discourse (i.e., the argumentative examination of problematized validity claims, which
is oriented toward reaching a "rationally motivated agreement").

With this brief analysis of the different foundational levels in
Habermas's project, there becomes clear the normative importance of the analysis of illocutionary force (more specifically, the
analysis of the contribution of illocutionary force to the meaning
of speech acts as such). In this way, the foundational problem
concerning the universalist claim of Habermas's project is transferred *away from* the level of the theory of communication (in
which what had to be demonstrated was the fundamental character of communicative action with respect to any other type of action). It is now transferred to the level of the formal-pragmatic
analysis of speech acts. Here, the equivalent foundational problem is not hard to identify if we take into account the normative
core of such an analysis. It is, namely, the necessary connection
between meaning and validity, which arises from the contribution
of the pragmatic meaning of illocutionary forces to the speech
act as a whole. This connection can only be asserted if one also
maintains the additional thesis that the literal meaning of illocutionary forces (i.e., in their "serious" use, as discussed above) is
more "fundamental" than displaced meanings (i.e., those pro-
ceeding from the "feigned" use of illocutionary forces, which
have no internal connection with validity). For obviously, *only
when the speaker says what she really means is it possible to reach "an
agreement on the pressuposed basis of validity claims that can be mutually
recognized"* (WIUP, p. 3; italics mine).

The need for this additional thesis only underscores further the
universalist claim of Habermas's project. Showing that the "serious" use of language is more than just one possible use of language among others is the singular path that Habermas's project
must take to demonstrate the universal character of communica-

tive rationality. For Habermas not only wants to show that communicative action is merely one possible (and contingent) praxis among others; he also wants to show that it contains an element that is "the necessary regulative for *any actual discourse*" (HCU, pp. 206–207).

Thus the foundational requirement arising from the universalist claim of Habermas's project falls squarely on the shoulders of the analysis of speech acts. But precisely for this reason, the metatheoretical demarcations that this project of "formal pragmatics" establishes cannot eliminate the normative weight inherent in the concept of "understanding" via definition. That is, it is an empty move *to restrict from the outset the success (the acceptability) of a speech act to the "serious" use of language*. However, this is precisely what Habermas does in "What Is Universal Pragmatics?" when he remarks:

I shall speak of the success of a speech act only when the hearer not only understands the meaning of the sentence uttered but also actually enters into the relationship intended by the speaker. And I shall analyze the conditions for the success of speech acts in terms of their "acceptability." Since *I have restricted my examination from the outset to communicative action*—that is, action oriented to reaching understanding—a speech act counts as *acceptable* only if the speaker *not merely feigns but sincerely makes a serious offer*. (WIUP, p. 59; italics mine)

Habermas himself points out the unacceptability of this maneuver in a footnote added in 1983, which I referred to earlier. There, he writes:[18]

At the time I did not realize the problems involved in this restriction mentioned in passing. The thesis that the use of language oriented to reaching understanding is the *original* mode of language use (which I then took to be trivial) requires careful foundational work.[19]

18. Translator's note: This added footnote is not contained in the published English version of "What Is Universal Pragmatics?" I have translated it from the original German version in *Vorstudien und Ergänzungen zur Theorie des kommunikativen Handelns,* p. 429.

19. As noted above, the debate between Searle and Derrida on this topic was initiated one year after the publication of "What Is Universal Pragmatics?" (see Derrida's and Searle's 1977 articles in *Glyph*).

The formulation of this thesis (which is essential to Habermas's theory of communicative action) seems to differ in scope with respect to the initial formulation at the beginning of the paper. The universalism of Habermas's project does not seem to be limited here to asserting the fundamental character of communicative action with respect to strategic action, but rather expands into a thesis about the use of language in general. This difference in scope points to another of the systematic improvements of the original project, improvements that Habermas carries out precisely in order to address the problem here discussed: namely, grounding his theory of communication in a theory of language in general (centered in a pragmatic theory of meaning). Such a theory will have to prove the fundamental character of the use of language oriented toward understanding with respect to any other use "derived" from it. This transformation of the original project, which is meant to preserve its universalism, will be examined in the next section, in which I will discuss the changes introduced in *Theory of Communicative Action*.

4.3   The Systematic Improvements Introduced in *Theory of Communicative Action*

In my discussion of the structural shortcomings of Habermas's project as formulated in "What Is Universal Pragmatics?" I anticipated two types of systematic improvements that *Theory of Communicative Action* incorporates for the formal-pragmatic analysis of action oriented toward understanding.

1. On the one hand, this analysis is now supplemented with a *new perspective*, which, as we saw, seems to overstep the narrow limits of the formal-pragmatic standpoint. The analysis of action oriented toward understanding is no longer restricted to the reconstruction of the unavoidable *pragmatic presuppositions* that constitute this type of action. Rather, going a step further and abandoning the perspective of participants in communication, this analysis involves an investigation of the conditions of possibility of communicative action as such, that is, those conditions that must always already be *given* for this type of action to take place in general.

As pointed out above, the upshot of this enriched combination of perspectives is the introduction of a concept that complements that of communicative action: namely, the concept of "lifeworld," undoubtedly one of the most obscure and problematic concepts of this theory.

This development clearly accentuates the close link between Habermas's account of action oriented toward understanding and the hermeneutic view. As I shall try to show in what follows (4.3.1), this link leads to problems in connection with the three traditional points of conflict between Habermas and hermeneutics, namely:

• with respect to the issue of *universalism.* For understanding now becomes dependent on a factual, particular element, which as we saw in Gadamer both (a) "places limits on the force of reflection" (owing to its holistic structure, not available at will), and (b) contextualizes the validity of understanding (making it relative to a prior and contingent "happening of truth");

• with respect to the issue of linguistic *idealism.* For the linguistic disclosure of the world is now recognized as playing a "constitutive" role in the fore-understanding that makes the explicit understanding between speakers possible; and

• with respect to the issue of *formalism.* For despite the methodological weight of the formal perspective for Habermas's universalist claim, his analysis is now limited by an element that cannot be formalized, given the properties assigned to it from the outset.

2. On the other hand, from the very introduction to *Theory of Communicative Action,* Habermas states the demand that the formal-pragmatic analysis of communicative action be understood as an essential component of a *theory of communicative rationality,* and not merely—as initially planned—as a metatheory directed toward a "foundation of sociology in terms of a theory of language."[20]

20. "Vorlesungen zu einer sprachtheoretischen Grundlegung der Soziologie," in *Vorstudien und Ergänzungen zur Theorie des kommunikativen Handelns,* pp. 11–126.

The universalist core of this demand requires that the scope of Habermas's formal-pragmatic analysis be broadened. This can no longer be understood as a reconstruction of the unavoidable presuppositions of *a particular praxis*—namely, the one he calls "communicative action." Rather, the universal character of communicative action must be proven by putting forward a hypothesis about *language in general:* more specifically, the thesis that the *original use* of language is its "use oriented toward understanding" (that without this use language as such would not be possible). In this way, the theory of communication initially projected leads to a theory of language in general. This forces Habermas to measure his formal-pragmatic analysis against other philosophical positions (without being able to adjudicate between them by appeal to "divisions of labor") (4.3.2).

4.3.1   The Complementarity of Communicative Action and Lifeworld

In chapter 1 of *Theory of Communicative Action,* Habermas introduces the concept of lifeworld as the "correlate of processes of reaching understanding" (p. 70). As he puts it,

Subjects acting communicatively always come to an understanding in the horizon of a lifeworld. Their lifeworld is formed from more or less diffuse, always unproblematic, background convictions. This lifeworld background serves as a source of *situation definitions* that are presupposed by participants as unproblematic. . . . The world-concepts and the corresponding validity claims provide the formal scaffolding with which those acting communicatively order problematic contexts of *situations,* that is, those requiring agreement, in their lifeworld, which is presupposed as unproblematic. (TCA, p. 70; italics mine)

From this brief discussion of the concept of lifeworld as the "correlate of processes of reaching understanding," we can infer that its central status cannot be derived from the trivial, empirical fact that every process of understanding takes place in a particular context, a "here and now." As we saw in "Remarks on the Concept of Communicative Action," Habermas defines the lifeworld as constitutive of processes of understanding (RCCA, p. 591).

The precise sense in which the ambiguous attribute "constitutive" should be understood is not difficult to specify if Habermas's conception of the lifeworld, as a "source of situation definitions that are presupposed by participants as unproblematic" (TCA I, p. 70), is situated in the context of Gadamer's analysis of the model of conversation.

As we saw, the recognition in this analysis of the symbolically mediated character of our relationship with the world (and hence of its intrinsic "variability") makes it necessary to trace the conditions of possibility of understanding to something that guarantees the *unity* of the world-disclosure shared by participants in communication. For understanding between interlocutors can be achieved only against the background of a prior agreement about the subject matter. That is, it can only be achieved when interlocutors talk about the same thing. It is for this reason that Gadamer claimed that "agreement is prior to disagreement" (GW 2, p. 187), that there is a "sustaining agreement" underlying every misunderstanding (GW 2, p. 223).

Thus, after recognizing the impossibility (as Searle saw) of appealing to a naively supposed "literal meaning," it is not surprising that Habermas is in need of a shared "source" from which participants in communication can draw "situation definitions." Identical meanings are not guaranteed by the mere fact that "speech acts are . . . self-identifying" (TCA I, p. 290). For this self-identification is only intelligible against the background of a prereflective knowledge shared by speakers. Therefore identical meanings can be guaranteed only by resorting to something prior, a particular lifeworld that, as a "nexus of meaning" shared by speakers, fixes "the framework of fundamental concepts within which we interpret everything that appears in the world in a specific way as something" (TCA I, p. 58). It is thus the lifeworld that makes it possible for speakers to talk about the same thing.

The model initially proposed by Habermas began by supposing merely (a) the telos of reaching understanding between speaker and hearer, (b) "on the presupposed basis of validity claims that can be mutually recognized" (WIUP, p. 3). But with his introduction of the lifeworld, this "formal reference system" (TCA I,

p. 69) is further situated (c) against the background of a shared "source of situation definitions."

Given this modification, though, it seems difficult to avoid the conclusion that the *counterfactual* agreement that Habermas proposes as the common basis required for reaching an understanding cannot guarantee such an understanding without ultimately appealing to the *factual* sustaining agreement of tradition that Gadamer proposes. That is, it seems unavoidable to appeal to the "linguistically organized stock of background assumptions, which is reproduced in the form of a cultural tradition" (RCCA, p. 591).

Therefore the presuppositions of possible understanding involve not only communicative competence (i.e., *"universal capabilities"*; WIUP p. 14), but also the belonging to a tradition. With this recognition, Habermas offers a more plausible picture (or "probable" picture; see footnote 8) of the specific dialectic that characterizes the "discontinuous intersubjectivity" of ordinary language. As already mentioned, this is the dialectic between an understanding that is *to be* achieved—threatened by an unlimited potential of problematization—and a "prior understanding guaranteed by the lifeworld" (ENT, p. 339), which serves as "the conservative counterweight to the risk of disagreement that arises with every actual process of reaching understanding" (TCA I, p. 70). Among other things, this picture is more plausible because it avoids the problems that result from examining the conditions of possibility of understanding solely from the point of view of the unavoidable presuppositions inherent in the communicative competence of speakers. As we saw with Humboldt, such an attempt necessarily runs into the difficulty of trying to explain understanding as arising *ex nihilo,* from a "zero context." The specific form that the difficulty takes in this view is the impossibility of appealing to a "literal meaning" (and as we saw, this is the root of Habermas's revision of his initial project).

It seems, then, that the way in which Habermas broadens his perspective should be considered as an unavoidable internal development of his project. I will try to show to what extent this is the case when I examine the difficulties underlying the "counterfactual agreement" that Habermas proposes (in his analysis of the conditions of possibility of understanding from the perspective of speakers). As we will see, these difficulties are bound up with the validity claim of "intelligibility" (see 4.4.2).

Clearly, this broadening of perspective brings Habermas's view closer to the theses of hermeneutics. But precisely for this reason, his account of how understanding is possible becomes more plausible only at the cost of endangering the two essential features of his initial project (which distinguish it from hermeneutics), namely its universalism and its formalism.

Regarding the issue of universalism, the problems inherent in the contextualization of the processes of understanding (resulting from this new perspective of analysis) arise at two different levels:

• On the one hand, problems arise with respect to *the very account of the conditions of possibility of understanding*. The introduction of the lifeworld as a constitutive element of the processes of understanding entails the *relativization of any understanding to the factual belonging to a particular tradition*. This unavoidably raises the issue of whether the "validity" of such understanding should not be regarded, as hermeneutics claims, as equally dependent on this factual element (which would thus be a "happening of truth," since it "determines" the prior interpretations of that which is to be assessed as valid or invalid; (see 4.3.1.a).

• On the other hand, these relativistic consequences affect the *scope of the analysis itself*. For according to Habermas's own theory, this analysis necessarily takes place *within* a particular cultural tradition. Therefore it is in danger of merely reconstructing the self-understanding characteristic of this particular tradition, illicitly elavating it to a supposedly universal dimension. This issue will be discussed in the next chapter (5.1.2).

The problem of how to maintain a formal standpoint arises from the inclusion, within Habermas's perspective, of a kind of knowledge characterized by features denoting that which is not susceptible to formalization par excellence. For this knowledge is "implicit," "holistically structured," and "not at the disposal of individuals" (i.e., not subject to thematization "at will"). Once this step is taken, any extension of formal analysis to the structures of this knowledge, or any hypothesis about these structures (or about their degree of "rationalization"), becomes problematic and difficult to discuss or decide (see 4.3.1.b).

4.3.1.a The Lifeworld and the Universalist Claim

So far, I have only sketched the difficulties concerning the introduction of the concept of lifeworld with respect to the *universalist* claim of Habermas's approach. To analyze these difficulties in more detail, I will situate them in the context of the discussion about formal pragmatics in which the concept of lifeworld was introduced.

As we saw in the previous section, the issue motivating Habermas's systematic reform of his project was the problem of literal meaning that arose for the standard theory of speech acts and led Searle to introduce similar changes. Habermas refers to this issue once again when he alludes to the "advantages" of the new perspective gained by the introduction of the concept of lifeworld for the analysis of communicative action:

The concept of action oriented to reaching understanding has the additional—and quite different—advantage of throwing light on this background of implicit knowledge which enters *a tergo* into cooperative processes of interpretation. Communicative action takes place *within a lifeworld* that remains *at the backs* of participants in communication. It is present to them only in the prereflective form of taken-for-granted background assumptions. . . . If the investigations of the last decade in socio-, ethno-, and psycholinguistics converge in any one respect, it is on the often and variously demonstrated point that the collective *background and context* of speakers and hearers *determines* interpretations of their explicit utterances *to an extraordinarily high degree.* Searle has taken up this doctrine of empirical pragmatics and criticized the long dominant view that sentences get *literal meaning* only by virtue of the rules for using expressions contained in them. . . . Searle . . . does defend the thesis that the literal meaning of an expression must be completed by the background of an implicit knowledge that participants normally regard as trivial and obvious. (TCA I, pp. 335–336; italics mine)

In what follows, Habermas goes on to discuss this revision of his initial project. But in this discussion, he indirectly alludes also to the "advantages" of the initial project. As he remarks:

I have also construed the meaning of speech acts as literal meaning [by virtue of the rules for using the expressions contained in them]. Naturally this meaning could not be thought independently of contextual conditions altogether; for each type of speech act there are *general* contextual conditions that must be met if the speaker is to be able to achieve illocutionary success. But these general contextual conditions *could* supposedly *be derived* in turn *from the literal meaning of the linguistic expressions employed in the standard speech acts.* And as a matter of fact, *if formal pragmatics is not to lose its object, knowledge of the conditions* under which speech acts may be *accepted as valid cannot depend completely on contingent background knowledge.* (TCA I, pp. 335–336; italics mine)

On the one hand, as we saw, the normative weight of the formal-pragmatic analysis of speech acts derives from the contribution of the pragmatic meaning to the global meaning of a speech act. That is, it derives from the fact that "we understand a speech act when we know what makes it acceptable." But on the other hand, the knowledge of acceptability conditions depends in turn, for systematic reasons, on a contingent background knowledge that ultimately predetermines the possible validity of the speech act itself. From this, there seem to follow two complementary and equally problematic implications.

In the first place, the attempt to reconstruct the general acceptability conditions of speech acts through a formal-pragmatic analysis faces a twofold difficulty: the reconstruction of these conditions from the perspective of the speakers' unavoidable presuppositions is necessarily incomplete. For those presuppositions may be necessary but in no way sufficient conditions. But a further reconstruction of the acceptability conditions determined by the background knowledge of the lifeworld is in principle impossible, given that its structure is holistic, implicit, and not available at will (see TCA, p. 336). Thus it is not surprising if Habermas fears that the recognition of the constitutive character of the lifeworld might result in the consequence that formal pragmatics will "lose its object" (TCA I, p. 335).

In the second place, a difficulty arises with respect to the scope of the connection between meaning and validity that this analysis makes explicit. For the attempt to establish an indirect link between every understanding of the meaning of an utterance and the assessment of the knowledge contained in such an utterance (i.e., the attempt to put meaning under the control of a constant assessment of its validity) now suffers a curious reversal. This attempt seems to run the risk of resulting in a relativization of "validity" to prior convictions, which determine meaning by distinguishing what is significant from what is absurd (in the sense that "beliefs that do not fit such convictions—convictions that are as beyond question as they are fundamental—appear to be absurd"; TCA, p. 336).

The dependence (or relativization) of validity with respect to a prior decision about meaning is implicit in the trivial fact that for something to be true or false, it must first be meaningful. This is what Wittgenstein alludes to in a remark cited by Habermas in the context of introducing the concept of lifeworld: "If the true is what is grounded, then the ground is neither *true* nor false."[21] It is a short step between this claim and Heidegger's and Gadamer's claim that "the ground" is therefore "the originary truth" (that is, a "happening of truth"). We already traveled this path when discussing the arguments of these authors in the previous chapter.

Once we recognize the constitutive status of the lifeworld, it is difficult to retrace our steps along this argumentative path in such a way as to avoid its consequences (as Habermas tries to do when he contends that the lifeworld does not "completely" determine validity conditions). This difficulty is analogous to that recognized in Gadamer's critique of Humboldt's project: When the linguistic world-disclosure prereflectively available to speakers as background knowledge is recognized as "constitutive" of what can appear in the world, the attempt to avoid the consequent relativization of intraworldly knowledge to linguistic world-disclosures seems hopeless. For this attempt either leads to Humboldt's incongruous attempt to restore the impossible ideal of reaching the "thing in itself," or else it is reduced (as in Habermas's case) to a mere lament, clinging to the (undoubtedly justified) intuition

21. L. Wittgenstein, *On Certainty*, sec. 205.

Language as Medium of Understanding

that such a reification of language is inadmissible, but without being able to say exactly why.

If we take into account the central features that were shown to be characteristic of the view of language in the German tradition, it is clear that the acceptance of the constitutive character of a linguistically structured background knowledge (which pre-interprets the situations in which speakers must reach an agreement) leads to the acceptance of two central theses, namely the thesis that meaning determines reference, and the thesis of meaning holism. In fact, the former was implicit already in Habermas's assumption that the intersubjectivity of communication (the possibility that speakers talk about "the same thing") can be guaranteed only by ensuring identical meanings (that is, by appealing to "literal meaning" or demanding that speech acts "identify" themselves).[22] This assumption becomes entangled with an additional difficulty arising from the recognition of the holistic character of meaning, namely the impossibility of appealing to a literal meaning detached from every context. This difficulty makes unavoidable the recourse to a prior (and unitary) linguistic world-disclosure that guarantees identical meanings de facto. Once this step is taken, the issue of linguistic idealism is brought to the forefront. This kind of idealism in fact already underlay the assumption that meaning determines reference, but it now becomes

22. This is the common assumption shared by hermeneutics and the defenders of a theory of indirect reference in the Anglo-American tradition (precisely those authors on whom Habermas relies). This assumption lies at the basis of the reification of language that has accompanied the linguistic turn in both traditions so far. Habermas does not realize that it is at the level of this basic assumption that there arises the linguistic idealism for which he reproaches hermeneutics, but whose source he does not succeed in identifying. (The reason for this is undoubtedly that he relegates to formal semantics the task of analyzing the cognitive use of language, that is, he relegates it to authors who share this central assumption with hermeneutics.) Precisely for this reason, Habermas *accepts* the conception of language as world-disclosure elaborated by Heidegger (and developed by Gadamer), only to try later to avoid its consequences (without realizing that the reification of language already lies *within* this conception). This central thesis of the present book will provide the topic of the next chapter.

explicit. In his analysis of the concept of lifeworld, Habermas remarks:

> If, as usual in the tradition stemming from Humboldt, we assume that there is *an internal connection between structures of lifeworlds and structures of linguistic worldviews, language and cultural tradition* take on a certain *transcendental* status in relation to everything that can become an element of a situation. . . . Language and culture are *constitutive for the lifeworld itself.* (TCA II, pp. 124–125; italics mine)

With this recognition, Habermas draws in an explicit way the same conclusions from the thesis that meaning determines reference as the authors of the "tradition stemming from Humboldt." What he arrives at is the inevitable view that language is responsible for world-disclosure, in the sense of being constitutive for that worldview which fixes "the framework of fundamental concepts within which we interpret everything that appears in the world in a specific way as something" (TCA I, p. 58).

Once this step is taken—once language is recognized as responsible for a world-disclosure that determines everything that can appear within it—it does not seem possible to avoid the consequence that the validity of our knowledge of the intraworldly depends on the validity conditions previously fixed by such a framework of fundamental concepts (which is subject to historical change). Habermas himself will show the internal logic of this argument when he later discusses the linguistic function of world-disclosure (which was already incorporated in *Theory of Communicative Action* with the concept of lifeworld but was not recognized as such; or which, as he puts it, was "negligently treated" [ENT, p. 336]). In *Nachmetaphysisches Denken* Habermas writes:

> From the theory of meaning we are already acquainted with the internal connection between meaning and validity: we understand the *meaning* of a speech act if we know the *conditions under which it may be accepted as valid. Semantic rules* thus lay down *the conditions of validity* for the sentences or speech acts *possible in a linguistic system. With such contexts of meaning language opens up a horizon of possible actions and experiences for those who belong to the linguistic system. World-disclosing language, as Heidegger says, allows something to be encountered as something in the world.* It is a different question, however, *whether these linguistically projected possibilities also prove their worth* in the intraworldly dealings. (NMD, p. 103; italics mine)

I will discuss later the difficulties connected with Habermas's attempt to retain the idea that language opens up possibilities while nonetheless holding that these possibilities may not prove their worth in the world. These difficulties will be the focus when I examine the structural problems that Habermas inherits from the view of language as responsible for world-disclosure (from his acceptance, more specifically, of the theses underlying this view, namely that meaning is holistic and determines reference; see 4.4).

4.3.1.b Lifeworld and the Formal Perspective
The problems entailed by the introduction of the notion of lifeworld with respect to the possibility of maintaining a formal perspective are even more evident than those concerning the viability of a universalist standpoint.

As already pointed out, the introduction of the lifeworld as constitutive of the processes of understanding poses an obvious problem for the formal-pragmatic analysis of action oriented toward understanding. The normative force of this analysis lies in showing, through a theory of meaning, the indissoluble connection between meaning and validity. But an essential element in this account of meaning is characterized as incapable of being formalized. Thus the prospects of elaborating this theory of meaning by extending the formal analysis to the structures of background knowledge seem, in principle, to be nil. This is owing to three features that Habermas attributes to background knowledge, features that preclude its formalization:

• In the first place, background knowledge is implicit. That is to say, it is not reducible to propositional knowledge. Habermas, like Searle before him, remarks that this implicit knowledge "cannot be represented in a finite number of propositions" (TCA I, p. 336).

• In the second place, "it is a *holistically structured* knowledge, the basic elements of which intrinsically define one another" (ibid.). Years later (see NMD pp. 63–105), Habermas will connect this characterization with the central motif of the discussion about meaning holism as already pointed out by Searle. Namely, there is no possibility of drawing a boundary, within background knowledge, between knowledge of language (or of "meaning") and knowledge of the world.[23] For this reason, Habermas makes the following remark in *Nachmetaphysisches Denken:*

If knowledge of the world is defined on the basis that it is acquired *a posteriori*, whereas knowledge of language, relatively speaking, represents an *a priori* knowledge, then the paradox may be explained by the fact that, in the background of the lifeworld, knowledge of the world and knowledge of language are integrated. (NMD, p. 94).

• In the third place, a further feature that follows from the others is that background knowledge is not at the disposal of speakers. That is to say, it is not susceptible to being brought to consciousness at will. It is on the basis of this feature that Habermas will discuss, in *Nachmetaphysisches Denken,* the "immediate certainty" that characterizes this "knowledge." In substantial agreement with the later Wittgenstein, he remarks:

Such background knowledge lacks an internal relation to the possibility of becoming problematic for it comes into contact with criticizable validity claims, thereby being transformed into fallible knowledge, only at the moment in which it is expressed in language. Absolute certainties remain unshakeable until they suddenly disintegrate; for, in lacking fallibility, they do not constitute knowledge in the strict sense at all. (NMD, p. 92)

When this last feature is added to the other two, what Searle remarked about the attempt to thematize this "knowledge" becomes explicitly clear. The difficulty for reconstructing such knowledge does not consist in a technical difficulty, but represents

---

23. Indeed, the crucial factor in the recognition of this consequence of meaning holism has been Quine's questioning of the distinction between analytic and synthetic knowledge (and hence also between a priori and a posteriori knowledge) in "Two Dogmas of Empiricism." This implication of meaning holism in turn calls into question the possibility of a theory of meaning, as later recognized by Putnam in "Meaning Holism." Habermas, however, recognizes the former implication but not the latter. As a result, certain difficulties ensue that I will discuss later (4.4.1.b).

an impossibility *in principle*. Habermas also makes explicit this consequence when he discusses the peculiarities of the attempt to reconstruct this "knowledge" systematically.

Habermas contends that the ideal method for carrying out this reconstruction is an "analysis of presuppositions." He remarks:

Unthematic knowledge [to which background knowledge belongs] is to be distinguished from merely *concomitantly thematized knowledge* [in a speech act] on the basis that it cannot be made accessible through a simple transformation of the participant's perspective into the observer's perspective; unthematic knowledge requires, rather, an analysis of presuppositions. (NMD, p. 86)

Immediately afterwards, Habermas reminds us of the need to carry out this analysis (in the context of formal pragmatics), when he observes: "it is those presuppositions that are unthematic that the participants in communication must make if a speech act in a given situation is *to be able to take on a specific meaning*, and *if it is to be capable of being valid or invalid* in the first place" (NMD, p. 86; italics mine).

To lend plausibility to this analysis of presuppositions, Habermas goes on to discuss Husserl's procedure of "eidetic variation" and Searle's kindred examples discussed above (his famous variations on the statement "the cat is on the mat"). Habermas describes this procedure as "the free—unrestrained—imagining of modifications of the world, or the projecting of contrasting worlds, that shed light on our expectations of normality—*as unconscious as they are unshakeable and unavailable*—and that may bring to light how the foundations of our everyday practices depend on a *Weltanschauung*" (NMD, p. 91; italics mine).

But the very formulation of this method contains the root of its own impossibility. If we are really dealing with "unshakeable and unavailable certainties," any attempt to find an ideal method to reconstruct them is by definition doomed to failure. Habermas cannot but recognize that

The method of free variation of unavoidable presuppositions soon meets its limits. The background of the lifeworld is just as little at our disposal as we are in a position to subject absolutely everything to abstract doubt.

Rather, Charles S. Peirce, with his pragmatic doubt about this Cartesian doubt, has reminded us that problems that severely unsettle lifeworld certainties come to meet us with the objective power of historical contingencies. (NMD, p. 91).

However, the recognition of this obvious consequence does not lead Habermas to give up the attempt to construct a theory of meaning (although such a theory seems to be forced to reconstruct what by definition cannot be reconstructed). The difficulties concerning Habermas's theory of meaning will be discussed later (4.4.1.b). The internal reasons for Habermas not renouncing this attempt will become clear in what follows, when we examine another systematic improvement introduced in *Theory of Communicative Action*.

4.3.2 The Need to Ground the Theory of Communication in a Theory of Language in General

In light of the analysis of Habermas's approach (at least as he has carried it out so far), it appears that even though language plays a central role in the theory of communicative action, this theory nonetheless does not contain an explicit account of the central theses of the conception of language on which it relies (an account equivalent to the one we found in the authors discussed previously). This is certainly owing to the fact that the goal of Habermas's initial project was not to develop a general account of language, but rather to construct a theory of communication. The construction of this theory does indeed need to be based on a particular conception of language, but it does not seem to require that this conception be made explicit.

However, as remarked above, the universalist core of Habermas's project commits him to a foundational enterprise of larger scope than he previously envisioned. Initially, Habermas's universalism was reflected in his equating of the presuppositions of action oriented toward understanding with the presuppositions of rational speech as such. In *Theory of Communicative Action* this universalism becomes explicit in Habermas's demand that his theory be understood as an attempt to construct a *theory of communicative rationality*. Habermas now needs not only to show that action oriented toward understanding should be understood as more fundamental than strategic action (since the latter cannot explain how the social order is possible); beyond this, as anticipated earlier, he needs to show that the use of language for reaching understanding is the "original" use of language. To substantiate this hypothesis, he is forced to ground his theory of communication in a theory of language in general (see NMD, p. 75).

The internal logic of this extension in Habermas's foundational commitment (which he already made explicit in the remark added to "What Is Universal Pragmatics?" in 1983) can be reconstructed in the following terms. He conceives the analysis carried out in *Theory of Communicative Action* as the attempt to derive "a concept of communicative rationality from the normative content of the general and unavoidable presuppositions of the insurmountable praxis of everyday understanding" (ENT, p. 368). That is, he understands it as the attempt to reconstruct "a voice of reason that cannot be silenced in everyday communicative praxis, whether we want to or not" (ibid.).

As we already saw in Habermas's modification of the initial project (as sketched in "What Is Universal Pragmatics?") the normative core of this reconstruction proceeds from the concept of understanding that it presupposes. Habermas always insists that "reaching understanding is a normatively laden concept that goes beyond the mere understanding of a grammatical expression" (NMD, p. 75). As we have seen, Habermas always uses this notion in the sense of "rationally motivated agreement."

However, the unavoidable presuppositions of "action oriented toward understanding," of that praxis in which participants pursue a rationally motivated agreement, cannot be considered "necessary" in a strict transcendental sense. For as Habermas points out in his "Entgegnung": "a) we can also act in non-communicative ways; and b) the unavoidability of idealized presuppositions does not imply its *de facto* fulfilment" (p. 346).

Therefore, to prove the "universality of communicative rationality" (ibid., p. 335), it is not sufficient to reconstruct the presuppositions of that particular praxis which is communicative action. These presuppositions must be shown to be inherent in the use of language itself (as "the necessary regulative for *all actual speech*"; HCU, pp. 206–207). To prove that the original use of language is its use for reaching understanding is the only path to guarantee precisely that "voice of reason that cannot be silenced in everyday communicative praxis, *whether we want to or not*" (ENT, p. 368; italics mine).

Thus Habermas is committed to showing that the structure of the praxis of communicative action, fraught with normative presuppositions, reflects in fact the structure of *every possible speech act*. That is to say, Habermas must show that the peculiar connection between meaning and validity disclosed by the analysis of action oriented toward understanding is inherent in the understanding of every possible speech act and that, therefore, "the dimension of validity is inherent in language" (ibid., p. 360). Here lies the foundational surplus required to maintain the universality of communicative rationality. Thus, in *Nachmetaphysisches Denken,* he remarks:

One can see from the very conditions for understanding linguistic expressions that *the speech acts* that can be formed with their help have a *built-in orientation toward a rationally motivated agreement with regard to what is said.* To this extent, an orientation toward the possible *validity* of utterances is part of the pragmatic conditions, *not just for reaching understanding but, prior to this, for linguistic understanding itself.* In language, the dimensions of meaning and validity are internally connected. (p. 76; italics mine)

The normative weight of Habermas's theory falls on the shoulders of this last thesis. It is this thesis that leads him to recognize that "the concept of communicative action provisionally introduced here is *based on a particular conception of language* and of reaching an understanding; it has to be developed in the context of theories of meaning" (ibid., p. 75; italics mine).

I will not discuss here to what extent a theory of meaning can render plausible the thesis that the orientation toward a rationally motivated agreement is inherent in linguistic understanding. The only goal of my reconstruction is to show which argumentative paths compel Habermas to develop an account of language as such.

Thus the new task that Habermas has to undertake is to construct a theory of meaning that can explain linguistic understanding (i.e., that can answer the basic question of "what it is to understand the meaning of a linguistic expression"; NMD, p. 76). The important question for our purposes is to what extent this task can be carried out solely with the means established by Habermas for the purposes of a *theory of communication*. In my opinion, this task cannot be tackled without supplementing the account of the *communicative* use of language with an account of its *cognitive* use (which was relegated from the beginning to formal semantics through a tacit division of labor).[24]

24. As pointed out above, the initial project of reconstructing the presuppositions of "action oriented toward understanding" did not encompass an account of language as such, beyond the limits of a theory of communication. This tacit assumption of Habermas's project is the source of his suggested "division of labor" concerning the cognitive and the communicative use of language (this is particularly clear in his early writings and progressively less apparent in later writings). From "the double cognitive/communicative structure of speech" (VSGS, p. 81), reflected in the general form of every speech act (*Mp*), Habermas rightly infers the interdependence of the two uses of language. However, the impact (still noticeable today) of the tacit "division of labor" I have underscored can be seen in the different tasks that Habermas assigns for the analysis of these two uses of language in his Christian Gauss Lectures, namely, a "theory of reference" (VSGS, p. 96) for the cognitive use and a "theory of speech acts" (ibid.) for the communicative use. In the "brief remarks" (ibid.) that Habermas has provided since then for the acccount of the cognitive use of language (i.e., the theory of propositional content), he simply mentions the double task that this account would have to carry out. More specifically, it would have to thematize "identification" and "predication" (which take place through the subject and the predicate of statements, respectively; (see *Vorstudien und Ergänzungen zur Theorie des kommunikativen Handelns*, pp. 96, 395, 413). From these more or less sporadic remarks we can only infer that Habermas takes as valid the traditional theory of reference (or theory of indirect reference, as I shall term it in the next chapter), and hence his implicit acceptance of the underlying thesis that meaning determines reference.

The need for this complementary account becomes evident in the methodological and thematic difficulties that render Habermas's analysis inadequate for carrying out the new task. These difficulties will form the topic of the next section, but they can be summarized briefly as follows:

• From a *thematic* point of view, the pragmatic theory of meaning contained in Habermas's analysis of speech acts does not address the issue of "linguistic understanding" as such. For it does not include (nor can it be extended to include) an account of the understanding of propositional contents (see 4.4.1).

• From a *methodological* point of view, the formal-pragmatic analysis of the validity basis of speech cannot tackle the issue of linguistic understanding. For, as a reconstruction of communicative competence, it relies on and presupposes *linguistic* competence. Action oriented toward understanding begins when "intelligibility" is already in place. But this is too late, as it were, if it is meant to have any bearing on the question of "what it is to understand the meaning of a linguistic expression" (NMD, p. 76; see 4.4.2).

However, these difficulties do not prevent us from tracing the basic premises of the conception of language presupposed by the theory of communicative action, though not yet made explicit by it. It is only in light of these premises that we can assess the prospects of defending the initial universalist claim.

4.4 Structural Problems in Habermas's Conception of Language: The Connection between Meaning and Validity

On the whole, Habermas's account of language as a medium of understanding as sketched so far endorses the fundamental premises of the conception of language found in the Hamann-Herder-Humboldt tradition, which extends down to hermeneutic philosophy.

As discussed at the beginning of this book, the common denominator for the linguistic turn in this tradition can be found in its *rejection of the conception of language as a tool* characteristic of the philosophy of consciousness. The common feature is the refusal to consider language through the model of the name that designates an independently existing object.[25] As we saw, this critique finds a new paradigm in the "concept," whose referent cannot be regarded as existing independently as can the referent of a name. This shift amounts to asserting the identity of language and thought, and thus to recognizing the symbolically mediated character of our relationship with the world.

As we saw, this recognition led to the abandonment of the traditional concept of world as the totality of language-independent entities. The world now appears only in a mediated way, as that

25. Habermas also identifies the linguistic turn with the overcoming of the view of language as a tool, a view characteristic of the philosophy of consciousness. In *Postmetaphysical Thinking*, he remarks: "Traditionally, language was conceived in terms of the model of assigning names to objects and was viewed as an instrument of communication that remained external to the content of thought. The new foundation, already marked out by Humboldt, depended upon turning away from this traditional conceptualization" (PMT, p. 45). The common denominator of the critiques of the instrumental conception of language, in both the German and Anglo-American traditions of the philosophy of language, is the rejection of the paradigm of the "name" as the model for explaining the functioning of language. Habermas also refers to this rejection in his remarks about the evolution of formal semantics. He writes:

> The approach of propositional semantics revolutionizes the older and long dominant referential semantics, according to which language is related to reality as the name is related to its object. The relation of the signified (the meaning) to the signifier (the sign) was thought to be explicable in terms of the relation of the symbol (the meaningful sign) to the designatum (the object referred to). This basic semiotic notion was suitable for the object-centered theory of knowledge in the philosophy of consciousness. In fact, names or designations, indeed all referential terms that we use to identify objects, do as it were establish contact between language and reality. If, however, this part is taken for the whole, a false picture arises. (PMT, p. 61)

What Habermas does not seem to recognize is that the "false picture" arising from the reification of language as world-disclosure that he regrets so much has its source in a symmetrical *pars pro toto* inference which is the opposite of the one he refers to, namely, the complete disregard for the designative function of language (in its internal connection with the possibility of cognitive learning). This issue will be discussed later (5.2).

about which subjects speak, that is, as the totality of possible states of affairs about which speakers must reach an agreement in each case.

With this transformation, language loses its purely empirical status and competes with the transcendental subject for authorship of the synthesis through which the world as such is constituted in its unity. The upshot of the critique of the view of language as tool was that we have access to a referent only through a linguistic sign. In other words, the identity of the referent can only be guaranteed *indirectly* through the identity of meaning (i.e., of the "mode" in which it is presented in language). The unity of the world to which we refer through language is thus necessarily grounded in the unity with which language opens (or "discloses") the world to us. Language, as bearer of the totality of meanings, fixes the categorial framework (the ontology, as it were) of everything that can be talked about, of everything that can "appear" within the world. For this reason, I consider the thesis that meaning determines reference to be the central assumption of the view of language as world-disclosure.

This assumption of the linguistic turn (in both the hermeneutic and Anglo-American traditions) is evident in many of Habermas's claims. This is implicit beginning in the early 1970s, in the strong connection he establishes between intersubjectivity and the identity of shared meanings.[26] But it becomes explicit in the 1980s, in his view of language as world-disclosure, as what makes it possible that "something appear to us as something."[27]

26. In his critique of the philosophy of consciousness in the Christian Gauss Lectures, Habermas remarks:

> Strictly speaking, an *intersubjectively shared experience* cannot be thought without the concept of a communicated *sense,* "shared" by various subjects. *Identical meanings* are not formed in the intentional structure of a solitary subject facing the world. It is only in virtue of the *identical validity* they possess for various subjects that we can assert, meaningfully, that meanings acquire identity. (VSGS, p. 58; italics mine)

27. As we saw above, this becomes patent in Habermas's remark about Heidegger in *Nachmetaphysisches Denken:* "*Semantic rules* thus lay down the conditions of validity for the sentences or speech acts possible *in a linguistic system.* With such

As we have seen, the innovation in Habermas's view from the 1970s to the 1980s is the amending of the initial assumption that the "identity of meaning" is guaranteed by the mere grammatical correction of the utterance. This made it possible to understand "intelligibility" as a validity claim sustained by "literal meaning." When Habermas renounces literal meaning, when he acknowledges the fact of meaning holism (which has always been underscored by hermeneutics against any formalist claim),[28] he has to resort to the same element as hermeneutics to guarantee identical meanings, namely the factual linguistic world-disclosure shared by the members of a given, particular lifeworld.

With this amendment to his initial view, Habermas also recognizes the hermeneutic *twofold perspective* for the analysis of the "discontinuous intersubjectivity" of ordinary language. According to this twofold perspective, intersubjectivity is to be considered not only (*a fronte*) as the result of a search for understanding among participants in conversation. It is also to be considered (*a tergo*) as the condition of possibility that must always already be given for that search to get off the ground.

---

contexts of meaning language opens up a horizon of possible actions and experiences for those who belong to the linguistic system. *World-disclosing language, as Heidegger says, allows something to be encountered as something in the world"* (NMD, p. 103; italics mine).

28. In "Zwischen Phänomenologie und Dialektik: Versuch einer Selbstkritik" Gadamer writes:

No one can reconstruct what it is in fact that contemporary linguistics calls "linguistic competence." Obviously what this is cannot be objectively represented as the set of what is linguistically correct. By "competence" it is meant that the speaker's linguistic capacity cannot be described as a mere application of rules and hence cannot be understood simply as the rule-governed use of language. . . . A fundamental part of my own attempt to defend hermeneutically the universality of linguisticity is that I consider language learning and the acquisition of a worldview as inextricable elements in the history of the formation of humanity. . . . We can use the analogy of learning a second language. In general, in this case we can only speak of an approximation to linguistic competence. . . . What this reveals is that we learn to look at the world through the eyes of our mother tongue and, conversely, that the first development of one's own linguistic capacity becomes articulated on the basis of the world by which one is surrounded. (GW 2, pp. 5–6)

But with this, Habermas seems to grant implicitly to hermeneutics that which was the essential core of his disagreement with it (and also the *raison d'être* of the very project of a theory of communicative action). That is, he seems to grant the insufficiency of including as the condition of possibility of understanding a counterfactual "sustaining agreement" that comprises the unavoidable presuppositions of action oriented toward understanding. For this action depends also on the prior existence of a factual sustaining agreement, transmitted by a cultural tradition and responsible for linguistic world-disclosure. Only this factual sustaining agreement can give unity to the world and thus render accessible that about which an understanding has to be reached.

By broadening his initial project in this way, Habermas endangers in a peculiar manner the connection between meaning and validity that constitutes the normative core of the formal-pragmatic analysis of the presuppositions of communicative action. For as we saw in the discussion of the hermeneutic view, the recognition of linguistic world-disclosure as constitutive of our intraworldly experience (that is, as the correlate of the transcendental subject after the linguistic turn) transforms the linguistically structured and culturally transmitted realm of meanings into a "happening of truth." That is, it confers normative authority upon this realm, treating it as the original source of the validity of all intraworldly knowledge, despite its contingency and variability (its detranscendentalized status as "cultural tradition").

Thus the constitution of meaning does not appear to be under the control of universal validity claims that are susceptible to cognitive examination and internally tied to reasons. Far from it: validity claims necessarily become relativized to a prior realm of meanings that prejudices every intraworldly experience without being in turn subject to the "control" of experience. Thus, as Habermas points out in *The Philosophical Discourse of Modernity,* "the internal connection between meaning and validity is . . . undone now from the other side and swallowed by the dimension of validity" (p. 321).

To avoid the relativistic consequences of this peculiar connection between meaning and validity (inherent in the view of languagc as world-disclosure), Habermas finds himself forced to *extend the scope* of the opposite connection between meaning and validity—a connection disclosed by the formal-pragmatic reconstruction of the presuppositions of action oriented toward understanding (that is, by his theory of communication). This extension encompasses a general theory of language itself, in which linguistic world-disclosure is placed under the control of universal validity claims presupposed in communication. (That is to say, it is placed under the control of the "yes/no" positions of participants, which establish a potential connection between their utterances and arguments about their validity). This extension is already made explicit by Habermas in his "Entgegnung," where he remarks:

The concept of communicative rationality, however, extends not only to the voluntary processes of consensus formation, but also to the structures of "being-already-in-agreement" in an intersubjectively shared lifeworld. Insofar as it is a horizon that determines context, this lifeworld limits the speech situation. At the same time, insofar as it is a prereflective, unproblematic background, it is constitutive of the resulting understanding. Lifeworld and communicative action complement each other. Therefore, *communicative rationality is as much embodied in the structures of the continuous intersubjectivity of "prior-agreement" guaranteed by the lifeworld, as in the structures of the discontinuous intersubjectivity of possible understanding, to be produced in each case by the agents themselves.* Since particular forms of life are reproduced through the medium of action guided by validity claims, the material a prioris of the linguistically constituted "worldviews," inherent in each form of life, are subject to a constant test. They must prove their worth in the intraworldly praxis and become transformed in the whirlpool of the processes of intraworldly learning. In the polarity between a prior "being-in-agreement" and an agreement to be produced there lies the dynamics of the communicatively structured lifeworld: its forms of reproduction move from one pole to the other over time. (ENT, pp. 339–340; italics mine)

Thus it appears once again that the normative element that controls linguistic world-disclosure is the "counterfactual sustaining agreement" inherent in everyday communicative praxis: the unavoidable presuppositions of action oriented toward understanding. As Habermas remarks in *Postmetaphysical Thinking*:

On the one hand, these subjects always find themselves already in a linguistically structured and disclosed world; they live off of grammatically projected interconnections of meaning. To this extent, language sets itself off from the speaking subjects as something antecedent and objective, as the structure that forges conditions of possibility. On the other hand, *the linguistically disclosed and structured lifeworld* finds its footing only in the practices of reaching understanding within a linguistic community. In this way, the linguistic formation of consensus, by means of which interactions link up in space and time, *remains dependent upon the autonomous "yes" and "no" positions that communication participants take toward criticizable validity claims.* (p. 43; italics mine)

In what follows, I will analyze the difficulties faced by Habermas's attempt to make this thesis plausible. More specifically, we will examine the unavoidable problems bound up with the attempt to place linguistic world-disclosure, which is "constitutive of the processes of understanding," under the control of these very processes. This analysis requires an examination of the normative core of the connection between meaning and validity claimed by Habermas. I will carry out this examination from two distinct but complementary perspectives.

In the first place, I will analyze the theory of language, or *pragmatic theory of meaning,* that Habermas proposes in order to justify the internal connection between meaning and validity. Here, I will try to make clear why the attempt to construct a theory of meaning that reduces meaning to possible validity is doomed to failure. Either this theory is limited to the analysis of the pragmatic meaning of illocutionary forces, in virtue of which speech acts are connected to validity claims; this would leave unanalyzed the background knowledge that determines the acceptability conditions and hence the very "understanding" of speech acts. Or alternatively, this theory may attempt to extend the analysis to background knowledge itself. In the first case, however, the restriction of the domain of analysis makes it impossible to maintain the connection between meaning and validity beyond the praxis of possible understanding: that is, at the level of "the understanding of language itself." But in the second case, the analysis runs into a difficulty inherent in meaning holism itself: the impossibility of a theory of meaning (4.4.1).

If the possibility of defending the connection between meaning and validity in this way turns out to be untenable, the only remaining possibility is to defend it along the second argumentative path pointed out by Habermas in relation to everyday communicative praxis. That is, it has to be defended through appeal to the dependence of the linguistic world-disclosure "upon the autonomous 'yes' and 'no' positions that communication participants take toward criticizable validity claims" (PT, p. 43).

In the second place, to assess the viability of this second line of argument, I will examine Habermas's *theory of communication*. That is, I will examine the formal-pragmatic analysis of the unavoidable presuppositions of communicative action. I will try to show why this second strategy for the defense of the connection between meaning and validity is also not feasible, why the background knowledge arising from the linguistic world-disclosure cannot be placed under the control of (discursively redeemable) validity claims. As already pointed out, the difficulty can be anticipated from a methodological point of view if we take into account that Habermas's theory of communication analyzes only the unavoidable presuppositions underlying the participants' search for understanding *intentione recta* (*a fronte*). In this sense his analysis starts too late, as it were, to give support to the thesis that communicative rationality is already "embodied in the structures of the continuous intersubjectivity of 'prior-agreement' guaranteed by the lifeworld" (ENT, pp. 339–340).

The negative results of this examination will lead us to search, not for a basis to undermine the normative weight given to the linguistic world-disclosure (as "constitutive" of our intraworldly experience), but for one that allows us to transfer the alleged normative character of particular, contingent world-disclosures, to the *formal structures inherent in language as such (in its cognitive use)*. Accordingly, this can be understood as the search for a correlate of the formalist and universalist perspective that Habermas defends with respect to the communicative use of language in the analysis of its cognitive use (chapter 5).

4.4.1   The Difficulties of a Pragmatic Theory of Meaning

The internal connection between meaning and validity disclosed by Habermas's formal-pragmatic analysis of communicative action found expression in the central claim of his *Theory of Communicative Action,* namely that "we understand a speech act when we know what makes it acceptable." Given the foundational requirements already discussed, this connection becomes the normative core of a formal-pragmatic theory of meaning intended to show that: "The dimension of validity thus inheres in language. The orientation toward validity claims belongs to the pragmatic conditions not only of possible mutual understanding, *but already of understanding language itself"* (NMD, p. 78; italics mine).

This important addition to Habermas's claim in *Theory of Communicative Action* requires going beyond a theory of communication (for the reconstruction of the pragmatic conditions of possible understanding), and articulating a theory of the "understanding of language itself," that is, a theory of meaning. This is what forces Habermas to defend the superiority of a formal-pragmatic theory of meaning over the alternatives available in the current philosophical discussion. This occurs in his "Entgegnung" (pp. 353–377), and more fully in *Nachmetaphysisches Denken* (pp. 63–152).

However, when we reflected on this broadening of Habermas's perspective, a fundamental issue arose. This issue will guide my discussion of the formal-pragmatic theory of meaning he proposes. The issue is as follows. Are the elements elaborated by Habermas in his *theory of communication* sufficient to develop a theory of meaning that can reconstruct not just the conditions of mutual understanding in communication, but also the conditions of the understanding of language as such? As I will try to show, this task requires complementing the analysis of the *communicative* use of language with an account of its *cognitive* use (which Habermas relegates from the outset to formal semantics). This necessary supplementation will enable us to question the reification inherent in the view of language as world-disclosure. However, we will thereby be forced to go beyond the (highly problematic) attempt to construct a theory of meaning in the manner of formal semantics (4.4.1.b), arguing for the need for a theory of reference (chapter 5). In light of this, I will discuss the difficulties inherent in Habermas's view, difficulties that in my opinion provide indirect support for my assessment of his theory of meaning. I will try to show that they cannot be solved by means of internal changes, but are rather difficulties *in principle,* of both a methodological and thematic character.

On the one hand, the methodological decision characteristic of the *pragmatic* approach is indeed adequate for a theory of communication developed by means of the analysis of speech acts. However, this decision cannot be extended with equal success to a theory of meaning; *understanding language is not an action.* This difficulty reveals the *internal reasons* that motivate the tacit division of labor, in virtue of which Habermas has always declined the task of carrying out an analysis of the propositional content of speech acts. However, if this analysis (repeatedly postponed) is not possible from a formal-pragmatic perspective, Habermas's pragmatic theory of meaning cannot aspire to be regarded *as* such a theory (4.4.1.a).

On the other hand, this theory of meaning faces the difficulty that threatens every attempt to articulate such a theory, and which has led most authors to regard as *impossible* the very task of articulating a theory of meaning. This is the thesis of meaning holism, which Habermas endorses without yet drawing any conclusions in this direction (although he relies on none other than Dummett, one of the few authors who deny meaning holism, *precisely* because its acceptance leads to the rejection of the possibility of a theory of meaning). This peculiarity of Habermas's position is internally related to his aforementioned systematic disregard for an analysis of propositional content (4.4.1.b).

4.4.1.a   The Standpoint of Formal Pragmatics

We need to analyze the scope of the formal-pragmatic perspective in order to assess whether it can answer "the basic question of a theory of meaning, namely: what it is to understand the meaning of a linguistic expression" (NMD, p. 76). To shed light on this issue, I will discuss Habermas's reconstruction of the development of perspectives in the theory of meaning in this century, which appears in his *Nachmetaphysisches Denken*. This reconstruction is entitled "The Pragmatic Turn in the Theory of Meaning"; its goal is to show the superiority of the formal-pragmatic perspective over the other standard approaches in the discussion of meaning.

Habermas argues that the superiority of this perspective lies in the fact that when the speech act is taken as the most basic unit of understanding, we can account for the three basic aspects of communication: "reaching understanding/with another/about something." These aspects are reflected in

the triadic relation between the meaning of a linguistic expression and (a) what is *meant* with it [*dem Gemeinten*], (b) what is *said* in it [*dem Gesagten*], and (c) the way in which it is used in a speech act. (NMD, p. 77)

We have to assess the scope of the formal-pragmatic perspective precisely in relation to this claim of completeness. The basic assumption of Habermas's pragmatic theory of meaning was already expressed in *Theory of Communicative Action* with the claim that "*we understand a speech act when we know what makes it acceptable*" (TCA I, p. 297). This claim seems to suggest that the "knowledge of meaning" (*Bedeutungswissen*) that a speaker must have in order to understand a speech act is knowledge of the "acceptability conditions" of the speech act in question. Thus, Habermas goes on to remark: "From the standpoint of the speaker, the *conditions of acceptability* are identical to the *conditions for his illocutionary success.* . . . A speech act may be called 'acceptable' if it satisfies the conditions that are necessary in order that the hearer be allowed to take a 'yes' position on the claim raised by the speaker" (ibid., pp. 297–298; italics mine).

However, with this last clarification, Habermas seems to reduce the conditions for understanding a speech act to one of the three aspects identified as constitutive of every speech act, namely reaching an understanding "with another." The relation of the meaning of a linguistic expression with (a) what is meant with it and (b) what is said in it disappears in Habermas's account of meaning, which is exclusively oriented toward the conditions for illocutionary success as such.[29]

With respect to the first aspect, the intentional dimension of communication, Habermas's exclusion is explicit (although not thereby less problematic, as discussed above; see footnote 18). Once again, Habermas appeals to the assumption of a "literal meaning" (this time in relation with the "serious use of language"), and solves the problem via definition:

> To be sure, formal pragmatics must also take measures to see that in the standard case *what is meant* does not deviate from *the literal meaning of what is said* [italics mine]. For this reason, our analysis is limited to speech acts carried out *under standard conditions*. And this is intended to ensure that the speaker means nothing else than the literal meaning of what he says. (TCA I, p. 297)

Putting aside the foundational problems that, as we have seen, arise for Habermas in relation to this prior "limitation," it could well be that this exclusion is productive (or even indispensable) for the construction of a theory of meaning. At any rate, I will not cast doubt on this methodological decision.

For the purposes of my discussion, I will focus on the second component of speech acts that seems to be excluded from Habermas's theory of meaning, namely, the relation of the meaning of a linguistic expression with "what is *said*" in a speech act. For as is well known, what constitutes the basic structure of *every speech act* (Mp) is not only its illocutionary force, but also and necessarily its propositional content.

Viewed in this light, the criterion of meaning that Habermas proposes seems to contain, at most, a *necessary* condition for understanding a speech act, but not a *sufficient* condition. The understanding of "acceptability conditions" (i.e., of the conditions for the "illocutionary success" of a speech act) does not guarantee the understanding of the speech act. For such an understanding necessarily requires that we know:

29. See footnote 31.

• the pragmatic meaning of the utterance (its illocutionary force), but certainly also

• the linguistic meaning of the propositional content.

However, as concerns this apparent difficulty involved in the criterion of meaning proposed by Habermas, we can already find an argument that he himself employs in "What Is Universal Pragmatics?"—namely, the peculiar "self-referentiality" of natural languages (which makes it possible to determine the relation between illocutionary force and propositional content). As Habermas says in *Postmetaphysical Thinking:*

The acts carried out in a natural language are always self-referential. They say both *how what is said is to be employed and how it is to be understood.* This reflexive structure of everyday language is tangible in the grammatical form of the individual speech act. *The illocutionary portion establishes the sense in which the propositional content is being employed* and the sort of action which the utterance should be understood as. (p. 64; italics mine)

This claim seems to suggest that not only the speech act *qua act,* but also its *content* can become determinate in virtue of the illocutionary component. What underlies this argument is the covert attempt to attribute self-transparency to speech acts (by reducing meaning to *pragmatic* meaning). But this attempt leads the formal-pragmatic theory of meaning into a blind alley: either it formulates a tautology, or it is false.

If the criterion of meaning implicit in the claim that "we understand a speech act when we know what makes it acceptable" only affects the pragmatic meaning (that is, the spectrum of illocutionary forces that connects a speech act with "validity claims" and "references to reality"), the content of this claim is vacuous. It is obvious, for example, that we understand an assertion when we know what asserting consists in, that we understand a command when we know what giving a command consists in, and so forth. (For this is always necessarily true, independently of how we explain these activities.) However, there is an obvious difference between this general understanding and the understanding of a particular assertion. One can identify a speech act as an assertion that, as such, lays a claim to truth and thus refers to the objective world (say, in the context of a lecture on nuclear physics), without one's having the faintest idea what is said in the assertion in question. (This would remain the case even if the "pragmatic" understanding enables one to determine what "kind of reasons" would support such an assertion, guaranteeing the illocutionary success of the speech act.) An analysis of this general understanding cannot claim, therefore, to be a theory of meaning.

On the other hand, according to Habermas's suggestion about the self-referentiality of speech acts, the illocutionary component of a speech act not only embraces the "pragmatic meaning" that determines "the sort of action which the utterance should be understood as." Further, it also establishes "the *sense* in which the propositional content is being employed" (italics mine). If we are to take this suggestion seriously, such a theory of meaning is simply false. The illocutionary component can determine itself as a *type of action,* but it cannot substitute or play the role of the background knowledge that, according to Habermas, enables speakers to understand "what is said" as such. This becomes clear in his own account of the ability of speech acts to "identify themselves":

Because in carrying out an illocutionary act a speaker simultaneously *says* what he *is doing,* a hearer *who understands the meaning of what is said* [italics mine] can, without further ado, identify the performed act as some specific action. (NMD, p. 64)

What this claim makes clear is simply that Habermas's pragmatic theory of meaning cannot account for that "strong presupposition" which lies at the basis of the formal-pragmatic analysis of speech acts (or better, of their "pragmatic meaning") carried out by his theory of communication. Habermas makes this presupposition explicit when he points out (against Searle's intentionalism), "what is always already presupposed in the intersubjectivist's description of the process of *communication* [is] the system of rules which fixes the meaning of a conventionally produced expression" (ibid., p. 137; italics mine).

Indeed, the pragmatic standpoint relies on this peculiar capacity of speech acts to "identify themselves." (That is, it relies on their *performative* character, as already shown by Austin and Wittgenstein.) On this basis, the pragmatic standpoint can reconstruct the presuppositions constitutive of communicative praxis (in the same way that we can reconstruct the rules underlying any intentional behavior). However, as soon as we direct our attention to the propositional content, *the pragmatic standpoint vanishes: understanding a language is not an action.* This is the internal explanation why the pragmatic perspective as such cannot be extended to account for meaning in general. This becomes explicit in one of Habermas's many remarks concerning the peculiarity of speech acts which, for him, makes this extension possible. As he remarks:

Speech acts interpret themselves: they have a self-referential structure. The illocutionary element establishes, as a kind of *pragmatic* commentary, the sense in which what is said is being *used.* Austin's insight that one does something by saying something has a reverse side to it: by performing a speech act one also says what one is doing. Admittedly, this performative sense of a speech act reveals itself only to a *potential hearer* who, in adopting the stance of a second person, has given up the perspective of an observer in favor of that of a *participant. One has to speak the same language and, as it were, enter the intersubjectively shared lifeworld of a linguistic community in order to benefit from the peculiar reflexivity of natural language.* (NMD, p. 65; italics mine)

If we take this insight seriously, it seems obvious that the criterion of meaning postulated by Habermas's formal-pragmatic theory would have to include this element of the shared lifeworld, and be formulated instead in the following terms: "We understand a speech act when we know what makes it acceptable and when we share a common language." The only problem with this extension of Habermas's principle concerns his attempt to make a (normative) claim about "the understanding of language itself" (NMD, p. 78). If this attempt aims at articulating a theory of meaning in the strict sense by saying that "we understand a speech act when we know what makes it acceptable and when we share a common language," it would appear that such an attempt comes dangerously close to stating that a theory of meaning is a definition of validity plus a theory of meaning (to paraphrase Putnam's critique of Davidson).[30]

This problem seems to substantiate our initial fear that what can be taken for granted in a theory of communication without landing in explanatory vacuity (namely, the existence of a shared language that lies concealed in the presupposition of intelligibility) can only be assumed in a theory of meaning at the risk of presupposing what is to be explained: "the understanding of language."

Keeping this problem in mind, let us look back to the starting point, to Habermas's thesis of the superiority of the formal-pragmatic perspective over all others (in virtue of its nonreductive standpoint that encompasses the three key aspects of communication). It now appears that with respect to the second aspect, "what is said," this perspective cannot compete with formal semantics, but actually *presupposes* it. The analysis of the pragmatic meaning of a speech act presupposes the analysis of the linguistic meaning of its propositional content. The former only reconstructs the "knowledge of meaning" shared by competent speakers with regard to the use of illocutionary forces (that is, of performative verbs); the latter reconstructs the rest of that "knowledge of meaning" (*Bedeutungswissen*).[31]

---

30. In "The Meaning of 'Meaning' " Putnam criticizes Davidson's thesis that a theory of meaning "might be modeled on . . . a *truth definition* for a formalized language" (pp. 258–259). He remarks: "This comes perilously close to saying that a theory of meaning is a truth definition plus a theory of meaning" (p. 260). The difficulties that Putnam points out with respect to "reductionist" attempts to articulate a theory of meaning certainly also affect Habermas's attempt to "reduce" meaning to "possible validity."

31. This is supported by some of Habermas's own claims such as the following:

A hearer understands the meaning of an utterance when, *in addition to grammatical conditions of well-formedness and general contextual conditions,* he knows those *essential conditions* under which he could be motivated by a speaker to take an affirmative position. These *acceptability conditions in the narrower sense relate to the illocutionary meaning* that [the speaker] expresses by means of *a performative clause.* (TCA I, p. 298; italics mine)

Wellmer takes the same line in his critical discussion of Habermas's pragmatic theory of meaning. In "What Is a Pragmatic Theory of Meaning?" he writes:

[Habermas's] principle of meaning for assertions is not the basic constructive principle for an incipient theory of meaning still to be worked out but rather indicates the manner by which insights of truth semantics should be "taken up" [*aufgehoben*] in a pragmatic theory of language. At the same time, the peculiar incommensurability of formal pragmatics and truth semantics finds its source here, inasmuch as formal pragmatics seeks to reconstruct a different *kind* of linguistic knowledge [*Sprachwissen*] than does truth semantics. In fact, one might say it does not meddle at all in the problematic details of truth semantics but simply says in a general way what *place* these problems have within a pragmatic theory of language. (p. 193; italics mine)

As pointed out earlier, this viewpoint does indeed restrict the scope of the pragmatic theory of meaning to an analysis of the illocutionary component of speech acts. Wellmer goes on to remark:

The formulation of those *general* acceptability conditions would be, to use Habermasian terminology, a formal pragmatics in the *narrow* sense, a theory of the meaning of pragmatic indicators, which are, roughly speaking, performative verbs. (ibid., p. 195).

The consequences of this restriction are obvious. As he adds:

Such a formal pragmatics would not necessarily compete with a truth semantics; one could rather view them as complementary, as Dummett has also proposed. (ibid.)[32]

32. In "What Is a Theory of Meaning? (II)" Dummett remarks:

The theory of reference and the theory of sense together form one part of the theory of meaning: the other, supplementary, part is the theory of force. The theory of force will give an account of the various types of conventional significance which the utterance of a sentence may have, that is, the various kinds of linguistic act which may be effected by such an utterance, such as making an assertion, giving a command, making a request, etc. (p. 74)

However, the difference between Dummett's and Habermas's views becomes clear when Dummett adds: "Such an account will take the truth condition of the sentence as given: for each type of linguistic act, it will present a uniform account of the act of that type which may be effected by the utterance of an arbitrary sentence whose truth condition is presupposed as known" (ibid.).

As discussed earlier, this "division of labor" between formal semantics and pragmatics is precisely what Habermas seemed to appeal to in his Christian Gauss Lectures. There, he distinguished between a *theory of speech acts* and a *theory of reference*. The task of the former would be to analyze "pragmatic universals" from the standpoint of the "production of interpersonal relations" (that is, to analyze the communicative use of language). The task of the latter would be to analyze such universals from the standpoint of the "constitution of object domains" (that is, to analyze the cognitive use of language) (see VSGS, p. 96). Since an analysis of the latter kind would investigate the "acts of reference and predication," it would try to reconstruct the knowledge of meaning (*Bedeutungswissen*) that forms the object of study of formal semantics. In "What Is Universal Pragmatics?" Habermas describes the theory of elementary propositions as follows:

The theory of elementary propositions examines the propositional content from the viewpoint of a formal-semantic analysis of statements. (p. 33)

However, in *Theory of Communicative Action* Habermas seems to deny categorically this supposed division of labor with formal semantics, when he gives a negative answer to the following rhetorical question:

Isn't a theory of speech acts, which hopes to explain the illocutionary binding effect through a warrant offered by the speaker for the validity of what he says and through a corresponding rational motivation on the part of hearer, dependent in turn on a theory of meaning that explains under what conditions the sentences employed are valid? In this debate we are not concerned with questions of territorial boundaries or of nominal definitions but with whether *the concept of the validity of a sentence* can be explicated independently of *the concept of redeeming the validity claim raised through the utterance of the sentence*. I am defending the thesis that this is not possible. (TCA I, p. 316)

Habermas's answer reveals that the incompatibility between formal semantics and pragmatics actually belongs to a different level than the one we have considered. If we situate this answer in the argumentative context of our discussion, it appears that the incompatibility that Habermas underscores actually indicates a deep compatibility, not only in *thematic* scope (where the issue of their relation becomes in fact a problem of demarcation), but also in *methodological* issues, where Habermas claims that formal semantics and pragmatics are in principle incompatible.

On the one hand, there is a clear compatibility in *thematic scope* between formal semantics and pragmatics in Habermas's pragmatic theory of meaning. It is obvious that he has never seriously tried to analyze the acts of reference and predication inherent in the propositional content of speech acts. This is not surprising, given that the systematic starting point of his theory is the assumption that by sharing a common language, speakers already understand the meaning of what is said (an analysis of which is left, therefore, to others). As we have seen, the problem of this assumption (which is more than adequate for a theory of communication) is that it undercuts Habermas's attempt to make any claim about "the pragmatic conditions not only of possible mutual understanding, but already of understanding language itself" (NMD, p. 78). Habermas cannot maintain the tacit division of labor with formal semantics (which, from the thematic point of view, he has assumed from the beginning) if his pragmatic theory of meaning is to be regarded *as* such a theory at all in the context of the current philosophical discussion. The extension of Habermas's analysis to the cognitive use of language (i.e., to "acts of reference and predication" inherent in propositional contents) would thus be the only path to prove the worth of the basic intuition of his theory of meaning, namely, that "the dimension of validity inheres in language" (ENT, p. 360). And the attempt to carry out this analysis would then perhaps lead to the conclusion that the path of formal semantics (i.e., the attempt to articulate a theory of reference through the detour of a theory of meaning) is by no means the best path. I will discuss this issue in the next chapter.

On the other hand, a deep compatibility between formal semantics and pragmatics can also be recognized with respect to *methodological* issues, where Habermas claims superiority for the pragmatic over the semantic standpoint. Habermas contends that as a result of its internal evolution, formal semantics is forced to take a pragmatic turn. His criticism of formal semantics thus makes clear a deep continuity with formal pragmatics (beyond the explicit break). This is underscored by Habermas himself, when he remarks:

My proposals [concerning a pragmatic theory of meaning] can be understood as an *internally motivated extension* of formal semantics. (ENT, p. 354)

According to Habermas's critical reconstruction of the evolution that has taken place in the philosophical discussion about meaning in this century, the normative core of the pragmatic theory of meaning (i.e., the connection between meaning and validity) finds its forerunner in the evolution of formal semantics starting from Frege, which tries to explain the meaning of statements in terms of their truth conditions. The verificationist approach to meaning currently defended by Dummett provides the basis for Habermas's attempt to show the need for a "pragmatic" turn. This becomes clear in his dispute with formal semantics mentioned above. Habermas's argument against Dummett's approach is as follows:

Semantic investigations of descriptive, expressive, and normative sentences, if only they are carried through consistently enough, force us to change the level of analysis. The very analysis of the conditions of the validity of sentences *by itself* compels us to analyze the conditions for the intersubjective recognition of corresponding validity claims. An example of this can be found in Michael Dummett's development of truth-conditional semantics. (TCA I, p. 316)

The development undergone by Dummett's approach points, in Habermas's opinion, in the direction of a formal-pragmatic theory of meaning. For in Dummett's view, truth-conditions are, in a first phase, epistemologized and interpreted in terms of "acceptability conditions," and in a second phase, relativized to an indirect knowledge of the reasons that warrant acceptability in each case. Concerning the last phase of Dummett's approach, Habermas remarks:

Truth-conditional semantics in its revised form takes into consideration the fact that truth conditions cannot be explicated apart from knowing how to redeem a corresponding truth claim. To understand an assertion is to know when a speaker has good grounds to undertake a warrant that the conditions for the truth of the asserted sentence are satisfied. (TCA I, 318)

The common assumption of formal semantics and formal pragmatics is, then, the intuition characteristic of a verificationist theory of meaning, according to which meaning can only be explicated in terms of acceptability conditions, that is, validity. The important extension of this perspective proposed by formal pragmatics occurs in two ways. On the one hand, it extends the connection between meaning and validity beyond truth to cover truthfulness and rightness. On the other hand, as a result, it does not restrict the analysis to assertoric sentences, but also extends it to expressive and normative sentences.

Therefore, if the basic assumption of truth-conditional semantics could be maintained, if it were possible to construct a theory of meaning on this ground, the plausibility of a pragmatic theory of meaning would be reinforced—if only by maintaining the weak version of the conflict between pragmatics and semantics pointed out by Wellmer. According to this version, formal pragmatics constitutes a broader perspective and allots to formal semantics its proper place (thereby tacitly relegating the "acts of reference and predication" involved in linguistic competence to the analysis of formal semantics). However, with this assumption, the pragmatic theory of meaning runs into difficulties of another kind which, as we shall see in what follows, threaten its plausibility even more.

4.4.1.b Meaning Holism

The goal of the formal-pragmatic theory of meaning is to reconstruct that "knowledge of meaning" which speakers have in virtue of the pragmatic and semantic presuppositions inherent in their speech acts. This knowledge enables speakers to understand "what is said" indirectly, through the knowledge of the acceptability conditions of speech acts.

Assuming that such a project for the reconstruction of the knowledge of meaning could avoid the limitations discussed so far, that is, assuming that it could account for the speech act in its entirety (including both its illocutionary component and its propositional content), it would still be faced with structural difficulties. These difficulties do not depend on the particular strategy chosen to carry out the analysis; rather, they are inherent in the very idea of reducing meaning to "possible validity" (reducing "knowledge of meaning" to "knowledge of acceptability conditions").

The structural difficulties at issue have been underscored in the multiple critiques directed against the different versions of the verificationist view of meaning in recent decades. But before discussing these difficulties, I want to call attention to a peculiar circumstance: The arguments raised against the possibility of a theory of meaning (emphatically rejected by the defenders of a verificationist standpoint, especially Dummett) are accepted and even developed at length by Habermas, who shows no indication of being aware of the challenge posed by these arguments for any attempt to construct a theory of meaning. In particular, what gives rise to this circumstance are the destructive consequences that result from Habermas's characterization of background knowledge as constitutive for understanding (since it determines meaning) and as having a holistic structure, which makes it impossible to draw a sharp boundary within this background knowledge between knowledge of meaning (*Bedeutungswissen*) and knowledge of the world (*Weltwissen*).

This circumstance certainly simplifies our discussion of the possibility of a theory of meaning in Habermas's case. For in the case of Dummett, it would be necessary to give arguments for meaning holism and against the "molecular" conception he defends. But in the case of Habermas, this is unnecessary, since he himself provides arguments for meaning holism.

The acceptance of meaning holism leads to difficulties of two different though interrelated kinds. On the one hand, with respect to the attempt to identify the speakers' knowledge of meaning with their knowledge of the acceptability conditions of speech acts, there emerges the same difficulty that is present for the understanding of standard speech acts. Thus Habermas remarks in *Nachmetaphysisches Denken:*

the *meaning of speech acts* remains *indeterminate* until their semantically fixed validity conditions have been supplemented by intuitively known, implicit *background assumptions* that remain unthematic and are presumed to be completely unproblematic. (p. 91; italics mine)

It is clear that the knowledge of the acceptability conditions of a speech act can only lead to the understanding of the speech act if the speaker also possesses the background knowledge inherent in the knowledge of language shared with other speakers. Therefore the reconstruction of the knowledge of meaning involved in the "understanding of language" would also have to include a reconstruction of the background knowledge that in each case determines the acceptability conditions of a speech act. For the presuppositions involved in this background knowledge are "presuppositions . . . that the participants in communication must make if a speech act in a given situation is to be able to take on a *specific meaning,* and *if it is to be capable of being valid or invalid* in the first place" (NMD, p. 86; italics mine).

The attempt to carry out a reconstruction of the knowledge of meaning must come to grips with the peculiar features of background knowledge. As we saw, this "knowledge" is holistically structured, implicit (hence not entirely expressible in propositional knowledge), and prereflective (hence not capable of being thematized at will). The peculiar character of background knowledge constitutes a challenge for any attempt to construct a theory of meaning for two different (though complementary) reasons.

In the first place, the last two features of background knowledge underscore its nonformalizable character, the methodological impossibility of carrying out a reconstruction of this knowledge. This is probably why Habermas considers it necessary to take as a starting point the fact that speakers *already share this background knowledge.*

But if this knowledge is recognized as constitutive for the understanding of language, and at the same time as something that must always already be taken for granted (as Habermas suggests), then it is difficult to understand the sense of the attempt to articulate a theory of meaning as such: that is, a theory that tries to *explain* the necessary conditions for the "understanding of language." If this theory contends that we understand a language when we share the background knowledge inherent in it (that is, the linguistic world-disclosure underlying a given lifeworld), it thus renounces the explanatory claim characteristic of every theory in precisely the same way hermeneutics does—namely, by taking as the basic unit of significance not just the speech act (nor such an act plus the yes/no position of a hearer), but *language as a whole.* If the "strong presupposition" that speakers share a common language is accepted not merely in the sense that they possess a grammatically regulated means of communication, but in the sense that they share a linguistic world-disclosure, the answer to the question of how it is possible for speakers to understand each other loses its enigmatic character. This answer is yet again the one provided by hermeneutics, namely, that speakers have "always already" understood each other.

This is precisely why, to save the possibility of a theory of meaning as such, Dummett is forced to reject meaning holism. Along these lines, he remarks in "What Is a Theory of Meaning?"

I am asserting that the acceptance of holism should lead to the conclusion that any systematic theory of meaning is impossible, and that the attempt to resist this conclusion can lead only to the construction of pseudotheories; my own preference is, therefore, to assume as a methodological principle that holism is false. (p. 121)

The reason Dummett cites for this claim supports the point I have been stressing. Thus in "What Is a Theory of Meaning? (II)" he writes:

I have argued that an acceptable theory of meaning must be at least molecular. . . . The difference between a molecular and a holistic view of language is not that, on a molecular view, each sentence could, in principle, be understood in isolation, but that, on a holistic view, *it is impossible fully to understand any sentence without knowing the entire language,* whereas, on a molecular view, there is, for each sentence, a determinate fragment of the language a knowledge of which will suffice for a complete understanding of that sentence. (pp. 76–79; italics mine)

The consequence that follows from accepting meaning holism, implicit in the view of language as the basic unit of significance (i.e., in the "strong intersubjectivist presupposition" that speakers "share a language"), points to a difficulty even more radical than the one concerning the possibility of a theory of meaning. As we saw, the acceptance of meaning holism implies the acceptance of the *impossibility of drawing a boundary between knowledge of meaning and knowledge of the world.*

This consequence of meaning holism makes Dummett's strong rejection of holism understandable. By recognizing this impossibility (as does Habermas; see NMD, pp. 94–97), the task of a theory of meaning not only becomes difficult, but also loses its very object. *The very attempt to abstract from the whole of our knowledge a "knowledge of meaning"* responsible for the understanding of language (a knowledge that could account for the necessary conditions of understanding, thus answering the basic question of a theory of meaning: "what is it to understand the meaning of a linguistic expression?" ibid., p. 76), *becomes illusory once meaning holism is accepted.* As Putnam puts it in "Meaning Holism":

We have an enormous number of "central" beliefs about almost anything; *there is no general rule* which decides in each case which of these to take as *part of the meaning* of a word in a given context and which to take as *"collateral information"* that will, given what speaker and hearer know, surely be conveyed by the use of the word. (1986, p. 292; italics mine)

The acceptance of meaning holism calls into question the possibility of a theory of meaning, not only because of the difficulties involved in articulating such a theory, but also because of the impossibility in principle of isolating its own object. Once meaning holism is accepted, the very notion of "meaning" loses the theoretical status (as well as the explanatory power) that it had acquired after the linguistic turn. It becomes reduced to a hopelessly vague notion that is useful in the context of translation from one language into another. Thus Putnam concludes:

The impossibility of a notion of "meaning" which agrees at all with our preanalytic intuitions about sameness and difference of meaning *and* which is invariant under belief-fixation dooms the notion to be exactly what it is: a vague but useful way of speaking when (by intuition and by experience) we correlate words and phrases in different languages and discourses. (1986, p. 291; italics mine)

Beyond the difficulties concerning the very attempt to articulate a theory of meaning, we have to see which consequences follow from accepting meaning holism (which is to say, from taking a "shared language" as the basic unit of significance that enables speakers to understand each other) for Habermas's central thesis about the internal connection between meaning and validity. If the background knowledge inherent in the understanding of language is recognized as "constitutive" for the processes of understanding—that is, as the guarantee of intersubjectivity in communication (for it is what determines identical meanings, and hence what enables speakers to talk about the same thing)—background knowledge becomes the final court of appeal for deciding the validity of what is said in communication. For the presuppositions of background knowledge are what make it possible that a speech act "be able to take on a *specific meaning,* and . . . *be capable of being valid or invalid* in the first place" (NMD, p. 86; italics mine). So it seems evident that what is being recognized is precisely what Habermas's theory tried to question, namely, that "semantic rules lay down the conditions of validity for the sentences or speech acts possible in a linguistic system" (ibid., p. 103), and hence that "as the linguistic horizon of meaning changes . . . the *conditions* for the validity of utterances change with it" (ibid.). The acceptance of meaning holism only worsens a situation that had already become problematic with the recognition of the particular background knowledge shared by speakers who belong to a given lifeworld, as the condition of possibility of understanding and hence also as what determines the acceptability conditions of such understanding.

The attempt to place meaning under the control of universal validity claims cannot be maintained by appealing to a knowledge of meaning that would enable the speaker to recognize the acceptability conditions of speech acts in each case. Rather, the conditions of acceptability are dependent on background knowledge, on a particular and contingent linguistic world-disclosure that is constitutive of the processes of understanding. Given this, the universalist claim of the theory of communicative action definitely appears to be indefensible. Habermas's claim that "the horizon of the understanding of meaning brought to bear on beings is not prior to, but rather subordinate to, the question of truth" (PDM, p. 154), which was supposed to resist the reification of language as world-disclosure, appears to be unfounded. It seems to follow from all this that, if the constitution of meaning inherent in language does have the constitutive character of a world-disclosure determining everything that can appear in the world, then the attempt to place this constitution of meaning under the control of the validity according to which we judge the intraworldly is, in principle, doomed to failure.

This difficulty proceeds not only from the attempt to extend the theory of communication to a theory of language in general. We can suspect as much once we take into consideration the deep continuity between the assumptions underlying Habermas's view of language and those of hermeneutics—continuity that has so far only been confirmed. In what follows, I will try to show that the same problems are reproduced at the core of Habermas's theory of communication (4.4.2). This will enable us to see to what extent an effective rupture with the hermeneutic view requires a much deeper break than Habermas has so far carried out, concerning the basic assumptions of the hermeneutic conception of language (chapter 5).

4.4.2 The Validity Claim of Intelligibility and the World-Disclosing Function of Language

As repeatedly pointed out, the initial project of reconstructing the unavoidable presuppositions of action oriented toward understanding through a formal-pragmatic analysis was limited to the examination of the functions of language in its communicative use, and did not involve an exhaustive analysis of language as such. For this reason, Habermas could impose certain limitations on his own approach. It should be understood as an attempt to reconstruct communicative competence (while presupposing linguistic competence) by regarding language exclusively as a "process": that is, as *speech* (not as a "structure"), and by focusing on the communicative use of language while disregarding its cognitive use.

As we have seen, the introduction of a shared background knowledge that constitutes the common interpretative framework within which speakers can understand each other "univocally" was a substantial extension of Habermas's initial approach. But this extension requires that the scope of the analysis be broadened beyond the functions of language in its communicative use, and that a global account of the various functions of language as such be carried out. However, that this broadened perspective did not figure as part of Habermas's initial project cannot be without consequences. For the formal-pragmatic perspective that reconstructs the unavoidable presuppositions inherent in communicative *action* cannot be transferred, without further ado, to the analysis of language as such.

This disparity between the role implicitly attributed to language (as guarantor of the intersubjectivity of communication) and the formal-pragmatic perspective in which language is analyzed merely as *speech,* that is, as "linguistic actions" carried out by participants in communication, was already brought to light in the provisional schema with which Habermas concluded "What Is Universal Pragmatics?" (p. 68; see table 4.1).

As we can see from table 4.1, Habermas's reconstructive perspective, whose starting point is the communicative use of language (and which tries to analyze the functions of language from the possible speech acts of participants in communication), cannot identify the function that language carries out as the guarantee of intersubjectivity at the level of analysis of the speech acts themselves. This difficulty simply reflects the initial assumption of Habermas's view: that speakers must already share a language in order to initiate communication.

Although Habermas does not make explicit all that is presupposed in his initial assumption, it can nonetheless be inferred

Table 4.1

Domains of reality	Modes of reference to reality	Implicit validity claims	General functions of speech acts
"The" world of external nature	Objectivity	Truth	Representation of states of affairs
"Our" world of society	Normativity	Rightness	Establishment of legitimate interpersonal relations
"My" world of internal nature	Subjectivity	Truthfulness	Disclosure of speaker's subjectivity
Language	Intersubjectivity	Intelligibility	———

from his schema if we take into account the validity claim that speakers raise with respect to this assumption, namely, the claim of intelligibility.

As we saw, Habermas's analysis of the validity basis of speech in "What Is Universal Pragmatics?" relied on the assumption of literal meaning and took intersubjectivity as a given (by appealing to a language shared by all speakers). Indeed the idea underlying this view was that the decision concerning the admissibility of a use of language on the part of speaker and hearer is tied to a discussion about its intelligibility, that is, a discussion about "the pragmatic meaning of the interpersonal relation . . . as well as the meaning of the propositional component of the utterance." For "an utterance is intelligible when it is grammatically and pragmatically well formed, so that everyone who has the mastery of the corresponding systems of rules can generate the same utterance" (VSGS, pp. 110–111). Thus, "when the intelligibility of an utterance becomes problematic, we ask questions such as 'What do you mean?', 'What is that supposed to mean?'. . . The answers to these questions can be called *interpretations*" (ibid.).

However, we can find clear differences between the two characterizations of intelligibility that Habermas offers in his Christian Gauss Lectures. For intelligibility seems to include everything from *grammatical errors* (resulting from linguistic incompetence) to *problems of interpretation* that point to a lack of "univocity" not reducible to mere grammatical incorrectness. If we take into account the kind of vindication that the validity claim of intelligibility involves, as described by Habermas, it seems clear that intelligibility cannot be reduced to issues decideable in terms of linguistic competence alone. As Habermas remarks:

If the background consensus is disturbed at this level in such a way that *ad hoc* interpretations do not suffice, we must resort to a hermeneutic discourse in which various interpretations can be subject to examination and the one considered as correct can be justified. (VSGS, p. 113)

However, there arises here an essential difference with respect to other validity claims. Habermas adds:

Here we cannot ignore a difference. Claims to truth and rightness work in everyday practice as *claims* which are accepted under the proviso that, if need be, they *could* be discursively redeemed. *Intelligibility,* however, is *a claim that is assumed to be factually redeemed* as long as communication runs undisturbed; it is not simply an accepted promise: unintelligible communication collapses. (VSGS; italics mine)

This passage emphasizes that the so-called validity claim of intelligibility is rather a *factual condition* of possibility for communication (that is, a condition that is not at the disposal of the speakers' discursive vindication, as emphasized by hermeneutics). In "Wahrheitstheorien" (1972) this difference is already explicitly included in Habermas's account. He observes:

When the linguistic formation rules of one speaker appear to another so obscure that she cannot understand the sentences uttered (whether at the semantic, grammatical, or even phonetic level), then they can both try to reach an agreement about the language to be used in common. In this respect intelligibility could figure among discursive validity claims. . . . But there is an obvious difference. . . . As long as communication runs undisturbed, intelligibility constitutes . . . a validity claim already factually redeemed; it is not simply a promise. Hence I will consider "*intelligibility*" among the *conditions of communication* and *not among the validity claims, whether discursive or nondiscursive, which are undertaken in communication.* (WT, p. 139; italics mine)

With this distinction within the broad range of "intelligibility" between mere linguistic competence (understood simply as the capacity to produce grammatically correct utterances) and the compatibility of interpretations arising from a "background consensus" without which communication indeed collapses, two obvious consequences are brought to the fore. On the one hand, it seems clear that the assumption of a shared language that makes the intersubjectivity of communication possible goes beyond the view of language as a "system of rules" for the generation of grammatically and pragmatically well-formed utterances. And on the other hand, it also seems clear that the "intelligibility" provided by such language is not questionable *in its validity*, but is rather a condition of possibility for communication itself. Intelligibility is a validity claim always already *factually* redeemed.

However, this consideration seems to threaten the connection between meaning and validity postulated by Habermas, that is, his attempt to identify "understanding" with "possible agreement." For with the assumption of a prior intelligibility that makes communication possible, Habermas is appealing to a "fore-understanding" that is necessarily given in every search for understanding, but whose validity is not in turn questionable in the process of communication itself. If this intelligibility is possible prior to any orientation toward validity (that is, prior to the identification of the references to reality and the validity claims at stake), it seems evident that there is some sense in which "we understand a speech act" *before* "we know what makes it acceptable." This is brought to light when in *Theory of Communicative Action* Habermas reproduces the classification of possible discourses or forms of argumentation according to the different validity claims (p. 23). as shown in table 4.2.

Putting aside the difficulty reproduced with respect to the formal-pragmatic orientation of Habermas's analysis (which leads him to postulate a discourse to which there corresponds no particular speech act or "problematic expression"), it is strange to suppose that a hermeneutic or explicative discourse (in which "various interpretations can be subject to examination and the *one* considered as *correct* can be justified"; VSGS, p. 113; italics mine), given a conflict of interpretations, can decide which interpretation is to be "considered as correct" *in virtue of the validity*

Language as Medium of Understanding

Table 4.2

Dimensions of Reference / Forms of argumentation	Problematic expressions	Controversial validity claims
Theoretical discourse	Cognitive-instrumental	Truth of propositions; efficiency teleological actions
Practical discourse	Moral-practical	Rightness of norms of action
Aesthetic criticism	Evaluative	Adequacy of standards of value
Therapeutic critique	Expressive	Truthfulness or sincerity of expressions
Explicative discourse	———	Intelligibility or well-formedness of symbolic constructs

claim of "intelligibility" alone. If "intelligibility" were the validity claim that constitutes the hermeneutic discourse, that is, if it exhausted the claims thematized in it, it is not clear why different interpretations have to compete in this discourse to be considered *the* only correct one (rather than fomenting the proliferation of consistent and hence intelligible interpretations, à la Rorty).

If we consider the problems inherent in the postulation of a validity claim of intelligibility from the point of view of its consequences for hermeneutic discourse, it becomes clear that this postulation calls into question precisely what Habermas's analysis tried to prove: the normative content of the connection between meaning and validity. This is precisely the point where Habermas's and Gadamer's positions converge in showing the impossibility of elaborating an interpretation without any reference whatsoever to the possible validity of what is to be interpreted. But this implies that the criteria inherent in hermeneutic discourse comprise not only "consistency" (which guarantees "intelligibility"), but also the other three validity claims.

In the end, the attempt to place "meaning" under the control of a validity claim of its own such as "intelligibility" is just a way of questioning the alleged connection between meaning and validity. However, it can hardly be questioned that a factual intelligibility is a condition of possibility of communication.

These difficulties reveal to what extent the initial assumption that speakers intersubjectively share a language (which makes possible the use of "identical meanings" and hence communication) cannot be understood in the "instrumentalist" sense that speakers possess a gramatically regulated medium for the transmission of information. In *Postmetaphysical Thinking*, Habermas points out the ultimate sense of his intersubjectivist starting point, that is, the premise of a shared language, in connection with the view of the later Wittgenstein:

Unlike the intentionalist approach, the use-theoretical approach does not emphasize the tool character of language but the interconnection of language with an interactive practice in which a form of life is simultaneously reflected and reproduced. . . . *The grammar of language games discloses the lifeworld dimension of intersubjectively shared background knowledge that supports the pluralized functions of language.* (NMD, p. 63; italics mine)

In this explanation, we find the internal necessity that leads Habermas to broaden the perspective of his initial project. Only from a conception of language as tool can the scope of the assumption that speakers share a natural language be reduced solely to the domain of linguistic competence that enables us to generate well-formed sentences.

By recognizing this, Habermas is led to remark that "in *Theory of Communicative Action* I treated the linguistic *function of world-disclosure* negligently" (ENT, p. 336). This remark is indirectly explained in Habermas's discussion of the most positive aspect of Taylor's theory of language, "which goes back to the Hamann-Herder-Humboldt tradition":[33]

[Taylor] frees the linguistic constitution of a "worldview" [*Weltansicht*] from the reductions to a semantic ontology which deals only with a grammatically regulated fore-understanding of reality. With Humboldt, Taylor shows *how every language opens a grammatically prestructured space in which the intraworldly can appear in a particular way.* (ENT, p. 336; italics mine)

33. Note that Habermas's observation is made in the context of his reply to Taylor's critique in "Sprache und Gesellschaft," in A. Honneth and H. Joas (eds.), *Kommunikatives Handeln.*

Language acquires a "constitutive" character when it is recognized in its world-disclosing function. But this constitutive character calls into question Habermas's claim that "the structures of a worldview, which through a prior understanding of meaning make possible our intraworldly praxis" (NMD, pp. 103–104), can be subject to control or questioned precisely in the very praxis that they make possible.

The structural impossibility of this claim becomes clear if we take seriously Habermas's analysis of the unavoidable presuppositions of action oriented toward understanding. Either communication involves the shared background knowledge that renders it intelligible (by allowing speakers to talk about "the same thing," as pointed out by hermeneutics) or, as Habermas's analysis shows, it "collapses." The assumption of a shared language (which, as responsible for world-disclosure, provides a unitary framework of reference for participants in communication) underscores that the participants' yes/no positions only become meaningful once the speakers already agree that they are talking about the same thing. The attempt to place this fore-understanding of the world (which is responsible for its "unity") under the control of validity claims, the attempt to connect it potentially with arguments or reasons, must run into the difficulty that had already become manifest in Habermas's characterization of the peculiar kind of knowledge that background knowledge is. As we saw above, Habermas gives the following account of the "immediate certainty" characteristic of this "knowledge":

The insistent, yet at the same time imperceptible presence of this background appears as an *intensified,* although nonetheless *deficient form of knowledge.* Such background knowledge *lacks an internal relation to the possibility of becoming problematic* for it comes into contact with criticizable validity claims, thereby being transformed into fallible knowledge, only at the moment in which it is expressed in language. *Absolute certainties remain unshakeable until they suddenly disintegrate; for, in lacking fallibility, they do not constitute knowledge in the strict sense at all.* (NMD, p. 92; italics mine)

If the only way to put the background knowledge arising from the linguistic world-disclosure under control were *the discursive problematization of this knowledge,* what is required is a sheer impossibility. For: (a) background knowledge is, by definition, shared by speakers, just like the language they speak (thus it is hardly capable of becoming problematic for those who share it without even being aware of it); and (b) insofar as it is constitutive of the processes of understanding, "background knowledge" is a condition of possibility of these processes, and hence it cannot be questioned in these very processes if the adjective "constitutive" is to have any meaning at all. This is underscored by the claim that, in a strict, fallibilist sense, background knowledge does not constitute any knowledge at all (and therefore cannot be directly connected with reasons).

It seems to follow that if the "constitution of meaning" inherent in language does have the constitutive character of a world-disclosure that determines everything appearing in the world, the possibility of "intraworldly learning" can only be understood as derived from that prior world-disclosure (and hence limited by it), but not as something that would be able to control its own condition of possibility. That is, once the view of language as world-disclosure is endorsed, Habermas's two "replies" to the advocates of this view can no longer be defended. These replies are:

• on the one hand, that "the horizon of the understanding of meaning brought to bear on beings is not prior to, but rather subordinate to, the question of truth" (PDM, p. 154); and

• on the other hand, that "the peculiar *uncoupling* of the horizon-constituting productivity of language from *the consequences of an intramundane practice* that is wholly prejudiced by the linguistic system" (ibid., p. 319) is not tenable.

To support this second reply, Habermas contends that "intramundane linguistic practice draws its power of negation from validity claims that go beyond the horizons of any currently given context." Thus he can trace the "excesses" of the reification of language to the fact that "the contextualist concept of language . . . is impervious to the very real force of the counterfactual, which makes itself felt in the idealizing presuppositions of communicative action" (PDM, p. 206).

1. Concerning Habermas's first reply, the discussion of the "force" of the idealizing presuppositions or of the counterfactual "sustaining agreement" inherent in communicative action, as he analyzes it, has already led us to identify a problem. This problem is that the attempt to place the constitution of meaning under the control of universal validity claims runs into an in-principle difficulty: for something to be true, truthful, or right, it must first of all be meaningful (not absurd). For only when something is already meaningful, only when speakers are already in agreement about the interpretative framework in which to consider that about which an understanding is sought (and hence when they make sure that they are talking about "the same thing"), can they question the truth, truthfulness, or rightness of each other's opinions about it. If the idealization of identical meanings prior to universal validity claims is not in turn factually redeemed, communication cannot yield any form of denial; it can only "collapse." What is thereby underscored is the internal connection between a prior "intelligibility" (required for communication in general to get off the ground), and the world-disclosing function that language must have always already carried out to guarantee the unity of the world and thus any communication about the intraworldly. In Habermas's theory of meaning, this circumstance resulted in the impossibility of isolating the acceptability conditions of speech acts from the background knowledge that determines these conditions and thus makes possible the understanding of speech acts.

And yet Habermas's attempt to trace the factual validity of world-disclosure back to the validity according to which we judge intraworldly experience (which allows for learning) certainly contains a correct intuition (which is, no doubt, what feeds the suspicion that the view of language as responsible for world-disclosure involves a crude reification of language). It is hardly plausible to suppose that language decides a priori what can appear in the world *in complete independence of what actually happens in it* (or it is at least difficult to explain how, given such a mechanism of adaptation, our species did not become extinct long ago).

2. Habermas appeals to this intuition in his second reply, concerning the implausibility of "the peculiar *uncoupling* of the

horizon-constituting productivity of language from *the consequences of an intramundane practice* that is wholly prejudiced by the
linguistic system" (PDM, p. 319).

The difficulty inherent in this line of argument already appeared in Humboldt's similar attempt to defend, in spite of the
linguistic turn, the possibility of objective knowledge (an attempt
systematically questioned by Gadamer). The attempt to postulate
an "intraworldly" element of control that can measure the linguistic world-disclosure (which is precisely what makes the intraworldly accessible as such) brings with it a problem already
identified by Habermas (see 2.2 above) in the "objectivist" re-
sponses to relativism, namely, "the problem of having to take up
a standpoint between language and reality" (PMT, p. 135), that
is, of having to adopt a "God's eye point of view."

This strategy appears to be untenable, for it is no longer plausible to reverse the linguistic turn once its fundamental premises
have been accepted. What this shows is that the attempt to justify
our fallibilist intuitions can succeed only if it can be carried out
through an analysis of *the functioning of language itself.* The alternatives that we are faced with seem to be the following: either we
can *ground the revisability* of the linguistic world-disclosure (which
would have to be dependent on its intraworldly consequences) *in
the structures inherent in language itself,* or we have to abandon once
and for all the attempt to justify consistently the fallibilist intuition
underlying Habermas's proposal.

But to ground this revisability in language itself, we would have
to question the constitutive character of the constitution of meaning inherent in language, which has to be amenable to revision.
This, however, seems to amount to a reversal of the linguistic turn
as such. For given that we cannot deny our symbolically mediated
relationship with the world (which thus dooms any attempt to
restore "the thing in itself") and given the holistic character of
our understanding of meaning (which makes it impossible to appeal to a literal meaning), it appears that the meaning of what is
explicitly said can only be determined against the background of a
constitution of meaning or world-disclosure that, by guaranteeing

identical meanings, establishes the common framework of reference on the basis of which speakers can talk about the same thing.

In what follows, I will propose an alternative to this apparent blind alley. It will be an attempt to *preserve the linguistic turn* while nevertheless *calling into question* the central thesis that stands in the way of any plausible defense of the revisability of the world-disclosures or "constitutions of meaning" inherent in natural languages: *the thesis that meaning determines reference.*

The analysis of the cognitive use of language, that is, of the "constitution of object domains" through the "acts of reference and predication" inherent in the propositional content of speech acts (an analysis that Habermas continually postpones), may well reveal that speakers need not rely on identical meanings (guaranteed by the world-disclosure inherent in language) in order to talk about "the same thing." That is, this analysis may lead to the articulation of a "new" theory of reference that does away with this hypothesis, which is defended by the traditional theory of indirect reference. If this turns out to be the case, such an analysis would be able to uncover those structures inherent in language as such by virtue of which language *contains in itself the possibility of its own revisability.*

An account of reference without the problematic detour through meaning can be found in the analysis of the cognitive use of language carried out by authors of the Anglo-American tradition such as Kripke, Putnam, and Donnellan. This analysis will support our initial suspicion that it is precisely the thesis that meaning determines reference that leads to the reification of language inherent in the view of language as world-disclosure.

Language as Medium of Learning: The Cognitive Use of Language

Having accepted the basic premises of the view of language as world-disclosure, Habermas encounters structural difficulties when he tries to resist the relativistic consequences of this view. These difficulties are underscored by the fact that he has not yet tried to respond to the challenge it poses, which would require a reflection on that "specific conception of language" (NMD, p. 75) lying at the basis of his theory of communicative action. He has only emphasized that such a reflection "has to be carried out in the context of a theory of meaning" (ibid.).

Since the linguistic turn, the normative burden of a theory of language has fallen squarely on the shoulders of the theory of meaning. The reason is as follows. As already mentioned, the recognition of the symbolically mediated character of our relationship with the world unavoidably challenges the traditional explanation of the possibility of objective knowledge. That is, it closes off the possibility of postulating a world-in-itself, accessible through perception to all speakers in an identical way. As a consequence, the conditions of possibility of intersubjective communication offer the only basis for explaining the possibility of objective experience. That is to say, the guarantee of such possibility can now only be obtained through the indirect means of explaining how it is that speakers are able to talk about the same things. The linguistic knowledge shared by all speakers appears to be the only common basis for such explanation. From this perspective, it seems clear that it is the identity of meanings shared by the speakers that guarantees the identity of the reference of the signs they use. Speakers who share a language share a knowledge of meanings that constitutes the unitary framework for all that can appear within the world (i.e., for all that can be the case). In this sense, knowledge of the meaning of signs is both a knowledge available to all speakers and the mechanism that guarantees the reference of the signs they use.

But this strategy entails paradoxical consequences for the explanation of the objectivity of experience. For once we consider different world-disclosures as constitutive of our access to the intraworldly, there necessarily arises the question of how to guarantee the *unity* of the world linguistically disclosed through that *plurality* of historically contingent world-disclosures. If the linguistic turn renders impossible any appeal to a world given independently of language, then the relativistic consequences of the incommensurability of different linguistic world-disclosures would seem inherent in the linguistic paradigm as such.

Thus it seems that precisely what gave the paradigm of language its apparent superiority over that of consciousness is ultimately responsible for this paradoxical conclusion. For the attempt to redefine the objectivity of experience in terms of the intersubjectivity of communication, and to explain the latter in terms of the identity of meanings arising from the realm of a shared language, leads to a series of problematic consequences:

• The *intersubjectivity* of communication can only be guaranteed *within the limits* of a given linguistic world-disclosure. To this extent, it can be argued that the linguistic paradigm fails to explain intersubjectivity every bit as much as the philosophy of consciousness fails. As Putnam puts it, the linguistic paradigm inaugurates a "*solipsism* with a 'we' instead of an 'I'" (1990, p. ix; italics mine).

• Furthermore, the linguistic paradigm can no longer guarantee the *objectivity* of experience. For it cannot account for that which the philosophy of consciousness was still able to take for granted, namely, the "unity" of the objective world that speakers refer to in communication. The *incommensurability* of linguistic world-disclosures turns reference and truth into intralinguistic notions dependent on a prior and contingent constitution of meaning that makes them possible.

• As a result, this paradigm cannot maintain a *universalist* perspective with respect to those world-disclosures. That is, the evolution of such world-disclosures cannot be conceived as a process of *learning* or rationalization (as Habermas would have it). For this would require appealing to an unattainable "God's eye point of view."

As mentioned in the preface, these problematic consequences of the linguistic turn gave rise to the initial suspicion at the basis of my research. I suspected that the basis of the anomalies that allegedly result from the transition to the linguistic paradigm as such are actually due to the thesis that meaning determines reference. That is, they stem from the attempt to explain the condition of possibility of reference, of speakers' talking about "the same things" *indirectly,* by way of appeal to the identical meanings that they share (5.1).

The critique of this theory of indirect reference, as carried out by authors such as Kripke, Putnam, and Donnellan, serves as a confirmation of my suspicion. The common denominator of the theories of direct reference that these authors defend is precisely the questioning of the thesis that meaning determines reference. In so doing, they underscore the crucial importance of the referential function of language to cognitive learning. That is, they highlight the crucial possibility of *revising* our knowledge, which is no doubt made accessible by a linguistic world-disclosure, but is not thereby immunized against refutation through subsequent experience. Only by recognizing the importance of this referential function can we reject the *incommensurabilist* consequences inherent in the reification of the linguistic function of world-disclosure (5.2).

Once the importance of the referential function of language is recognized, we can address the issue of whether the universalist viewpoint, inherent in Habermas's thesis about the rationalization of worldviews or "linguistic world-disclosures," can be maintained after the linguistic turn. Can a universalist perspective be defended by avoiding the linguistic reification intrinsic to the view of language of hermeneutics? In my opinion, this would necessitate considering the world-disclosing and referential functions of language *jointly*. For this task, I rely on the analysis of the formal conditions of "discourse" that Habermas provides in chapter 1 of his *Theory of Communicative Action*. In this analysis, the possibility of questioning or revising what is said by speakers is grounded in the acquisition of a *formal system of reference*. This system is developed in three directions: in relation with the objective world, as well as with the social and subjective worlds. If the possibility of developing such a formal system could be grounded in the structures of language as such, the need to appeal to particular historical constitutions of meaning as the basis for talking about the same things could be called into question (5.3).

As a result of the linguistic turn, the importance of the referential function of language has been displaced from the center of philosophical attention. Its "rediscovery" is, in my opinion, the only possible corrective for the reification of the world-disclosing function.

5.1 Some Paradoxes of the Thesis That Meaning Determines Reference

As I have emphasized throughout, the thesis that meaning determines reference not only underlies the linguistic turn in the German tradition of the philosophy of language. It also serves as the basis for the analytic tradition initiated by Frege. This shared presupposition relies on the crucial distinction between *meaning* and *reference* and its consequent epistemologization, by which the meaning (or "mode of presentation" of the designatum) is regarded as the condition of our access to the referent.

The transition from the paradigm of perception to that of understanding entails the idea that our access to the referent is mediated by the meaning through which this referent is understood. Insofar as language is responsible for the way in which referents appear, thereby determining how they are to be considered in each case, it contains the framework of reference (the ontology, as it were) for all that can appear in the linguistically "disclosed" world.

The view of language as responsible for world-disclosure is not based on the model of the designation of an object by means of a name, as was usual for the philosophy of consciousness with its view of language as a tool. Rather, it stems from the model of the attribution of a property to an object, through which this object is interpreted "as something." As we saw in our discussion of Heidegger, the ascription of a name to some entity is actually seen as an indirect *attribution* of what that entity "is." This is why Heidegger remarks, in his "Hölderlin und das Wesen der Dichtung," that the designation of beings by means of names cannot be understood in the sense that "something already known beforehand is given a name, but [in the sense] *that only through that naming is it established what that entity is*" (p. 41; italics mine).

On this view, the act of referring is made possible by a linguistic meaning that situates the referent in the conceptual scheme inherent in a given language, and to that extent establishes what that entity is. This represents a version of the classical theory of reference in analytic philosophy, as developed by Frege[1] and Russell[2] (the view that names are synonymous with descriptions), and still maintained in revised form by authors such as Strawson[3] or Searle.[4]

We also find a defense of this classical theory of reference in Habermas's scattered remarks about the direction that the analysis of the cognitive use of language ought to take. This is located, more specifically, in his brief explanation of the "acts of identification and predication." In his Christian Gauss Lectures, Habermas observes:

I will only make a few remarks about *the pragmatics of the cognitive use of language*. At least two presuppositions are associated in the elementary

1. G. Frege, "Über Sinn und Bedeutung," in *Funktion, Begriff, Bedeutung*.
2. Russell (1905), (1976).
3. Strawson (1950), (1959).
4. Searle (1958), pp. 166–173.

predicative sentences which we utter in constative speech acts. We presuppose the existence of an object about which we say something; and we presuppose the truth of the proposition, that is, of that which we say about the object. . . . The first presupposition is justified if speaker and hearer are able to *identify univocally the object designated* by the grammatical subject of the assertoric sentence. . . . [For] *the referential expression, whether a singular term or a definite description, can be understood as an indication as to how the object can be identified.* (VSGS, p. 96; italics mine)

As is clear from this version of the theory of indirect reference, the condition of possibility of speakers being able to refer to the same thing lies in the fact that they share the meaning of a referential expression, an expression that "can be understood as an indication as to how the object can be identified." In "What Is Universal Pragmatics?" Habermas gives an example to illustrate this point:

A hearer can understand the meaning of the sentence with the *propositional content:* "the being yellow of Peter's new car" under the condition that the hearer has learned to use the propositional sentence correctly in the assertion:

5) "I'm telling you, Peter's new car is yellow. . . ." A proper use of the propositional sentence in (5) demands (at least) the following of the speaker:

a) The existence presupposition—there is one and only one object to which the characteristic "Peter's new car" applies.

b) The presupposition of identifiability—the (denotatively employed) propositional content contained in the characterization "Peter's new car" is a sufficient indication, in a given context, for a hearer to select the (and only the) object to which the characteristic applies. (WIUP, p. 47)

This explanation, reminiscent of Russell's analysis of definite descriptions, involves the conflation of referential expressions with attributes. That is to say, as Quine[5] explains following Russell, what the speaker asserts by using such a sentence is that "there exists one and only one object which is a car, is new, belongs to Peter and is yellow." Therefore the referent of that assertion is that

---

5. Quine (1953), pp. 1–20, especially p. 13.

which satisfies the description "Peter's new car is yellow." The hearer needs to know the meaning of the expressions used by the speaker in order to identify the referent (that is, to speak about "the same thing"), for the meaning provides the necessary and sufficient conditions for univocally identifying the referent. Thus the designating relation is assimilated to the attributive relation; the subject of the assertion is eliminated and becomes just one more predicate.

The difficulties that have mounted for the classical theory of reference in this century can be summarized in the form of three basic problems:

• If the sets of descriptions that constitute the meaning of the terms used by speaker and hearer do not coincide (because of differences in their "background knowledge"), they *cannot refer to the same thing*. If the descriptions that, for the speaker, constitute the meaning of the definite description "the new car of Peter" and enable her to identify the referent (e.g., the car that Peter drove yesterday, that is yellow and has five doors, etc.), do not coincide with the descriptions that the hearer associates with that description (e.g., the car that Peter bought in France, that is blue and has four doors, etc.), speaker and hearer are certainly not talking about "the same thing." For, if we suppose that Peter has two cars, the differences in their descriptions could lead them to identify different objects in the world. This supposition points to a related further problem, namely,

• If speaker and hearer do not agree on the descriptions suitable for the referent, they cannot argue about who is right. For *each of them talks precisely and only about that which satisfies her descriptions, whatever this may be*. If the speaker is saying that what is yellow is that object and *only* that object which satisfies the description "Peter's new car," that is, "the car that Peter drove yesterday," and (to simplify the example) the description that the hearer associates with the expression "Peter's new car" is "the (blue) car that Peter bought in France," they can hardly decide whether or not "Peter's new car" is yellow. To argue meaningfully about this issue, they would have to *refer to the same car, however it might be best described, and not to that which satisfies the description, whatever that may be.*

• If the speaker makes a mistake in the descriptions that her use of the referential expression presupposes, she *may be referring to something completely unknown to her.* If it so happens that the Peter who was driving a car yesterday is not the Peter who bought a new car on this view, the speaker has made an assertion about a referent whose existence is completely unknown to her, but which *happens to satisfy her description.*

Hence we can see the unwelcome consequences of making reference dependent upon meaning. Any difference in the descriptions that are associated with an expression and also enable speakers to identify the referent implies that, *by definition,* they are not talking about the same thing. Thus speaker and hearer cannot possibly correct each other's beliefs.

The intersubjectivity of communication is precisely what was supposed to be guaranteed by the appeal to identical meanings. But on a closer look, this strategy leaves as an inexplicable mystery the question of how speakers might be able to talk about the same thing. As we can see, the problem of incommensurability or solipsism already emerges *within* a community of speakers who share the same linguistic world-disclosure. Indeed, if the background knowledge shared by speakers in virtue of the world-disclosing function of language determines that to which they refer with their linguistic signs, but the holistic character of this background knowledge makes it impossible to draw a boundary between knowledge of meaning and knowledge of the world, then the slightest difference in the speakers' background knowledge will prevent them from talking about the same thing. And given the contribution of speakers' knowledge of the world to their background knowledge, differences are bound to arise. As a result of meaning holism, then, the anticipations of meaning of speaker and hearer are unavoidably different. To this extent, such supposed knowledge of meaning does not seem to be responsible, as Heidegger claimed, for "one and the same thing being unveiled." On the contrary, it seems instead to be the reason why "to under-

stand is always to understand differently,'' as Humboldt and Gadamer pointed out. The "solipsism with a we" leads, by its own
logic, to a "solipsism with an I."

The situation is not improved when the strong version of the
classical theory (as developed by Frege and Russell) is revised in
the direction of the so-called cluster-theory. This theory holds
that speakers do not have to share *all* of the descriptions associated with the referential expression, but only the *majority* of them.
But the essential assumption shared by both versions of this theory
is the epistemologization of reference, namely, the thesis that "referring" means "identifying" univocally. Therefore addressing
the problems that ensue from the impossibility of postulating a
de facto identity of meaning for all speakers who share a common
language by saying that only an *approximate* convergence is required can only make things worse if the *telos* of the *univocal "identification"* is maintained. This revised version of the classical theory
of reference shows even more clearly the incapacity of this classic
paradigm to account for how speakers can refer to the same thing.

To uncover the root of these difficulties, I will draw on authors
of the Anglo-American tradition who have challenged this classical theory of indirect reference. Their method is to question
the adequacy of the view that referring depends on sharing the
meaning of referential terms that enable speakers to identify
the designatum. Far from assimilating referential acts to acts of
"identification," the theories of direct reference[6] try to explain
the act of referring as one of direct designation (or *rigid* designation, as Kripke puts it).[7] The degree of elaboration these views
have received so far does not allow them to be described as an
articulated "theory," in the strict sense. But without a doubt, the
principal benefit yielded by these views has been their radical

6. See the preface, footnote 3.

7. Reference is direct *not* because there is a direct epistemic way of identifying
the referents (without shared "meanings," i.e., without identity criteria), but
rather because reference is nonepistemic. That is to say, the linguistic conditions
for successful reference are not identical with the epistemic conditions for successful identification of the referents (i.e., *knowledge* of them). See footnote 27.

critique of the basic assumptions of the classical theory (i.e., of the thesis that meaning determines reference).

To analyze this critique, I will focus on the views of K. Donnellan and H. Putnam. In my opinion, these views capture the leading intuitions of this new perspective, without succumbing to the metaphysical ballast of Kripke's position. My discussion of these views is not meant to be exhaustive, a task that would lead us beyond the bounds of this work. My aim is only to draw attention to the necessity of taking into account the referential function of language, which has been every bit as neglected *since* the linguistic turn as the world-disclosing function was *before* it. In the wake of the linguistic turn, the instrumental view of language, which reduces all functions of language to the single function of designation, becomes inadmissible. But we should regard as equally inadmissible the *reduction of all functions of language to predication*, to its world-disclosing function. For it is precisely this reification that prevents us from grasping the internal connection between language and the possibility of cognitive learning. I will try to demonstrate this in what follows.

5.2 Donnellan's and Putnam's Theories of Direct Reference: The Referential Function of Language

As already mentioned, the core of the theories of direct reference can be found in their critique of the thesis that meaning determines reference (i.e., that constancy of meaning guarantees constancy of reference). The unrestricted validity of this thesis is placed into question by showing that the descriptive content of referential expressions does not determine the identity conditions of their referents. Put differently, it is shown that the referents of such expressions are not necessarily *those things that satisfy their descriptive content.*

This claim raises two separate questions. One concerns the normative presuppositions bound up with the practice of designation as opposed to predication. In my opinion, this analysis is the most relevant consequence of the theories of direct reference for the problems discussed in this book (incommensurability, linguistic relativism, etc.). The other is the factual, epistemic question concerning how we know what a speaker is referring to. Namely, how is reference determined in particular cases if not through the meanings of referential expressions (i.e., through the semantic satisfaction-conditions implied by the descriptive content of these expressions)? Some of the attempts to answer this second question, by giving a positive account of what determines reference in particular cases, have led theories of direct reference to be identified with *causal* theories.[8] This has happened *in spite* of the fact that many defenders of such theories (especially Donnellan[9] and Putnam[10]) have often denied that causality can be of any help in such an explanation.[11] In any event, my use of these new theories will touch exclusively on their answer to the first question,[12] which

8. A clear defender of the causal theory of reference is M. Devitt (1981).

9. See K. Donnellan (1974), pp. 3–32.

10. See H. Putnam (1975b), p. 203; also (1988), p. 118. More explicit is Putnam's remark in *Renewing Philosophy:*

> I should note here in passing that Krikpe and I have both denied quite consistently that what we are proposing is . . . a definition of reference in causal terms. What Kripke and I have defended is the idea that certain sorts of words can refer only if there is a causal connection between them and certain things or certain kinds of things. But we have never tried to *reduce* reference to causation. (p. 221)

11. Another author who calls into question whether the causal theory *is* the prevailing view among the defenders of the theory of direct reference is H. Wettstein (1991), pp. 70ff.

12. For various reasons, I am not going to enter into the second question. First of all, a systematic treatment of this question would make it unavoidable that we enter into a much more general discussion of the Anglo-American philosophy of language, a theme that lies outside the focus of this work. Second, and more specifically, the positive explanations given by most of these authors of how reference is determined in different cases are not sufficiently developed as to offer a general account. Third, and perhaps more decisively, I have the impression that once the idea that the identity of meanings fixes the identity of reference is rejected (i.e., the idea of a supposedly analytic knowledge of meanings, shared by all speakers, which fixes in advance the necessary and sufficient conditions that referents have to satisfy to be referred to by them), no general (i.e., context-independent) explanation about how reference is determined in all particular cases can be given. In this sense the question itself loses much of the philosophi-

in my opinion entails no particular answer to the second question, and a fortiori no commitment to a causal theory of reference.[13]

5.2.1 Donnellan's Distinction between the Referential and Attributive Uses of Definite Descriptions

To elucidate the important shift in perspective of the new theories of reference *vis-à-vis* their classical counterpart, I will first analyze K. Donnellan's distinction between the "attributive" and "referential" uses of definite descriptions. For on the basis of this distinction, it is possible to clarify the limitations and paradoxes of the theory of indirect reference. The key motivation behind Donnellan's distinction is the rejection of the idea that referential expressions can be interpreted as "attributes" that enable us to understand something *as* something (as Heidegger puts it). This idea had always been crucial for maintaining the thesis that meaning determines reference (as is made clear by the systematic rejection of the view of linguistic signs as mere names for designating independently existing objects). Thus, once Donnellan's distinction is drawn, we can identify the difficulty underlying the reification of language as world-disclosure that has been analyzed throughout this book: This view can only account for the attributive use of referential expressions, but not for the referential use of these expressions. This is the core of the critique of Russell's view accomplished by Donnellan's distinction, a critique applicable to any view of language that relies on the assumption that meaning determines reference.

Donnellan introduces his distinction in "Reference and Definite Descriptions,"[14] with the following words:

---

cal appeal it had in a Fregean conception of semantics. In my opinion, this is an argument for explaining reference by going beyond semantics toward pragmatics, but not necessarily toward a causal explanation of reference.

13. The best way to account for the insights of the theories of direct reference is rather by remaining realist (defending reference and truth as nonepistemic) within an internalist, pragmatist perspective. In my view, this is what *internal realism* amounts to.

14. In Schwartz (1977), pp. 42–65.

I will call the two uses of definite descriptions I have in mind the *attributive use* and the *referential use*. A speaker who uses a definite description *attributively* in an assertion states something about whoever or whatever is the so-and-so. A speaker who uses a definite description *referentially* in an assertion, on the other hand, uses the description to enable his audience to pick out whom or what he is talking about and states something about that person or thing. In the first case the definite description might be said to occur *essentially,* for the speaker wishes to assert something about whatever or whoever fits that description; but in the referential use the definite description is merely one *tool* for doing a certain job—calling attention to a person or thing—and in general any other device for doing the same job, another description or a name, would do as well. In the attributive use, the *attribute* of being so-and-so is all important, while it is not in the referential use. (p. 46; italics mine)

The example Donnellan then uses to illustrate this distinction consists in the different uses we can make of the sentence "Smith's murderer is insane." In one case someone observes Smith's corpse, destroyed beyond recognition, and asserts that "Smith's murderer is insane," for whoever committed such an atrocity *must* be insane. In this case, being Smith's murderer is a necessary attribute of the person to whom the speaker refers. A completely different case is one in which the speaker is present in the courtroom at the trial for Smith's murder, and notices the defendant of the case behaving in an extremely odd way. This odd behavior leads the speaker to assert: "Smith's murderer is insane."

In the latter case, the definite description "Smith's murderer" is used referentially, and not attributively. For to talk about the odd behavior of the defendant, the speaker could have used another description, or the name of the defendant, or even a pointing gesture to indicate the person to whom she refers.

The importance of this distinction becomes clear when we consider the implications that can be drawn if we suppose that Smith was not murdered, but rather run over by a train. In the first scenario, where the definite description "Smith's murderer" was used attributively, the speaker will have referred to no one at all. To this extent, her speech act collapses (in the same way as would an assertion about the present king of France).[15] But in the second scenario, the speaker can succeed in referring to someone with her speech act even though the definite description is not satisfied by the referent, provided of course that the hearers understood to whom the speaker wanted to refer with her description. The implication, then, is that the speaker can be *corrected* by a hearer who already knows (or believes) that the defendant is not Smith's murderer, or even that *there is no such murderer.*

Donnellan clarifies this insight by means of a second example, which also helps illuminate the core of his argument:

Suppose you are at a party and, seeing an interesting-looking person holding a martini glass, one asks, "Who is the man drinking a martini?" If it should turn out that there is only water in the glass, one has nevertheless asked a question about a particular person, a question that it is possible for someone to answer. Contrast this with the use of the same

15. Donnellan's example of "Smith's murderer" is undoubtedly the most famous illustration of his distinction. But his examples concerning orders (rather than mere assertions) perhaps illustrate even better the possible success of communication. To show the different implications that follow from these uses of definite descriptions with respect to the possible success of communication, Donnellan provides the following example in "Reference and Definite Descriptions" (in Schwartz 1977): Consider the order,

"Bring me the book on the table." If "the book on the table" is used referentially, it is possible to fulfill the order even though there is no book on the table. If, for example, there is a book *beside* the table, though there is none *on* it, one might bring that book back and ask the issuer of the order whether this is "the book you meant." And it may be. But imagine we are told that someone has laid a book on our prize antique table, where nothing should be put. The order, "Bring me the book on the table" cannot now be obeyed unless there is a book that has been placed on the table. There is no possibility of bringing back a book which was never on the table and having it be the one that was meant, because there is no book that in that sense was "meant." In the one case the definite description was a device for getting the other person to pick the right book; if he is able to pick the right book even though it does not satisfy the description, one still *succeeds* in his purpose. In the other case, there is, antecedently, no "right book" except one which fits the description; the *attribute* of being the book on the table is *essential.* Not only is there no book about which an order was issued, if there is no book on the table, but *the order itself cannot be obeyed.* (p. 9; italics mine)

question by the chairman of the local Teetotalers Union. He has just been informed that a man is drinking a martini at their annual party. He responds by asking his informant, "Who is the man drinking a martini?" In asking the question the chairman does not have some particular person in mind about whom he asks the question; if no one is drinking a martini, if the information is wrong, no person can be singled out as the person about whom the question was asked. Unlike the first case, the attribute of being the man drinking a martini is all-important, because if it is the attribute of no one, the chairman's question has no straightforward answer. . . . In the referential use of a definite description we may succeed in picking out a person or thing to ask a question about even though he or it does not really fit the description; but in the attributive use if nothing fits the description, no straightforward answer to the question can be given. (1966, pp. 48–49)

It is for just these reasons that Donnellan calls this latter use the "attributive" use. For in this use of the description, the attribute of *being the man who is drinking the martini* seems to be essential. That is, this attribute cannot be replaced by a non-synonymous one and still express the same proposition. Rather, the attribute is constitutive of whether the speaker referred to anything at all with his proposition—and if so, to *whom* it was that he referred. On the other hand, in the referential use of the description, what is decisive is that the description is only a means for picking out one determinate person among all others for the purpose of saying something about him. The point of Donnellan's distinction is precisely to show that *what is expressed* in the referential use is never what is expressed in the attributive use. Whether or not the description we use actually describes the object correctly, we have two different ways of referring to objects. On the one hand, we may want to refer to "whatever satisfies such and such conditions." On the other, we may want to refer to some particular object that we try to describe the best we can, so as to allow the hearers to identify the object to which we are referring.

The differences between these two uses of definite descriptions are clarified in Donnellan's analysis at three different levels.

First, he tries to show the difference in what is expressed in the attributive and referential uses by pointing to the different truth-conditions of statements containing definite descriptions used in either way. Take Donnellan's example "the murderer of Smith is insane." Whether or not the description actually applies to the referent, in the attributive case the truth-conditions of the statement can be made explicit à la Russell, whereas in the referential case they cannot. When the definite description is used *attributively,* the truth-conditions of "The murderer of Smith is insane" amount (roughly) to: "there is one and only one person who murdered Smith and that person is insane." By contrast, when the definite description is used *referentially,* the truth-conditions of the statement amount (roughly)[16] to: "that person there is insane." Obviously, both statements do not need to be true in the same cases, and hence, they are understood differently by the hearers.

Second, as we have seen, Donnellan tries to show what this difference amounts to in the pragmatic context of actual communication. Given that the conditions for satisfying a description play a different role in the two different uses, the consequences of being or not being something that satisfies the description in question are completely different in each case. In the attributive use, when the satisfaction-conditions of the description are not fulfilled, the consequence is a failure of reference, and hence an unsuccessful speech act. As we saw earlier (see footnote 15), Donnellan exhibits the difficulties of such cases not only as regards the truth-conditions of assertions, but also as regards the obedience-conditions of orders, questions, and the like. In the referential use, however, there is no such consequence, precisely because the satisfaction-conditions of the description *are not the decisive factor for determining its referent.* When there is something that satisfies the description, the consequences in both cases are also different.

16. Here I follow Wettstein's suggestion of understanding definite descriptions used referentially as functioning semantically as demonstratives, i.e., as a device for demonstrative reference (see 1991, pp. 51 ff.). His explanation of "The murderer of Smith is insane" in the referential case is the following: "Since Jones was demonstrated and insanity predicated of him, what was asserted was that *that one, Jones, is insane,* a singular proposition, true with respect to a possible world w just in case Jones, the individual demonstrated in the actual world, is insane in w" (p. 54).

Language as Medium of Learning

If the description was used attributively, the referent is whatever fits that description, independently of whether it is known to the speaker and whether the speaker meant to refer to it. However, if the description was used referentially, it is not appropriate to identify the referent merely on the basis of the satisfaction conditions of the speaker's description. From a failure in description (in the opinion of the hearer), there follows the possibility of correcting the speaker about her mistake, or at least the possibility of expressing disagreement by redescribing the referent in a way the hearer considers appropriate. In the attributive case, these two possibilities are excluded as meaningless.

With the possibilities of correction and redescription available in the referential use of descriptions, we encounter the third level of analysis employed by Donnellan for showing the genuine difference between the two possible uses of definite descriptions. The difference becomes especially clear by considering the meaningfulness of the hearers' redescription of the referent for reporting what the speaker said in both cases. In the attributive use, a nonsynonymous redescription is obviously unacceptable, whereas in the referential use it is not. As Donnellan remarks in "Reference and Definite Descriptions":

When a speaker says, "The F is Y," where "the F" is used attributively, if there is no F, we cannot correctly report the speaker as having said *of* this or that person or thing that it is Y. But if the definite description is used referentially we can report the speaker as having attributed Y to something. And *we* may refer to what the speaker referred to, using whatever description or name suits our purpose. Thus, if a speaker says, "Her husband is kind to her," referring to the man he was just talking to, and if that man is Jones, we may report him as having said *of Jones* that he is kind to her. If Jones is also the president of the college, we may report the speaker as having said *of the president of the college* that he is kind to her. And finally, if we are talking to Jones, we may say, referring to the original speaker, "He said of you that *you* are kind to her." It does not matter here whether or not the woman has a husband or whether, if she does, Jones is her husband. If the original speaker referred to Jones, he said of him that he is kind to her. Thus where the definite description is used referentially, but does not fit what was referred to, we can report what a speaker said and agree with him by using a description or name which does fit. In doing so we need not . . . choose a description or name which the original speaker would agree fits what he was referring to. (p. 188)

As long as speakers and hearers use the terms referentially (i.e., as long as they consider that the satisfaction conditions of the descriptions they use are not the decisive factor for reference), the same content *can* be expressed in spite of the different descriptive means used to express it. This possibility of redescription, which is only meaningful if speakers understand the use of the definite description referentially rather than attributively, gives further support to Donnellan's claim that something completely different is expressed in the referential and attributive uses. If the analysis is correct, there are far-reaching implications.

Given this distinction, it seems clear that the classical theory of reference covers only the *attributive* use of referential expressions. This limitation is reflected in the conflation of names with attributes implicit in the logical analysis of sentences containing referential expressions in terms of existential quantification. The obvious consequence of this analysis is as follows. The paradigmatic case for explaining reference in the classical theory is precisely a case in which it is impossible to refer to something in particular, impossible to name it. That is to say, it is a case in which it is only possible to make general assertions about the world. This is what Donnellan criticizes about the theory of indirect reference in his discussion of Russell's theory of descriptions. In "Speaking of Nothing," Donnellan explains:

On [Russell's] theory of definite descriptions the singular expression, the definite description, is really a device that introduces quantifiers and converts what might seem at first sight a simple proposition about an individual into a general proposition. "The Φ is Ψ" expresses the same proposition as "There is a Φ and there is at most one Ψ and all Φs are Ψs"; and the latter clearly would express a general proposition about the world. . . . Now if we contrast these singular expressions with ones, if there are any, that do not introduce quantifiers, that when put as the subject of a simple subject-predicate sentence do not make the sentence express a general proposition, then I think there is a strong temptation to say that only the second kind of singular term can be used to really mention an individual. Russell clearly believed that there must be the possibility, at least, of singular terms that do not introduce quantifiers, that seems in large part to be his reason for believing in "genuine" names. (p. 224)

Donnellan gives a pragmatic twist to Russell's point of view, adding:

Whether or not there is some argument that shows the necessity of such singular terms, I believe that prior to theory the natural view is that they occur often in ordinary speech. So if one says, for example, "Socrates is snub-nosed," the natural view seems to me to be that the singular expression "Socrates" is simply a device used by the speaker to pick out what he wants to talk about, while the rest of the sentence expresses what property he wishes to attribute to that individual. This can be made somewhat more precise by saying, first, that the natural view is that *in using such simple sentences containing singular terms we are not saying something general about the world—that is, not saying something that would be correctly analyzed with the aid of quantifiers;* and, second, that *in such cases the speaker could, in all probability, have said the same thing, expressed the same proposition, with the aid of other and different singular expressions, so long as they are being used to refer to the same individual.* (pp. 224–245; italics mine)

Donnellan shares Russell's insight concerning the different kinds of propositions that can be expressed in both cases. But he disregards Russell's conviction that the linguistic means for referring to some particular thing in the world, to the referent as such, should not contain any descriptive content.[17] Otherwise, Russell thought, the use of these means would unavoidably introduce the generality shown by his own analysis of definite descriptions in terms of existential quantification. But if Donnellan's analysis of the distinct uses of definite descriptions is correct, the possibility of referring to something in particular in the world does not depend on the *semantic* characteristics of the expressions used, but on the *pragmatic* competence of the speakers. As soon as speakers interpret the descriptions in a statement in a referential way, as designating something particular in the world, they recognize *the logical independence of the referent from our ways of describ-*

17. This seems to be why Russell held that the only "genuine names in a logical sense" were demonstratives (such as "that" and "this").

ing or identifying it. This normative presupposition implicit in the practice of referring belongs to the speakers' pragmatic competence. Precisely for this reason, they do not have to *avoid* the use of referential expressions with descriptive content in order to refer to something in particular, as Russell mistakenly thought. They only have to *consider them as (contingent) means for picking out the referent rather than as necessary conditions of the referent's identity.* Obviously, what has to be identical for the speakers to be able to talk about the same things are the *referents* they are talking about. There does not also have to be an identity in their ways of describing them, an identity of the *meanings* of the expressions used. But precisely to the extent that *synonomy* in the expressions used is not the condition for *sameness of reference,* the descriptive content of the expressions employed does not *determine what* is being referred to, but only *expresses the different ways* in which the referent is described—ways that can always be incorrect or a matter of disagreement. In this sense, a successful description of the referent is not the condition for successful reference.[18] As Donnellan's examples of the referential use of designative expressions show, speakers are not committed to a successful description of the referents[19] in order to be able to refer to them. At most, they have

18. Successful reference (i.e., the possibility that speakers talk about the same thing) seems actually to depend more on the *factual* agreement of the speakers about how to describe the referents in a particular context (*even if it is a mistaken one*) than on some description of the referents being actually correct but, say, *unknown* to the other speakers.

19. The difficulties of such a commitment will become especially clear in the context of Putnam's discussion of the use of theoretical terms in science. In this context, it is easier to recognize the inadmissible consequences of epistemologizing reference, i.e., the absurdity of believing that *we cannot refer to things until our beliefs (or theories) about them, and their identity, are correct.* Had this been the case, how could we ever have improved our knowledge about them? That is to say, how could we first have disagreed about their identity (by developing alternative conceptions of them) and then have changed our beliefs about them? As Putnam's arguments will show, what may seem a harmless requirement in the context of ordinary communication has as an unavoidable consequence the thesis of incommensurability when applied to a scientific context. Such epistemic considerations provide the best arguments for recognizing reference (and hence truth) as nonepistemic.

to be willing to redescribe the referents, in case their assumptions about them are proved to be inappropriate, which always remains an open question.

Thus what the referential use of designative expressions shows is the sense in which the meaning of these expressions is not always constitutive of the identity of the referent. Rather, this meaning is only one device among others for referring to it. If this device ceases to be adequate, it can be questioned and replaced by another. As Donnellan puts it:

We saw that when a definite description is used referentially, a speaker can be reported as having said something *of* something. And in reporting what it was of which he said something, we are not restricted to the descriptions he used, or synonyms of it; we may ourselves refer to it using any descriptions, names, and so forth, that will do the job. Now this seems to give *a sense in which we are concerned with the thing itself and not just the thing under a certain description* [italics mine], when we report the linguistic act of a speaker using a definite description referentially. (1966, pp. 64–65)

In this genuine sense of referring, what we want to designate is not "whatever satisfies our description," but rather that whose existence we suppose—"however it might be correctly described." The significance of this sense of referring is that it enables speaker and hearer to communicate despite their differences in beliefs. They can talk about the same thing even if they do not agree on how it is best described, if the level of their knowledge of the referent is vastly unequal, or even if what the referent "is" is not yet sufficiently known.

In this sense, the *normative* presupposition behind the referential use of referring to "the thing itself" rather than to "the thing under a certain description" *does not have any epistemic content.* And a fortiori, it does not imply the *epistemic* postulate of immediate access to the thing in itself.[20]

Without the use of linguistic signs, names, definite descriptions, and the like, reference is indeed impossible. But this does not

---

20. If anything epistemic follows from this analysis of the referential use of linguistic expressions, it is rather the insight of fallibilism, as I will try to show in the next section.

signify that the meanings inherent in the expressions we use (which undoubtedly imply an indirect attribution of properties to the referent) have to be regarded as "constitutive" of that to which we want to refer with them (as suggested by the conception of language as world-disclosure).

What follows from Donnellan's distinction for the explanation of reference in general is that referential expressions have a more decisive component than their descriptive content. That is to say, what is decisive for their use is their demonstrative or "indexical" component (as Putnam puts it), rather than the satisfaction conditions implicit in their descriptive content. And this component is precisely what has been completely neglected by the theories of indirect reference. However, for establishing this crucial objection against such theories, the arguments mentioned thus far may not suffice.

As we have seen in Donnellan's examples, an easy way to show the independence of these two components is to show cases in which they *diverge,* and in which the demonstrative component is the decisive factor for a correct understanding of the expression being used (for understanding it in the referential and not in the attributive sense). In fact, this is the strategy followed by Donnellan in most of his examples of the referential/attributive distinction.

However, as the discussion concerning this distinction has made clear, this strategy leads to certain difficulties. Examples based on the divergence between the demonstrative and the descriptive component of expressions seem to be structurally identical with examples of a completely different distinction: that between "speaker's reference" and "semantic reference" (which is understood as a particular case of the distinction between speaker's meaning and sentence meaning). In this sense, this *divergence* (possible in cases of referential use) has been understood by many authors as just a particular case of *improper use* of linguistic expressions. That is, it is understood as a case in which the speaker manages to assert something different from what the terms mean when used literally. For this reason, they have considered both distinctions to be one and the same, and have consequently declared that the referential/attributive distinction has no semantic significance.[21] In my opinion, this is a confusion.[22] The referential/attributive distinction is *genuine* and cannot be conflated with the distinction between speaker's meaning and sentence meaning (i.e., speaker's assertion and semantic content).

In the present context, however, it is essential to show that this distinction is genuine. That is, it is essential to make it visible for those who still cannot see anything in the referential use other than a case of improper use of linguistic expressions. For the problem with this "blindness" is not just the conflation of the referential/attributive distinction with the distinction between speaker's meaning and sentence meaning. More than this, the real problem is that such a conflation makes it possible to retain the view that the attributive use of linguistic expressions is the paradigm case of referring. And if this is the case, then meaning ultimately determines reference, as the theory of indirect reference has always maintained. In this sense, it seems that the question of whether the insights behind the theories of direct reference stand or fall depends on whether the referential/attributive distinction is genuine.

Some defenders[23] of the semantic significance of Donnellan's distinction have argued that his recourse to examples of improper use of descriptions confuses rather than clarifies the real point behind his distinction. The point, they hold, is to show that *what is expressed* by the two different uses of definite descriptions (or of referential expressions in general) diverges; the difference can easily be seen in cases of improper use of descriptions, but this is not an essential characteristic of the distinction as such. However, my attempt to show that the referential/attributive distinction is genuine, that it is not a case of the general distinction between speaker's meaning and sentence meaning, will follow a

21. See Searle (1979b), Salmon (1982), Kripke (1977), Bertolet (1986).

22. Many authors have emphasized the essential differences between the two distinctions. See Loar (1976), Wettstein (1991), Recannati (1981) and (1993).

23. Recannati argues in this direction (1993, pp. 278 ff.).

different path. My arguments will not only aim to show that the *divergence* on which Donnellan's examples are based is a merely contingent element of his examples. More importantly, I will try to demonstrate that this divergence *is not a case of improper use* of linguistic expressions at all.

To show that the referential use is not a case of improper use of linguistic expressions, but rather a genuine way of referring, it may be useful first to show what is peculiar in the distinction between proper and improper uses of linguistic expressions when *reference* is at issue.

In a general sense, the distinction between speaker's meaning and sentence meaning points to cases in which the speaker is not aware of the proper meaning of a word and thus uses it wrongly. (These cases can range from simple malapropism to insufficient knowledge of a language, or even to the more complicated cases of irony, metaphor, particular idiolects, etc.) What is essential to this distinction is the presupposition of a general agreement about the *proper use* of words among speakers, on the basis of which these other cases are essentially exceptional (and, in this sense, of no philosophical impact whatsoever). On the other hand, what is special about cases that involve reference (as opposed to cases related exclusively to grammatical rules internal to the language) is that such agreement is not only *intralinguistic.* More than this, as Wittgenstein made clear, it is an agreement in judgments about *how the world is.* From this point of view, to speak of the distinction between speaker's reference and semantic reference or, more precisely, to speak of semantic reference is actually a metaphor. Given the generality of language, linguistic expressions convey general possibilities of description, but they obviously do not refer by themselves to any particular thing. In this sense, what is meant by "semantic reference" is, actually, something like "a *linguistic community's* reference." Given the agreement in a linguistic community about how to describe objects in the world properly, it is easy to exemplify the distinction between speaker's reference and semantic reference by appealing to clear cases of errors by particular speakers about something in the world. But as opposed to cases that involve only grammatical rules,

speakers might very well agree about what the descriptions mean. But the question would still be whether their application to a particular referent is appropriate or not. And this can never be settled simply by appealing to linguistic conventions. But there is more. What becomes clear by considering such cases is not only that such a *cognitive* divergence or disagreement is not just linguistic. It also becomes clear that such a disagreement is essentially open: that is, it allows us neither to assume a privileged perspective nor to appeal to a final authority (of conventions or rules), as is possible in the case of linguistic meaning.

The question is how to explain the possibility of such disagreements with respect to reference. How can speakers meaningfully disagree about the *correct* way of describing *the same referents?* Furthermore, how can they *express such disagreement* so that the attempt at reaching an agreement can be meaningfully pursued? More generally, what are the conditions given in our referential practices that allow for meaningful disagreement and mutual learning about the way the world is? *This* is where the referential/attributive distinction becomes essential. If we consider once more Donnellan's explanation of the different possibilities of redescription of the referents in the two different uses, and if we take into account that the disagreement between speakers can be *cognitive* and not merely *linguistic,* then it is easy to recognize the indispensability of the referential use of designative expressions.

To the extent that the attributive use of descriptions implies that we understand them as referring to "whatever satisfies the description," such a case does not allow for disagreement concerning the correct ways of describing the referent. If the hearers disagree with the description, if they believe that there is nothing that satisfies it, this means *eo ipso* that the speaker has failed to refer to anything at all. From the hearers' point of view, there is nothing to be redescribed; the speaker's statement expresses only a *de dicto* belief.[25] But as Donnellan has shown, in the case of refer-

---

25. The distinction between *de dicto* and *de re* beliefs is usually explained as the difference between a belief in a *dictum* or saying in the first case, and a belief about some *res* or thing in the second. There are different cases that motivate

ential use of descriptions, the hearers can *disagree* with a description as inappropriate *for the referent* that they themselves would describe in a different way. Consequently, they can also *express* their disagreement by redescribing the speaker's statement in *de re* form. (In Donnellan's example, if the hearers do not consider Jones to be the murderer of Smith, they might reply to the speaker as follows: "You have said *of Jones* that he is insane, but this is not true, and—by the way—the fact that he is accused of Smith's murder does not mean that he is the murderer of Smith.") [26] Such a redescription shows that the hearers can meaningfully commit themselves to the *existence of the referent,* but not to *the particular way the speaker describes it. This possibility is what cannot be accounted for by the theory of indirect reference* (i.e., by neglecting the referential use of linguistic expressions or by denying their genuine sense). The importance of such a communicative possibility should not be understated. For it is only by learning the referential use of linguistic expressions, that is, the *nonepistemic sense of the practice of referring,*[27] that speakers can understand the *independence of the*

---

this distinction. The most interesting one for our purposes is the one that allows us to distinguish general beliefs about the world from beliefs concerning a particular individual. In Quine's example, "Ralph believes that someone is a spy" can be understood as expressing a belief either *de dicto,* namely, "Ralph believes there are spies," or *de re,* namely, "There is someone whom Ralph believes to be a spy" (see Quine 1971). What is interesting for our purposes is that ascribing a belief *de re* to someone commits the ascriber to the existence of the referent the belief is about. For this reason, if the ascriber believes that there is nothing the speaker was talking about, he cannot ascribe a belief *de re.* But on the other hand, precisely to the extent that this commitment concerns the existence of the referent, it does not also include an epistemic commitment to the particular way of describing it by the original believer.

26. The essential openness of such possibilities of redescription is pointed out by R. Brandom in his explanation of the de re / de dicto distinction from a pragmatic point of view in *Making it Explicit,* pp. 495–520.

27. The de-epistemologization of reference can be viewed as the key of the anti-Fregean revolution of the theories of direct reference. As H. Wettstein expresses it, "linguistic contact with things—reference, that is—does not presuppose epistemic contact with them" (1991, p. 158). It seems clear to me that, if the condition for successful reference (i.e., linguistic contact with things) were successful

referent from the linguistic means used to refer to it. And only on the basis of this understanding is the possibility of disagreement at this level meaningful (i.e., feasible for the speakers). Only in this way is it possible for them to consider and discuss *alternative ways* of conceiving the same referents, and to learn from each other about *the best way of describing them.* This kind of *cognitive disagreement* is clearly essential for learning processes in general. Thus it should not be excluded in a theoretical account of our referential practices by assimilating it to a case of *improper use* of linguistic expressions.

Insofar as the scientific domain is especially sensitive to the openness and instability of our epistemic situation, a discussion of the use of theoretical terms in the sciences may offer a better basis for showing the significance of the referential/attributive distinction.[28] It is not difficult to apply Donnellan's analysis to the specific case of concept-formation in scientific theories. In so doing, we will be able to see more clearly the important consequences of the genuine sense of "referring" vindicated by the theories of direct reference. Thus, I now turn to a brief discussion of Putnam's analysis of the functioning of scientific concepts. This analysis lies at the center of his development of a new perspective from which reference can be explained.

---

knowledge of them (so that we would not be able to refer to things before we *know* their actual identity), the amount of things to which we could refer would be extremely limited. Or rather, taking into account that the correction of our knowledge is in principle always possible, their number would perhaps even be null.

28. As we shall see, in such a context the cases of cognitive *divergence* cannot be explained away as cases of *improper use* of linguistic expressions, i.e., as examples of the (merely linguistic) distinction between speaker's meaning and sentence meaning. Or rather, even worse, if such a strategy is allowed in this case, the epistemic problem of incommensurability follows unavoidably. From this perspective, incommensurability is simply the consequence of conflating a divergence or disagreement about the appropriate way of describing the referents with a merely conventional matter, i.e., with a divergence between the conventional rules of different languages or theories.

5.2.2 Putnam's Explanation of the Functioning of Theoretical Terms in the Empirical Sciences

In the present context, a discussion of the view of direct reference contained in Putnam's analysis of the use of theoretical terms in the sciences is interesting for two reasons. On the one hand, this discussion will enable us to analyze the incommensurabilist consequences of the theory of indirect reference. These were underscored by our discussion of the conception of language as world-disclosure, although they have not yet been analyzed in detail. On the other hand, a discussion of the use of theoretical terms in science has another distinct advantage. For these terms constitute the paradigmatic case in which the thesis that meaning determines reference seems most plausible. Scientific terms, in contrast with ordinary-language terms, are usually introduced by (more or less) precise definitions. As a result, it seems clear that these definitions, which constitute the "meaning" of the terms, fix in advance what the referents of those terms are. They provide the necessary and sufficient conditions for the identification of the referents. To this extent, it seems obvious that what is designated by these concepts is necessarily that which satisfies the definitions used to introduce them. In the case of scientific concepts, at least, it seems evident that their use is attributive (i.e., that their meaning is constitutive of that which they designate).

However, it is precisely this assumption about scientific terms that Putnam calls into question in his reflections on reference. The core of Putnam's critique of the theory of indirect reference lies in his analysis of the functioning of a specific kind of term. These are the so-called natural kind terms: terms such as "lemon," "tiger," "water," or "gold," as well as theoretical concepts used in inductive contexts in the natural sciences, such as "electron," "atom," "momentum," or "multiple sclerosis." In Putnam's opinion, what is specific about these terms is that they are not definable. That is, it is impossible to provide a set of descriptions that constitute the necessary and sufficient conditions for identifying the members of the class that they designate. The "meaning" of these terms, no matter how precise the available descriptions, does not allow the univocal identification of that which they designate. For all natural kinds have abnormal members that do not satisfy the prototypical or "paradigmatic" descriptions, and yet nobody would question that they belong to those classes. A green lemon is still a lemon, a tiger with three legs is still a tiger, and so forth. Thus Putnam's analysis of the functioning of these terms allows him to attain a decisive insight against the theory of indirect reference, namely, that "the extension of a term is not fixed by a concept."[29] Instead,

extension is, in general, determined *socially*—there is a division of linguistic labor as much as of "real" labor—and . . . extension is, in part, determined *indexically*. The extension of our terms depends upon the actual nature of the particular things that serve as paradigms, and this actual nature is not, in general, fully known to the speaker.[30]

The indexical component of natural kind terms is Putnam's equivalent of the referential use of definite descriptions analyzed by Donnellan. Putnam explains it in the following way:

We have maintained that indexicality extends beyond the *obviously* indexical words and morphemes. . . . Our theory can be summarized as saying that words like "water" have an unnoticed indexical component: "water" is stuff that bears a certain similarity relation to the water *around here*. Water at another time or in another place or even in another possible world has to bear the relation same$_L$ to *our* "water" *in order to be water*. Thus the theory that (I) words have "intensions," which are something like concepts associated with the words by speakers; and that (II) intension determines extension cannot be true of natural-kind words like "water" for the same reason the theory cannot be true of obviously indexical words like "I."[31]

In Putnam's opinion, it is this mostly unnoticed but irreducible indexical component of natural kind terms that precludes the analysis of such terms along the lines of the theory of indirect

29. Putnam (1975a), p. 245.
30. Ibid.
31. Ibid., p. 234.

reference. This is so for the same reason that this theory traditionally regarded genuine indexicals as exceptions, namely, indexical
or implicitly indexical expressions *do not contain any descriptive necessary and sufficient conditions* that must be *satisfied by objects* in order
to refer to them. Given that it is impossible to supply necessary
and sufficient conditions for membership in the natural kind designated by a specific term, the reference to an object belonging
to a natural kind cannot be equated with the *ascription to it of a
determinate property that would be regarded as a criterion for membership
in that kind.* This observation immediately speaks against conflating designation with attribution or predication. For it is merely a
result of the aforementioned characteristic property of the classes
named by natural kind terms—the fact that they can have abnormal members. Putnam explains this in his "Is Semantics Possible?" (in 1975d) in the following terms:

With any natural understanding of the term "property," it is just *false*
that to say that something belongs to a natural kind is just *to ascribe to it
a conjunction of properties* [italics mine]. To see why it is false, let us look
at the term "lemon." The supposed "defining characteristics" of lemons are: yellow color, tart taste, a certain kind of peel, etc. Why is the
term "lemon" *not* definable by simply conjoining these "defining characteristics"? The most obvious difficulty is that a natural kind may have
abnormal members. A green lemon is still a lemon—even if, owing to some
abnormality, it *never* turns yellow. A three-legged tiger is still a tiger. Gold
in the gaseous state is still gold. It is only normal lemons that are yellow,
tart, etc.; only normal tigers that are four-legged, etc. . . . There are no
analytic truths of the form *every lemon has P.* (pp. 140–141)

The reference of natural kind terms, then, is not determined
by the descriptions associated with those terms. But it might seem
that we cannot say the same about *theoretical* concepts, for these
are usually introduced precisely through definitions, which can
be as exact as a mathematical formula (e.g., "momentum *is* mass
times velocity" in Newtonian physics). In this case, for once, it
seems clear that the referential expression "momentum" is used
attributively. That is, it is employed to designate *that which is* mass
times velocity, whatever it may be. But this is exactly what Putnam
denies. As he contends later in his article: "*theoretical terms* in

science have no analytic definitions, for reasons familiar to every reader of recent philosophy of science" (p. 146).

With this contention, Putnam does not try to question the obvious fact that many theoretical terms are *introduced* in scientific discussions by means of a precise, even mathematical, definition. What he does call into question is the idea that the point of such introduction is *to define* the necessary and sufficient conditions to be met by that which falls under the classification of those concepts. As he observes in "The Meaning of 'Meaning'":

[I]t is beyond question that scientists *use terms* [italics mine] as if the associated criteria were not *necessary and sufficient conditions,* but rather *approximately* correct characterizations of some *world of theory-independent entities.* (p. 237)

Putnam's distinction does not concern the de facto exactness or degree of approximation of the terms when they are introduced in theories. Rather, he appeals to a distinction in the *use* made by scientists of these terms (just as Donnellan distinguished between the referential and attributive use). The task is to analyze, from a *pragmatic* point of view, what scientists attempt to *do* when these concepts are used in scientific discussions. Undoubtedly, the point of introducing these concepts is to designate entities (in the real world) whose existence is supposed to be theory-independent. On this issue, Putnam later remarks as follows:

[W]e may give an "operational definition," or a cluster of properties, or whatever, but the intention is never to "make the name *synonymous* with the description." Rather "we *use* the name *rigidly*" to *refer* to whatever things share the *nature* that things satisfying the description normally possess. (ibid., p. 238; italics mine)

To assess the plausibility of Putnam's thesis that theoretical concepts in science are used referentially rather than attributively, we have to take into account the implications of each of these uses.

As we saw, if the use of theoretical concepts (or of any designative expression) is supposed to be purely attributive, it is not possible to correct the knowledge contained in the definitions of these concepts. Indeed, if by "momentum" we meant "mass times velocity," it would be impossible by definition to "discover" that momentum is *not* mass times velocity. First, theories would conventionally establish, by means of definitions, an ontology that would be inherent in them. (They would, so to speak, "disclose" worlds that are related to them.) And then, they would simply deduce all of the consequences that apply to everything that has been previously defined in that way. But obviously, this view of scientific theories as relying on truths by definition (or stipulation) involves a radical conflation of the empirical sciences with the mathematical paradigm. The problem with this conflation is clear. It is hard to understand why scientists should be interested in deriving theoretical consequences that apply to those entities that satisfy their definitions, *in complete independence of whether or not these entities exist in the real world.*

The incorrigibility of the mathematical paradigm, inherent in the attributive use of designative expressions, has a counterintuitive consequence, namely, that scientific theories cannot be corrected according to what actually happens in that world to which they refer through their concepts. In this sense, the attributive use of theoretical concepts seems to be incompatible with the method that distinguishes the natural sciences from mathematics: induction. The inductive method requires that the initial postulates of a theory be revisable in the light of subsequent discoveries.

The revisability required by the inductive method explains why the referential use of theoretical concepts is constitutive for scientific practice. Although from the point of view of their *genesis* these concepts may be introduced by way of definitions (that is, attributions of properties to the entities that fall under their scope), this does not mean that these attributions become constitutive, in a *normative* sense, of what these concepts designate. The significance of introducing a concept in a theory through a designative expression is that we thereby *postulate the existence* of a referent whose constitution is usually not entirely known, and for which we therefore cannot provide necessary and sufficient conditions of identification. With such an expression, we refer to an entity that we assume (counterfactually) to be *independent of the theory* used to describe it, so that the theory is not "true by definition," but rather can be revised in light of other hypotheses or other theories that talk about the same thing but explain it better. Given actual scientific practice, it seems implausible that scientists, beyond postulating the existence of entities and explaining their behavior, would postulate their "essence" (what these entities "are," as Heidegger puts it).[32] At the very least, it would be implausible to think that they do this in complete independence of whether such postulation is tenable in view of alternative theories or eventual improvements in the same theory.

But to allow for transtheoretic terms, the attributions implied by the introduction of concepts in theories have to be distinguished from their primarily referential function. For if these attributions are to be considered as constitutive of what the concepts designate, whatever that may be, the internal improvement of theories would be impossible. It would only be possible to reject them wholesale, constructing new and radically incommensurable theories in their place.

In his "Explanation and Reference," Putnam illustrates the problematic consequences of the thesis that the meaning of terms is constitutive of what they designate. He does this by means of an example drawn from the history of science:

Bohr assumed in 1911 that there are (at every time) numbers p and q such that the (one-dimensional) position of a particle is q and the (one-dimensional) momentum is p; if this was a part of the meaning of "particle" for Bohr, and in addition, "part of the meaning" means "necessary condition for membership in the extension of the term," then electrons are *not* particles in Bohr's sense, and, indeed, there are *no* particles "in Bohr's sense." (And no "electrons" in Bohr's sense of "electron," etc.) *None of the terms in Bohr's 1911 theory referred* [italics mine]! It follows on this account that we cannot say that present electron theory is a better theory of the same particles that Bohr was referring to. (p. 197)

That is, the traditional theory of reference seems to render scientific progress impossible. Taking this consequence into ac-

32. Textual evidence of the incommensurabilist interpretation of the evolution of scientific theories defended by Heidegger can be found in his lectures from the winter semester of 1935–36, published in English under the title *What Is a Thing?*

count, we can see the importance that the designative function of language has for cognitive processes. Or in other words, we can sense the fundamental role that the referential use of designative expressions plays in these processes. Putnam's example leads to quite a different conclusion if expressions such as "electron" are considered in their referential function, as designating theory-independent entities that may be described with greater or lesser accuracy. For, as Putnam remarks later, according to this interpretation of the use of the term "electron,"

Bohr would have been referring to electrons when he used the word "electron," notwithstanding the fact that some of his beliefs about electrons were mistaken, and *we* [italics mine] are referring to those same particles notwithstanding the fact that some of our beliefs—even beliefs included in our scientific "definition" of the term "electron"—may very likely turn out to be equally mistaken. (ibid.)

It is this peculiarity of designative expressions, the fact that they enable us to refer *directly* to that which is assumed to have an independent existence, that allows for transtheoretic terms. This is precisely what cannot be explained by the traditional theory of reference, with its interpretation of designative expressions as disguised predicates. The true function of designative expressions is obliterated by such a conflation. For indeed, with the predicate of a sentence we do not designate an entity, but attribute a property to it. To this extent, the attribution is necessarily constitutive of the use of such a predicate. But this is not necessarily the case in the use of a name, or in that of a designative expression used referentially.

An indirect confirmation of this interpretation of the use of theoretical terms in science can be found in yet another example from the history of science. Here again, Putnam wants to explain why the fundamental role of these concepts is simply to designate, and not to attribute something to what is designated (i.e., in Heidegger's terms, to make something appear *as* something). In *Representation and Reality,* Putnam writes:

Even if a term is originally *introduced* into science via an explicitly formulated *definition,* the status of the resulting truth is not forever a *privileged* one, as it would have to be if the term were simply a synonym for the *definiens*. An example from the history of physics may help to clarify this all-important point. In Newtonian physics the term *momentum* was defined as "mass times velocity". . . . But with the acceptance of Einstein's Special Theory of Relativity a difficulty appeared. Einstein did not challenge the idea that objects have momentum. . . . But he showed that the principle of Special Relativity would be violated if momentum were *exactly* equal to (rest) mass times velocity. What to do? Einstein studied the case of "billiard balls". . . . Can there be a quantity with the properties that (1) it is conserved in elastic collisions, (2) it is closer and closer to "mass times velocity" as the speed becomes small, and (3) its direction is the direction of motion of the particle? Einstein showed that there *is* such a quantity, and he (and everyone else) concluded that that quantity is *what momentum really is*. The statement that momentum is *exactly* equal to mass times velocity was revised. *But this is the statement that was originally a "definition"!* And it was *reasonable* to revise this statement; for why should the statement that momentum is conserved not have at least as great a right to be preserved as the statement "momentum is mass times velocity" when a conflict is discovered? . . . As Quine puts it, *truth by stipulation is not an enduring trait of sentences.* When the statements in our network of belief have to be modified, we have "trade-offs" to make; and what the best trade-off is in a given context cannot be determined by consulting the traditional "definitions" of terms. (pp. 9–10; italics mine)

What this example makes clear is that revision would undoubtedly be impossible if the theoretical terms of science were not used referentially. That is, there could be no revision if the attributions associated with theoretical terms were understood not as hypotheses in need of confirmation concerning theory-independent entities, but as stipulated "definitions" of intratheoretic entities. For a mere difference between theories would force us to conclude that these theories do not refer to the same things (by definition). The incommensurability between theories (or paradigms) is a necessary result of interpreting the use of theoretical concepts as attributive. This becomes manifest in the paradoxical structure of the formulation of the incommensurability thesis itself.

To be able to assert the incommensurability between concepts belonging to different paradigms or theories, we must assume precisely that which the incommensurability thesis wants to deny, it is clear that in most cases an agreement about reference is not merely *conventional*. Rather, it depends essentially on the epistemic situation of a particular linguistic community at a given time.[24] In this sense, an agreement about reference is by no means merely an agreement as to linguistic meaning.

This can be shown by looking more carefully at Donnellan's examples. It seems clear that the cases in which the speaker uses descriptions like "Smith's murderer" or "the man drinking the martini" can only be considered examples of improper use of linguistic expressions *given the stipulation* that the referent did not actually murder Smith or was not drinking a martini. This stipulation, however, has nothing to do with linguistic meaning. That is to say, it is not derived from the rules of the language. Precisely to the extent that the *divergence* present in such cases is actually based on an *epistemic* stipulation, and not on *linguistic* conventions, it is wrong to understand this *divergence* as a case of the *improper use* of linguistic means.

An easy way to see this is to think of some modifications of the examples above. It is not difficult to imagine these examples becoming more and more difficult to state in such terms once they involve more difficult cases and are rendered more faithful to the actual epistemic situations in which human beings can find themselves. (This would happen, for example, if we renounced the appeal to a deus ex machina who fixes once and for all what the real facts are.) In such a case, it would become clear that the question concerning what is a proper use and what an improper use of a description for referring to something cannot be settled by appealing to the semantic rules of a language. In most cases, the

24. This epistemic situation is an unstable one, and in the interesting (hard) cases is essentially an open one. The presupposition of general agreement here can lead to wrong conclusions. Whereas in the case of the grammatical rules of a language, such a presupposition, in spite of its obviously idealized character, can be regarded as unavoidable (i.e., as methodologically identical to the presupposition that the community speaks the same language), in the epistemic case such a presupposition would be not an innocent idealization, but an extremely harmful one. As I will argue in what follows, it would amount to the exclusion of the possibility of cognitive learning.

namely, a common framework of reference underlying these concepts. For the very choice of appropriate examples requires more than the contrast between different theories in general. Obviously, the difference in the framework of reference or object domain of two theories, per se, does not imply the incommensurability of these theories but, in principle, their *indifference*. One clear example would be the attempt to compare the reference of the concepts of the Freudian theory of the unconscious with those of the concepts of quantum mechanics. To distinguish the alleged cases of incommensurability from those of mere indifference, we must choose for our examples theories that really are *in conflict*. That is, we must reckon with theories that aim to explain the *same* phenomena, and at least in this sense attempt to talk about the *same* things (such as Newtonian and quantum mechanics in physics, or the Mendelian and DNA models of heredity in biology, etc.). In other words, the reference of the fundamental concepts of allegedly incommensurable theories must be assumed to have a transtheoretic character in order to show their absolute divergence.

This structural incoherence clearly underscores the *negative* character of the argumentation behind the incommensurability thesis. What this argumentation actually shows is the explanatory gap in the attempt to analyze the behavior of scientific theories relying on a theory of indirect reference. Indeed, if that to which theoretical concepts refer has to be explained in the manner proposed by this theory (so that by "referent" we understand "whatever falls under the concepts used in the theory in question"), it is impossible to suppose that different theories with concepts used in different ways refer to the same things. (For according to this theory, any difference in the meaning or intension of the terms implies, by definition, a difference in their extension.) This supposition, however, is what underlies the choice of examples of alleged incommensurability. For it is indispensable to the distinction between incommensurability and mere indifference. The fact that we *can* clearly distinguish them (especially in order to assert the former) indicates that we need to revise the basic thesis assumed in the wake of the linguistic turn, namely, that meaning determines reference.

Certainly, the inclusion of a system of concepts within the framework of a theory confers upon them a "world-disclosing" function. That is, these concepts set the frame of reference for everything that is encompassed by the theory. But an essential function of the use of concepts is precisely to refer to entities that we assume to have an extratheoretic existence, and that must be designated directly by these concepts. The counterfactual assumption of direct designation is not a denial that these concepts *in fact* indirectly attribute certain properties to the entities they designate. The only implication of the referential use of designative expressions, is that those implicit attributions (originating in the "meaning" of the terms) cannot be understood as *constitutive* of what these terms designate. Instead, they are understood as more or less correct descriptions that can be revised if they enter into conflict with other descriptions or with our intraworldly praxis.[33]

33. There is an ambiguity in the view of reference as an intratheoretic notion. Such a view is defended by Quine, for example, when he states that "terms and reference are local to our conceptual scheme" (1960, p. 53), or that "reference is nonsense except relative to a coordinate system" (1969, p. 200); and that therefore "meaning determines reference within each fixed ontology" (1990, p. 22). It is not clear what is meant by these statements. If they are meant in the *factual* sense that we can only *know* what the different terms of a language or theory refer to if we know the whole system of classification or ontology of the language or theory to which it belongs, they seem to be trivially correct. To know what a term refers to (i.e., to be able to discriminate between the referents of different terms), it is necessary to know by contrast at least some other things to which the term does *not* refer. Otherwise, it would refer to everything or nothing. But if these theses are meant in the *normative* sense that the referents of our terms are also local to our conceptual scheme, i.e., not the real referents but intralinguistic (merely postulated or theoretically constructed) entities, they are obviously wrong. The point (i.e., the normative sense) of the activity of referring is irreducibly language-transcendent. Those objects to which our terms refer (or should aim to refer) are obviously the real referents, however they ought to be appropriately described. In this sense, *referring* to them is not an epistemic activity, as is *ascribing* properties to them, describing them, or classifying them. That is to say, "satisfaction" (the semantic relationship for predication) cannot be understood as the decisive semantic relationship (or as the indirect channel) for reference.

As already mentioned, this presupposition should not be understood in epistemic terms. That is, it does not amount to an attempt to reach the "thing in itself" or to go beyond the realm of language. Rather, it simply amounts to the negative *fallibilist* intuition

---

However, Quine's strategy of eliminating singular terms (i.e., his "no-name" theory) seems to imply this second, normative interpretation of the thesis that meaning determines reference. As Quine puts it:

> What the disappearance of singular terms . . . means is that all reference to objects of any kind . . . is channeled through general terms and bound variables. We can still say anything we like about any one object or all objects, *but we say it always through the idioms of quantification:* "There is an object *x* such that . . ." and "Every object *x* is such that . . .". The objects whose existence is implied in our discourse are finally *just the objects which must, for the truth of our assertions, be acknowledged as "values of variables".* . . . To be is to be a value of a variable. . . . Except when we are concerned with philosophical issues of linguistic reference and existence, on the other hand, there is no point in depriving ourselves of the convenience of singular terms. (1950, p. 282)

The point of the theories of direct reference can be said to consist in the attempt to emphasize that *precisely when we are concerned with philosophical issues of linguistic reference,* we also cannot deprive ourselves of the "convenience" of singular terms. That is, the rationale of the practice of referring (and its peculiar character as opposed to predication) can only be made clear through an analysis of singular terms that shows that reference is *irreducible* to satisfaction plus quantification. Reference is not intratheoretic, precisely to the extent that in our theories we *use* terms referentially and not attributively. That is, we do not refer (as would follow from Quine's strategy) to whatever satisfies our descriptions, to whatever renders our statements true. Rather, our descriptions are true if that to which we refer is in fact correctly described by our theories—which may not be the case. This language-transcendent, non-epistemic sense of the activity of referring can be explained only by taking into account the difference between the attributive and the referential use of designative expressions, a difference necessarily lost by Quine's strategy of eliminating singular terms. It is only on the basis of this difference that we can explain how speakers are able to learn that their descriptions of the referents (whether used in their predications or just for referring) are incorrect, to realize that the referents' identity may be different than they assumed it to be. Naturally, they cannot discover this by trying to step *outside* all systems of reference or descriptions, but only by being confronted (*from within* their epistemic practices, so to speak) with *alternative* descriptions or theories. This confrontation is *sufficient* for learning that *none of these descriptions* can be considered *constitutive* of the referents' identity.

constitutive of cognitive processes of learning, namely, that knowledge is not knowledge unless it is revisable.

Precisely because the use of language rests on designation just as much as on predication (or more specifically, because we have designative expressions that can be used referentially), we can refer to things whose structure we do not yet know with precision, things about which our assumptions can turn out to be false. Designative expressions are used referentially whenever learning or the possibility of revision is inherent in a praxis.[34] For that which underlies the referential use of designative expressions is the as-

---

34. Mathematics is a domain in which the attributive use of designative expressions may be appropriate, that is, where the thesis that meaning determines reference seems prima facie tenable. As Putnam remarks:

> "Objects" in constructive mathematics are *given through descriptions.* Those descriptions do not have to be mysteriously attached to those objects by some non-natural process (or by metaphysical glue). Rather, the possibility of *proving* that a certain construction (the "sense," so to speak, of the description of the model) has certain constructive properties is what is asserted and *all* that is asserted, by saying that the model "exists." In short, *reference is given through sense, and sense is given through verification procedures and not through truth conditions.* The "gap" between our theory and the objects' simply disappears—or, rather, it never appears in the first place. (1983, p. 21)

Another domain that may seem to underscore the contrast between the logic characteristic of the attributive use and that of the referential use is jurisprudence. Terms pertaining to the social world through which we *regulate* juridical relations (whether kinship terms like "father," "son," and the like, or interactions such as "murder," "robbery," etc.) can be considered to function mostly attributively, precisely in order to be able to accomplish their regulatory function. That is, they must be regarded as definable—or at least they must be in fact defined despite the unavoidable conventionality or arbitrariness involved in many cases. However, there are also clear limits to the arbitrariness of the attributive use admissible in this domain. In chapter 7, in which I defend an internal-realist strategy for explaining the cognitive status of moral questions, I will try to show, even if only indirectly, that the possibility of discovery—implicit in the referential use—cannot be completely alien to law, as for example in cases where questions of justice are at issue. A very plausible defense of direct reference as the best semantic account for the legal domain is offered in N. Stavropoulos (1996). Unfortunately, I became aware of this work after the present book was completed.

sumption that there is something that has to be *discovered* rather than *legislated*. That is, the referential use requires the assumption that there is something in relation to which our knowledge can be corrected.[35]

This perspective brings out the *potential for rationality inherent in the referential function of language*. As we saw in chapter 3, Gadamer recognized the reflective effort inherent in the evolution through which the word became "sign," a pure univocal "designator," independent of that which it designates (an evolution through which the possibility of the referential use of language is grasped). Despite Gadamer's rejection of this evolution, the difference between his reconstruction and Humboldt's is important for our assessment of the significance of the referential function of language.

Humboldt held that the view of language "natural" to man is to regard it as a mere tool for designating objects that exist independently of it. But Gadamer rightly points out that the initial relation with language is, in fact, the *lack* of differentiation between word and thing. (This seems to be true from both a phylogenetic and an ontogenetic point of view.)[36] An essential feature of mythical worldviews is precisely this initial undifferentiatedness between language and reality, between "sign" and "designatum." This entails a lack of distance with respect to one's own language, and thus a lack of reflective distance with respect to the symbolically mediated character of our relationship with the world. As

35. This central aspect of the referential function of language is emphasized by Føllesdal (1986). He remarks that

names are normally introduced for the following three purposes:

(i) When we are interested in *further features* of the object beyond those that were mentioned in the description that was used to draw our attention to the object.
(ii) When we want to follow the object through *changes*.
(iii) When we are aware that some or many of our beliefs concerning the object are *wrong* and we want to correct them. (p. 108)

36. Regarding the ontogenetic case see J. Piaget, *The Child's Conception of the World*, chapters I and II.

Habermas puts it in his *Theory of Communicative Action,* this lack of distance implies that

a linguistically constituted worldview can be identified with the world-order itself to such an extent that it cannot be perceived *as* an interpretation of the world that is subject to error and open to criticism. (p. 50)

The counterpoint to this situation is the reflection initiated by "the Greek enlightenment," in which the differences between "sign," "designatum," and "concept" become explicit. It is precisely this differentiation that underlies the distinction between an interpretation of the world, and the world that is assumed to be independent of this interpretation. The assumption of a single world, identical for everyone, which first renders meaningful the attempt to revise our interpretations of it, can only come about by learning the referential function of language (i.e., the referential use of designative expressions). This function allows us to differentiate language itself from the reality to which we can refer, of course, only by means of it.

In what follows, I will discuss Habermas's comparison of the features of the mythical with those of the modern worldview, a comparison that seems to lend support to my hypothesis. This discussion will serve two purposes. On the one hand, I will try to show that Habermas's analysis of the conditions of possibility of the rationalization of worldviews can be seen as indirect confirmation of the view I have defended in this chapter (through my brief discussion of the central tenets of the theory of direct reference). In this way, I will also try to show the theoretical standpoint through which, working within Habermas's own framework, we could do away with the view of language that hypostatizes its world-disclosing function at the expense of its referential function. Surprising as it may sound, it is precisely Habermas's analysis that provides us with the means to question, from a different standpoint, the thesis that meaning determines reference. This remains the case even though he himself has granted the thesis in question to hermeneutics, with his view of the lifeworld as "constitutive" of understanding (that is, with his view of background knowledge as unrevisable), without knowing later on how to block the consequences of this thesis.

5.3 The Condition of Possibility of Discourse: The Referential Function of Language and the Formation of a Reflective Concept of World

In chapter 1 of *Theory of Communicative Action*, Habermas analyzes the conditions of possibility of "discourse." This analysis, though, is based on a strategy different from the one he employed for his formal-pragmatic analysis of communicative action in "What is Universal Pragmatics?" The concept of discourse is introduced implicitly through a comparison of the features of the mythical with those of the modern world-view. As a result of this comparison, Habermas contends:

Validity claims are in principle open to criticism because they are based on *formal world-concepts*. They presuppose a world that is identical for *all possible* observers, or a world intersubjectively shared *by all the members of a group* and they do so *in an abstract form freed of all specific content*. (p. 50; italics mine)

To uncover this condition of possibility of discourse, Habermas analyzes those aspects of the mythical worldview that, from a modern point of view, are regarded as resulting from the structures of a deficient rationality. For through this contrast, "the heretofore unthematized presuppositions of modern thought should become visible in the mirror of mythical thinking" (p. 44).

This comparison of the mythical and modern worldviews is undertaken in connection with Habermas's attempt to "inquire into the conditions that the *structures of action-orienting worldviews* must satisfy if a *rational* [italics mine] conduct of life is to be possible for those who share such a worldview" (pp. 43–44). The ultimate goal of this analysis is to defend the universalistic position behind Habermas's theory of communicative action. In this context, he writes:

The universalistic position forces one to the assumption that the rationalization of worldviews takes place through learning processes. . . . If we are to conceive historical transitions between differently structured systems of interpretation as learning processes, however, we must satisfy the demand for a formal analysis of meaning constellations that makes it possible to reconstruct the empirical succession of worldviews as a series of steps in learning that can be insightfully recapitulated from the perspective of a participant and can be submitted to intersubjective tests. (pp. 66–67)

This hypothesis provides the appropriate background for understanding the guiding assumption of Habermas's comparison of the mythical and modern worldviews: "mythical worldviews are far from making possible rational orientations of action in our sense" (p. 44). Habermas traces this assumption back to the fact that "in a mythically interpreted world we cannot, or cannot with sufficient precision, make certain *differentiations* [italics mine] that are fundamental to our understanding of the world" (p. 48). The differentiations to which he alludes are the following:

• the distinction between culture and nature:

In a mythical worldview, there is a peculiar confusion between culture and nature. That is, there is

a mixing of two object domains, physical nature and the sociocultural environment. Myths do not permit a clear, basic, conceptual differentiation between things and persons, between objects that can be manipulated and agents—subjects capable of speaking and acting to whom we attribute linguistic utterances. Thus it is only consistent when magical practices do not recognize the distinction between teleological and communicative action. . . . The *ineptitude* to which the technical or therapeutic failures of goal-directed action are due falls into the same category as the *guilt* for moral-normative failings of interaction in violation of existing social orders. (p. 48)

Habermas sets out to explain the process for differentiating these object domains, the process resulting from "the demythologization of worldviews" that leads to "the desocialization of nature and the denaturalization of society" (ibid.). He proposes to understand this differentiation in terms of the distinction between "*basic attitudes toward worlds*" (p. 49). These are explained by Habermas in the following terms:

Regarded as object domains, nature and culture belong to the world of facts about which true statements are possible; but as soon as we are to specify explicitly wherein things are distinct from persons, causes from motives, happenings from actions, and so forth, we have to go beyond differentiating object domains to differentiating between a *basic attitude toward the objective world of what is the case* and a *basic attitude toward the social world of what can be legitimately expected,* what is commanded or ought to be. (TCA, p. 49; italics mine)

What underlies the undifferentiatedness of nature and culture (and hence what precludes the development of these differentiated basic attitudes) is the lack of a more fundamental distinction, namely,

• the differentiation between language and world:

That is, there is not a sufficient differentiation "between language as the medium of communication and that *about which* [italics mine] understanding can be reached in linguistic communication" (TCA, p. 49). Concerning this distinction, Habermas writes:

In the totalizing mode of thought of mythical worldviews, it is apparently difficult to draw with sufficient precision the familiar (to us) semiotic distinctions between the *sign-substratum* of a linguistic expression, its *semantic content,* and the *referent* to which a speaker can refer with its help. The magical relation between names and designated objects, the concretistic relation between the meaning of expressions and the states-of-affairs represented give evidence of systematic confusion between *internal connections of meaning* and *external connections of objects.* Internal relations obtain between symbolic expressions, external relations between entities that appear in the world. . . . Evidently there is not yet any precise concept for the nonempirical validity that we ascribe to symbolic expressions. Validity is confounded with empirical efficacy. . . . [I]n mythical thought diverse validity claims, such as propositional truth, normative rightness, and expressive truthfulness are not yet differentiated. (TCA, pp. 49–50; italics mine)

Of special interest in the present context is the consequence of this confusion between language and world, between "sign" and "designatum." As pointed out above, "the linguistically constituted worldview can be identified with the world-order itself to such an extent that it cannot be perceived *as* an interpretation of the world that is subject to error and open to criticism" (TCA, p. 50).

By way of contrast with this lack of differentiation characteristic of the mythical worldview, Habermas can then establish the "formal presuppositions of intersubjectivity," which underlie the processes of understanding regulated by validity claims typical of the modern worldview. As already mentioned at the beginning of this section: "Validity claims are in principle open to criticism because they are based on *formal world-concepts.* They presuppose a world that is identical for *all possible* observers, or a world intersubjectively shared *by all the members of a group* and they do so *in an abstract form freed of all specific content*" (TCA, p. 50; italics mine).

The important thing to note is the condition that Habermas then singles out as indispensable to the development of such world-concepts:

Actors who raise validity claims have to avoid *materially prejudicing* the relation between language and reality, between the medium of communication and that about which something is being communicated. Under the presupposition of formal world-concepts and universal validity claims, the *contents* of a linguistic worldview have to be *detached from the assumed world-order itself.* (TCA, pp. 50–51; italics mine)

After discussing the unfolding of this presupposition in ontogenesis (relying on Piaget's account), Habermas points out the need to form "a reflective concept of 'world.'" For such a concept would make possible the "access to the world through the medium of common interpretative efforts, in the sense of a cooperative negotiation of situation definitions" (TCA, p. 69).

Putting the conclusions of the previous section in the context of Habermas's analysis, my claim about the potential for rationality inherent in the referential function of language seems to be confirmed. Learning the referential use of designative expressions, and thus the distinction between sign and designatum, is essential for forming a reflective concept of "world"—that is, the concept of a single world intersubjectively shared by all participants in communication "in an abstract form freed of all specific content" (TCA, p. 50). As we have seen, it is this counterfactual presupposition of a *single objective world* that enables speakers "to avoid *materially prejudicing* the relation between language and reality, between the medium of communication and that about which something is being communicated." In this way, it allows that "the contents of a linguistic worldview [become] *detached from the assumed world-order itself*" (TCA, pp. 50–51; italics mine).

To learn this distinction by mastering the referential use of designative expressions does not involve any rejection of the world-disclosing function of language. That is, such learning does not question the symbolically mediated character of our relationship with the world. Our access to this world (to the referents) is of course always de facto *prejudiced* by the choice of linguistic means through which we refer to it. But insofar as we have learned to use these linguistic means referentially, thanks to the designative function of language, we have also learned a *normative* distinction. We can distinguish, however counterfactually, between the implicit attributions (or background knowledge) underlying these linguistic means and the world assumed to be independent of them. This distinction, in turn, allows speakers to assume that they refer to "the same things" even when their interpretations differ.[37] This is underscored by Habermas when he writes:

The function of the formal world-concepts, however, is to prevent the stock of what is common from dissolving in the stream of subjectivities repeatedly reflected in one another. They make it possible to adopt in common the perspective of a third person or a nonparticipant. Every action oriented to reaching understanding can be conceived as part of

37. This consequence of the theory of direct reference makes it clear that it is not necessary to appeal to a specific and shared background knowledge, constitutive of the processes of understanding, *in the hermeneutic sense*, as the ground that determines what speakers refer to and hence as the condition of possibility for talking about "the same thing." This theory of reference gives support to the Habermasian thesis cited above, namely, that communicative rationality is already embodied "in the structures of uninterrupted intersubjectivity of the 'pre-agreement' guaranteed by the lifeworld" (ENT, pp. 339–340), and hence, that a "counterfactual [and formal] sustaining agreement" is a sufficient condition of possibility for understanding, at least given a certain degree of rationalization (or *Dezentrierung*) of worldviews.

a cooperative process of interpretation aiming at situation definitions that are intersubjectively recognized. The concepts of the three worlds serve here as the commonly *supposed* system of coordinates in which the situation contexts can be ordered in such a way that agreement will be reached about what the participants may treat as a fact, or as a valid norm, or as a subjective experience. (TCA, pp. 69–70; italics mine)

Here we find not only indirect confirmation of the importance of the referential function of language (as well as of the counterfactual and formal nature of the "sustaining agreement" that makes possible the praxis of understanding and communication); we also find the key to recognizing the source of the reification of language characteristic of hermeneutic philosophy. The thesis that meaning determines reference underlying the hermeneutic view of language is not understood in a purely factual sense. That is to say, it is not understood as the mere *fact* that our relationship with the world is always symbolically mediated. Rather, this thesis is taken in the *normative* sense that what is disclosed by language *must necessarily be identified with the assumed world-order itself.*

As we have seen in this chapter, to make language responsible for world-disclosure *in this sense* implies questioning a distinction inherent in the referential function of language, one which sustains the structures of our rationality—namely, the distinction between language and the world.

III

Habermas's Theory of Communicative Rationality from an Internal Realist Point of View

Introduction

In chapter 4, I pointed to Habermas's central thesis concerning the internal connection between meaning and validity, his claim that "the dimension of validity is inherent in language." On the basis of the discussion in chapter 5, there now seem to be sufficient grounds for believing that this thesis could be properly defended with the aid of a theory of direct reference. That is, it could be supported by an explanation of the unavoidable normative presuppositions already anchored in the use (and understanding) of referential expressions. This is so insofar as these presuppositions are required not only for the *communicative* use of language, i.e., for understanding particular speech acts. Rather, they are already required for its *cognitive* use, that is, for understanding the propositional content expressed in *any* kind of speech act. Such an explanation emphasizes that the crucial distinction for reference (that between sign and object) presupposes that these terms are logically independent. In this sense, reference as a nonepistemic activity is obviously language-transcendent, and thus interpretation-transcendent. It is the activity of referring, then, that compels speakers to recognize the *factual* rather than "constitutive" character of their interpretations against *that of which* they are interpretations. It is in this sense that speakers unavoidably transcend the context of their own interpretations (i.e., traditions) for the validity claims they raise in their speech acts. They cannot transcend their factual epistemic situation in the sense of being able to reach a privileged epistemic perspective; there is no "God's eye point of view." But *to the extent that their knowledge claims purport to be about a (nonepistemic) reality,* we can always ask about the appropriateness of any factual epistemic means for expressing these claims. Whenever speakers raise universal validity claims (i.e., cognitive claims), their particular epistemic ways of expressing them can *in principle* always be corrected. It can be criticized or put into question from an alternative epistemic perspective, interpretation, or the like. For their cognitive claims concerning reality, speakers know that such a correction *always makes sense in principle.* As Habermas's analysis of discourse makes clear, the formal, realist presuppositions implicit in our cognitive claims are conditions for the intelligibility of a practice (i.e., the practice of communicating about something in the world). These are not substantial beliefs about reality with a specific content.[1] The purely formal notion of a single objective world is not just one particular belief among others that the speakers might happen to have, but is rather a formal presupposition anchored in the practices of discourse concerned with knowledge claims (i.e., universal validity claims).[2]

As we have seen, such normative presuppositions of the activity of referring are crucial to Habermas's explanation of the very possibility of discourse (and therefore of the use of language oriented toward understanding). To this extent, the insights behind the theories of direct reference not only seem compatible with Habermas's approach, but even appear implicitly *contained* in it.[3]

But as can already be inferred from chapter 4, things are not so straightforward. For to take seriously this line of thought, which

1. J. R. Searle argues in the same way when he explains the meaning and status of the thesis of "external realism"—that "there is a way that things are that is independent of all representations of how things are." He remarks that this is not an empirical thesis but a condition of possibility of maintaining certain sorts of theses, i.e., a condition of intelligibility for certain kinds of linguistic practices (1995, pp. 177ff.). But Searle does not explicitly state what these different kinds of linguistic practices have in common, i.e., which "large areas of discourse" are the ones for which such a presupposition is a condition of intelligibility. In Habermas's analysis, as we will see, it becomes clear that the linguistic practices at issue are the ones concerned with knowledge claims.

2. Only to the extent that speakers purport to refer to something in the objective world for saying something true about it can their claim be an objective knowledge claim (as opposed to a merely subjective belief). But owing to the meaning of such claims, speakers know that they are unavoidably subject to criteria of success (objective correctness) that transcend their particular epistemic situation—i.e., that these criteria are logically independent of this situation. See footnote 13, this chapter.

3. Habermas himself has recently expressed his agreement with the crucial insight of the theories of "direct" reference discussed in the previous chapter: namely, the connection between the possibility of mutual agreement and learning and the realist, normative presupposition of a single objective world implicit in the referential use of linguistic expressions. See Habermas, "Reply," p. 1527; "Rorty's Pragmatic Turn," pp. 14, 17.

is undoubtedly already present in Habermas's theory of communicative rationality, we have to recognize the indispensable *normative* role played in the practice of discourse by such *realist* presuppositions.

As we have seen, the practice of discourse is based on the distinction between *interpretations* and what they are interpretations *of,* and thus on their logical independence (that is, the independence of realist and epistemic presuppositions). However, to recognize this is to recognize that the conditions for the validity of such interpretations cannot be exclusively epistemic. With their knowledge claims as such, speakers unavoidably transcend the context of their own interpretations. But by the same token, the validity of these claims is context-transcendent *precisely because it also depends on non-epistemic conditions.* That is, it depends on conditions that either obtain or do not obtain, regardless of the speakers' given epistemic situation.

Thus, to recognize the normative weight of such presuppositions, it is necessary to pursue a realist strategy that would understand reference (and thus truth) as non-epistemic. Naturally, such a strategy implies the renunciation of an antirealist approach.

As already mentioned in the preface, Habermas's approach oscillates between two distinct strategies. The first is an antirealist strategy, constructivist through and through. The second is one that could be called "internal realism";[4] it incorporates realist elements in a generally pragmatist perspective.

This oscillation is possible owing to the peculiar perspective from which Habermas's theory is developed. As a result of his

---

4. As mentioned earlier, I borrow this term from Putnam. I understand this expression as an attempt to assert our *realist* intuitions from within a pragmatist perspective, and thus without leaving the *internal* perspective of the participants in communicative practices (adopting the observer's or God's eye point of view). As Putnam states it: "If we succeed in remaining realists while giving up the idea of the Mirror of Nature, we will have become what I call 'internal realist'" (1994, p. 288). Understood in this way, internal realism is actually incompatible with antirealism (and is not itself a form of it, as has sometimes been held), i.e., it requires us to understand reference and truth as nonepistemic. In this sense, I consider Putnam's recent rejection of epistemic truth to be nothing more than a consistent step in his defense of internal realism (see 1994, pp. 242–295).

formal-pragmatic perspective, Habermas's approach attempts to reconstruct the normative presuppositions implicit in the communication processes oriented toward mutual understanding, from the *internal* perspective of the speakers themselves. But as a reconstruction of *communicative* presuppositions, such a formal-pragmatic perspective does not per se predetermine a realist or antirealist account. (That is to say, it excludes metaphysical realism but does not demand antirealism.) In fact, until quite recently,[5] Habermas's own development of his theory of communicative rationality relied heavily on an antirealist account of the connection between meaning and validity. The main strategy has been to interpret the universal validity claims of "truth" and "moral rightness" in epistemic terms, that is, to reinterpret both claims in terms of the notion of "rational acceptability under ideal conditions." This has been followed by an appeal to the normative presuppositions implicit in such epistemic notions, so as to explain the common normative basis for a valid understanding among speakers concerning these validity claims. In my opinion, this antirealist strategy has served as the basis for most of the criticisms directed at Habermas's approach from the outset.[6] For as we shall see, the attempt to defend the universalist core of a theory of communicative rationality by means of an antirealist strategy presents this theory with a thorny difficulty. Either it allows us to give an account of normative validity only at the price of a metaphysical idealism incompatible with fallibilism (and with pluralism, for that matter); or else, to avoid such metaphysical ballast, it would have to accept the relativism implicit in a consistently antirealist position. As I will try to show in what follows, only an internal-realist strategy allows for a consistent defense of the normative elements unavoidably contained in a theory of communicative rationality (universalism, fallibilism, cognitivism, etc.). Moreover, it does this from an entirely pragmatic, postmetaphysical point of view.

5. See footnote 7.

6. See E. Tugendhat (1992), pp. 275–314 and (1993), pp. 161–176; also A. Wellmer (1986), pp. 51–172.

In fact, Habermas has recently acknowledged the difficulties implicit in an antirealist strategy with respect to the validity claim "truth" (i.e., the attempt to explain this notion in terms of the epistemic notion of "rational acceptability").[7] For this reason, I offer only a summary[8] of the main problems involved in such an antirealist strategy (chapter 6). This will allow me, in a second step, to show how an equivalent internal-realist strategy could be articulated for the validity claim of "moral rightness." In this way, the universalism and cognitivism of discourse ethics can be defended, free of accompanying metaphysical baggage. And by the same stroke, it can be made compatible with the pluralism characteristic of modern societies (chapter 7).

7. Habermas's rejection of his epistemic conception of truth can be found in his article "Rorty's Pragmatic Turn."

8. I have argued against this strategy in a more detailed way in the following articles: "Spannungen im Warheitsbegriff"; "Truth, Knowledge and Reality"; and "Pluralism and Universalism in Discourse Ethics." A. Wellmer had already criticized Habermas's conception of truth on similar grounds—even if it is not completely clear to me whether Wellmer considers truth as non-epistemic, nor whether he would agree with my interpretation of the internal connection between truth and rational acceptability (see footnote 24). His critique can be found in Wellmer (1986), pp. 51–174; (1992), pp. 171–219; and (1993), pp. 157–177.

6

Rational Acceptability and Truth

To show that Habermas's theory of communicative rationality can actually be made *more* defensible by use of an internal-realist rather than an antirealist strategy, it will first be helpful to consider what his theory aims to explain in the most general sense. It can then be shown how this aim might be preserved, and defended even more convincingly, by such a change of general strategy.

As seen in previous chapters, Habermas's approach tries to explain the peculiar kind of rationality presupposed in those communicative practices in which participants attempt to reach a mutual understanding. To participate in such practices, speakers must be able, if asked, to *justify* their own speech acts. That is, they must be capable of participating in argumentation processes or "discourses." Habermas's formal-pragmatic analysis of the general normative presuppositions of such processes is, therefore, a discourse-theoretic interpretation of the notion of rational acceptability (or rational justification). What is distinctive about this interpretation is its general formal-pragmatic approach, that is, the claim that the appropriated explanation of such a notion is a *procedural* one. For as this explanation shows, the rational acceptability of our beliefs becomes all the more contingent on the rationality of our argumentation *procedures* the less it can rely on any *substantive content* that is precluded a priori from being problematized. Given the unavoidable *openness* of the communicative practices oriented toward mutual understanding (an understanding dependent on the explicit, unforced assent of the participants), only the formal conditions of rational argumentation *procedures* can be regarded, in advance, as *necessary* conditions for their outcome being rationally acceptable or justified. Thus the insight behind his approach is that our convictions are rational not so much because they are part of a *system* of unrevisable, absolutely grounded beliefs; instead, the decisive factor is that they are the result of an open, self-correcting *process* that allows for permanent revisability. Habermas expresses this in the following terms:

Whoever shares views that turn out to be false is not *eo ipso* irrational. Someone is irrational if she puts forward her opinions dogmatically, clinging to them although she sees that she is not able to justify them. In order to qualify an opinion as rational, it is enough that it can be held true for good reasons in the relevant context of justification, i.e., that it is rationally acceptable. (CCCR, p. 312).

Given Habermas's general aims, one of the virtues of such a procedural characterization of "rational acceptability" is clear. The *formal* features that belong to rationally acceptable argumentation-*procedures* as such are *neutral* with respect to the *kind of content* (i.e., the kind of *questions*) to which such a practice can meaningfully be applied.[1] In this sense, Habermas's analysis shows that we essentially have *one procedural notion* of rational acceptability and *different substantial criteria* for justification. The latter vary in different contexts (owing to the different kinds of questions at issue), and at different times (through the unfolding of cognitive learning-processes). Actually, it is in this sense that our notion of rational acceptability is at bottom *procedural.* For given that we can only infer the correctness of our beliefs from the convincingness of our reasons,[2] and given fur-

1. As we will see in chapter 7, this opens up the possibility of arguing that not only theoretical questions concerning the truth of statements can be decided rationally, but moral and political questions as well.

2. This is true given that no direct confrontation with a nonconceptualized reality is possible for us or, as Habermas expresses it, that "direct access to uninterpreted truth conditions is denied to us" (RPT, p. 26).

ther that no substantial criteria for justification can be precluded a priori from being problematized,[3] it follows that we
can only infer the convincingness [4] of our reasons from the results of a rational process of argumentation—that is, a process
taking place under the conditions of an ideal speech situation.[5]
The procedural conditions that guarantee the rational acceptability of our ways of achieving knowledge are *necessary* conditions for the validity of their outcome *only to the extent* that no
substantial criteria of justification can be a *sufficient* condition
for the *correctness* of such an outcome (i.e., that we can only infer
its correctness from its intersubjective *convincingness*). Only if
this is the case can the central insights behind the discourse-
theoretic explanation of rational acceptability be correct, namely,
that

3. As Habermas expresses it: "procedures and reasons are so closely interwoven
with each other that there cannot be any evidence or criteria of assessment that
are completely *prior* to argumentation, that do not have to be justified in turn
in argumentation and validated by rationally motivated agreement reached in
discourse under the presuppositions of argumentation" (EDE, p. 165). Only to
the extent that we do not allow *any substantial criteria* of justification to be regarded as a *sufficient condition for convincingness* can we mantain a general *fallibilist*
attitude in our cognitive practices (toward any possible belief, any epistemic criteria for justification, etc.).

4. The discourse-theoretic explanation of the notion of rational acceptability
or justification is based on two characteristics of the notion of convincingness: its intersubjectivity (subjective certainty is no guarantee of general convincingness), and its "unforceability" (only under non-coercive conditions is
it possible to tell whether an argument is genuinely convincing or not. These
conditions can then be analyzed in terms of the structural or formal characteristics required for a rational procedure of argumentation). See footnote
24.

5. I use the expression "ideal speech situation" in the same way that Habermas introduced it in his article "Wahrheitstheorien," namely, as a *label* for the
totality of normative presuppositions of the argumentation practices that
constitute his discourse-theoretic explanation of rational acceptability. By
using this label, I avoid having to mention all of these different presuppositions every time. Concerning the analysis of these presuppositions, see sections
IV and V from "Wahrheitstheorien," and also *Theory of Communicative Action*
(pp. 44ff.).

a. our notion of rational acceptability is essentially procedural, characterizable in formal terms; and,

b. the procedural conditions for rational acceptability are *necessary* conditions for the validity of our epistemic practices.

Thus speakers are rational in this sense in virtue of two capacities. First, they are rational insofar as they can consider *the force of arguments as the only determining factor* for the strength of their convictions. Second, as a result, they are rational to the extent that they can regard the force of counterarguments as *binding* for the determination of such convictions. These attitudes, and the argumentative practice that is based on them, can be considered rational precisely (and only) to the extent that *no epistemic means can guarantee the correctness* of the outcome of our cognitive practices (truth, moral rightness, and so forth).[6] In this sense, a discourse-theoretic explanation of rational acceptability stands or falls with its ability to explain the *fallibilism* in which our argumentative practices of testing and revising knowledge claims are rooted.

Taking into account the central insights of a discourse-theoretic explanation of the notion of "rational acceptability" (or justification), we can now reflect on Habermas's discourse theory of truth. This will allow us not only to see whether this theory gives a plausible account of the notion of truth; it will also clarify the implications of the antirealist strategy, which identifies this notion with the epistemic notion of rational acceptability under ideal conditions. Does this strategy preclude the possibility of defending a procedural, discourse-theoretic explanation of the notion of rational acceptability? The answer is important, since this discourse-theoretic explanation makes up the very core of Habermas's theory of communicative rationality.

6. Were this a possibility, whoever would have access to such epistemic means could not possibly be rational in mantaining a *fallibilist* attitude vis-à-vis beliefs obtained through such a necessarily successful method. A dogmatic (i.e., fundamentalist) attitude would be rather more appropriate.

6.1 Truth as an Epistemic Notion

In his article "Wahrheitstheorien,"[7] Habermas tries to explain the internal connection between truth and rational acceptability. To do this, he adopts a *pragmatic* perspective, trying to show the insufficiencies of any attempt to explain the notion of truth without relating it to the practices of revision of our beliefs. For he shares one of the crucial insights behind all epistemic explanations of truth, namely, that no merely *semantic* analysis of the truth predicate à la Tarski is exhaustive. That is, it cannot tell us everything we always wanted to know about the sense and function of such a predicate for our epistemic practices of evaluating and revising beliefs. As long as the internal connection between truth and knowledge is not shown, the philosophically relevant analysis of truth has not been provided. If, from a semantic point of view, Tarski's Convention T ("'p' is true if and only if p") exhausts the meaning of the truth predicate, restricting ourselves to such a point of view renders unavoidable the conclusion that asserting "p is true" does not add anything to the mere assertion "p". The disquotational use seems to be the only use of the truth predicate. This observation leads to the outcome, suggested by Ramsey's redundancy theory,[8] that such a predicate is logically superfluous. It would follow that a theory of truth is also superfluous, as suggested in recent years by deflationists.[9] If on the contrary, Habermas argues, one adopts a *pragmatic* perspective, if one considers in what contexts we use such a predicate, the difference between the two assertions becomes evident. To add "is true" (or "is false") to other speakers' assertions ceases to be superfluous as soon as we situate ourselves in the context of putting them into question. For in such a context, the truth claim (which undoubtedly is already implicit in the assertion of some statement p)

7. J. Habermas, "Wahrheitstheorien," in *Vorstudien und Ergänzungen zur Theorie des kommunikativen handelns.*

8. F. P. Ramsey (1931).

9. See M. Williams (1986), pp. 223–242; S. Leeds (1978), pp. 111–130; P. Horwich (1982), pp. 181–201.

becomes explicit through remarks of the type "p is true/p is false," precisely in order to indicate the controversial character or the need for justification of these assertions. Such remarks point to the need for an explicit thematization (in a "discourse") of the truth claim contained in the problematized assertion, in order to analyze its degree of justification. From this perspective, it is possible to see the other uses of the predicate "true," over and above the disquotational use. We can adopt Rorty's names for these additional uses.[10] With the "endorsing" use, we assent to what is said by someone, committing ourselves to it. And with the "cautionary" use, we contrast "true" with "justified," warning of the possibility that a statement that seems justified may turn out not to be true. By analyzing these uses, it becomes evident that such a predicate is not only not superfluous. More than this, the use of the predicate "true" is *crucial*, at least for the epistemic practices of revising our knowledge.

From this perspective, it is understandable that the discourse theory of truth grounds itself in a formal-pragmatic analysis of constative speech acts (i.e., assertions). For even though statements are that to which we ascribe truth or falsity, these statements taken in isolation merely express possible states of affairs. For a statement to be true, however, the expressed state of affairs must be a fact. Habermas remarks in this context that

we call statements true or false in relation to the states of affairs that are expressed or reproduced in them. . . . To each statement we can assign a state of affairs, but a statement is true if and only if it reproduces a real state of affairs or a fact—and not if it presents a state of affairs as if it were a fact. (WT, p. 128)

Thus Habermas remarks that only when a statement "is placed in relation with the external reality of that which can be observed"

---

10. In "Pragmatism, Davidson, and Truth" (pp. 333–355), Rorty distinguishes along with the *disquotational* use of the truth predicate two other uses of it: the *endorsing* use and the *cautionary* use. Returning to this distinction in "Universality and Truth" (unpublished manuscript), Rorty holds that the cautionary use is the only use that cannot be eliminated from our linguistic practices—for in his opinion, the other two uses can easily be paraphrased in terms that do not require the truth predicate.

through an *assertion* does this statement actually remain tied to the validity claim "truth." For such a statement, "inasmuch as it is a non-situated sentence, a mere grammatical construction, neither requires nor can satisfy" such a claim.[11] To this extent, the meaning of the predicate "true" is interpreted correctly only if it is understood as a validity claim that we attach to statements *when we assert them.*[12] Now, the fact that someone asserts a statement means at the same time that he or she *believes* or *knows* that such a statement is true. In this sense, statements that may be true or false express beliefs that, if true, can be regarded as knowledge. For this reason, the validity claim "truth" linked to our statements becomes explicit (through remarks of the type "*p* is true/false") in the context of knowledge claims being called into question and revised.

These methodological considerations are reflected in the three theses with which Habermas characterizes the discourse theory of truth:

First thesis. We call truth the validity claim that we attach to the constative speech acts. A statement is true when the validity claim of the speech acts with which . . . we assert that statement is justified.

Second thesis. Questions of truth are posed only when validity claims are problematized. . . . For this reason, in discourses in which hypothetical validity claims are examined, the remarks concerning the truth of statements are not redundant.

Third thesis. . . . Whether a state of affairs is the case or is not the case, is not decided by the evidence of experiences, but by the result of an argumentation. The idea of truth can only be developed with reference to the discursive cashing in of validity claims. (WT, pp. 135–136)

The second thesis expresses the intuition, undoubtedly justified, that truth cannot be considered as radically nonepistemic. This is so at least insofar as "true" is a predicate that we attribute

11. Habermas (WIUP), pp. 388–389.

12. The point in Habermas's argument is that understanding Convention T is parasitic on a prior understanding of what assertions are. Without an understanding of what it means to assert "*p*," the right-hand side of the biconditional would remain unintelligible. See also Habermas's "Rorty's Pragmatic Turn," (pp. 19ff.).

to our *beliefs;* in this sense, there is an internal connection between truth and knowledge. This, in turn, justifies the third thesis: the consideration that only an explanation of the function of such a predicate in the praxis of testing our knowledge claims can exhaustively account for the meaning and function of this predicate without leading us to the conclusion either that the predicate is completely superfluous (in the sense of a theory of redundancy) or that any attempt to explain it makes no sense (as deflationists hold).

The first thesis, however, contains the germ of an epistemic interpretation of the concept of truth. For it not only affirms that there is an internal connection between truth and knowledge (insofar as the candidates for truth and falsity are our *beliefs*); it also makes the decisive step that leads to an epistemic conception of truth. For this thesis allows Habermas to reformulate the necessary and sufficient condition for truth stated at the start, namely, that "a statement is true if and only if it reproduces a real state of affairs or a fact." Accordingly, he can now claim that "the truth condition of statements is the potential agreement of everyone else. . . . The truth of a proposition means the promise to reach a rational consensus over what is said" (WT, p. 137). To evaluate the justification of such an epistemic conception of truth—in which truth depends not on what is the case but rather on the rational acceptability of what is said[13]—one

13. Beyond all the general problems of any attempt to equate truth and rational acceptability that we are going to discuss in this chapter, there is a problem peculiar to Habermas's theory of communicative rationality, namely, that one of the main targets of this theory is to show that there are questions other than those of truth (such as moral questions) that can also be *decided* in a rationally acceptable way. Taking this into account, it is clear that "rational acceptability under ideal conditions" (i.e., "the promise to reach a rational consensus over what is said") cannot explain the meaning of "truth" *if it also has to explain the meaning of "moral correctness"*—as we will see in the next chapter. Had we not been told, at the beginning of the article, that the consensus in the case of truth claims has to be *about the existence of states of affairs in the objective world* (and not, for example, about the generalizability of interests preserved by a norm as in the case of moral claims), we would never be able to know by means of the proposed definition alone how the participants in discourses can tell what they

must analyze in detail the argument that lies at the basis of such a thesis.

The connection between assertability and truth that is expressed in the thesis at hand is justified by the following reflection: "truth is a validity claim that we attach to statements when we assert them. . . . In asserting something I make the claim that the statement that I assert is true. This claim I can make with reason or without reason" (WT, p. 129). From this there follows, as Habermas subsequently points out, that "*assertions can be neither true nor false, but rather they are justified or not justified*" (ibid., italics mine). This is undoubtedly correct, because the justification or rational acceptability of assertions does not indeed depend *only* on the truth of the corresponding statement. When I assert something, I not only make the claim that what is asserted is true. I also claim that I *know* it to be true, and that if necessary, I could give reasons supporting my belief as to its truth. As traditionally stated,[14] the necessary and sufficient conditions for establishing that someone *knows* something are the following:

---

have to look for in the case of "truth" claims (as opposed to other, different cases). It is the internal connection between assertability and truth, underlined by Habermas, that makes it impossible to interpret the realist meaning of the notion of truth in epistemic terms. Precisely to the extent that with assertions (as opposed to other kinds of speech acts like requests or commands) we aim to state what is the case (i.e., to state *the existence of states of affairs in the objective world*), the truth or falsity of the statements asserted cannot depend on anything other than this existence. The very *sense* of the practice of assertions unavoidably determines the conditions of its success. As we will see later, "truth" and "falsity" merely express the two possible outcomes of this practice, the success or failure of the attempted goal (given the *point* of making *assertions* rather than any other speech acts—namely, to say how things are). The very *meaning* of assertions, as assertions *about reality,* is therefore what introduces the element of context-transcendent validity into such a linguistic game by which speakers subject themselves to standards which transcend their own attitudes, epistemic situation, and so forth.

14. Although the conditions for knowledge that I point out here are usually attributed to Plato (*Theatetus* 201a and perhaps also *Meno* 98a), my recapitulation of these conditions follows (with slight variations) the one given by A. J. Ayer (1956), p. 35, and R. M. Chisholm (1957), p. 16.

Chapter 6

S knows that *p* if and only if

(1) *S* believes that *p;*

(2) *S* is justified in believing that *p;* and

(3) *P* is true.

The irreducibility of these conditions is clear. The fact that my statement is de facto true (condition 3) does not imply that I know what is expressed in it. That is, it does not imply that I can give reasons for my belief in it, and therefore that this statement is justified or rationally acceptable (condition 2). Conversely, it is not sufficient that I have convincing reasons to support my belief in such a statement (condition 2) for it to be true (condition 3).

If we keep this in mind with respect to Habermas's first thesis (i.e., that "a statement is true when the validity claim of the speech acts with which . . . we assert this statement is justified"), we find that this thesis is either trivially correct or outright false. If the truth condition of the statement is that its assertion be justified, in the sense that it can be regarded as "knowledge," then the thesis is trivially correct. For keeping in mind the conditions of knowledge mentioned above, this thesis would amount only to the assertion that the condition under which a statement is true is that, among other things, it is true. Nevertheless, if what one is asserting as the truth condition of the statement is that the corresponding assertion is justified in the sense that there are convincing reasons that support it, then the thesis is false. The truth of the statement cannot depend on the justifiability (or rational acceptability) of the assertion. That is, condition 3 cannot be reduced to condition 2, as is claimed by all epistemic theories of truth.[15] That the three theses imply such a reduction is clear from

15. In general terms, the difficulty implicit in all these attempts is that either justification (or rational acceptability) falls short of guaranteeing truth, in which case such an epistemic reduction would call into question the unconditional validity of truth; or, if it guarantees truth (if it already includes truth as a condition), it cannot help to explain this notion. The attempted explanation remains empty.

Habermas's aforementioned conclusion, namely, that "the truth condition of statements is the potential agreement of everyone else. . . . The truth of a proposition means the promise of reaching a rational consensus over what is said" (WT, p. 137).

One obvious difficulty in identifying "truth" with "rational acceptability" is the *unconditional validity* that we attribute to the former but not the latter. This difference goes back to two characteristic traits of our use of the notion of "truth," traits that cannot be found in the use of the notion of rational acceptability. The first is the *binary* use of the true/false opposition. By contrast, rational acceptability is a matter of degree. The second is the *fixed* character that we ascribe to truth as opposed to justification or rational acceptability—the fact that we consider truth to be a property of statements that *cannot be lost.*

The combination of these two features results in what Habermas calls the "premise of 'a single right answer.'"[16] To any clearly stated question concerning the truth of statements, there can only be one right answer. We cannot say that a statement was true and now is false. This explains why we cannot say that we *knew* something that turned out to be wrong, whereas we can say without contradiction that we were *justified* (i.e., epistemically responsible) in believing something that turned out to be false. That there is something to be known about certain questions means that there is a fact of the matter as to their answers. It means that what can be known *is* either one way or the other. Accordingly, it cannot be the case that an answer and its opposite are both correct. This impossibility is precisely what suggests the context-transcendence of the validity of such absolute notions.

However, if we try to explain this context-transcendence by appealing to the notion of "idealized rational acceptability," we have to transfer the unconditional validity of truth to this epistemic notion. In so doing, we have to regard our particular interpretations and ways of justifying the statements held to be true as endowed also with absolute validity. Our evaluation of these inter-

16. See Habermas, "Reply," pp. 1477–1559.

pretations also has to be regarded as constrained by the characteristic binary use of the notion of truth. That is, it is limited by the
either-or of the premise of "a single right answer." Just as we are
required to presuppose that "if a statement is true it cannot be
false at the same time," we are also required to accept that "if a
statement is rationally acceptable under ideal conditions it cannot
be false at the same time."[17] The consequence of closing up the
gap between truth and rational acceptability (even if only counterfactually) is that it will not only be the case that if a statement is
true it cannot be false, but also that our particular way of justifying
the statement also cannot be wrong. Thus the particular interpretation or theory through which we understand and justify the
truth of the statement must be *absolutely* correct. It must be the
single correct interpretation. The fact that the absolute validity of
truth has to be derived from the absolute validity of what is rationally acceptable under ideal conditions implies presupposing a
particular kind of consensus about what is rationally acceptable:
in view of its absolute validity, this consensus must be seen as definitive or *unrevisable.* It is in this sense that the notion of idealized
rational acceptability unavoidably seems to involve anticipating an
end to the argumentation process. Understood in this way, the
claim of rational acceptability for our reasons and arguments implies anticipating that they "will stand up to all possible objections" (R, p. 1508). Thus these reasons are definitive—they result
from the *single correct interpretation.*[18] But if *this* is the notion of

17. Putnam (1978) explains the internal conection between such a notion of
"idealized rational acceptability" and the idea of "an absolutely 'unrevisable'
truth as an idealization" (p. 138), when he says: "The supposition that even an
'ideal' theory . . . might *really* be false appears to collapse into *unintelligibility*"
(p. 126). Putnam has recently rejected such an epistemic conception of truth
(as "idealized rational acceptability") precisely because of its antifallibilist consequences. See also Putnam (1994), pp. 242–295.

18. The main problem with such a metaphysical-idealist strategy is not only how
to *justify* the epistemic commitment to an "infinite rational consensus" (Habermas) or an "ultimate opinion" (Peirce)—i.e., the "One True Theory" (Putnam), or a "privileged conceptual scheme" (Searle). This is, indeed, already
difficult given the interpretative character of our epistemic practices (given the

rational acceptability lying behind our knowledge claims, two consequences follow that are equally devastating for a defense of Habermas's general approach. On the one hand, this notion is not at all related to our capacity for reasoning under the conditions of an ideal speech situation (i.e., our capacity to be epistemically responsible). For it is related not to the *procedure* of argumentation, but to its *content*. In such a case, a discourse-theoretic explanation of "rational acceptability under ideal conditions" is not possible. We have no idea whatsoever as to what makes the ideal conditions *such* that under them (and contrary to any possible human experience) reasoners are not just epistemically responsible, but necessarily *successful*.[19] And, on the other hand, this very notion would make the discourse-theoretic explanation of rational acceptability false. For in such a case, the rationality of an argumentation process does not depend on following the unforced force of the better argument under the conditions of an ideal speech situation. Rather, it depends on having the actual

---

plurality of languages and conceptual schemes, meaning holism, conceptual relativity, etc.). The crucial problem, though, is how to *motivate* such a commitment (i.e., why of all our theories only *one* can be rationally acceptable under ideal conditions, and therefore true, if it is not because there is only one reality). For in providing an answer to this question, such an epistemic strategy is sooner or later forced to smuggle in realist presuppositions, as can be seen especially clearly in Peirce's recourse to the idea of correspondence. But once the realist source of the validity of truth is recognized, it is no longer plausible that the *realist* commitment to one objective world (or reality) should imply the *epistemic* commitment to one valid conceptual scheme (or theory). A realist commitment, as such, cannot predetermine in *how many epistemic ways* we will be able to express the *same* reality, the same states of affairs. Conceptual relativity is indeed compatible with realism (see 7.3). The dilemma of a metaphysical-idealist strategy seems to be, then, that the very attempt to motivate such a position renders it unjustified.

19. As Habermas recognizes in his article "Rorty's Pragmatic Turn": "[W]ith regard to the argumentative presuppositions of general inclusiveness, equal rights of participation, freedom from repression, and orientation to reaching understanding, we can imagine *in the present* what an approximate satisfaction in an ideal way would look like. This does not hold for the anticipation of the future, for the anticipation of a future corroboration" (p. 26)—i.e., the anticipation of *correctness*.

correct arguments, the one correct interpretation. Then, as mentioned earlier, such an idealization calls into question the status of rational acceptability in the discourse-theoretic sense as a *necessary* condition. If what is rationally acceptable under ideal conditions also possesses the *absolute* validity that we ascribe to truth, our commitment to rationality is not a commitment to fallibilism or discursive rationality. On the contrary, it is a commitment to incorrigibility.

According to this strategy, accepting the (logical) premise of "a single right answer" unavoidably implies accepting a further commitment to the (epistemic) premise of "a single correct interpretation." But precisely because of this epistemic commitment, the difficulties of this strategy go further than just the counterintuitive explanation of the meaning of truth. They concern the problematic move of reading antifallibilist idealizations into the notion of rational acceptability. As I will try to show, such a move necessarily undermines a discourse-theoretic explanation of this notion.

In his recent rejection of the epistemic conception of truth, Habermas himself has pointed out this general difficulty:

[N]o matter how the value of the epistemic conditions is enhanced through idealizations, either they satisfy the unconditional character of truth claims by means of requirements that cut off all connection with the practices of justification familiar to us; or else they retain the connection to practices familiar to us by paying the price that rational acceptability does not exclude the possibility of error even under these ideal conditions, that is, does not simulate a property that "cannot be lost." (RPT, p. 366)

This dilemma is inescapable for any epistemic conception of truth. We can see this in more detail by considering some new accounts of the notion of knowledge. These new approaches have emerged in response to the challenge to the traditional accounts by E. Gettier's article "Is Justified True Belief Knowledge?"

Given the logical gap between truth and justification, one way to avoid the possibility—shown by Gettier—that S knows that p even if S believes the true statement p for the wrong reasons (*per accidens*, so to speak), is to interpret the truth condition of the traditional accounts of knowledge in epistemic terms. Thus, following R. Fogelin,[20] we could say that

S knows that p if and only if

(1) S believes that p;

(2) S is justified in believing that p; and

(3) S's grounds establish the truth of p.

With such an interpretation of the truth condition in epistemic terms, two different senses of "justification" (or "rational acceptability") necessarily emerge. Using Fogelin's terminology, in the sense expressed in condition 2, someone is justified by dint of being *epistemically responsible*. (Or, in discourse-theoretic terms, they are justified by following the unforced force of the better argument, under the conditions of an ideal speech situation.) But in the sense expressed in condition 3, someone is only justified if her reasons are *actually correct*. Now, it is of course possible to give a characterization (formal, procedural, or otherwise) of the notion of justification in the sense of condition 2, namely, that a statement is justified if it can be considered *convincing for everyone*[21] (under the conditions of an ideal speech situation, or however else). But this is by no means possible for a notion of justification in the sense of condition 3, that a statement is only justified if it is *actually correct*. What is evaluated in this case is not the *soundness of the procedure*, but the *success of the outcome*. Used in this sense, the notion of justification has to be applied exclusively to the succesful case. But it does not contain any indication whatsoever about how to tell whether this is the case for any given statement. It is a criterially *empty* notion. For this reason, it cannot replace the epistemically operational sense of justification expressed in condition 2, with the help of which we judge the soundness of our ways of achieving knowledge (i.e., of the procedures of belief-formation).

Habermas's attempt to identify truth with rational acceptability under ideal conditions compels him to understand such ideal

---

20. R. Fogelin (1994), pp. 15–30.

21. See footnote 4, this chapter.

conditions as *sufficient* conditions for truth. Therefore he is forced to interpret the notion of rational acceptability not in the sense expressed in condition 2, but in the sense of condition 3. Under this version of the theory,[22] discursive rational acceptability is not a *criterion* for truth (condition 3 is not reduced to condition 2). Instead, it allows us to explain the normative *sense* of the validity of truth in terms of the anticipation of an infinite rational consensus (truth is explained in the epistemic terms expressed in condition 3). But this renders his explanation of truth trivially correct, to the extent that condition 3 already *entails* truth as a condition. A discourse theory of truth states, then, that a statement is true if it can be considered rationally acceptable under ideal conditions based on grounds that "stand up to all possible objections" (R, p. 1508), that is, that establish its truth. This would make the theory of truth correct, though obviously empty. But in so doing, the idealization of the notion of rational acceptability required for this strategy unavoidably transforms *the very content of this notion*, as explained by the discourse theory. As a result of this transformation, the new notion no longer has a connection with the discourse-theoretic explanation of rational acceptability. (That is, it cannot possibly be characterized in discourse-theoretic terms.) Moreover, owing to the unconditional validity of the notion of truth, it entails an idealization of epistemic incorrigibility that would *render superfluous the requirement of rationality* (i.e., epistemic responsibility) *in the discourse-theoretic sense.* For now, what is rationally acceptable under ideal conditions is not what is justified in the sense of being *convincing* for everyone under discursive conditions, but only what is actually *correct.* Yet if the commitment to rationality is ultimately a commitment to incorrigibility,[23] then it is

22. Habermas developed this new interpretation of his theory of truth as a consequence of Wellmer's criticism (in Wellmer 1986, pp. 51–174). See Habermas, "Entgegnung," pp. 351ff.

23. It does not seem immediately obvious to hold that when we claim to be justified in believing something, what we commit ourselves to is not to be *convincing* but to be *right* (i.e., to have the ultimate reasons or arguments, the actually correct ones). The only sense in which we can say that we are committed to having the correct arguments seems to be that, if we do not, we would have to

not clear why there should be a further commitment to discursive requirements of any kind. The attempt to interpret rational acceptability as a *sufficient* condition for truth calls into question precisely the central thesis behind Habermas's theory of communicative rationality. That is, it challenges the claim that *discursive* rational acceptability is a *necessary* condition for the validity of our epistemic practices of testing and revising knowledge claims.[24]

---

withdraw our claim of being justified. As we will see in the following analysis of "achievement words," a commitment to correctness in any other sense can only be as *empty* as any commitment to success in general. Whenever we claim to be justified in our beliefs, we rely on our epistemic responsibility rather than on a (mysterious) guarantee of success. Our commitment thus entails only that our reasons can be (or *could* be) regarded as *convincing reasons by everyone*—naturally, only as long as no counterargument (or counterevidence, etc.) appears. In order to prove the soundness of our arguments, we commit ourselves to presenting them to all possible participants in a discourse, to adopting a hypothetical attitude toward their validity, and to following exclusively the logic of "the unforced force of the better argument." These commitments make clear the normative (or idealized) content of the notion of justification or rational acceptability *in the discourse-theoretic sense*. The use of such a notion can only be meaningful under the presupposition that, if all these conditions were fulfilled (i.e., under the conditions of an ideal speech situation), "the unforced force of the better argument" would be a *universal* force, or as Habermas puts it in *Moral Consciousness and Communicative Action*, that "each person, who participates in argumentative practices in general, can in principle arrive at the *same* judgements" (p. 131). Obviously, it would make no sense to participate in an argument or discourse without the presupposition that under discursive conditions all the participants would evaluate the convincingness of the arguments *in the same way*. In this sense, the notion of "rational acceptability" implies the possibility of a transcultural convergence in our criteria of rationality. The universalism implicit in such a presupposition about the *unity of reason* can be considered controversial in itself, but at least not as much as it would be if it also had to support the further presupposition of the *necessary success of our reason*. Our fallibilist intuitions tell us that there is no guarantee of such success.

24. Wellmer (1986), pp. 70ff., argues on similar grounds against Habermas's theory of truth. In developing his arguments, though, he seems to infer from the incorrectness of a discourse theory of *truth* (the fact that the rationality and the truth of consensus need not coincide) the incorrectness of a discourse theory of *rational acceptability* as well. He holds that the rational acceptability of a consensus depends on the correctness of the reasons given and not on their convincingness under an ideal speech situation. It seems doubtful, though, that this can

Beyond its general implausibility as an explanation of the notion of *truth,* this move is even incompatible with Habermas's discourse-theoretic account of *rational acceptability.*[25] As mentioned

---

be our actual use of the term "rational," given that we are never in a position to know (definitively) whether our reasons are the correct ones. If, as Wellmer correctly points out, no content can be given to such a notion (i.e., if there is nothing we can say in advance concerning what makes our interpretations, justifications, etc. actually correct), it seems that we can have no possible use for a notion of rational acceptability in this sense (namely, as an achievement word). Or at least this notion cannot possibly replace the operational notion of justification with the help of which we actually judge the soundness of our ways of achieving knowledge—given that, as a matter of fact, we always have to infer the correctness of our reasons from their intersubjective convincingness.

Given this fact, and given that we can assure ourselves of such convincingness

a. neither alone (for in such a case—to paraphrase Wittgenstein—we could not possibly distinguish between "being convincing" and "seeming convincing to me"),

b. nor under coercive or asymmetrical conditions (for under anything less than the conditions of an ideal speech situation, we cannot tell whether something is genuinely convincing or not)—

given all this, a discourse-theoretic explanation of rational acceptability indeed seems to capture the epistemic, operational sense of this notion as we use it.

If this is accepted, Wellmer's critique of the discourse theory of truth does not apply to a discourse theory of *rational acceptability.* For an explanation of *this* notion (understood as expressing operational, epistemic criteria) cannot be wrong on the grounds of falling short of guaranteeing correctness, for *no* epistemic criteria can possibly give such a guarantee. That is, the epistemic criteria offered by a discourse-theoretic explanation of rational acceptability cannot be wrong by *being epistemic criteria,* but only by being the *wrong* ones. *This* is what has to be shown. But as long as we regard rational acceptability in the operational sense as a necessary condition for accepting knowledge claims, it seems difficult to argue that the basic idea behind the discourse-theoretic explanation of rational acceptability is wrong.

25. By questioning the gap between the two conditions, a discourse theory of truth endangers the plausibility of a discourse theory of rational acceptability (i.e., the status of *necessary* condition of a discursive rational acceptability for our practices of revision of knowledge claims). Some critics, such as Wellmer and Tugendhat, have criticized the alleged status of discursive rational acceptability as a *sufficient* condition for knowledge in order to conclude that it is therefore not a necessary condition either. But for this conclusion, no specific argument has been offered. In his reaction against these critics, Habermas sometimes also

at the outset, the crucial insight behind Habermas's approach is that rational acceptability in the sense of condition 2 is a *necessary* condition for a sound practice of testing and revising knowledge claims. But this is the case precisely insofar as no *sufficient* condition in the sense of condition 3 is epistemically accessible to us, insofar as the notion behind condition 3 has to remain *criterially empty*.[26] But to recognize this (i.e., to acknowledge that the truth condition cannot be interpreted in epistemic terms) is no more than to recognize the non-epistemic sense of the notion of truth. This can be shown by analyzing the different general categories to which the notions expressed in conditions 2 and 3 belong.

6.2 Truth as an Achievement Word

As we saw before, there is one obvious difference between the sense of justification expressed in each of the two conditions, namely, that when we use it in the sense of condition 2, we evaluate the *correctness* of the *procedure*. But in the sense of condition

---

seems to accept the stated inference—namely, the inference that to concede that rational acceptability is not a *sufficient* condition for the validity of our epistemic practices amounts to conceding that it is not a *necessary* condition either. Under this supposition it seems, then, that if the discourse theory of rational acceptability is not at the same time an explanation of the notion of truth, then it also cannot be a correct explanation of the notion of rational acceptability. But the real issue in Habermas's approach is obviously whether a discourse-theoretic explanation of rational acceptability gives a correct account of our notion of rational acceptability. For if it does, no special argument is needed to show that rational acceptability, in turn, is a necessary condition for knowledge. Not because it *guarantees* it (for *nothing* does—there is no sufficient condition for knowledge epistemically accessible to us), but because it is what *entitles* us to make knowledge claims.

26. The fact that we can only infer the correctness of our claims from their convincingness (under discursive conditions) is the crucial argument supporting Habermas's defense of an internal connection between truth and discursive rational acceptability. This is the point of his third thesis: "Whether a state of affairs is the case or is not the case, is not decided by the evidence of experiences, but by the result of an argumentation. The idea of truth can only be developed with reference to the discursive cashing in of validity claims" (WT, pp. 135–136).

3, we evaluate only the *success* of its *outcome*. With this second notion, as with knowledge and truth, we thereby express a *status*—the *successful* outcome of a practice. With the first notion, by contrast, we evaluate the *process*, the *attempt* to achieve such a status. To gain a sense of what this difference amounts to, we can examine the two categories of expressions distinguished by G. Ryle in *The Concept of Mind* as *achievement* versus *task* words.

In *The Concept of Mind*, Ryle analyzes the different logic in the use of "achievement verbs" (and their antitheses, the "failure verbs") as opposed to that of "task verbs." For example: "win" or "lose" as opposed to merely "participate"; "cure" or "worsen" as opposed to merely "treat"; "know" or "be mistaken" as opposed to merely "believe."

The central difference between these complementary types of expressions is as follows. Whereas the first category of expressions is concerned with the *status* of the possible outcomes of an activity (success or failure), the second refers to the procedure or *process* by means of which an activity is performed:

One big difference between the logical force of a task verb and that of a corresponding achievement verb is that in applying an achievement verb we are asserting that *some state of affairs obtains over and above that which consists in the performance,* if any, of the subservient task activity. For a runner to win, not only must he run but also his rivals must be at the tape later than he; for a doctor to effect a cure, his patient must both be treated and be well again; for the searcher to find the thimble, there must be a thimble in the place he indicates at the moment when he indicates it; and for the mathematician to prove a theorem, the theorem must be true and follow from the premises from which he tries to show that it follows. (p. 150)

The distinction between achievement words and task words is needed whenever the goal of a task does not consist solely in its (correct) performance (i.e., whenever a correct attempt does not guarantee success). For this reason, achievement words as such express the status of the successful case and say nothing about the process of trying to achieve it. This makes clear why this kind of expression has a *fixed* character, with no room for changing over time. If we discover that in a particular case there was actually no success, we cannot continue using achievement words to describe such a case. Ryle explains this consequence by pointing out a peculiar characteristic of their use: "It has long been realised that verbs like 'know,' 'discover,' 'solve,' 'prove,' 'perceive,' 'see' . . . are in an important way incapable of being qualified by adverbs like 'erroneously' and 'incorrectly' " (p. 152). On the basis of his analysis, he later offers the following explanation for this peculiarity of such expressions:

Just as a person cannot win a race unsuccessfully, or solve an anagram incorrectly, since "win" means "race victoriously" and "solve" means "rearrange correctly," so a person cannot detect mistakenly or see incorrectly. . . . It is not that the perceiver has used a *procedure* which prevented him from going wrong or set a Faculty to work which is fettered to *infallibility,* but that the perception verb employed itself connotes that he did not go wrong. . . . The fact that doctors cannot cure unsuccessfully does not mean that they are infallible doctors; it only means that there is a contradiction in saying that a treatment which has succeeded has not succeeded. (p. 238)

Thus one important consequence of the use of "achievement words" is that they can only preserve their meaning by being *criterially empty.* By ascribing them to particular cases, we do not refer to the correctness of the procedure (i.e., of the attempt to obtain the achievement). Rather, we qualify the case as one of achievement. As Ryle explains, this feature does not mean that when we apply these expressions to a particular task or procedure we hold them to be infallible.[27] Rather, we use these expressions and their

27. The point of Ryle's analysis is precisely to show that the use of achievement words has been misunderstood by interpreting them as a special kind of task word. He remarks:

Automatically construing these and kindred verbs [achievement verbs] as standing for special kinds of operations or experiences, some epistemologists have felt themselves obliged to postulate that people possess certain special inquiry procedures in following which they are subject to no risk of error. They need not, indeed they cannot, execute them carefully, for they provide no scope for care. The logical impossibility of a discovery being fruitless, or of a proof being invalid, has been misconstrued as a quasi-causal impossibility of going astray. If only the proper road were followed, or if only the proper

opposites (win/lose, knowledge/error, true/false) to evaluate the two possible outcomes of the corresponding procedures or tasks. For that reason, their use already anticipates the possibility of correction. Therefore the *consequence of their fixed character* is not the presupposition of infallibility, but rather *the obligatoriness of correction*. Ryle continues:

> This is why a person who claims to have seen a linnet, or heard a nightingale, and is then persuaded that there was no linnet or nightingale, at once *withdraws his claim* to have seen the linnet, or heard the nightingale. He does not say that he saw a linnet which was not there, or that he heard an unreal nightingale. Similarly, a person who claims to have solved an anagram and is then persuaded that that is not the solution, withdraws his claim to have solved it. (p. 239)

It thus seems that, for all the tasks or procedures that can succeed or fail, we can find complementary expressions of the two kinds described. That is, we need descriptive expressions (task words) for identifying the kind of performance or procedure at issue, but also need normative expressions (achievement words) for referring to the different possible outcomes of such a performance.[28] On the one hand, these normative expressions thereby express the *sense* or goal of the corresponding activity (that of par-

---

faculty were given its head, incorrigible observations or self-evident intuitions could not help ensuing. So men are sometimes infallible. Similarly *if hitting the bull's eye were construed as a special kind of aiming, or if curing were construed as a special kind of treatment,* then, since neither could, in logic, be at fault, *it would follow that there existed special fault-proof ways of aiming and doctoring.* There would exist some temporarily infallible marksmen and some occasionally infallible doctors. (pp. 152–153)

28. We may also need normative expressions for evaluating the correctness of the procedure, but they are not the same as those for evaluating the success of the outcome. The task of achieving knowledge is a paradigmatic case in which we can find all three kinds of expressions. As we saw earlier, the three conditions for knowledge contain the corresponding kinds of expressions discussed here. condition (1) contains the descriptive expression ''believes'' for describing the *task* at issue; condition (2) contains the normative expression ''justified'' for evaluating the *correctness* of the *procedure;* and condition (3) contains the normative expression ''true'' for evaluating the *success* of the *outcome.*

ticipating in a race is to win; that of acquiring beliefs is to achieve knowledge, i.e., truth). But on the other hand, precisely in order to preserve this normative sense, their meaning *cannot depend in turn on anything concerning this activity or procedure other than its outcome.* These expressions do not contain any reference to the possible adequate ways of trying to arrive at the different outcomes to which they apply. They are criterially empty.

These general characteristics of achievement words can help clarify why the unconditional validity of notions like truth or knowledge does not imply an epistemic commitment to incorrigibility. As we saw previously, the commitment made by the speaker in asserting that a statement is true manifests itself in a trivial assumption: the speaker must necessarily suppose that in the future, such a statement also will not turn out to be false. Such a commitment obviously proceeds from the binary functioning of the true/false opposition. Given the two possible outcomes of an assertion (success or failure), to assert that a statement is true implies a commitment to the belief that such a statement is not false. Precisely because of this, such a commitment does not actually imply any evaluation of the quality of the evidence supporting the assertion of the statement. That is, it cannot be understood as an *epistemic* anticipation (of my infallibility) but only as a condition of a logical nature. That is, it implies that the statement will not turn out to be false, *if* it is true. This condition as such only commits us to the recognition that the statement is *either true or false.* Thus any testing of the reasons supporting it will have to be directed toward the exclusion of one of the two possibilities. Such a supposition, though, is too modest to contain an epistemic promise of incorrigibility. For the epistemic sense inherent in the supposition not only does not imply the unrevisability of my beliefs, but actually anticipates *the obligation* to revise the acceptability of contrary beliefs. If the statement turns out to be false, if the reasons submitted for examination show this, I will not be able to continue asserting that it is true (or even that it *used* to be true). In any case, if I continue to affirm that it is true, in spite of my inability to give reasons for its rational acceptability, no one will accept that *I myself* know this statement.

But the question that remains open concerns the rationale behind the binary use of the true/false opposition, which motivates this epistemic obligation. The either/or implicit in our use of the true/false opposition cannot itself be motivated by epistemic reasons—not if it is only on the basis of the binary use that the obligation to revise the acceptability of contrary beliefs makes sense in the first place. The answer to this question seems to lie in the distinctive character of achievement expressions.

6.2.1 The Non-Epistemic Sense of Achievement Words

As Ryle observed, the epistemic obligations that follow from the use of achievement words in general are due precisely to the *nonepistemic sense of the achievement itself*. That is, in such cases no epistemic condition of our attempts (to achieve the task's goal) is immune to correction, precisely because the achievement as such depends exclusively on whether "some state of affairs obtains over and above that which consists in the performance" (Ryle 1984, p. 150). S's knowledge of "p" depends on whether S's grounds do in fact establish the truth of "p";[29] the truth of "p" depends on whether it is the case that p, and so forth.

Thus the *realist* sense of the achievement is what excludes any *epistemic* condition of the performance to be considered in advance as *sufficient* for the *obtaining* of the outcome. This explains why justification in the sense of condition 3 is criterially empty, and at the same time, it also clarifies why we are obliged to consider any epistemic condition as in principle *fallible*. Therefore the aforementioned exclusion is not due to epistemic considerations of any kind—such as the skeptical suspicion that we suffer from a chronic epistemic disability. It is not that our epistemic condi-

---

29. It is important to note that the nonepistemic sense of achievement words is owing not to the activity evaluated being nonepistemic (this *can* be the case, as with "win," "find," "cure," but does not *need* to be, as seen from the examples of "know," "prove," "solve"), but rather to the fact that the *obtaining* of its conditions of success are not, as such, an epistemic matter. See the following footnote.

tions are not "ideal" enough to achieve a correct outcome (who says that they aren't?). Rather, it is that the correctness of the outcome depends *exclusively* on the *obtaining* of a state of affairs. *And this is not an epistemic matter.*[30] Habermas expresses this clearly enough in his "Rorty's Pragmatic Turn." In connection with his retraction of the epistemic interpretation of truth, he writes:

A truth claim raised for "*p*" implies that the truth conditions for "*p*" are satisfied. We have no other way in which we can establish whether or not this is the case except via argumentation, for direct access to uninterpreted truth conditions is denied to us. But the fact that the truth conditions are satisfied does not itself amount to an epistemic fact just because we can only *establish* whether these conditions are satisfied via the discursive vindication of the truth claim. (pp. 367–368)

Habermas's recognition of the realist sense of the notion of truth amounts to a retraction of his original interpretation of this notion as rational acceptability under ideal conditions. But as is also clear from the above passage, this retraction by no means implies or requires revoking the crucial insight behind his explanation of the internal relation between truth and rational acceptability. There is no need to deny that (discursive) rational acceptability is a necessary condition for the vindication of truth claims. It seems, therefore, that maintaining *realist* intuitions in an explanation of *epistemic* matters (i.e., adopting an internal-realist strategy) by no means endangers a defense of the crucial insights behind Habermas's theory of communicative rationality. Moreover, as we saw in the previous chapter, such a *realist* insight is in fact already contained in Habermas's own explanation of the

30. It is this intuition that lies behind externalist explanations of knowledge. The fact that the validity of knowledge depends on conditions that must obtain does not mean that it depends on our knowing that they obtain. As Michael Williams expresses it in *Unnatural Doubts:* "If 'How do you know. . .?' means 'How do internal cues ensure that the beliefs induced track the truth?' the answer is that they don't. You know if you track, otherwise not. There need be no answer to 'How do you know . . .?' that lives up to internalist . . . standards" (p. 345). It seems that, if our fallibilist intuitions are right, there *should* be no answer to the question in this sense (i.e., in the sense of an *epistemically accessible guarantee* of knowledge).

conditions of possibility of discourse. This remains the case even if up till now he has never mobilized it in the context of his explanation of the notion of truth. As we saw in that connection, speakers can only regard the obligation to revise their different beliefs in a discourse as meaningful under a specific condition, namely, under the presupposition that these beliefs are about the *same* reality, the *same objective world*. In this connection, as we saw, Habermas pointed out that

validity claims are in principle susceptible to critique because they are based on *formal concepts of world*. They presuppose an identical world for *all possible* observers or a world that is intersubjectively shared by *all members* of a group, and this *in an abstract form, that is, disconnected from all concrete contents*. (TCA I, p. 82)

Here, in the context of the analysis of the validity claim "truth," the correctness of this insight seems especially clear. For only under the supposition of *one* objective world is it possible to understand why a statement *must be either true or false*. So too, only in this way can it be understood why the search for a rational justification of the statement *must adopt the precise form of excluding one of the two cases*. The counterfactual supposition of *one objective world* renders meaningful the binary use of the true/false opposition. It is also this supposition that is responsible for the context-transcendent validity that we ascribe to truth. Only because truth, as an achievement word, is regarded as depending *exclusively* on what is the case can it preserve its unconditional validity *with respect to any epistemic criteria whatsoever* of rational acceptability. And, vice versa, only because these criteria are necessarily dependent on a *nonepistemic* circumstance are they inevitably conceived as, in principle, fallible. It is the presupposition of a single objective world, then, that makes the unconditional validity of truth compatible with a fallibilist understanding of our knowledge.[31] And *only this*

31. On the one hand, it is what obligates us to accept in advance the correctness of the (logical) premise of "a single right answer." But on the other hand, because it does not include any epistemic content, it also does not include the epistemic commitment to the premise of a single correct interpretation. The presupposition of one objective world does not predetermine in how many epis-

fallibilist understanding justifies the epistemic requirement of discursive rational acceptability with respect to our practices of testing and revising validity claims. If our analysis is correct, only a *realist* strategy allows us to combine these two central insights lying behind Habermas's explanation of the internal connection between truth and rational acceptability: the unconditional validity of truth can be combined (free from paradox) with the requirement of discursive rational acceptability for the vindication of truth claims. The internal relationship of these two insights can also be explained on the basis of the general analysis of achievement words discussed earlier.

6.2.2 The Epistemic Requirements for the Use of Achievement Words

As we have already seen, achievement words entail by virtue of their meaning *that* a certain state of affairs obtains. But they do not also specify *how to tell* whether this is the case on any particular occasion. Then, to grasp their meaning, to grasp the necessary and sufficient conditions that have to *obtain* for such words to be used appropriately, does not entail grasping any epistemic criteria for recognizing the obtaining of such conditions (i.e., for being *infallible* in applying it to any particular case). But this, in turn, is precisely why their *use* in any given context raises additional epistemic questions. When we *claim* such a normative status (truth, knowledge, etc.) for any particular belief, we have to be able to justify if necessary that this status *actually applies* to the belief at issue. And it is this justification that is subject to epistemic requirements of rational acceptability, which has to be intersubjectively convincing.[32]

---

temic ways we will be able to describe the same reality. On the compatibility between realism and conceptual relativity, see 7.3.

32. The internal connection between these epistemic requirements and the use of achievement words becomes clear by taking into account that they appear only when we use achievement words, and disappear at the moment when we reduce our claims to avoid the use of such terms (i.e., if one reduces the claim "I know that *p*" to simply "I believe that *p*," or the claim "*p* is true" to the claim

Therefore the internal connection between truth and rational acceptability implicit in this second question is not due to a *semantic* requirement for *grasping the meaning* of truth (as it would have to be if truth were an epistemic notion). Rather, it is a *pragmatic* requirement for its *application to any particular belief*. Thus, to recognize the internal connection between truth and rational acceptability by no means requires our reducing one notion to the other.

If this is correct, a *semantic* analysis of the notion of truth cannot be considered *insufficient* for grasping its *meaning* (such that a deeper epistemic meaning beyond Convention T would have to be found). Rather, precisely in virtue of its meaning, as an achievement word, this notion is *epistemically empty*.[33] For this reason, from

---

"*p* seems true to me," etc.). As soon as we reduce a claim of success to the claim of a mere *attempt*, we are not subject to epistemic requirements precisely to the extent that our reduced claim is no longer binding for the others (i.e., by accepting it they do not commit themselves to anything). On the other hand, the fact that these claims are beyond the requirement of justification does not therefore mean that they entail any special infallibility: We cannot be *wrong* about how things seem to us for the simple reason that on the basis of it we cannot be *right* either. And as long as we are not right, there is nothing to be justified. See W. Sellars (1997), pp. 32ff.; also R. Brandom (1994), pp. 293–1297.

33. The fact that we do know the necessary and sufficient conditions that fix the meaning of "truth," but that at the same time these conditions are epistemically empty (i.e., that they do not tell us how to know if in a particular case the conditions are fulfilled or not), can be shown by recourse to an argument similar to Moore's open question argument. That "truth" as an achievement word is epistemically empty can be shown (just as Putnam did when arguing against Dummett's epistemic interpretation of truth as "warranted assertability") by indicating that whatever epistemic criteria we choose to explain truth, the question will always remain open (i.e., meaningful): "It is rationally acceptable (coherent, justified, etc.) that *p*, but is it true that *p*?" The meaningfulness of this question explains the "cautionary" use of the truth predicate: that the contrast between truth and any epistemic notion is always meaningful makes us conscious of the fallibility of any particular belief, any epistemic criteria of justification, etc.

But the epistemic (i.e., criterial) emptiness of the notion of truth does not mean that we do not grasp its meaning (i.e., the necessary and sufficient conditions for truth). This can also be shown by using the same argument, but taking into account the realist sense of the notion of truth. The fact that the question: "It is the case that *p*, but is it true that *p*?" is not open (i.e., not meaningful) is all we need to know in order to understand the notion of truth.

the *pragmatic* point of view of its *application* to any particular belief, its appropriate use requires additional epistemic conditions, conditions of the kind expressed by epistemic notions like justification (or rational acceptability). The internal relationship between the *use* of these two kinds of notions obviously cannot be grasped from a semantic point of view. That is, it cannot be grasped by merely explaining the meaning of any of these notions. (This is the correct insight behind the epistemic approaches to truth.) But on the other hand, the *pragmatic* analysis of the epistemic conditions for applying the notion of truth cannot end up transforming its meaning in terms of *other* (epistemic) *notions.*

Understood in these terms, the semantic and pragmatic points of view seem to be complementary rather than opposed. It is not the case that a *semantic* analysis of the notion of truth fails to exhaust its *meaning.* As deflationists insist, Convention T seems to be *all we can know about the meaning of the notion of truth.* Rather, it is that such an analysis still tells us nothing about the *pragmatic* conditions (i.e., the additional epistemic conditions) for applying such a notion to any particular belief. *In this sense,* as every defender of an epistemic account of truth complains, Convention T is indeed trivial. That is, it is *epistemically empty.* But quite obviously, to regard Convention T as trivial can only mean to view it as *trivially correct.* That is, any explanation of the pragmatic use of this notion in our epistemic practices has to *contain* Convention T, among other things, but cannot *exclude* Convention T or render it *wrong.*[34] As we have seen, if the notion of truth can fulfill any

34. Given that the correctness of Convention T is never called into question by the defenders of an epistemic explanation of truth, it seems that all of their explanations unavoidably have the following structure: First, it is recognized that " 'P' is true if and only if it is the case that *p,*" and then an epistemic explanation has to be offered in the sense that: "It is the case that *p* if and only if . . . ('*p*' is rationally acceptable, coherent, justified, etc.)." The difficulty with such an attempt is that our notion of reality is obviously (or, as Searle puts it, "radically") nonepistemic. That there is nothing epistemic that could meaningfully be put after the "if and only if" is probably all we need to know about the notion of reality (together with its uniqueness, with the either/or behind the absolute and binary oposition of real/unreal). That is to say, this is what the formal notion of *one objective world* amounts to.

epistemic function in the context of testing and revising our beliefs, then this can only be in virtue of its actual, *realist* sense.

The acknowledgment of the realist sense of the notion of truth—that is, that the only necessary and sufficient condition of the truth of a statement "*p*" is that "*p*" be the case—loses its aparent triviality precisely when such a condition is situated in the epistemic context of the practices of testing our beliefs. It is precisely because the unconditional validity of truth is *not* due to epistemic conditions that this notion can play the "cautionary" role of a fallibilist reserve, *vis-à-vis* the validity of any such epistemic conditions, criteria of justification, and the like. That truth cannot be equated with any epistemic notion, that the conditions for truth cannot be reduced to epistemic conditions, is what teaches us that the inference from "convincing" to "correct" *can fail.* This makes us conscious, in turn, of the permanent possibility of having to revise our beliefs or the epistemic criteria of acceptability that support them.

On the one hand, it is owing to the *realist meaning* of the notion of truth that this notion can play the epistemic role of *fallibilist reserve* with regard to the validity of any of our beliefs or epistemic criteria for justification. On the other hand, it is also owing to the requirements of its *adequate application* that truth *claims* are always in need of *epistemic justification.* The irreducibility of truth to justification (or to rational acceptability) expresses the context-transcendent validity of the former as opposed to the latter. This context-transcendence leaves open the possibility of discovering a way to defend the truth of a particular statement that here and now appears utterly unjustifiable. (This might happen in light of new information, a new interpretative strategy, or even an entirely new categorization.) Contrariwise, the irreducibility of justification to truth is what compels us to *prove* our claims to truth to be acceptable as justified. This is therefore what compels us to *withdraw our knowledge claim* as long as this proof is not available (i.e., as long as our reasons or justifications are not intersubjectively convincing).

In light of this analysis, it becomes clear that it is not necessary to defend the counterintuitive thesis that the truth of a statement depends on the possibility of agreement about it in order to defend the undeniable thesis that our *knowledge claims* are dependent on argumentative practices (in which we prove the convincingness of our reasons and arguments by exposing them to a public discussion, to all the available counterarguments). As Habermas explains in *Theory of Communicative Action:* "[T]he learning processes by which we acquire theoretical knowledge and moral insight, revise and extend our evaluative language, overcome self-deceptions and difficulties of understanding, depend on argumentative practices" (p. 44). But for this very reason, if the argumentative practices have to allow for *learning,* they can only *entitle* us to hold our beliefs as valid. They cannot *guarantee* their validity. As I will try to show in what follows, this is equally the case with respect to our moral insights.

7

Rational Acceptability and Moral Rightness

Given the scope of Habermas's theory of communicative rationality, the attempt to argue that an internal-realist strategy offers the best basis for defending the crucial insights behind this theory stands under a requirement of completeness. That is, it is not enough to show what such a strategy would look like for an explanation of the argumentative processes concerned with the truth of statements (i.e., theoretical discourses). The same must be shown too for an explanation of arguments concerned with the moral rightness of norms (i.e., practical discourses). This second, riskier[1] attempt requires that

---

1. This further step is difficult for several reasons. On the one hand, there is considerably less philosophical agreement concerning moral questions in general than there is with respect to questions of truth. Whereas theoretical questions concerning the truth of statements are *the* cognitive questions par excellence, to argue that practical questions concerning the moral rightness of norms are cognitive as well is hardly uncontroversial. In this context, however, I am only concerned with the attempt to interpret discourse ethics in internal-realist terms; for this reason, I take its goals as given and will not try to argue directly in favor of the assumption of moral cognitivism as such. On the other hand, to defend the notion that a realist strategy can help explain the universal validity of moral questions (implicit in regarding them as cognitive questions) can wrongly but easily be associated with the moral realism defended by intuitionists like Moore or Sidgwick at the beginning of this century. Realism can be understood as an ontological position concerning the existence of the objects

we first recall the central theses of Habermas's approach to moral questions.

Discourse ethics can be characterized as an attempt to analyze the internal connection between moral rightness and rational acceptability. It can be viewed, in Habermas's words, as an attempt to explain "the moral point of view based on general communicative presuppositions of argumentation" (EDE, p. 119).

The aim is to show how the general, discursive conditions for rational acceptability contained in his theory of communicative rationality, which as such are morally neutral[2] (i.e., are motivated by cognitive and not moral reasons), impose restrictions on the possible answers to moral questions. This is the case at least insofar as *these questions are treated as cognitive* (and, therefore, in need of justification) by the participants in moral discourses. The practice of justifying moral norms subjects

---

of a given discipline: in the same sense in which a realism about numbers can be defended in mathematics, a realism about, say, values can be defended in moral theory (usually together with the postulate of the corresponding human capacity of intuition of such ideal, moral facts). The kind of realism that I will try to defend in what follows, however, is not meant as an *ontological* position; actually, the kind of facts I will appeal to are by no means postulated ideal entities or controversial moral facts at all, but simply the objects of moral judgments, which anyone discussing them would trivially accept. It is not the assumption of the existence of, say, human interests that is at dispute in this case. For if there were no human interests to be regulated by moral norms, there would simply be no need for moral norms (and no moral judgments concerning them). The realism defended here, in keeping with the previous chapter, is rather a position within *epistemology*, which stands in oposition to antirealism *concerning the best explanation of the source of the objectivity of cognitive questions in general.* The issue, therefore, is not whether there exist human interests or not, but instead whether their existence is the source of the validity of moral judgments, or whether this validity depends rather on epistemic conditions (on our evidence or decisions concerning them). In continuity with the previous chapter, the general issue is again whether truth or moral rightness can be explained in epistemic terms (i.e., whether ideal justification is the necessary and sufficient condition for them) or whether their sense is instead non-epistemic.

2. See Habermas, *Between Facts and Norms*.

its possible outcomes to general, *necessary conditions* of rational acceptability. If moral questions can be meaningfully regarded as cognitive questions, and if the discourse-theoretic account of the notion of rational acceptability contained in Habermas's theory of communicative rationality is correct, then the discursive conditions for rational acceptability analyzed in this theory are necessary conditions for the validity of our knowledge claims regarding the moral rightness of norms (just as they are for our knowledge claims concerning the truth of statements).

Two important consequences follow from this approach. On the one hand, it yields a positive achievement for moral theory by explaining the historical evolution of our moral insights as the result of an internally motivated learning process. Taking into account the general discursive requirements for rational acceptability, it is possible to understand why the practice of justifying moral norms (under historical conditions of a given plurality of moral codes) has influenced the evolution of our moral insights toward an egalitarian morality, that is, a morality guided by principles.[3] On the other hand, a moral theory such as discourse ethics does not and cannot aim to answer substantive moral questions; it does not sanction or privilege any particular moral code. This is owing to the distinctive traits of this approach.

To the extent that communicative rationality only contains general discursive requirements for rational acceptability (i.e., communicative presuppositions for rational argumentation), it cannot be equated with practical reason in the classical sense. Habermas explains in *Between Facts and Norms:*

Unlike the classical form of practical reason, communicative reason is not a source for norms of action. . . . Communicative reason thus makes an orientation to validity claims possible, but it does not itself supply any substantive orientation for managing practical tasks—it is neither informative nor immediately practical. (pp. 4–5)

3. See Habermas, "Discourse Ethics: Notes on a Program of Philosophical Justification."

It is in this sense that communicative rationality can be considered morally neutral.[4] For as regards the discursive conditions for rational acceptability, we have to recognize that:

a. They are not informative. As *formal, procedural* conditions, they are insufficient for generating true judgements or just norms. Thus they are necessary but not sufficient conditions for the validity of the outcomes of practical or theoretical discourses.

b. They are not practical, for the following reasons:

1. They are basically the same for all kinds of cognitive questions, even *theoretical* questions concerning the truth of statements. That is, they are not *specifically* practical.

2. They are motivated by *cognitive* rather than by specifically moral reasons.

3. As such, they can have only a *cognitive impact* (with respect to the rational acceptability of moral judgments), *and not a motivational one*. As Habermas explains it:

On the one hand, [communicative reason] stretches across the entire spectrum of validity claims: the claims to propositional truth, the truthfulness of the subject, and normative rightness; to this extent, it reaches beyond the realm of moral-practical questions. On the other hand, it pertains only to insights—to criticizable utterances that are accessible in principle to argumentative clarification—and thus falls short of a practical reason aimed at motivation, at guiding the will. (BFN, p. 5)

As Habermas points out in his "Erläuterungen zur Diskursethik," "a cognitivist ethical theory ascribes to practical reason exclusively epistemic capacities" (EDE, p. 187). As we have seen, discourse ethics does not aim to provide substantial criteria for generating morally right norms, or correct arguments and reasons

---

4. In the sense mentioned previously, though, it is obviously *not* morally neutral: Its own normativity, even if derived exclusively from general (discursive) conditions of rational acceptability, has an obvious moral impact. The characteristics already mentioned in the previous chapter that belong conceptually to a requirement of convincingness (namely, its *intersubjectivity* and *unforceability*) contain clear moral implications. See Habermas's discourse-theoretic justification of human rights in *Between Facts and Norms* (esp. section III).

for them. It only explains the conditions *under which alone* those criteria (arguments, reasons, and the like) can achieve *justificatory force*.[5] That means, obviously, that moral insights obtained under such conditions only have "the weak force of rational motivation" (EDE, p. 192). That is, whoever acquires such insights "knows that he has no good reason to act *otherwise*" (EDE, p. 135).[6]

Thus discourse ethics offers a rule of argumentation (but no substantive content) for moral discourses, in which the *justification* (but not the application) of norms is at issue. This rule of argumentation is the so-called principle of universalization (U), a principle expressing the condition that any norm has to fulfill in order to be valid—that is, *justified*:[7]

(U)   All affected can accept the consequences and the side effects its general observance can be anticipated to have for the satisfaction of everyone's interests (and these consequences are preferred to those of known alternative possibilities for regulation). (DE, p. 65)

An analysis of the different elements contained in this rule of argumentation or moral principle allows us to see it as a discursive interpretation of the moral point of view. In strict parallelism with

5. This approach, then, contests any attempt to explain the moral point of view that either aims to give the actors *substantive criteria* for obtaining valid moral judgments (e.g., Rawls's principles of justice, utilitarianism, etc.) or that does not include *discursive* conditions as necessary conditions for their validity (e.g. Kant's categorical imperative). See Habermas, *Moral Consciousness and Communicative Action* (p. 133).

6. That is, as Habermas remarks in this context, "insight does not exclude weakness of will" (EDE, p. 135). But on the other hand, that "the weak force of rational motivation," as a source of moral insight, is an insufficient (motivational) source for moral actions does not mean that it is no source at all. Habermas explains further: "The weak motivating force of moral insights is manifested empirically in the fact that someone who acts against his better judgment must not only face the moral rebukes of others but is also prey to self-criticism, and thus to 'bad conscience'" (EDE, p. 135).

7. Given that (U) is a rule of argumentation for the *justification* of moral norms, it seems clear that it expresses the condition under which moral norms are valid in the sense of *justified*—but not necessarily in the sense of being in fact morally right. See the following footnote.

Habermas's discourse theory of truth, discourse ethics can be seen as the attempt to explain the internal relationship between moral rightness and (discursive) rational acceptability. In this sense, (U) is formed from two different components.

On the one hand, (U) expresses general discursive conditions for justification or rational acceptability. The claim that a norm is morally right (like the claim that a given statement is true) can be considered justified if it could be accepted as convincing *for everyone* under the conditions of an ideal speech situation. The discursive interpretation of rational acceptability, when applied to any kind of norm, results in what Habermas calls the discourse principle:

D: Just those action norms are valid to which all possibly affected persons could agree as participants in rational discourses. (BFN, p. 107)[8]

On the other hand, beyond general discursive conditions, the moral principle (U) specifies what the moral point of view consists in. To claim that a norm is morally right means to claim that it is equally in everyone's interest.[9] As Habermas explains in *Between Facts and Norms:*

8. The expression "valid" is ambiguous here. There are two senses in which the agreement of the participants in practical discourses is a condition for the validity of social norms. On the one hand, the agreement expresses the general *volitional* element of an autonomous decision (for whose risks, because of the limitations of our knowledge, we ourselves assume the responsibility). This is the political sense of *legitimacy* (i.e., the *principle of democracy*) that is at issue no matter what kinds of norms are under discussion as regards their enforcement. The other, more specific sense in which the agreement is a condition for the validity of norms *from a moral point of view* is the *cognitive* sense of a rationally acceptable *justification* that the conditions for moral rightness are satisfied by a given norm. In both cases, though, the fact that the norms satisfying the condition of agreement are valid means that they are therefore *rationally acceptable,* but not necessarily that they are for this reason actually *morally right.* This further sense of validity cannot, in turn, be conditioned by the agreement of the participants. Depending on how the expression "valid" in (U) and (D) is interpreted, i.e., depending on what kind of validity is supposed to be guaranteed by them (legitimacy, justification, or moral rightness), completely different conceptions of discourse ethics arise. I will discuss them in what follows (see 7.2).

9. See footnote 12.

The moral principle first results when one specifies the general discourse principle for those norms that can be justified if and *only* if equal consideration is given to the interests of all those who are possibly involved. (p. 108)[10]

These general characteristics of discourse ethics can be considered as derived from two basic insights that serve as support for the very attempt to give a discursive explanation of the moral point of view. Habermas summarizes them in his "Discourse Ethics: Notes on a Program of Philosophical Justification":

Discourse ethics . . . stands or falls with two assumptions: (a) that normative claims to validity have *cognitive* meaning and can be treated *like* claims to truth and (b) that the *justification* of norms and commands requires that a real *discourse* be carried out and thus cannot occur in a strictly monological form, i.e., in the form of a hypothetical process of argumentation occurring in the individual mind. (DE, p. 68; italics mine)

This characterization offers an adequate basis for approaching the question of whether and to what extent the internal-realist

10. Given that all rational discourses (theoretical and practical) are subject to the same procedural conditions, the different contents of the different kinds of discourses are derived from the different kinds of questions placed within them, and are also what allow the participants to know what they have to look for in them (what the discourse is about, viewed in terms of its content). This is what allows us to distinguish good from bad arguments, relevant from irrelevant contributions, and so forth. As Habermas remarks: "[T]he kind of reasons results from the logic of the given question" (BFN, 139).

For practical questions in general, discourse ethics defends a deontological approach and considers that moral questions concerning the justice of norms are *autonomous* with respect to ethical-political questions concerning the good life (i.e., what is good for me or for us). Whereas moral questions can be considered cognitive in the strict sense (and therefore, claims of moral rightness are supposed to have unconditional validity and to be in need of justification), ethical-political questions have validity only relative to a given political community. For this reason, whereas a rationally acceptable decision of ethical-political questions depends exclusively on the factual will of a given community, in the case of moral questions it depends on a context-transcendent rightness that cannot be equated with any factual will. A claim of moral rightness, then, goes beyond any claim of factual legitimation; it requires, further, cognitive justification (see EDE, p. 100).

perspective that I defend as the strongest interpretation of Habermas's theory of communicative rationality can also be applied to discourse ethics (i.e., to practical questions concerning the moral rightness of norms).[11]

In what follows, I will try to show not only how these two assumptions or theses, crucial for discourse ethics, can be interpreted on the basis of a general internal-realist strategy. But more than this, I will also try to show that only such a strategy offers a firm basis for defending them against its critics, enabling us at the same time to avoid some misunderstandings contained in Habermas's own defense of his position.

The aim is to show that, in the same way as it is possible to explain the internal relation between truth and (discursive) rational acceptability without reducing one to the other, it is possible to explain the internal relation between moral rightness and (discursive) rational acceptability without ignoring the specific sense (and function) of both notions.

7.1 Cognitivism: Moral Rightness and Truth

First, it is important to notice that the two assumptions mentioned by Habermas do not stand on the same level. That is, the second assumption only makes sense if the first is correct. Any proposal for identifying the decisive (i.e., necessary and sufficient) conditions for the justification of moral norms can make sense only once it has been established that such norms can be meaningfully justified at all. Only if moral questions can be considered cognitive does it make sense to attempt to justify which answers to such questions are morally right and which are not. Otherwise, the issue of justification would not appear in the first place.

To explain why participants in moral discourses consider moral judgments to be in need of justification (i.e., to explain the ratio-

11. F. J. Davis (1994) offers an interesting attempt to interpret discourse ethics from a realist point of view. I agree completely with his analysis of the realist presuppositions implicit in discourse ethics, but I draw very different conclusions concerning the internal relationship between these presuppositions and discourse.

nale of accepting requirements of justification as appropriated for moral questions), it is first necessary to explain in what sense (i.e., in virtue *of what*) moral questions can be meaningfully considered as *cognitive* questions. Only if the analysis of what moral questions are about can explain the presupposition that there is something *to be known* about them does it then make sense to ask for the most rational way to discover the right answer to such questions. In other words, we have to see how far the comparison goes between truth claims and moral claims, in order to see how defensible the cognitivism of discourse ethics really is.

Against the claim of an internal relationship between morality and rationality, it is usually pointed out that one who acts immorally is not thereby necessarily irrational. Immoral actions can be considered rational in at least one clear sense, namely, in the sense of instrumental rationality. An immoral action or norm may very well be an extremely rational, that is, *efficient* means for reaching one's own goals. However, there is a different but equally clear sense in which such actions or norms cannot be considered rational. Namely, they cannot be considered rationally acceptable, that is, publicly *justifiable*. As long as we do not claim justification for an immoral action or norm, a requirement of rationality in this latter sense is obviously not operative for us. But as soon as we claim that the action or norm is justified, or are required to do so by others, we also have to claim (and attempt to show) that it is not immoral at all.

The fact that speakers consider it appropriate to justify moral judgments or norms, as well as to ask others for justification, speaks precisely in favor of regarding moral questions as cognitive. For the requirement of justification makes sense only under the supposition that such questions can be decided in a rational way—that there is a correct answer to them that can be known.

Now, the presupposition that there is something to be known about a given kind of question, as we saw already concerning the truth of statements, means that there is a fact of the matter as to their answers. It means that that which can be known is either one way or the other—and therefore it cannot be the case that an answer and its opposite are both correct. If moral questions are indeed cognitive, participants in moral discourses have to pre-suppose that to (clearly stated) moral questions there can only be "a single right answer," just as they suppose to be the case for questions about truth.

This requirement does seem to be built into the *unconditional validity* that speakers ascribe to moral statements or norms. They are *binarily* coded, for we cannot say that a norm is *more* or *less* just, but only that it is just or unjust. They also have a *fixed* character, not allowing for changes over time, since we cannot say that a norm was once just and is now unjust. Our use of the just/unjust opposition thus seems to be structurally identical to our employment of the true/false opposition.

Undoubtedly, there are differences between the meaning of the two validity claims from the point of view of the *content* (differences also reflected in the obvious distinction between assertions and commands). Still, both have something in common that explains the structural similarities in our uses of them: the cognitivist presupposition of "a single right answer" is meaningful in both cases, to the extent that we know the *necessary and sufficient conditions for the satisfaction of both validity claims*. This makes both validity claims discursively redeemable. As much as we know the necessary and sufficient condition for truth ('P' is true if and only if p), we also know the necessary and sufficient condition for moral rightness: a norm N is morally right ("just") if and only if it is equally in everyone's interest.[12] Grasping the meaning of these

---

12. It is debatable whether moral questions should be *reduced* to questions of justice (as done by deontological approaches) or if they also include, in Habermas's terms, ethical questions concerning the good life. Moreover, it is also debatable whether questions of justice can be *isolated* from questions of goodness at all. All of this is, however, not pre-empted by an explanation of what "just" means (i.e., by an explanation of the minimal sense of this notion). If we apply Moore's open question argument in this context it is possible to see that an explanation of the meaning of "just" along these lines is prima facie plausible. The following does not seem to be an open (i.e., meaningful) question: "The norm N is equally in everyone's interest, but is it just?"

The proposed explanation is general enough (indeed, it is *criterially empty*) not to favor any particular conception of justice above others, but only to express what all of them have in common *as conceptions of justice*. To claim that a norm is just is to claim that it is equally in everyone's interest; what, in turn, can be

validity claims is what enables the participants in a theoretical or practical discourse to *know what they are looking for.* As Habermas explains in "Erläuterungen zur Diskursethik": "Just as the assertoric mode of utterance can be explained through the fact that the asserted states of affairs exist, so too the deontological mode can be explained through the fact that the demanded actions are in the common interest of all possibly affected" (p. 130).

The realist presuppositions behind both validity claims explain why our discussion concerning both kinds of questions is restricted in advance by the premise of "a single right answer." Our knowledge concerning the truth of statements depends on the existence of the asserted states of affairs in the objective world. Depending on what happens to be the case, the statement must be either *true* or *false*. Similarly, our knowledge concerning the moral rightness of norms depends on the existence of common interests among all individuals in the social world. In virtue of what happens to be the generalizable interests among all human beings,[13] a norm can only be *just* or *unjust*.

---

claimed to be equally in everyone's interest is not itself included in such an explanation. That is to say, it could in principle be *anything* (for it depends on the shared general beliefs, criteria of justification, etc., of the relevant speakers at any given moment in time, as history teaches us). In this sense, such a condition by no means favors an egalitarian morality, that is, it does not offer a sufficient basis for justifying such a morality. As can be clearly seen in discourse ethics, some other source of normativity is needed in order to obtain egalitarian outcomes from such a criterially empty condition. Only when moral claims are bound up with requirements of (discursive) rational acceptability (and under historical conditions of a given plurality of moral codes) can the development toward an egalitarian moral be considered likely, or even to some extent unavoidable.

13. The presupposition that there are generalizable (universalizable) interests among all human beings (and therefore that no norm that makes it impossible to preserve them can be morally right) goes beyond the presupposition that some interests may happen to be shared by all human beings at a given time. To be more exact, what it presupposes is that some of those shared interests are *unrenounceable* for all human beings. They are those, to paraphrase Rawls, that "a rational human being wants whatever else she wants" (see Rawls 1971, p. 92). Only when those interests are at issue does the question of the moral rightness of a norm arise.

On the one hand, these realist presuppositions have a crucial *formal role* as *conditions of possibility for a meaningful theoretical or practical discourse.* For just as the presupposition of the existence of states of affairs in the objective world is the condition of possibility of a meaningful discussion about the truth of statements, the presupposition of the existence of generalizable interests among the individuals in the social world is the condition of possibility of a meaningful discussion about the moral rightness of social norms. This presupposition of existence is indispensable for practical discourses, not because it is necessarily the case that there are such interests common to all human beings, rather, it is because if we came to the conclusion that there *are not* such interests, that accordingly this presupposition makes no sense (which is obviously an open, empirical question), then the question of the moral rightness of social norms would also become meaningless.[14] If, as a matter of fact, there were no interests common to all human beings, we could not understand what it means to consider a norm as just or unjust.[15] But as long as we can reasonably presuppose

14. As J.-J. Rousseau remarks in *The Social Contract:* "If the establishment of societies was made necessary because individual interests were in opposition, it was made possible because those interests concur. *The social bond is formed by what these interests have in common; if there were no point at which every interest met, no society could exist.* And it is solely on the basis of this common interest that society must be governed" (p. 63; italics mine).

15. In his *Ethik und Dialog,* Wellmer correctly identifies this presupposition as crucial for Kant's ethics as well: "Kant has evidently always already seen in the will of those who can or cannot will a maxim as general law the expression of a *common* will; the cognitivism of Kant's ethics—i.e., the claim of general in the sense of *intersubjective* validity of moral judgements—stands or falls with this presupposition" (p. 38). But his critique of this presupposition shows that he does not correctly identify its status. He criticizes it with the following argument: "That this presupposition is problematic is obvious: the expression 'can will' contains an irreducible 'empirical' moment; we have to reckon with the possibility that different people can will *different* ways of action as general" (ibid.). This objection is intended as a criticism of the categorical imperative, in the sense that "it cannot be seen at all how a moral consensus could be guaranteed with the help of the categorical imperative" (ibid., p. 39). It seems right that reckoning with the possibility pointed to by Wellmer (namely, that different people can will different ways of action as general) immediately yields an objection to

that there are such interests, as long as we can thereby consider it meaningful to discover which norms are "equally in everyone's interest," there can only be *one* right answer. That is to say, every norm either safeguards those interests for everyone, or it does not.

On the other hand, however, these realist presuppositions as such have no epistemic content.[16] As we saw in the previous chapter, the true/false opposition is used to evaluate the two possible outcomes of the practice of asserting how things are. And precisely because its use depends exclusively on the *outcome,* it does not in turn contain any indication about how to know which of the two outcomes obtains for any particular statement. Similarly, the just/unjust opposition evaluates the two possible outcomes of the practice of establishing social norms (for regulating conflicts between the interests of the human beings). But it does not in turn contain any indication about how to know which of the two outcomes obtains for any particular norm. Precisely because those normative expressions are *criterially empty,* their use raises additional questions concerning the justification of applying them to any particular norm or statement. By grasping the meaning of these normative expressions, we know *what* has to be found out (in the respective cases), but not *how* to find it out. This unavoid-

---

the assumption that we can generalize, from our subjective certainty concerning our own interests, to what others "can will." But if this possibility is understood as an objection to the presupposition that common, generalizable interests could be found at all (by whatever epistemic means), it immediately poses the question of whether after seriously reckoning with this possibility we could still continue with a meaningful practice of raising and justifying moral claims (i.e., with a meaningful use of the distinction just/unjust for evaluating social norms). If we take into account that this presupposition is not an empirical one, but rather a condition of meaningfulness for moral claims, it seems that what would fall under the empirical possibility pointed to by Wellmer would not only be Kant's cognitivism (or the categorical imperative), but rather the meaningfulness of the moral point of view in general.

16. Therefore they commit us to the (logical) premise of a single right answer but not to the (epistemic) premise of a single correct interpretation. Their unconditional validity, then, is compatible with epistemic pluralism (i.e., with conceptual relativity). See 7.3 below.

ably raises the further *epistemic* question concerning the most appropiate ways to achieve successful results in these practices.[17] As we saw already, the internal relationship between these two questions explains the two different sources—realist and epistemic[18]—that build up the necessary and sufficient conditions for knowledge. That is, it explains the internal relationship between the validity claims "truth" or "moral rightness," and rational acceptability or justification.

Habermas offers a highly similar explanation of this internal relationship in his defense of the moral cognitivism of discourse ethics against Rawls's constructivism in "Erläuterungen zur Diskursethik":

A validity claim says that the conditions of validity of an utterance—be it an assertion or a moral command—are satisfied, something which cannot be shown by direct appeal to decisive evidence but only through discursive redemption of the claim to propositional truth or normative rightness. The conditions of validity that are not directly accessible are interpreted in terms of reasons that can be advanced in discourse; and the kind of reasons relevant to discursive redemption of a validity claim cast light on the specific meaning of the validity claim raised in a given instance. Just as the assertoric mode of utterance can be explained

17. All conceptions of justice (i.e., all explanations of the moral point of view) are attempts to provide an answer to *this* question—whether we think of Kant's categorical imperative, Rawls's original position, Habermas's rule of argumentation (U), etc.

18. Knowledge claims, as we saw in the previous chapter, are built up from a mixture of realist and epistemic requirements. For *us* to *know* that *p*, on the one hand, objective conditions have to *obtain*—"*p*" has to be, in fact, true (i.e., it has to be the case that *p*). But on the other hand, *we* have to be able to *justify the fact that they do*. The same applies to knowledge claims concerning the moral rightness of norms. In order for us to know that *N* is morally right, on the one hand, objective conditions have to obtain (i.e., *N* must in fact be equally in everyone's interest), but on the other hand, we have to be able to justify the fact that they do. In strict parallelism with the case of truth claims, we can say that

S knows that *N* is morally right if

(1) *S* believes in the rightness of *N*,

(2) *S* is justified in his belief about *N*, and

(3) *N* is morally right.

through the fact that the asserted states of affairs exist, so too the deontological mode can be explained through the fact that the demanded actions are in the common interest of all possibly affected. (EDE, p. 130)

A realist interpretation of both validity claims seems to be not only *compatible* with Habermas's discursive explanation of rational acceptability, but already *contained* in it *in germ*. However, although it is possible to find this kind of explanation of the structural similarities between the validity claims "truth" and "moral rightness," wherever Habermas tries to defend the cognitive status of moral questions, he has recently begun to insist on a dissimilarity between both validity claims. It is crucial to analyze this dissimilarity in order to determine which interpretation of discourse ethics he actually favors, and consequently, how defensible the assumption of moral cognitivism is if such a dissimilarity is accepted.

7.2 Moral Discourse and Moral Rightness

While retracting his epistemic conception of truth in "Rorty's Pragmatic Turn," Habermas adds a cautionary note. Whereas a realist strategy can be adopted for explaining the validity claim of "truth," this is not possible concerning "moral and other normative validity claims that have a built-in orientation toward discursive vindication" (p. 381). This is so because:

They lack the property of "transcending justification" that accrues to truth claims through the supposition of a single objective world built into the communicative use of language. Normative validity claims are raised for interpersonal relationships within a social world that is not independent of "our own making" in the same way as is the objective world. The discursive treatment of normative claims is, however, "analogous to truth" insofar as the participants in practical discourse are guided by the goal of a commanded, permitted or forbidden "single right answer." The social world is intrinsically historical, that is, constitued ontologically in a different way than the objective world. For this reason, in the case of the social world, the idealization of the justificatory conditions cannot include an "anticipation of a future corroboration," in the sense of an anticipated refutation of future objections . . .; rather it can be understood only in the critical sense of a proviso regarding convergence, that is, a proviso concerning the actually achieved state of decentering of the justification community. The discursive vindication of a truth claim says that the truth conditions, interpreted as assertibility conditions, are satisfied. In the case of a normative validity claim, the discursively achieved consensus grounds the corresponding norm's worthiness to be recognized; *to this extent the consensus itself contributes to the satisfaction of the norm's conditions of validity. Whereas rational acceptability merely indicates the truth of a proposition, it provides a constructive contribution to the validity of norms.* (RPT, p. 381; italics mine)

Here, Habermas insists on an epistemic interpretation of the validity claim "moral rightness" as "rational acceptability under ideal conditions." That is, contrary to the interpretation offered earlier, the rule of argumentation (U) does not state the epistemic conditions under which our claim of moral rightness for a norm is *justified*. Rather, this rule states that these epistemic conditions (i.e., the discursive consensus among those affected) are the conditions for the norm to be *morally right*.

In all the various expositions of the central insights of discourse ethics, (U) is introduced as a condition for the *validity* of norms (from a moral point of view). But it always remains ambiguous just *what kind* of validity is meant. To the extent that (U) is supposed to be a rule of argumentation for the *justification* of moral norms in practical discourses, it seems natural to think, as I did above, that the norms that satisfy (U) are valid in the sense that they are *justified*. But if the epistemic (antirealist) interpretation offered in the previous citation is accepted, that is to say, if claims of moral rightness do not transcend justification, then the fact that a norm is justified (i.e., satisfies (U)) is *all that "to be morally right" means*. Moral rightness, then, signifies nothing more than rational acceptability under ideal conditions.

7.2.1 Moral Discourse as a Sufficient Condition for Moral Rightness

As we saw earlier, the second assumption mentioned by Habermas as crucial for a successful defense of discourse ethics commits him only to the thesis that "the *justification* of norms and commands requires that a real *discourse* be carried out" (DE, p. 68). Nonetheless, under the interpretation offered above, discourse ethics would be committed to an *additional* assumption. It would have to be assumed, namely, that the discursive justification of norms is all that their moral rightness consists in. Accordingly, moral discourses would have to guarantee not only moral *justification,* but also moral *rightness.*

Taking into consideration our discussion in chapter 6 of the equivalent assumption concerning the identification of discursive rational acceptability and truth, we can anticipate that to defend the strong claim that the notion of discursive rational acceptability *explains* the notion of moral rightness, we must understand the first notion not in an operational sense but as an achievement word. That is, such a notion has to include moral rightness as a condition: Discursive rational acceptability is not the best epistemic way for us to *infer* the moral rightness of a norm but rather what *establishes its moral rightness.* Habermas follows this strategy in "Erläuterungen zur Diskursethik," where he shows what the idealization of (discursive) rational acceptability amounts to:

Moral-practical discourse represents the ideal extension of each individual communication community from within. In this forum *only those norms proposed that express a common interest of all affected can win justified assent.* (EDE, p. 113)

This characterization of moral discourse allows us to understand rational acceptability under ideal conditions in two different ways. On the one hand, we could take it in a *realist* sense. This would mean that under such ideal conditions, the affected parties would agree only on those norms that *in fact* express a common interest, shared by all of them. On the other hand, we could interpret it in an antirealist, that is, *decisionist* sense. This would mean that under the aforementioned ideal conditions, the norms the affected parties would agree on, *whatever they might be,* would deserve to be called "equally in the interest of all" owing *solely to the fact that they were agreed upon in this way.*

In the antirealist sense, however, it is impossible to defend the cognitivism and unconditional validity of the claims of moral rightness. If to be in the common interest of all the affected parties means to be the outcome of the discursive agreement among the affected, once they have *in fact decided*[19] what are the norms they all agree on, no possibility of revision or criticism makes any sense. As Tugendhat[20] remarks in his critique of discourse ethics:

[W]hat is finally decisive is the factual agreement, and we have no right to disregard it by arguing that it was not rational. . . . Here we do have an act which is irreducibly pragmatic, and this precisely because it is not an act of reason, but an act of the will, an act of collective choice. The problem we are confronted with is not a problem of justification but of the participation in power, of who is to make the decisions about what is permitted and what not. (1981, p. 11)

In such a case, whether a norm is just or not depends upon a factual agreement. It is therefore not unconditionally valid, but valid only relative to a specific community at a specific time. In this case, as Tugendhat argues convincingly, the significance of moral discourses cannot be cognitive. For they do not enable *impartiality of judgment,* but rather *autonomy of will-formation.* Against Tugendhat's interpretation, Habermas has always insisted on the cognitive significance of moral discourses, since they allow for moral insight (and hence for rationally motivated consensus) and not merely for fair decisions (i.e., compromises; see DE, pp. 78ff.). Such a strong (antirealist) interpretation of the assumption concerning the role of moral discourses would thus render impossible any defense of the prior assumption concerning moral cognitivism.

Taking into account that discourse ethics is, first of all, an attempt to defend moral cognitivism, the aforementioned charac-

---

19. But naturally, regardless of *how* and *for what reasons.* For under this interpretation, it is not possible to appeal, in turn, to the point of view of universalizable interests as a factor that the participants in moral discourses have to take into account, *independently of their agreement.*

20. The quote comes from an unpublished manuscript from 1981 quoted by Habermas in "Discourse Ethics" (p. 83). Tugendhat's critique of discourse ethics can be found in "Sprache und Ethik" and "Die Diskursethik" (in *Vorlesungen über Ethik,* pp. 161–176).

terization of the ideal conditions for moral discourses can only preserve a cognitivist sense if moral rightness is understood in the first (realist) sense and is then *explained in epistemic terms* through the notion of "rational acceptability under ideal conditions" (instead of reducing it to "factual acceptance under fair conditions"). As mentioned previously, under this characterization rational acceptability under ideal conditions (or justification) can no longer be interpreted in an operational sense (i.e., in the sense of epistemic responsibility), but only as an achievement word. That is, a norm is only justified (rationally acceptable under ideal conditions) if it is in fact morally right. But the introduction of this further restriction on what can be considered rationally acceptable under ideal conditions has the same disadvantages that we encountered earlier in the equivalent strategy with respect to truth.

Regarding the explanatory force of Habermas's approach, the first difficulty is that this strategy would render discourse ethics completely empty. There are at least two reasons for this. On the one hand, such a discursive explanation of "moral rightness" would be trivially correct, insofar as ideal rational acceptability *already entails moral rightness as a condition.* Thus (U) states that a norm is morally right if under ideal conditions all those affected could accept it on the basis of grounds that establish its moral rightness. But on the other hand, there is no possibility of giving a discourse-theoretic interpretation of the third of these restrictions. As we know, moral discourses are characterized in formal, procedural terms; accordingly, they can at most guarantee the correctness of the *procedure* but not of the *content* (whether of the arguments used, the substantial criteria of justification accepted at any given time, etc.). For this reason, the idealization of rational acceptability that makes it possible to guarantee moral rightness *from the point of view of the content* cannot be explained in discourse-theoretic terms (i.e., epistemic terms). We have no idea what the conditions would look like under which the participants in moral discourses would be not only intersubjectively convincing (i.e., epistemically responsible), but also infallible. The anticipation of correctness would require the participants in moral discourses to be in an epistemic situation transcending their human condition. That is, they would have to have infinite knowledge about the consequences and side effects of a norm, about the full range of possible learning processes in moral argumentation, about human interests themselves, and so forth.

Independently of whether such an idealization could ever be given any content, the real problem concerning discourse ethics would remain. For once such an anticipation is allowed—even if only counterfactually—as a sound normative requirement behind our claims of moral rightness, then all restrictions stemming from the operational (i.e., discursive) sense of rational acceptability would be *superfluous*.[21] As we saw earlier in the case of truth claims, if what is rationally acceptable under ideal conditions is not what is justified in the sense of being convincing for everyone, but is rather *what is actually correct*, then it is unclear what the point could be of a further commitment to discursive requirements of any kind. Once one is right, one does not *also* need to be intersubjectively convincing, or *anything else*. The conditions of rational acceptability that are sufficient to guarantee moral rightness, whatever these may be, would render the discursive conditions of rational acceptability unnecessary for the practice of testing moral claims. Put differently, discursive conditions are necessary for epistemic reasons that would not be given if rational acceptability (in the achievement sense) were the right anticipation behind our

---

21. This argument lies at the basis of Wellmer's critique of Habermas (see Wellmer, 1986, pp. 69ff.). Wellmer argues that, to the extent that the correctness of the reasons used to justify a moral claim does not depend on discursive conditions, these conditions are not necessary or constitutive of the rationality of our justifications of moral claims. This criticism is only correct, however, if Habermas insists on understanding (ideal) discursive conditions as *sufficient* to *guarantee* moral rightness. But if we understand discourse ethics in its more plausible interpretation, i.e., if (U) is understood as offering an *operational* epistemic criterion for (rational) moral justification, Wellmer's critique is incorrect. That discursive conditions are not necessary for the *correctness* of the reasons does not show (as Wellmer seems to presuppose) that discursive conditions are not necessary *for us to tell whether the reasons are correct or not*. If they are not, it has to be for other (epistemic) reasons not offered by Wellmer; see chapter 6, footnote 25.

claims of moral rightness: If infallibility could possibly be epistemically guaranteed, any additional discursive requirement would
be superfluous.

For the very reasons already cited in the parallel discussion of
truth claims, discursive requirements for rational acceptability can
be justified as a *necessary* condition for a sound practice of testing
moral claims only to the extent that no *sufficient* condition for
moral rightness is epistemically accessible to us. Only to the extent
that "justified" ("rationally acceptable") in an achievement
sense can only be *criterially empty,* is an *operational* sense of "justified" necessary for evaluating *here* and *now* whether a given norm
can be considered right or not.

Precisely such an *operational* rule of argumentation is what discourse ethics means to offer with (U), its principle of universalization. As Habermas remarks:

[T]he principle of universalization, as a rule of argumentation, must
retain a reasonable, and thus operational, sense for finite subjects who
make judgments in particular contexts. Hence it can demand at most
that in justifying norms those consequences and side effects be taken
into account which general adherence to a norm can be *anticipated* to
have for the interests of each on the basis of the information and reasons
available to them at a particular time. (EDE, p. 139)

In this operational sense, however, the results are *obviously not infallible.* But if the procedure allows for error, then its results cannot be considered morally right per se. To meet the procedural
conditions does not *constitute what "morally right" means.* Rather,
it simply offers the best epistemic support for the supposition that
the norms at issue are *in fact* morally right. Such a procedure cannot *guarantee* the moral rightness of a norm—nothing can. But
it *can entitle us* to claim moral rightness for the norm, as long as
no counterarguments appear (whether on the basis of new experiences, consequences, side effects or learning processes in general). As Habermas correctly remarks: "the validity claim of a
norm that has withstood the universalization test bears a 'time
and knowledge index'" (EDE, p. 139).[22] Therefore the only

22. See footnote 25.

validity claim that can possibly be meant is the claim of rational acceptability (or justification). For the claim of moral rightness, due to its unconditional validity, is incompatible with any time index.

Given that such a "time and knowledge index" is not only due to the difficulty of satisfying the discursive conditions for (ideal) justification but *also to our cognitive limitations and capacity for learning*, moral rightness unavoidably *transcends justification*. For only the logical difference between them renders meaningful the obligation of (discursive) justification and perhaps even revision of our moral claims.

But Habermas had offered an additional argument against the assumption that moral rightness can transcend justification. Given the peculiar nature of the conditions for moral rightness, given that it is not possible to separate completely what is equally in everyone's interest from our evidence concerning what is in our own interest, the satisfaction of the conditions for moral rightness seems unavoidably to have an epistemic component that makes moral claims completely different from truth claims. The truth of a statement depends on what is the case, whereas the moral rightness of a norm depends on what we want to be the case— that is, it depends upon a general *will*. In this sense, the social world is not independent of "our own making" in the same way as the objective world is.

It seems clear, however, that if regarding moral issues we subject our *will* to the *insight* in a context-transcendent correctness (something that, according to Habermas, we do not do with respect to ethical-political questions), it can only be because we regard the will in the first case as in some sense independent of "our own making," or at least of our *arbitrary* making. As Habermas remarks, against decisionist explanations of the moral point of view, "a moment of passivity always attaches to convictions, they *take shape* and are not produced by us like decisions" (EDE, p. 122). There are many factors that explain why, with respect to moral claims, we subject our practices to objective conditions that can transcend our given epistemic situation.

First of all, it seems that regarding the question of what makes up our unrenounceable interests, we believe that the answer depends less on "our own making" than on our human condition. In this sense, we seem to recognize a (possible) gap between our own unrenounceable interests and the evidence we have of them at any particular time. If we keep looking for those norms that are in fact equally in everyone's interest, despite all the difficulties in overcoming our epistemic disagreements, it can only be because given any suspicion concerning whether a norm is just, *the option of changing the affected interests instead of the norm is not a viable option.*[23]

But even under the presupposition of an ideal transparency of *our own unrenounceable interests,* this provides no guarantee concerning the knowledge of the unrenounceable interests of others. Yet it is obviously on such knowledge that the condition of being "equally in everyone's interest" also depends.[24]

Moreover, even if all of us could never possibly be mistaken concerning our own unrenounceable interests, this would not guarantee infallible knowledge concerning the objective consequences that a norm in the long run and under changing (i.e., currently unpredictable) circumstances would have for all those who are possibly affected.[25] Discrimination is not always a

---

23. Our feelings concerning moral issues (which are by no means a sign of cognitive disagreement, but rather primarily of violated interests) do sometimes come before the related arguments (and the consequent cognitive agreement or disagreement). But this can be the case only insofar as the interests we have, and our sensitivity toward them, are not entirely dependent upon our epistemic situation (concerning those interests as well as the foreseeable consequences and side effects of the norms). If epistemic agreement (even under discursive ideal conditions) were a sufficient condition for justice, so that as Habermas affirms, "the consensus itself contributes to the satisfaction of the norm's conditions of validity" (RPT, p. 41), we would not need to *discover* just norms. That is to say, we would not need to discover norms that in fact satisfy those conditions, given whatever interests among human beings happen to be the universalizable ones. But rather, we could *change our interests* so as to make any possible norm agreed upon *just* (by definition).

24. This, by the way, is the crucial argument of discoure ethics against Kant's categorical imperative. (See EDE, pp. 156–157, 107.)

25. The fallibility of our epistemic situation can affect not only our judgment concerning the appropriate conditions of application of the different prima facie valid norms, which it obviously does. It can also affect our judgment

consequence of the repressed will of those affected by it. It can also result from our incapacity to foresee the side effects of a norm in the long run, or even from our inability to imagine a more satisfactory norm, despite all our best intentions. It does not seem meaningless to say that we might find out that a norm, despite our general agreement (based on our prior epistemic situation) as to its moral rightness, has actually turned out to be morally wrong (i.e., *in fact* unfair, discriminatory, or the like). As Habermas claims against decisionist explanations of the moral point of view, "just social orders are not constructed but also discovered" (EDE, p. 159).[26]

However, Habermas's objection leaves us with the following question. Does an explanation of the presupposition of objectivity behind our moral claims have to be achieved at the price of conflating them with truth claims, of conflating the social with the objective world?

But what both validity claims have in common, if the analysis offered here is correct, does not depend in the least on any such conflation. As could be seen from our earlier analysis of achievement words, the sense in which the outcome of an *activity* can be judged from the point of view of its *objective success or failure* (i.e., from the point of view of whether the necessary and sufficient conditions that orient the activity at issue in fact obtain or not) does not depend on the *content* of the activity being related with the objective or social world. As a question concerning the outcome of *our activities,* these conditions are in no sense independent of the goals (sense) of the activities that are decided by us—

concerning the actual consequences and side effects of a norm under its *standard* conditions of application. Once these consequences or side effects become clear, we can learn that what all of us considered a prima facie valid norm is actually not valid at all.

26. Naturally, just social orders are constructed as *social* orders in the sense that they are not a natural phenomenon. They are created first of all by the introduction (i.e., enforcement) of norms. But as *just* social orders, they are not created in this sense: whether they are just or not depends on whether they in fact satisfy the necessary and sufficient conditions of what it means to be just.

that are indeed of "our own making." With the predicates true/ false we evaluate the outcomes of *our activity* of asserting how things are. This activity and its goal are both of our own making: *We establish* the necessary and sufficient conditions of its success ("P" is true if and only if it is the case that *p*). But once they are established, the question of whether these conditions in fact obtain in any particular case *cannot also be decided by us ourselves,* cannot be "of our own making" in the same sense.[27] Similarly, with the predicates just/unjust we evaluate the outcomes of *our activity* of establishing generally binding norms for regulating social conflicts. This activity and its goal *are* of our own making: *We establish* the necessary and sufficient conditions of its success (*N* is just if and only if *N* is equally in everyone's interest). But once they are established, the question as to whether these conditions in fact obtain or not in any particular case cannot also be decided by us.[28] It cannot be made dependent on our given epistemic situation. As we saw already concerning any activity evaluated by achievement words, the correctness of the outcome depends *exclusively* on the *obtaining* of a state of affairs. And *this is not an epistemic matter.* By the same token, the validity (i.e., justice) of a norm depends, as Habermas puts it, on "the circumstance that the norm is equally in everyone's interest" (EDE, p. 67). And again, *this is not an epistemic circumstance.* Viewed in this light, Habermas's recognition, in

27. In some cases, we can even establish *arbitrarily* the conditions for the success of an activity—for example, for someone winning the lottery (an extremely conventional activity, and therefore "of our own making" in all possible senses). But we cannot in the same way decide arbitrarily whether or not someone has won.

28. The *formal* notion of one objective world (expressed in the either/or of the opposition obtains/does not obtain) should not be preempted by a naturalist prejudice in favor of a natural or physical world. Taking into account that it is our orientation toward what is the case that first motivates the presupposition of a formal objective world, as Habermas demonstrates in his theory of communicative rationality, and also taking into account that for this reason we adopt it (i.e., we apply the distinction obtains/does not obtain) for judging social matters as well, it is clear that *in this sense* there are as many social facts as there are natural facts. This is also clear in the formal expression of Convention T, which remains correct no matter what the statement "*p*" is about.

"Rorty's Pragmatic Turn," of the distinction between epistemic and realist conditions concerning truth claims might be paraphrased in precisely the same terms with respect to moral claims. This would read as follows:

A claim of moral rightness raised for the norm "*N*" implies that the rightness conditions for "*N*" are satisfied (i.e., that *N*, in fact, is equally in everyone's interest). We have no other way in which we can *establish* whether or not this is the case except via argumentation (with all possible affected), for direct access to uninterpreted rightness conditions is denied to us. But the fact that the rightness conditions are satisfied does not itself amount to an epistemic fact just because we can only *establish* whether these conditions are satisfied via the discursive vindication of the claim of "moral rightness." (paraphrase of a passage from RPT, pp. 367–368) [29]

7.2.2 Moral Discourse as a Necessary Condition for Moral Justification

Under this interpretation, (discursive) rational acceptability is a *necessary* condition for a valid practice of evaluating moral claims *on epistemic grounds* and not because it *constitutes* what "moral rightness" means. *What has to be found out* concerning the moral rightness of norms is not whether all those affected under ideal discursive conditions would accept them (as would be the case concerning their legitimacy). Rather, what must be determined is whether the norm is, in fact, equally in everyone's interest. But

29. Undoubtedly, access to "uninterpreted truth conditions" and to "uninterpreted conditions of moral rightness" is denied to us for different reasons. In the first case it is because of the underdetermination of our theories by data. But in the second case the indetermination is not only owing to the different possible interpretations of our own interests but also owing to our (relative) freedom to choose them, their (possible) changeability, etc. It is clear that, in this sense, the social world is "more" of our own making than the objective world is. But I think that it is also clear that this difference does not affect the argument at all. It is still the case that the conditions that have to obtain for us to consider a norm just are not epistemic (i.e. they do not depend on our agreement; they depend on whether the possibilities of action prescribed by the norm at issue are, in fact, fair, non-discriminatory, etc.)

to know *what* "moral rightness" means does not provide us with any answer as to the question of *how* to find out which of the two cases obtains for any given norm.[30] Therefore *any* answer to this

30. The difference between (and logical independence of) the two questions explains both what all the various conceptions of justice (Kantian, Habermasian, Rawlsian, etc.) have in common—as conceptions of *justice*—and what they all disagree about—as alternative *conceptions,* alternative answers to the *epistemic* question regarding the best way to find out whether a norm is just (whether it be the categorical imperative, (U), the original position, etc.).

A confusion between the two different questions seems to lie at the basis of Tugendhat's critique of discourse ethics (see 1992, pp. 275–314, esp. pp. 291–292 and pp. 305–306). Tugendhat's arguments seemingly aim to show that because the (discursive) agreement of the affected does not belong to the semantic conditions for moral rightness, to what "moral rightness" means (namely to be equally in everyone's interest), it also cannot be a condition for finding out whether a norm is morally right. He seems to understand the *semantic* conditions that fix *what* has to be the case for a norm to be morally right as *at the same time expressing epistemic* conditions concerning *how* to find out whether this is the case or not for a given norm. Based on this confusion, though, he admits (see pp. 291–292) that to be "equally in everyone's interest" is a very imprecise criterion for a decision beyond the easiest cases—which may support the suspicion that moral questions are not cognitive after all. But such a semantic condition is not just epistemically imprecise, but epistemically *empty*—every bit as empty as Convention T is regarding truth. As we have seen, the meaning of these normative expressions fixes the conditions that have to obtain for its proper application. But given this normative function, they cannot at the same time express a factual procedure or criterion that competes with other possible ones. To grasp the semantic conditions of these expressions is indeed a necessary (and prior) condition for discovering appropriate epistemic criteria. An answer to the question of *how* to find something out obviously presupposes a prior answer to the question regarding *what* has to be found out but *is not already contained in it.* The fact that the discursive agreement of all those affected does not belong *as an epistemic criterion for moral justification* to the semantic conditions for moral rightness cannot serve as an argument against discourse ethics (just as it could not against any other propposed criteria, whether Kantian, Rawlsian or otherwise). To the extent that (U) indeed contains the semantic condition for moral rightness (i.e., an indication of what the moral discourse is about), it cannot be wrong on semantic grounds, but only on epistemic ones. That is to say, it cannot be wrong by expressing an epistemic criterion but only by expressing a *wrong* one. Tugendhat's criticism, however, seems to have motivated Habermas's attempt to somehow introduce the (discursive) agreement of those who are affected in the semantics of "moral rightness," i.e., to interpret (U) as a *sufficient*

epistemic question would have to be defended on epistemic grounds. At this level, then, the question is: Given what has to be found out, and given our epistemic limitations, what would be the best way to find it out? Discourse ethics can defend the rule of argumentation, (U), as the best epistemic way to justify the moral rightness of norms if it is able to argue that (discursive) rational acceptability is a *necessary* condition for moral justification—against those conceptions that do not contain such a condition (such as Kant's categorical imperative or Rawls's original position, for example). As we saw, this is precisely what Habermas indicated as the second crucial assumption of discourse ethics: "the *justification* of norms and commands requires that a real *discourse* be carried out and thus cannot occur in a strictly monological form" (DE, p. 68; italics mine).

But it is difficult to see why in order to argue that (discursive) rational acceptability is a *necessary* condition for moral justification (on epistemic grounds) it is also necessary to contend that it is a *sufficient* condition for moral rightness. Moreover, in some of his replies to his critics, Habermas seems to suppose that defending the second claim is the only way to defend the first.[31] But if our analysis is not completely wrong, the second claim is not only implausible, but extremely *harmful* precisely when it is a question of defending an approach of the characteristics of discourse ethics.

As I will try to show in more detail in what follows, discourse ethics can plausibly contend that (discursive) rational acceptability is a *necessary* condition for moral *justification* only to the extent that no *sufficient* condition for *moral rightness* is epistemically accessible to us.

---

condition for moral rightness (and not as the epistemic procedure for moral justification that it is supposed to be). As the analysis of this attempt in the foregoing section has shown, (U) cannot have it both ways for the same reasons that weaken Tugendhat's criticism. Either it expresses what moral rightness means in epistemic terms (and thus is criterially empty), or it offers an operational criterion for moral justification (but then cannot guarantee moral rightness).

31. See the previous footnote; see also chapter 6, footnote 25.

I cannot go into detail regarding the alternative approaches to discourse ethics, which directly or indirectly call into question the requirement of discursive conditions for a valid justification of our moral claims. But on the basis of the analysis offered in these chapters, we can distinguish roughly between two general ways of questioning this crucial assumption of discourse ethics.

One obvious way to challenge the thesis that a consensus under ideal discursive conditions is a necessary condition for moral justification is to deny the requirement of (cognitive) justification for moral claims altogether. One could either defend some kind of moral emotivism (or relativism in general), or interpret the requirement of justification in a noncognitive sense, as a mere requirement of legitimation (such as in Tugendhat's decisionism). These revisionary positions, however, do not represent a specific criticism of the *epistemic* assumption of discourse ethics. Rather, they call into question its prior assumption concerning moral *cognitivism* in general.[32] They do not address the question of *how to find out* what is morally right, but only what it *means* to be morally right. Therefore no way of interpreting the epistemic assumption can be of any help in settling this prior discussion.[33]

There is another, more specific way to question the appropriateness of (U) (i.e., of discursive rational acceptability) as a *necessary* condition for moral justification. This would consist in an appeal to a *sufficient condition* for moral rightness that does not

32. The first, emotivist strategy denies the assumption of cognitivism behind our practices of justifying norms questioning that "just" means anything like "equally in everyone's interest." It proposes, instead, that we recognize that by judging a norm as "just" we can actually only mean something like "I approve of this; do likewise." The second, decisionist alternative interprets the cognitivist assumption as a deceit for what can only be more or less fair conditions of collective decision; what appears to be a good "reason" in our justification practices is in fact only a successful participation in power.

33. Unless one opts for arguing that discursive consensus is a *sufficient* condition for moral rightness in the antirealist sense that it explains what "morally right" actually means, namely, that we all would agree on it under ideal discursive conditions. As we have seen, such a defense of the assumption concerning the role of moral discourses means to accept the decisionist critique—i.e., to give up the assumption of moral cognitivism.

depend in turn on discursive conditions. It could be either a *substantial criterion* for moral justification (e.g., the utilitarian maxim), or it could be a criterion derived from an *authority* able, in virtue of some capacity, to adopt a privileged epistemic position for guaranteeing moral rightness. (This could be a moral code handed down by God, obtained on the basis of first-person certainty as in Kant's categorical imperative, or on the basis of philosophical knowledge as in Rawls's theory of justice.) In any such case, discursive requirements (i.e., actual moral discourses) could be considered superfluous.

Although in this context the question seems to be a specifically moral one, what is actually at issue is the general thesis behind Habermas's theory of communicative rationality concerning the *procedural* sense of our notion of rational acceptability.[34] This the-

---

34. Rawls's criticism of Habermas concerning the distinction between procedural and substantive conceptions of justice (in his "Reply to Habermas") seems to be based on a confusion as to which notion is explained in procedural terms in Habermas's approach. Rawls interprets discourse ethics as attempting to offer a procedural notion of "justice" and provides convincing arguments against the plausibility of such an attempt. Essentially, he argues that the conditions for agreement in practical discourse can serve at best as conditions for the legitimacy of its outcome but not for its justice (i.e., its moral rightness). He thus concludes that it is not the notion of justice, but rather the more general notion of legitimation, that may be procedural. Even though Rawls's interpretation gains some support from the inconsistencies of Habermas's exposition as discussed here, it is clear that his criticism misses the point of Habermas's theory of communicative rationality. As already indicated, what the theory offers is indeed not a procedural interpretation of the notion of justice (or truth) but of the notion of rational acceptability. This notion is not only more general than the notion of justice (as Rawls observes); more importantly, it does not have a *specifically moral* content. This is precisely the virtue of the theory, and not at all its shortcoming. For one of the crucial aims of Habermas's theory is to show that the vindication *both* of our truth-claims and of our claims concerning the justice of norms depend on *one and the same basic conception of rational acceptability understood in procedural terms* (i.e., as the outcome of a discussion taking place under the conditions of an ideal speech situation). In this sense, the discourse-theoretical interpretation of "rational acceptability" can explain *simultaneously* both the conditions under which truth-claims can be considered *justified,* and the conditions under which moral claims can be considered *legitimate.* It is precisely on the basis of this explanatory strategy that Habermas can claim that moral ques-

sis has been misunderstood by many critics as stating that procedural (i.e., discursive) conditions are *sufficient* for guaranteeing truth or moral rightness, as if theoretical or moral discourses were able to generate correct arguments and true statements or morally right norms in virtue of their procedural conditions alone. To the extent that they are not, (U) has been criticized for being unable to offer "a sufficiently determinate procedure. The argumentation procedure cannot ensure the choice of correct answers solely on the basis of presuppositions of communication" (EDE, p. 164). Habermas's thesis, however, is that such procedural conditions are *necessary* but not sufficient conditions for a valid justification practice. That is, they do not compete with the substantive criteria for justification (or kinds of arguments, etc.) used at any given time, but are complemented by them. The difference in status between the procedural conditions and any substantive criteria of justification lies elsewhere. Whereas the former are *necessary* conditions, implied in the very notion of justification, any substantive criterion can be considered as a sufficient condition for justification *only as long as there is a (factual) general agreement as to its validity.*[35]

Given that any justification depends conceptually on its convincingness for those who have asked for justification, discursive

---

tions are just as *cognitive* as theoretical questions. Habermas himself explains this in " 'Vernünftig' versus 'wahr'—oder die Moral der Weltbilder," as follows: "I agree with Rawls's remarks about procedural vs. substantive justice (Reply 170–180); these reflexions, though, fail to capture the sense in which I use the expressions 'procedure' and 'procedural rationality' when I affirm that an argumentative practice organized in a particular way justifies the supposition of *the rational acceptability of its outcomes*" (in *Die Einbeziehung des Anderen,* p. 119; italics mine).

35. As Habermas remarks concerning "sacred world-views" and their "spellbinding authority," it is not so much that a justification based on authority is not oriented toward the convincingness of those who have asked for it. Rather, only because they in fact accept the authority's reliability can the justification gain binding validity in the first place: "This archaic form of authority was not based on the fact that normative beliefs remained in the background, that they could not be thematized and connected with reasons; it was based, rather, on a prescriptive choice of themes and the rigid patterning of reasons" (BFN, p. 36).

conditions are actually *never* superfluous. For any process of justification as such has to take place under conditions in which it is possible to tell how genuinely convincing the arguments are (i.e., under non-coercive conditions). If these conditions do not obtain, the practice at issue is something other than a process of argumentation or justification. In such a process, the appeal to an authority or to any other substantive criterion of justification can only work given the (factual) general acceptance of the authority's reliability or of the criterion's validity by the participants in the argument.[36] Given a general agreement and abundant shared convictions among the participants in this process, they can take discursive conditions (of rational acceptability) for granted, to such an extent that they remain completely inconspicuous. But as already mentioned in the previous chapter, given the unavoidable openness of the orientation toward mutual understanding (an understanding dependent on the explicit and *unforced assent* of their participants) proper to justification practices, the burden of proof for any proposal of a sufficient criterion for justification (whether utilitarian, Kantian, or whatever) is to show its immunity to any present or future critique by the participants in argumentation processes. Interestingly enough, the very attempt to show this, independently of its success, would confirm the validity of discourse ethics's epistemic assumption concerning practical discourses. As Habermas remarks:

Any content, no matter how fundamental the action norms in question may be, must be made subject to real discourse (or advocatory discourses undertaken in their place). The principle of discourse ethics prohibits singling out with philosophical authority any specific normative content (as, for example, certain principles of distributive justice) as the *definitive* content of moral theory. Once a normative theory like Rawls's theory of justice strays into substantive issues, it becomes just *one contribution to practical discourse* among many—even though it may be an especially competent one. (DE, p. 122)[37]

36. See footnote 37, this chapter.

37. In view of the actual development of Rawls's philosophical self-understanding, these remarks seem less a critique than a premonition. See Rawls (1985) and (1993). There is an internal reason for the correctness of this premonition

It was in this vein that I remarked earlier that the attempt to interpret (ideal) discursive conditions as *sufficient* for guaranteeing moral rightness weakens the position of discourse ethics. For it jeopardizes the insight that (discursive) rational acceptability is the only acceptable *necessary* condition for moral justification, precisely to the extent that *no sufficient condition* for moral rightness is *epistemically accessible to us* (i.e., no substantive criterion for moral rightness can be regarded in advance as immune to critique or definitive). This is precisely what we understand when we understand (U). This insight represents the impact of (discursive) rational acceptability on moral questions.[38] And it is also what

---

that is interesting in the present context. Precisely to the same extent that Rawls's approach aims to offer *sufficient* criteria for justice it remains tied to the background consensus of beliefs factually shared in the present time. In this sense, Rawls's own interpretation of the status of his *Theory of Justice* (i.e., of its lack of universal validity) is an unavoidable consequence of the theory's task as he conceives it. As Rawls states it: "justice as fairness seeks to identify the kernal of an overlapping consensus, that is, the shared intuitive ideas which when worked up into a political conception of justice turn out to be *sufficient* to underwrite a *just* constitutional regime. This is the most we can expect, not do we need more" (1985, pp. 246–247; italics mine).

Thus Rawls's approach aims to provide substantive criteria for justice (i.e. conditions that would be *sufficient* to *guarantee* the justice of the outcome). However, as he himself came to realize, any such conditions or criteria can only be sufficient *based on the particular background beliefs factually shared by the citizens of a given society at a particular time* (in this case the citizens of democratic societies). Given these shared beliefs, such citizens would agree on the principles singled out by Rawls, if he is right. But obviously under other system of background beliefs (i.e., other conceptions of the person, of what counts as a good reason, as valid criteria of justification, etc.) the results would be different. For this reason, any conception that wants to offer a decision procedure that satisfies *sufficient* conditions for justice can aim to be at the most "the conception we regard—here and now—as fair and supported by the best reason" (1985, p. 238). It is in this sense that it cannot claim universal validity.

38. The further impact concerning the egalitarian consequences that we can see as implied in (U) depends on an additional factor, namely, the given historical situation from which we interpret (U): a situation marked by a plurality of moral codes and ethical convictions. Only after the affected themselves (as a consequence of such a situation) do not recognize any authority concerning their own interests as unquestionably valid can egalitarian consequences follow from (U).

differentiates discourse ethics from any moral theory that aims to offer *sufficient conditions for moral rightness* (i.e., moral criteria beyond any requirement of justification, beyond the requirement of validation in real moral discourses). But it is necessary to discuss an additional question in order to be able to judge what is the most plausible interpretation of discourse ethics.

7.3 Moral Cognitivism and Ethical Pluralism

As can be seen from Habermas's discussion of the dissimilarities between truth claims and moral claims, there is at least one clear feature of both validity claims that allows them to be compared. This feature marks *the* difference between moral cognitivism and decisionism (i.e., between moral universalism and relativism). As Habermas remarks, "the discursive treatment of normative claims is, however, 'analogous to truth' insofar as the participants in practical discourse are oriented toward the goal of a commanded, permitted or forbidden 'single right answer'" (RPT p. 381).

On the basis of what has been discussed so far, it is possible to specify the different consequences that follow for the crucial "premise of 'a single right answer,'" depending on which strategy (realist or epistemic) is chosen for defending moral cognitivism. Recently, Thomas McCarthy has pointed out a crucial consequence of Habermas's attempt to defend this premise within the (epistemic) strategy of identifying moral rightness with "idealized rational acceptability."[39] He argues that the premise of "a single right answer" entails, as a "regulative idea" for moral discourse, that there has to be *a single correct interpretation* of moral questions. Thus the premise implies excluding certain kinds of pluralism and disagreement that are perfectly rational alternatives to rational agreement on practical questions.

This consequence might seem implausible in its own right. But beyond this, it presents an internal difficulty for discourse ethics. The problem, briefly, is as follows. The assumption of moral cognitivism depends essentially on the possibility of defending the

39. See McCarthy (1991) and (1996).

autonomy (*Entkoppelung*) of questions of justice from questions of goodness. Whereas moral questions concerning the justice of norms are restricted by the premise of "a single right answer," ethical-political questions concerning what is good for us (or for me) obviously are not. But if the moral rightness of a norm is explained in epistemic terms as its (discursive) rational acceptability under ideal conditions, then the fact that a norm is morally right means that the interpretation on the basis of which it is justified would be accepted by all those affected as correct under ideal (discursive) conditions. The moral rightness of the norm, then, depends on the correctness of the interpretation that justifies it. Such an interpretation, however, cannot be independent of ethical considerations in the way that the norm itself (or the commanded, permitted, or forbidden action) may be.[40] Nevertheless, as we have already seen, to preserve the validity of the premise of "a single right answer" within an epistemic strategy, it would be necessary not only to argue that if a norm is morally right it cannot be wrong at the same time, but also to contend that the particular way of justifying it cannot be wrong either. The particular ethical interpretation through which we justify the moral rightness of the norm would have to be absolutely correct; it would be the single correct interpretation. Moral universalism would turn out to be incompatible with ethical pluralism. Thus, if discourse ethics does not question such pluralism, if it mantains that there are no unconditionally valid answers for ethical questions, then it would also be unable to defend moral universalism.

But if this analysis is plausible, the difficulty seems internal not to the general assumptions of discourse ethics per se but only to

---

40. One clear difficulty of all attempts to explain normative notions such as "truth" (or "justice") with the help of epistemic notions such as "idealized rational acceptability" (or coherence, justification, etc.) is that whereas it is meaningful to apply the first notions to individual statements (or norms), to statements or norms considered in isolation, the epistemic notions can only be applied holistically. A statement (or a norm) is individually true (or just), but it cannot be "rationally acceptable" or coherent taken in isolation. Statements or norms can be rationally acceptable or coherent only in relationship to a general *interpretation* or justification.

the specific attempt to explain moral rightness in terms of (discursive) rational acceptability. It could be avoided, however, if the unconditional validity of moral norms (on which the correctness of the premise of "a single right answer" depends) could be explained without appealing—not even counterfactually—to the presupposition of a single correct interpretation. In my opinion, this can be achieved within the frame of discourse ethics by following the realist strategy sketched in this chapter—that is, by explaining the source of the validity of the norms (their "moral rightness") not in *epistemic* but in *realist* terms.

As pointed out earlier, the unconditional validity implied in the binary use of notions like truth or moral rightness can be explained as a consequence of a trivial condition. Namely, if a statement is true, it cannot at the same time be false; if a norm is morally right, it cannot at the same time be wrong. By using the oppositions true/false or morally right/morally wrong (just/unjust), we thereby commit ourselves to accepting that the statement at issue is *either true or false,* that the norm is *either just or unjust.* And hence the evaluation of the reasons supporting such a statement (or norm) will have to be directed toward the exclusion of one of the two possibilities.

This logical condition, however, seems to be less a consequence of particular epistemic considerations than of the existence presuppositions implicit in the meaning of the notions of truth and moral rightness analyzed earlier. The truth of a statement depends on whether the described state of affairs obtains, and the moral rightness of a norm on whether the regulated actions are equally in everyone's interest. Owing to these existence presuppositions, whenever we use such binary notions, we have to accept in advance that there is a single right answer. But precisely because these *existence* presuppositions have *no epistemic content,* our commitment to the premise of a single right answer (and therefore to the unconditional validity of these notions) does not include an epistemic consequence, such as the premise of a single correct interpretation. That is, this commitment does not predetermine *in how many epistemic ways* we will be able to express *the same existing states of affairs,* or to safeguard *the same existing generaliz-able interests.* In this sense, the (logical) premise of a single right answer per se does not imply the (epistemic) premise of a single correct interpretation. Only by taking into account the realist sense of the validity of these normative notions is it possible to understand why their unconditional validity does not seem to depend on the absolute validity of our epistemic means for expressing true statements or just norms. Epistemic pluralism seems to be compatible with the premise of a single right answer.

In what follows, I will try to show with the aid of Putnam's arguments how a realist strategy can indeed explain the unconditional validity of truth without questioning the fact of epistemic pluralism (i.e., conceptual relativity). This will allow me to explain how, analogously, a realist strategy can make ethical pluralism compatible with moral universalism.

7.3.1   Realism and Conceptual Relativity

Putnam's debate with Bernard Williams in *Realism with a Human Face*[41] can be reformulated for our purposes in the following way. It may be read as an attempt to make clear that, to defend the rationale of the premise of a single right answer, we do not need to introduce the presupposition of a single correct interpretation, or—in Putnam's terms—of an "absolute conception of the world" (RHF, p. 173).

In his defense of this thesis, Putnam appeals to the actual state of the empirical sciences:

At the level of space-time geometry, there is the well-known fact that we can take points to be individuals *or* we can take them to be mere limits. States of a system can be taken to be quantum mechanical superpositions of particle interactions . . . or quantum mechanical superpositions of field states. . . . Not only do single theories have a bewildering variety of alternative rational reconstructions (with quite different ontologies),

41. See Putnam (1990), chapter 11; especially the section on "Absoluteness," pp. 170–174. Concerning the compatibility of realism and conceptual relativity, see also Putnam (1992) and Searle (1995).

but there is no evidence at all for the claim . . . that science converges to a *single* theory. . . . That convergence to one big picture is required by the very concept of knowledge is sheer dogmatism. Yet, without the postulate that science converges to a single definite theoretical picture with a unique ontology and a unique set of theoretical predicates, the whole notion of "absoluteness" collapses. (RHF, p. 171)[42]

If this is correct, a defense of the premise of a single right answer does not seem to require accepting the epistemic presupposition of a single correct interpretation. We only need to be able to recognize, across the different ontologies contained in the different theories or interpretations at issue, that these alternative interpretations are interpretations of the *same* phenomena. Therefore the truth-values of statements that are (in this sense) equivalent will have to be distributed across these alternative conceptualizations or theories *in the same way*. As Putnam puts it in *Renewing Philosophy:* "If a sentence in one version is true in that version, then its correlate in the other version is true in the other version" (RPH p. 118). This requirement, derived from what he calls the "useful idealization" of "the principle of bivalence" (p. 123), underlies our use of the true/false opposition. However, this cannot be understood to mean that, to be equivalent, the sentences of two different theories must be synonyms in a trivial sense, as if they were not, so to speak, *genuinely alternative* ways of conceptualizing the same phenomena—as if they were in the end only one theory. As Putnam shows, they are not synonyms at all. They cannot preserve *meaning*, for they can only acquire their meaning in the holistic context of their respective theories or conceptualizations, and these indeed cannot be reduced to one another: "But to ask if these two sentences [in the example cited earlier] have the same meaning is to try to force the ordinary-

---

42. Putnam continues his argument by drawing the consequences for ethical knowledge in the following terms: "It is, indeed, the case that ethical knowledge cannot claim absoluteness; but that is because the notion of absoluteness is incoherent. Mathematics and physics, as well as ethics and history and politics, show our conceptual choices; the world is not going to impose a single language upon us, no matter what we choose to talk about" (RHF, p. 171).

language notion of meaning to do a job for which it was never designed. . . . We should simply give up the idea that the sentences we have been discussing preserve something called their 'meaning' when we go from one such version into another such version" (RPH, p. 119). As Putnam later makes clear, what they actually preserve is *reference:* "Seemingly incompatible words may actually describe the same situation or event or the same physical system" (RPH, p. 124).

Only by taking this possibility into account can we recognize the fallacy of considering the epistemic premise of a single correct interpretation as necessarily contained in the premise of a single right answer. We can thus recognize that epistemic pluralism by itself does not entail relativism. As Putnam points out: "The fact that the real system allows itself to be talked about in these two very different ways does not mean either that there is no real physical system being talked about, or that there are two different physical systems in two different Goodmanian worlds being talked about. . . . It is absolutely clear, it seems to me, that the two descriptions are descriptions of *one and the same world,* not two different worlds" (RPH, p. 122). Putnam concludes: "The whole point . . . is that very *different* sentences can describe the very same state of affairs" (RPH, p. 117).

It is this possibility that leads Putnam to draw the further conclusion: we have "to recognize that there are many true descriptions of the world in many different vocabularies, without trying to privilege one of those descriptions as the 'absolute' one" (RPH, p. 103). As long as we can "claim that our conceptual schemes are just different 'descriptions' of what are in some sense 'the same facts'" (RPH, p. 110) (which is always a revisable claim), we can concede that "there is no one uniquely true description of reality" (RPH, p. 110). That is, we can abandon the dubious presupposition of an "absolute conception of the world."

It should be kept in mind that to maintain such a claim, it is not necessary to postulate the possibility of access to reality in itself. On the contrary, we only need to be able to recognize the different conceptualizations as conceptualizations *of the same phenomena*. Habermas explains what this capacity involves in his ''Reply'':

> If we want to do justice to the transcendental fact of learning then we must indeed reckon with . . . a communicative reason that no longer prejudges the contents of a particular view of the world. This entirely procedural reason operates with context-transcending validity *claims* and with pragmatic *presuppositions* about the world. But the presupposition of an objective world that is the same for all participants in communication only has the formal meaning of an ontologically neutral system of reference. It only implies that we can refer to the same—reidentifiable—entities, even as our descriptions of them change. (R, p. 1527)

The connection between this formal capacity and the possibility of learning becomes clear once we take into account that such a capacity is the condition of possibility of discourse as such. It is what is required to evaluate the rational acceptability of alternative interpretations in a discourse, since it is precisely this capacity that allows the participants to adopt a hypothetical attitude toward their own interpretations or conceptualizations. As already mentioned, Habermas remarks in his *Theory of Communicative Action* that ''validity claims are in principle open to criticism because they are based on *formal concepts of world*. They presuppose a world that is identical for *all possible* observers, or a world intersubjectively shared by *all members* of a group, and this *in an abstract form, freed from all specific contents*'' (p. 82).

From this perspective, the existence presuppositions bound to truth claims and moral claims (i.e., the existence of states of affairs in the objective world and of generalizable interests shared by all the members of the social world) have a purely *formal role*. They are conditions of possibility for a meaningful theoretical or practical discourse. But precisely the formal character of these realist presuppositions shows that the premise of a single right answer derived from them does not include any epistemic presupposition of absoluteness for the particular *content* at issue. That is, it does not imply the premise of a single correct interpretation. If this can also be shown with respect to moral claims, it seems plausible to mantain that the fact of ethical pluralism is not an argument against moral universalism.

7.3.2 Pluralism: The Right and the Good

As in the case of questions about truth, maintaining the commitment involved in the use of the binary opposition "morally right/morally wrong" in the evaluation of social norms requires only that the participants in a practical discourse, with the help of their own (perhaps different) interpretations of their common interests, try to reach a consensus about the *either/or* concerning the moral rightness of the norm at issue. This agreement, however, is not contingent on a previous agreement on their own interpretation of why the interests safeguarded by the norm are worth having, unrenounceable, or the like.

McCarthy's argument against the meaningfulness of the premise of a single right answer is cogent only on the assumption that this premise necessarily implies the premise of a single correct interpretation. The central argument seems to be the following. Insofar as our access to our own needs and interests is symbolically (i.e., culturally) mediated, whenever our descriptions and interpretations of these needs and interests are different (to whatever extent), we would have to conclude that they cannot be different descriptions or interpretations of the *same* interests and needs. Thus we would have to conclude that there is no way of considering the symbolically interpreted needs as the same ones across alternative interpretations. However, only if the participants in practical discourses did not have this possibility available, only if they operated under the premise of a single correct interpretation, would the pluralism of ethical interpretations (characteristic of multicultural societies) lead them unavoidably to accept relativism.

Habermas seems to see this[43] when he replies to McCarthy in "Erläuterungen zur Diskursethik":

43. Habermas seems to recognize the non-epistemic origin of the premise of a single right answer at different points in his "Reply"; for example, when he writes: "Each national constitution represents a historically different way of construing *the same*—theoretically reconstructible—basic rights, and each positive legal order implements *the same* basic rights in a different form of life. But the identity of the meaning of these rights—and the universality of their content—

It remains an empirical question how far the sphere of strictly generalizable interests extends. Only if it could be shown in principle that moral discourses *must prove unfruitful,* despite the growing consensus concerning human rights and democracy, because there is no way at all of *identifying common interests as such in the light of incommensurable languages,* would the deontological endeavor to uncouple questions of justice from context-dependent questions of the good life have failed. (EDE, pp. 202–203)

However, if we grant the possibility of identifying the same needs and interests even under (relatively) different interpretations of them, then it is not clear that the premise of a single right answer requires presupposing "the premise that a single correct interpretation has to be found" (R, p. 1498). The only requirement seems to be that, independently of the different cultural ways of interpreting these interests and needs historically, the participants in practical discourses should be able to reach an agreement about the norms to be considered morally right (insofar as they safeguard the common, unrenounceable interests that all of them happen to have). As long as the participants find it feasible to identify the interests safeguarded by the norms at issue as the same common interests that they share, it is meaningful—even if extremely difficult—to look for an agreement on the social norms that can be considered morally right (even if they accept the multiple ways of articulating these common interests by different cultures). Such a hermeneutic task, required by the participants in

---

must not be lost in the spectrum of these different interpretations" (R, p. 1498). But under his use of the expression "identity of meaning" is concealed the epistemic premise of a single correct interpretation, as becomes clear when he continues: "This contest of interpretations makes sense only on the premise that it is necessary to find a single correct reading that claims to *exhaust* the universalistic content of these rights in the present context" (R, p. 1498).

The claim that the identity of the content of human rights comes from an ideal, identical *sense* or interpretation of them, waiting to be discovered, seems dubious. I think rather that the identity of the content of human rights depends on their *reference* to the interests presupposed as existent among all human beings. That is just what it means to say that different interpretations can express the *same* interests.

Rational Acceptability and Moral Rightness

practical discourses, is already difficult enough. For they have to bridge the gap between their different interpretations in order to identify, even if under alternative conceptualizations, the same unrenounceable interests.[44] It would be downright hopeless if the participants were also required to reach agreement on the particular way of interpreting the interests at issue.

But as is known from Habermas's defense of the cognitivism implicit in discourse ethics, the premise of a single right answer involves the additional requirement that the participants in a practical discourse have to agree about the moral rightness of a norm *for the same reasons*. Otherwise, their agreement would be merely a compromise. This, however, seems to require "the premise that a single correct interpretation has to be found" (R, p. 1498). I think that the requirement of an agreement *for the same reasons* is correct. But I have the impression that there is an ambiguity in the formulation of the requirement that makes it difficult to distinguish between the premise of a single right answer and the premise of a single correct interpretation. However, in this context, such a distinction seems to be crucial to Habermas's defense of the autonomy of questions of rightness from questions of goodness.

The requirement in question can be understood in two different ways. In my view, one of these ways is important for discourse ethics. The other, I suggest, is what provokes the criticism of the absoluteness of the premise of a single correct interpretation. Like

---

44. But not as difficult as it may sound. It would be hopeless if it should take place at this abstract level, if it should be a general (and definitive) ethical agreement about the admissible alternative interpretations of the common interests of all human beings (as opposed to the inadmissible ones). The fact that practical discourses are centered on social norms (on prohibited or permitted actions) gives to the participants a relatively independent, operationalized way of *identifying their own interests* by attending to the consequences of a general observance of the norm at issue, as is made clear by the discursive interpretation of (U). Precisely because this identification is not fixed once and for all (especially if it has to take place through different cultural interpretations), the decision about the moral rightness of a norm depends on the possible acceptance of all those affected by it.

this premise, the second way of understanding the requirement does not belong among the normative presuppositions of a universalist or cognitivist point of view. This way of understanding the requirement seems to imply that the participants in a practical discourse can come to share conclusions only if they share the evaluative backgrounds or ethical self-understandings from which they take the reasons for the justification of moral norms. But in multicultural societies, the participants in practical discourses are not likely to have these evaluative commitments in common. It follows that in discussions of whether a norm is "equally in everyone's interest," even if the participants come to common conclusions, they do not do so *for the same reasons.*

However, a universalist or cognitivist perspective on moral questions does not rest on such a strong (or substantive) view of the requirement. Such a perspective requires only:

a. that all participants agree on the moral rightness or wrongness of the norm at issue; and therefore,

b. that all of them assent to the validity of the norm *for the reason that* the norm preserves a generalizable interest, that it is "equally in everyone's interest" (as opposed to being, say, a "fair compromise" or an efficient regulation).

This first level of agreement expresses only what it means for a norm to be just. In this sense, it is identical with the unavoidable requirement that the participants in a practical discourse have to be able to adopt the moral point of view. But beyond this level of consensus, it is not necessary that they agree also about the further substantive reasons as to why the needs or interests regulated by the norm are worth safeguarding, are unrenounceable, or whatever the case may be. The universalist or the cognitivist recognizes, in fact, that the value of morally right social regulations can be understood only from the internal perspective of such an ethical self-understanding. Such a perspective, *as the interpretative framework through which the participants are aware of their own needs and interests,* is a necessary condition for participating in practical discourse. However, participants need not share these interpretative frameworks. For they could agree that the norm at issue

does in fact preserve the interests they all consider unrenounceable (and, therefore, universalizable), even if they describe these
interests (and their reasons for being unrenounceable) by means
of different interpretations contained in their different cultural
traditions.

In fact, discourse ethics excludes the absolutist presupposition
that the participants cannot agree on the moral rightness of a
particular norm (by evaluating whether it preserves a generalizable interest or not) unless they also agree on the particular way
of understanding these interests at large. It does so precisely to
the extent that it defends the autonomy of questions of rightness
from questions of goodness.

But for that reason, it seems possible to keep an epistemic pluralism of interpretations without collapsing into a relativist point
of view *only if* we explain the universalist intuition about the unconditional validity of the moral rightness of social norms in terms
of the existence of common interests among all human beings.
Because (and so long as) there are such interests among all human beings, we can in principle find norms able to preserve these
interests. Only such norms can be considered morally right.
The either/or of the absolute opposition between morally right
and morally wrong need not be extended beyond the norms at
issue to the interpretations themselves—interpretations in
light of which the participants understand their own needs and
interests.

As pointed out earlier, the presupposition of common interests
is unavoidable precisely to the extent that, without it, it makes *no
sense at all* to attempt to determine whether or not a norm is
equally in everyone's interest. In this sense, the issue does not
seem to be whether such a presupposition is implied by our claims
to moral rightness—for the participants do not have such a
choice. Rather, the issue is whether, in addition to presupposing
the existence of such common interests (however they may be
interpreted), the participants also have to presuppose that,
among the different ways of understanding these interests by different people and at different times, one and only one particular interpretation is correct. *This kind of absoluteness* is actually

neither necessary nor desirable for a consistent defense of moral cognitivism.

In fact, some participants in communicative practices may naively presuppose that their own interpretation is the only correct one. However, as soon as they are confronted by *alternative* interpretations *of the same subject matter* (as is unavoidable in multicultural societies) they would have to adopt a hypothetical attitude toward their own interpretation in order to be able to participate in a discourse. This, in turn, requires the participants to distinguish intuitively between competing interpretations and *that of which* they are interpretations (whatever this may be in each case). That is, they must be able to identify, across these different interpretations, the *same interests* that they themselves are trying to articulate with the help of their own interpretations.

The fact that this identification can actually take place only across the different interpretations, and not *beyond* all interpretation, does not mean that the participants in communicative practices cannot understand them as alternative ways of conceptualizing *the same reality* (on which they understand that their knowledge claims depend). The context-transcendent validity of their cognitive claims is neither the promise of abandoning their epistemic situation for a direct confrontation with reality, nor an epistemic blindness concerning the fallibility of their own epistemic means or interpretations, but an essential component of the very sense of these claims. The realist conditions *to which they subject their own cognitive practices* allows them to learn of the fallibility of their epistemic situation without ever abandoning it. The limits of their languages are never the limits of their world, because of the crucial role the world plays in the use of their languages.

Bibliography

Anz, W. (1977) "Die Stellung der Sprache bei Heidegger," in Gadamer, H.-G. (ed.), *Das Problem der Sprache*, pp. 467–482. Munich: Wilhelm Fink Verlag.

Apel, K.-O. (1963) *Die Idee der Sprache in der Tradition des Humanismus von Dante bis Vico*. Bonn: Bouvier Verlag.

———— (1976) *Transformation der Philosophie*. Frankfurt: Suhrkamp.

———— (1989) "Sinnkonstitution und Geltungsrechtfertigung. Heidegger und das Problem der Transzendentalphilosophie," in Forum für Philosophie Bad Homburg (ed.), *M. Heidegger: Innen- und Außenansichten*, pp. 131–175. Frankfurt: Suhrkamp.

Aristotle. (1984) *De Interpretatione*, J. L. Ackrill (transl.), in *The Complete Works of Aristotle [Vol. 1]*. Princeton: The Princeton University Press.

Ayer, A. J. (1956) *The Problem of Knowledge*. London: Penguin.

Baumann, H.-H. (1971) "Die generative Grammatik und W. von Humboldt," in *Poetica* 4/1:1–13.

Beiser, F. C. (1987) *The Fate of Reason. German Philosophy from Kant to Fichte*. Cambridge, MA: Harvard University Press.

Berlin, I. (1993) *The Magus of the North. J. G. Hamann and the Origins of Modern Irrationalism*. Cambridge: Cambridge University Press.

Bertolet, R. (1986) "Donnellan's Distinction," *Australasian Journal of Philosophy* 64:477–487.

Blanke, F. and Schreiner, L. (eds.) (1956) *J. G. Hamanns Hauptschriften erklärt*. Gütersloh: Carl Bertelsmann Verlag.

Bollnow, O. F. (1938) "W. von Humboldts Sprachphilosophie," in *Zeitschrift für deutsche Bildung* 14:102–112.

Borsche, T. (1981) *Sprachansichten. Der Begriff der menschliche Rede in der Sprachphilosophie W. von Humboldt.* Stuttgart: Klett-Cotta.

———— (1990) *W. von Humboldt.* Munich: Beck.

Brandom, R. (1994) *Making It Explicit.* Cambridge, MA: Harvard University Press.

Brown, R. L. (1967) *Wilhelm von Humboldt's Conception of Linguistic Relativity.* The Hague: Mouton.

Bühler, K. (1934) *Sprachtheorie.* Jena: Fischer.

Cassirer, E. (1923) "Die kantischen Elemente in W. von Humboldts Sprachphilosophie," in *Festschrift für P. Hensel,* Greiz, pp. 105–127.

Chisholm, R. M. (1957) *Perceiving: A Philosophical Study.* Ithaca: Cornell University Press.

Culler, J. (1982) *On Deconstruction.* Ithaca: Cornell University Press.

Davis, F. J. (1994) "Discourse Ethics and Ethical Realism: A Realist Realignment of Discourse Ethics," *European Journal of Philosophy* 2:125–142.

Derrida, J. (1977a) "Signature, Event, Context," *Glyph* 1:172–197.

———— (1977b) "Limited Inc," *Glyph* 2:162–254.

Devitt, M. (1981) *Designation.* New York: Columbia University Press.

Donnellan, K. S. (1966) "Reference and Definite Descriptions," pp. 42–65 in Schwartz (1977).

———— (1972) "Proper Names and Identifying Descriptions," in Davidson, D. and Harman, G. (eds.), *Semantics of Natural Language,* pp. 356–379. Dordrecht: Reidel.

———— (1973) "Substances as Individuals," *The Journal of Philosophy* 70/19:711–712.

———— (1974) "Speaking of Nothing," pp. 42–65 in Schwartz (1977).

Droescher, H. M. (1980) *Grundstudien zur Linguistik. Wissenschaftstheoretische Untersuchungen der sprachphilosophischen Konzeptionen Humboldts, Chomsky und Wittgenstein.* Heidelberg.

Dummett, M. (1975) "What Is a Theory of Meaning?" in Guttenplan, S. (ed.), pp. 97–138. *Mind and Language.* Oxford: Oxford University Press.

——— (1976) "What Is a Theory of Meaning? (II)," in G. Evans and J. McDowell (eds.), *Truth and Meaning*, pp. 67–137. Oxford: Oxford University Press.

——— (1986) " 'A Nice Derangement of Epitaphs': Some Comments on David-son and Hacking," in E. LePore (ed.), *Truth and Interpretation: Perspectives on the Philosophy of Donald Davidson*. Oxford: Blackwell, 1986.

Eschbach, A. and Trabant, J. (eds.) (1983) *History of Semiotics*. Amsterdam: John Benjamins.

Fogelin, R. (1994) *Pyrrhonian Reflections on Knowledge and Justification*. Oxford: Oxford University Press.

Føllesdal, D. (1986) "Essentialism and Reference," in Hahn, L. and Schilpp, P. (eds.), *The Philosophy of W. V. Quine*, pp. 97–113. La Salle.

Frege, G. (1980) *Funktion, Begriff, Bedeutung*, ed. by G. Patzig. Göttingen: Vanden-hoeck and Ruprecht.

——— "Über Sinn und Bedeutung," pp. 40–65, in Frege (1980).

Gadamer, H.-G. (1967) "Rhetorik, Hermeneutik, und Ideologiekritik. Metakrit-ische Erörterungen zu Wahrheit und Methode," republished as pp. 232–250 in Gadamer (1986).

——— (1971) "Replik zu Hermeneutik und Ideologiekritik," republished as pp. 251–275 in Gadamer (1986).

——— (1980) "The Universality of the Hermeneutical Problem," in J. Bleicher (ed.), *Contemporary Hermeneutics*, pp. 128–140. London: Routledge and Paul.

——— (1986) *Gesammelte Werke*, vol. 2. (GW) Tübingen: Mohr.

——— (1994) *Truth and Method* (TM), transl. by J. Weinsheimer and D. Marshall. New York: Continuum.

Gajek, B. (ed.) (1987) *Hamann, Kant, Herder*. Marburg: P. Lang.

Geach, P. T. (1962) *Reference and Generality*. Ithaca: Cornell University Press.

Gethmann, C. F. (1974) *Verstehen und Auslegung*. Bonn: Bouvier Verlag.

Gettier, E. (1963) "Is Justified True Belief Knowledge?" *Analysis* 23/6:121–123.

Gipper, H. (ed.) (1972) *Gibt es ein sprachliches Relativitätsprinzip?* Stuttgart: Fischer.

Görtzen, R. (1986) "Bibliographie zur *Theorie des kommunikativen Handelns*," pp. 406–416 in Honneth and Joas (1986).

Bibliography

———— (1990) "J. Habermas: A Bibliography," in D. M. Rasmussen (ed.), *Reading Habermas.* Cambridge, MA: Blackwell.

Goosens, W. (1977) "Underlying Trait Terms," pp. 133–154 in Schwartz (1977).

Gründer, K. (1982) *Reflexion der Kontinuitäten.* Göttingen: Vandenhoeck and Ruprecht.

———— (1956) "Geschichte der Deutungen," pp. 9–140 in Blanke, F. and Schreiner, L. (1956).

Habermas, J. (1980) "The Hermeneutic Claim to Universality" (HCU), in J. Bleicher (ed.), *Contemporary Hermeneutics,* pp. 181–211. London: Routledge and Paul.

———— (1979) "What Is Universal Pragmatics?" (WIUP), in *Communication and the Evolution of Society,* pp. 1–68. Boston: Beacon Press.

———— (1984b) "Vorlesungen zu einer sprachtheoretischen Grundlegung der Soziologie" (VSGS), pp. 11–26 in Habermas (1984a).

———— (1984c) "Wahrheitstheorien" (WT), pp. 127–186 in Habermas (1984a).

———— (1981) "Urbanisierung der Heideggerschen Provinz," in Habermas, *Philosophisch-politische Profile.* Frankfurt: Suhrkamp.

———— (1984/1987) *Theory of Communicative Action,* (TCA), vols. 1 and 2, transl. by Th. McCarthy. Boston: Beacon Press.

———— (1984a) *Vorstudien und Ergänzungen zur Theorie des kommunikativen handelns* (VETKH), Frankfurt: Suhrkamp.

———— (1982) "Reply to My Critics," in J. Thompson and D. Held (eds.), *Habermas: Critical Debates,* pp. 219–283, Cambridge, MA: MIT Press.

———— (1985a) "Dialektik der Rationalisierung," in pp. 167–208 Habermas (1985b). Frankfurt: Suhrkamp.

———— (1985b) *Die Neue Unübersichtlichkeit.* Frankfurt: Suhrkamp.

———— (1985c) "Remarks on the Concept of Communicative Action" (RCCA), pp. 151–178 in G. Seebass and R. Tuomela (eds.), *Social Action.* New York: Reidel.

———— (1986) "Entgegnung" (ENT), pp. 327–405 in Honneth and Joas (1986).

———— (1987) *The Philosophical Discourse of Modernity* (PDM), transl. by F. Lawrence. Cambridge, MA: MIT Press.

———— (1988b) *On the Logic of the Social Sciences* (LSS), transl. by S. W. Nicholsen and J. A. Stark. Cambridge, MA: MIT Press.

Bibliography

—— (1988a) *Nachmetaphysisches Denken* (NMD). Frankfurt: Suhrkamp.

—— (1990b) *Moral Consciousness and Communicative Action,* transl. by Ch. Lenhardt and S. W. Nicholsen. Cambridge, MA: MIT Press.

—— (1990a) "Discourse Ethics: Notes on a Program of Philosophical Justification" (DE), pp. 43–115 in Habermas (1990b).

—— (1992) *Postmetaphysical Thinking: Philosophical Essays* (PMT), transl. by W. M. Hohengarten. Cambridge, MA: MIT Press.

—— (1991b) "Erläuterungen zur Diskursethik" (EDE), pp. 119–226 in Habermas (1991a).

—— (1991a) *Erläuterungen zur Diskursethik.* Frankfurt: Suhrkamp.

—— (1996a) *Between Facts and Norms* (BFN), transl. by W. Rehg. Cambridge, MA: MIT Press.

—— (1996c) "Reply"(R), *Cardozo Law Review* 17/4–5:1477–1559.

—— (CCCR) "Some Further Clarifications of the Concept of Communicative Rationality," pp. 307–342, in Habermas (1998).

—— (1996b) *Die Einbeziehung des Anderen.* Frankfurt: Suhrkamp.

—— (1998) *On the Pragmatics of Communication,* Cambridge, MA: MIT Press.

—— "Rorty's Pragmatic Turn" (RPT), pp. 343–382, in Habermas (1998).

Hamann, J. G. (1949–1957) *Sämtliche Werke,* 6 vols., ed. by J. Nadler. Vienna.

—— (1988a) "Metakritk über den Purismus der Vernunft" (MK), in Hamann (1988b).

—— (1988b) *Vom Magus im Norden und der Verwegenheit des Geistes. Ein Hamann-Brevier,* J. Majetschak (ed.). Munich: Deutscher Taschenbuch Verlag.

Heeschen, V. (1972) *Die Sprachphilosophie W. von Humboldts.* Bochum.

Heidegger, M. (1962) *Being and Time* (BT), transl. by J. Macquarrie and E. Robinson. San Francisco: Harper and Row.

—— (1967a) "Vom Wesen des Grundes," in Heidegger, *Wegmarken.* Frankfurt: Klostermann.

—— (1986b) *Vom Wesen der Wahrheit.* Frankfurt: Klostermann.

—— (1980) "Der Ursprung des Kunstwerkes" (UKW) in Heidegger, *Holzwege.* Frankfurt: Klostermann.

———— (1944) "Hölderlin und das Wesen der Dichtung" (HWD) in Heidegger, *Erläuterungen zu Hölderlins Dichtung.* Frankfurt: Klostermann.

———— (1967b) *What Is a Thing?* transl. by W. B. Barton and V. Deutsch. Chicago: Regnery.

———— (1986a) *Unterwegs zur Sprache* (UzS) Pfuellingen: Neske.

———— (1988) *Zur Sache des Denkens.* Tübingen: Niemeyer.

———— (1976) *Logik. Die Frage nach der Wahrheit.* Marburger Vorlesung Wintersemester 1925–26. *Gesamtausgabe* vol. 21. Frankfurt: Klostermann.

———— (1984) *Grundfragen der Philosophie. Ausgewählte "Probleme" der "Logik."* Freiburger Vorlesung Wintersemester 1937–38. *Gesamtausgabe* vol. 45. Frankfurt: Klostermann.

———— (1989) *Beiträge zur Philosophie (Vom Ereignis),* 1936–38. *Gesamtausgabe* vol. 65, Frankfurt: Klostermann.

———— (1991) *Über Logik als Frage nach der Sprache.* Freiburger Vorlesung Sommersemester 1934. Madrid: Anthropos.

Heintel, E. (1959) "Gegenstandskonstitution und sprachliches Weltbild" in Gipper, H. (ed.), *Sprache. Schlüssel zur Welt,* pp. 47–55. Düsseldorf: Pädagogischer Verlag.

Herder, J. G. (1881–1913) Sämmtliche Werke, ed. by B. Suphan, Berlin: Weidmann.

Hermeneutik und Ideologiekritik. (1971) Mit Beiträgen von Apel/Bormann/ Bubner/Gadamer/Giegel/Habermas. Frankfurt: Suhrkamp.

Herrmann, F. W. v. (1964) *Die Selbstinterpretation M. Heideggers.* Meisenheim.

———— (1974) *Subjekt und Dasein. Interpretationen zu "Sein und Zeit."* Frankfurt: Klostermann.

Holenstein, E. (1980) *Von der Hintergehbarkeit der Sprache.* Frankfurt: Suhrkamp.

Honneth, A. and Joas, H. (1986) *Kommunikatives Handeln.* Frankfurt: Suhrkamp.

Honneth, A., McCarthy, T., et al. (eds.) (1992) *Philosophical Interventions in the Unfinished Project of the Enlightenment.* Cambridge, MA: MIT Press.

Horwich, P. (1982) "Three Forms of Realism," *Synthese* 51:181–201.

How, A. R. (1980) "Dialogue as Productive Limitation in Social Theory: The Habermas-Gadamer Debate," *Journal of the British Society for Phenomenology* 11/2: 131–143.

Humboldt, W. v. (1903–36) *Gesammelte Schriften,* die königlich Preussischen Akademie der Wissenschaften (ed.), 17 vols. Berlin: B. Behr's Verlag.

—— (1963) *Schriften zur Sprachphilosophie,* vol. 3 of *Werke in fünf Bänden,* Flitner, A. and Giel, K. (eds.) Darmstadt: Klett-Cotta.

—— (1957) *W. von Humboldt,* ed. by Weinstock. Frankfurt: Fischer.

—— (1988) *On Language. The Diversity of Human Language-structure and Its Influence on the Mental Development of Mankind.* Cambridge / New York: Cambridge University Press.

Ingram, D. (1983) "The Historical Genesis of the Gadamer-Habermas Controversy," *Auslegung: A Journal of Philosophy* 10 / 1–2:86–151.

Jakobson, R. (1960) "Linguistics and Poetics," in T. A. Sebeok (ed.), *Style and Language,* pp. 350–377. New York: Wiley.

Jay, M. (1982) "Should Intellectual History Take a Linguistic Turn? Reflections on the Habermas-Gadamer Debate," in LaCapra, D. and Kaplan, S. L. (eds.), *Modern European Intellectual History. Reappraisals and New Perspectives,* pp. 86–110. Ithaca: Cornell University Press.

Kant, I. (1956) *Groundwork of the Metaphysics of Morals,* transl. by H. J. Patton. New York: Harper.

—— (1965) *Critique of Pure Reason,* transl. by N. K. Smith. New York: St. Martin's Press.

Kawohl, I. (1969) *W. von Humboldt in der Kritik des 20. Jahrhunderts.* Düsseldorf.

Kripke, S. A. (1972) "Naming and Necessity," in D. Davidson and G. Harman (eds.), *Semantics of Natural Language.* Dordrecht: Reidel.

—— (1977) "Speaker's Reference and Semantic Reference," *Midwest Studies in Philosophy* 2:255–276.

Kutschera, F. v. (1975) *Sprachphilosophie.* Munich: Fink.

Lafont, C. (1993) "Die Rolle der Sprache in *Sein und Zeit,*" *Zeitschrift für philosophische Forschung* 47 / 1:41–59.

—— (1994a) *Sprache und Welterschließung. Die linguistische Wende der Hermeneutik Heideggers.* Frankfurt: Suhrkamp. (*Heidegger, Language, and World-Disclosure,* Cambridge Univ. Press, forthcoming.)

—— (1994b) "World-disclosure and Reference," *Thesis Eleven* 37:46–63.

—— (1994c) "Referencia y verdad," *Theoria* 9 / 21:39–60.

———— (1994d) "Spannungen im Wahrheitsbegriff," *Deutsche Zeitschrift für Philosophie* 42/6:1007–1023.

———— (1995) "Truth, Knowledge, and Reality," *Graduate Faculty Philosophy Journal* 18/2:109–126.

———— (1997) "Pluralism and Universalism in Discourse Ethics," in A. Nascimento (ed.), *A Matter of Discourse: Community and Communication in Contemporary Philosophies,* pp. 55–78. London: Avebury Press.

Leeds, S. (1978) "Theories of Reference and Truth," *Erkenntnis* 13:111–130.

Liebrucks, B. (1965) *Sprache und Bewußtsein,* vol. 2, *Sprache.* Frankfurt: Akademische Verlagsgesellschaft.

Linsky, L. (ed.) (1971) *Reference and Modality.* Oxford: Oxford University Press.

Loar, B. (1976) "The Semantics of Singular Terms," *Philosophical Studies* 30:353–377.

Löwith, K. (1960) "Die Sprache als Vermittler von Mensch und Welt," in H. Höfling (ed.) *Beiträge zur Philosophie und Wissenschaft. Festschrft für W. Szilasi.* Munich: Francke.

Lorenz, K. and Mittelstraß, J. (1967) "Die Hintergehbarkeit der Sprache," *Kantstudien* 58:187–208.

Majetschak, S. (1989) "Metakritik und Sprache. Zu J.G. Hamanns Kant-Verständnis und seinen metakritischen Implikationen," *Kantstudien.*

Manchester, M. L. (1985) *The Philosophical Foundations of Humboldt's Linguistic Doctrines.* Amsterdam: John Benjamins.

Martens, E. and Schnädelbach, H. (eds.) (1989) *Philosophie. Ein Grundkurs.* Hamburg: Rowohlt.

McCarthy, T. (1978) *The Critical Theory of Jürgen Habermas.* Cambridge, MA: MIT Press.

———— (1991) "Practical Discourse: On the Relation of Morality and Politics," in McCarthy, *Ideals and Illusions,* pp. 181–99. Cambridge, MA: MIT Press.

———— (1996) "Legitimacy and Diversity: Dialectical Reflections on Analytical Distinctions," *Cardozo Law Review* 17/4–5:1083–1127.

Miller, R. L. (1968) *The Linguistic Relativity Principle and Humboldtian Ethnolinguistics.* The Hague: Mouton.

Misgeld, D. (1976) "Critical Theory and Hermeneutics: The Debate between Habermas and Gadamer," in J. O'Neill (ed.), *On Critical Theory.* New York: Seabury Press.

Bibliography

Moore, G. E. (1903) *Principia Ethica*. Cambridge: Cambridge University Press.

Mumm, S. (1977) "Zur Propädeutik der Linguistik: Wort und Zeichen. Mit einem Beitrag zur hermeneutischen Humboldt-Rezeption," *Germanistische Linguistik*: 102–170.

Nassen, U. (1982) "Hans-Georg Gadamer und Jürgen Habermas: Hermeneutik, Ideologiekritik, und Diskurs," in *Klassiker der Hermeneutik*. Paderborn: Schöningh.

Piaget, J. (1929) *The Child's Conception of the World*. London: Routledge.

——— (1970) *Genetic Epistemology*. New York: Columbia University Press.

Plato. (1961) *Thaetetus* and *Meno*, in *The Collected Dialogues of Plato*, E. Hamilton and H. Cairns (eds.). Princeton, NJ: Princeton University Press.

Putnam, H. (1962) "The Analytic and the Synthetic," pp. 33–69 in Putnam (1975d).

——— (1970) "Is Semantics Possible?" pp. 139–152 in Putnam (1975d).

——— (1975a) "The Meaning of 'Meaning,'" pp. 215–271 in Putnam (1975d).

——— (1975b) "Explanation and Reference," pp. 196–214 in Putnam (1975d).

——— (1975c) "Language and Reality," pp. 272–290 in Putnam (1975d).

——— (1975d) *Mind, Language, and Reality: Philosophical Papers*, vol. 2, Cambridge: Cambridge University Press.

——— (1976) "'Two Dogmas' revisited," pp. 87–97 in Putnam (1983).

——— (1977) "Models and Reality," pp. 1–25 in Putnam (1983).

——— (1978) *Meaning and the Moral Sciences*. London: Routledge.

——— (1981) *Reason, Truth, and History*. Cambridge: Cambridge University Press.

——— (1983) *Realism and Reason: Philosophical Papers*, vol. 3. Cambridge: Cambridge University Press.

——— (1986) "Meaning Holism," in A. Schilpp and E. Hahn (eds.), *The Philosophy of W. V. Quine*, pp. 405–426. La Salle, IL: Open Court.

——— (1988) *Representation and Reality*. Cambridge, MA: MIT Press.

——— (1990) *Realism with a Human Face*. (RHF) Cambridge, MA: Harvard University Press.

———— (1992) *Renewing Philosophy*. (RPH) Cambridge, MA: Harvard University Press.

———— (1994) "Comments and Replies," in P. Clark and B. Hale (eds.), *Reading Putnam*, pp. 242–295. Cambridge, MA: Blackwell.

Quine, W. v. O. (1950) *Methods of Logic*. Cambridge, MA: Harvard University Press.

———— (1953b) "Two Dogmas of Empiricism," pp. 20–46 in Quine, *From a Logical Point of View*. Cambridge, MA: Harvard University Press.

———— (1953a) "On What There Is," pp. 1–19 in Quine, *From a Logical Point of View, op. cit.*

———— (1960) *Word and Object*. Cambridge, MA: MIT Press.

———— (1969) *Ontological Relativity and Other Essays*. New York: Columbia University Press.

———— (1971) "Quantifiers and Propositional Attitudes," in L. Linsky (ed.), *Reference and Modality*, pp. 101–111.

———— (1990) "The Elusiveness of Reference" in Sukale, M. (ed.), *Sprache, Theorie, und Wirklichkeit*, pp. 13–24. Frankfurt.

Ramsey, F. P. (1931) "Facts and Propositions," in *The Foundations of Mathematics*. London: K. Paul, Trench, Tubner and Co.

Rawls, J. (1971) *A Theory of Justice*. Cambridge, MA: Harvard University Press.

———— (1985) "Justice as Fairness: Political not Metaphysical," *Philosophy and Public Affairs* 14:227–251.

———— (1993) *Political Liberalism*. New York: Columbia University Press.

———— (1995) "Reply to Habermas," *The Journal of Philosophy* 92/3:132–180.

Recannati, F. (1981) "On Kripke on Donnellan," in Parret, H., Sbisa, M., and Verschueren, J. (eds.), *Possibilities and Limitations of Pragmatics*, pp. 595–630. Amsterdam: John Benjamins.

———— (1993) *Direct Reference: From Language to Thought*. Oxford: Blackwell.

Riedel, M. (1978) *Verstehen oder Erklären? Zur Theorie und Geschichte der hermeneutischen Wissenschaften*. Stuttgart.

———— (1990) *Hören auf die Sprache. Die akroamatische Dimension der Hermeneutik*. Frankfurt: Suhrkamp.

Rorty, R. (1986) "Pragmatism, Davidson, and Truth," in E. LePore (ed.), *Truth and Interpretation*, pp. 333–355. Oxford: Blackwell.

—— (1991) "Wittgenstein, Heidegger und die Hypostasierung der Sprache," in *Der Löwe spricht . . . und wir können ihn nicht verstehen. Ein Symposion an der Universität Frankfurt anläßlich des hundersten Geburtstags von L. Wittgenstein*. Frankfurt: Suhrkamp 1991.

Rousseau, J.-J. (1994) *The Social Contract*. Oxford: Oxford University Press.

Ryle, G. (1984) *The Concept of Mind*. Chicago: University of Chicago Press.

Runggaldier, E. (1985) *Zeichen und Bezeichnetes. Sprachphilosophische Untersuchungen zum Problem der Referenz*. Berlin: W. de Gruyter.

Russell, B. (1905) "On Denoting," *Mind* 14:479–493.

—— (1976) "Knowledge by Acquaintance and Knowledge by Description," in Russell, *Mysticism and Logic*, pp. 152–67. New Jersey: Barnes and Noble.

—— (1994) "The Philosophy of Logical Atomism," in Russell, *Logic and Knowledge*. London and New York: Routledge.

Salmon, N. (1981) *Reference and Essence*. Princeton, NJ: Princeton University Press.

—— (1982) "Assertion and Incomplete Definite Descriptions," *Philosophical Studies* 42:37–45.

Sapir, E. (1949) *Culture, Language and Personality, Selected Essays*, D. G. Mandelbaum (ed.). Berkeley: University of California Press.

Scharf, H. W. (1977) *Chomskys Humboldt-Interpretation. Ein Beitrag zur Diskontinuität der Sprachtheorie in der Geschichte der neueren Linguistik*. Düsseldorf.

—— (1983) "Das Verfahren der Sprache. Ein Nachtrag zur Chomskys Humboldt-Reklamation," in Eschbach and Trabant (1983).

Schmitt, W. H. (1982) "Die logische Spannweite von Hamanns Satz: 'Vernunft ist Sprache,'" in Scheer, B. and Wohlfart, G. (eds.), *Dimensionen der Sprache in der Philosophie der deutschen Idealismus*. Würzburg: Königshausen and Neumann.

Schnädelbach, H., see E. Martens.

Schwartz, S. (1977) *Naming, Necessity, and Natural Kinds*. Ithaca: Cornell University Press.

Searle, J. R. (1958) "Proper Names," in *Mind* 67:166–173.

—— (1969) *Speech Acts*. Cambridge: Cambridge University Press.

———— (1977) "Reiterating the Differences: A Reply to Derrida," in *Glyph* 1: 198–208.

———— (1979a) *Expression and Meaning*. Cambridge: Cambridge University Press.

———— (1979b) "Referential and Attributive," pp. 137–161 in Searle (1979a).

———— (1979c) "Literal Meaning," pp. 117–136 in Searle (1979a).

———— (1983a) "The Background," pp. 141–159 in Searle (1983b).

———— (1983b) *Intentionality*. Cambridge: Cambridge University Press.

———— (1995) *The Construction of Social Reality*. New York: The Free Press.

Seils, M. (1978) "Wirklichkeit und Wort bei J. G. Hamann," pp. 314–339 in Wild (1978).

Sellars, W. (1997) *Empiricism and the Philosophy of Mind*. Cambridge, MA: Harvard University Press.

Simon, J. (1979) "Vernunftkritik und Autorschaft," pp. 135–168, in Gajek, B. (ed.), *J. G. Hamann*. Frankfurt: Klostermann.

———— (1987) "Spuren Hamanns bei Kant?" in Gajek, B. (ed.), *J. G. Hamann*.

Spreu, A. (ed.) (1986) *Sprache, Mensch, und Gesellsachft. Werk und Wirkungen von W. von Humboldt und J. W. Grimm in Vergangenheit und Gegenwart*. Berlin.

Stavropoulos, N. (1996) *Objectivity in Law*, Oxford: Oxford University Press.

Stegmüller, W. (1987) *Hauptströmungen der Gegenwartsphilosophie*, vol. 2. Stuttgart: Kröner.

Strawson, P. (1950) "On Referring," *Mind* 59:320–344.

———— (1959) *Individuals*. London: Routledge.

Taylor, Ch. (1985) "Theories of Meaning," in *Human Agency and Language: Philosophical Papers*, pp. 248–292. Cambridge: Cambridge University Press.

———— (1986) "Sprache und Gesellschaft," pp. 35–52 in Honneth and Joas, *Kommunikatives Handeln*.

Trabant, J. (1983) "Ideelle Bezeichnung. Steinthals Humboldt-Kritik," in Eschbach and Trabant (1983).

———— (1986) *Apeliotes oder der Sinn der Sprache. W. von Humboldts Sprach-Bild*. Munich: Fink.

———— (1990) *Traditionen Humboldts*. Frankfurt: Suhrkamp.

Tugendhat, E. (1970) *Der Wahrheitsbegriff bei Husserl und Heidegger.* Berlin: de Gruyter.

—— (1976) *Vorlesungen zur Einführung in die sprachanalytische Philosophie.* Frankfurt: Suhrkamp.

—— (1992) "Sprache und Ethik," in *Philosophische Aufsätze,* pp. 275–314. Frankfurt: Suhrkamp.

—— (1993) *Vorlesungen über Ethik.* Frankfurt: Suhrkamp.

Wellmer, A. (1977) "Kommunikation und Emanzipation. Überlegungen zur sprachanalytischen Wende der kritische Theorie," in U. Jaeggi and A. Honneth (eds.), *Theorien des historischen Materialismus.* Frankfurt: Suhrkamp.

—— (1986) *Ethik und Dialog.* Frankfurt: Suhrkamp.

—— (1992) "What Is a Pragmatic Theory of Meaning? Variations on the Proposition 'We Understand a Speech Act when We Know What Makes It Acceptable,'" pp. 171–219 in A. Honneth, T. McCarthy, C. Offe, and A. Wellmer (eds.), *Philosophical Interventions in the Unfinished Project of the Enlightenment,* Cambridge, MA: MIT Press.

—— (1993) *Endspiele: Die unversöhnliche Moderne.* Frankfurt: Suhrkamp.

Wettstein, H. (1991) *Has Semantics Rested on a Mistake? And Other Essays.* Stanford: Stanford University Press.

Wild, R. (ed.) (1978) *J. G. Hamann. Wege der Forschung.* Darmstadt: Wissenschaftliche Buchgesellschaft.

Williams, M. (1986) "Do We (Epistemologists) Need a Theory of Truth?" *Philosophical Topics* 14:223–242.

—— (1996) *Unnatural Doubts.* Princeton, NJ: Princeton University Press.

Wittgenstein, L. (1969) *On Certainty.* Oxford: Blackwell.

—— (1958) *Philosophical Investigations.* Oxford: Blackwell.

Whorf, B. L. (1956) *Language, Thought, and Reality,* J. B. Carroll (ed.). Cambridge, MA: MIT Press.

Wolf, U. (ed.) (1985) *Eigennamen. Dokumentation einer Kontroverse.* Frankfurt: Suhrkamp.

Wohlfahrt, G. (1984) "Hamanns Kantkritik," *Kantstudien.*

Wright, K. (1986) "Gadamer: The Speculative Structure of Language," in B. R. Wachterhauser (ed.), *Hermeneutic and Modern Philosophy.* New York: State University of New York Press.

Name Index

Name Index

Studies in Contemporary German Social Thought
Thomas McCarthy, general editor

Jürgen Habermas, *Moral Consciousness and Communicative Action*

Jürgen Habermas, *The New Conservatism: Cultural Criticism and the Historians' Debate*

Jürgen Habermas, *The Philosophical Discourse of Modernity: Twelve Lectures*

Jürgen Habermas, *Philosophical-Political Profiles*

Jürgen Habermas, *Postmetaphysical Thinking: Philosophical Essays*

Jürgen Habermas, *On the Pragmatics of Communication*

Jürgen Habermas, *The Structural Transformation of the Public Sphere: An Inquiry into a Category of Bourgeois Society*

Jürgen Habermas, editor, *Observations on "The Spiritual Situation of the Age"*

Axel Honneth, *The Critique of Power: Reflective Stages in a Critical Social Theory*

Axel Honneth, *The Struggle for Recognition: The Moral Grammar of Social Conflicts*

Axel Honneth and Hans Joas, editors, *Communicative Action: Essays on Jürgen Habermas's* The Theory of Communicative Action

Axel Honneth, Thomas McCarthy, Claus Offe, and Albrecht Wellmer, editors, *Cultural-Political Interventions in the Unfinished Project of Enlightenment*

Axel Honneth, Thomas McCarthy, Claus Offe, and Albrecht Wellmer, editors, *Philosophical Interventions in the Unfinished Project of Enlightenment*

Max Horkheimer, *Between Philosophy and Social Science: Selected Early Writings*

Tom Huhn and Lambert Zuidervaart, editors, *The Semblance of Subjectivity: Essays in Adorno's Aesthetic Theory*

Jans Joas, *G. H. Mead: A Contemporary Re-examination of His Thought*

Michael Kelly, editor, *Critique and Power: Recasting the Foucault/Habermas Debate*

Hans Herbert Kögler, *The Power of Dialogue: Critical Hermeneutics after Gadamer and Foucault*

Reinhart Koselleck, *Critique and Crisis: Enlightenment and the Pathogenesis of Modern Society*

Reinhart Koselleck, *Future Past: On the Semantics of Historical Time*

Cristina Lafont, *The Linguistic Turn in Hermeneutic Philosophy*

Harry Liebersohn, *Fate and Utopia in German Sociology, 1887–1923*

Herbert Marcuse, *Hegel's Ontology and the Theory of Historicity*

Larry May and Jerome Kohn, editors, *Hannah Arendt: Twenty Years Later*

Christoph Menke, *The Sovereignty of Art: Aesthetic Negativity in Adorno and Derrida*

Pierre Missac, *Walter Benjamin's Passages*

Shierry Weber Nicholsen, *Exact Imagination, Late Work: On Adorno's Aesthetics*

Gil G. Noam and Thomas E. Wren, editors, *The Moral Self*

Guy Oakes, *Weber and Rickert: Concept Formation in the Cultural Sciences*

Claus Offe, *Contradictions of the Welfare State*